Early Advaita Vedānta and Buddhism

SUNY series
in Religious Studies
Harold Coward, editor

Early Advaita Vedānta and Buddhism

The Mahāyāna Context of the Gauḍapādīya-kārikā

Richard King

State University of New York Press

Published by
State University of New York Press, Albany

Printed in the United States of America

For information, address State University of New York Press,
State University Plaza, Albany, NY 12246

Production by Cynthia Tenace Lassonde
Marketing by Fran Keneston

Library of Congress Cataloging-in-Publication Data

King, Richard, 1966–
Early Advaita Vedānta and Buddhism : the Mahāyāna context of the Gauḍapādīya-kārikā / Richard King.
p. cm. — (Suny series in religious studies)
"Running translation of the Gauḍapādīya-kārikā"—Appendix.
Includes bibliographical references and index.
ISBN 0-7914-2513-4(hc) — ISBN 0-7914-2514-2(pbk.)
1. Gauḍapāda Ācārya. Gauḍapādīyakārikā. 2. Advaita. 3. Gauḍapāda Ācārya—Knowledge--Mahayana Buddhism. 4. Gauḍapāda Ācārya—Sources. 5. Philosophy, Indic. 6. Hinduism—Relations—Buddhism. 7. Buddhism—Relations—Hinduism. I. Gauḍapāda Ācārya. Gauḍapāda-kārikā. II. Title. III. Series.
B132.A3K53 1995
181'.482—dc20 94-24728
CIP

10 9 8 7 6 5 4 3 2 1

For my mother, Lillian Richardson,
and Juli

Contents

Acknowledgments

This monograph is a revised version of my Ph.D. thesis, The *Gauḍapādīyakārikā*: A Philosophical Analysis of the Mahāyāna Buddhist Context of Early Advaita Vedānta (University of Lancaster, England, 1992). I would like to take this opportunity to thank a number of people who have helped, both directly and indirectly, in the production of this book. First, Dr. David Smith of the University of Lancaster for his many helpful comments, particularly on the Vedānta tradition and the translation of the *kārikās*; Dr. Andrew Rawlinson for early encouragement when first attempting to make sense of Nāgārjuna and the Prajñāpāramitā, and to Dr. Daniel Mariau of the University of Hull for first introducing me to the world of Indian philosophy as an undergraduate. I would also like to thank Jeremy Carrette for his close friendship, support, and intellectual stimulation. These acknowledgments would not be complete without mentioning my partner, Juli Stewart, for her constant love and encouragement. Not only did this involve financially supporting me for a year while researching in London, but also for showing me the importance of grounding philosophical insights in the world of everyday experience. This work is a testimony to her continued love and support.

Chapter 1 will appear as "Early Advaita Vedānta: The Date and Authorship of the *Gauḍapādīyakārikā*" in the *Indo-Iranian Journal* (forthcoming). Chapter 5 is a revised and expanded version of material originally published as "*Asparśayoga*: Meditation and Epistemology in the *Gauḍapādīyakārikā*" in the *Journal of Indian Philosophy* 20 (March 1992), pp. 89–131. Most of the discussion pertaining to the Yogācāra school, however, has not been published before. Chapters 4 and 6 contain some revised material which was originally published as "*Śūnyatā* and *Ajāti*: Absolutism and the Philosophies of Nāgārjuna and Gauḍapāda" in *Journal of Indian Philosophy* 17 (Dec 1989), pp. 385–405.

Abbreviations

BS	Brahmasūtra
BSBh	Brahmasūtra-bhāṣya of Śaṅkarācārya
BU	Bṛhadāraṇyaka Upaniṣad
BUV	Bṛhadāraṇyaka Upaniṣad Vārttika of Sureśvara
CU	Chāndogya Upaniṣad
GK	Gauḍapādīyakārikā
GKBh	Gauḍapādīyakārikābhāṣya, attributed to Śaṅkarācārya
Kośa	Abhidharmakośa of Vasubandhu
MĀ	Madhyamakāvatāra of Candrakīrti
MHK	Madhyamakahṛdayakārikā of Bhāvaviveka
MMK	Mūla-Madhyamaka-kārikās of Nāgārjuna
MU	Māṇḍūkya Upaniṣad
NS	Naiṣkarmyasiddhi of Sureśvara
RGV	Ratnagotra-vibhāga-śāstra
TSN	Trisvabhāvanirdeśa, attributed to Vasubandhu

Introduction

There is always the risk that in the study of the thought forms of a philosopher one will superimpose a level of systematic development that does not exist. This has happened to a certain degree in the study of Śaṅkara. Much of the debate about what is or is not an authentic Śaṅkarite work stems from two different attitudes to the study of individual Indian philosophers and their various scholastic works. The first attitude, a somewhat rigid model, upholds the "monolithic" principle. On this view Śaṅkara = "the author of the *Brahmasūtra-bhāṣya*" and any deviation from the doctrines and linguistic forms of that work are taken to be firm evidence for the non-authenticity of a text. The second model proposes that an Indian philosopher, as a human being, has undergone some development in both linguistic and doctrinal realms. Despite the tradition which affirms that Śaṅkara died at a very young age, upholders of the second approach have attempted to classify texts into "early," "middle," and "late" compositions. For instance, if the *Gauḍapādīya-kārikā-bhāṣya* is an authentic work of Śaṅkara's then it would seem to be one of his earliest works since it displays an immaturity and uncertainty that is not found in the commentary on the *Brahmasūtra*. The GK's commentator is either ignorant of Buddhist terminology and doctrines, or naively careless in his attempts to "cover up" their appearance in this Vedāntic text.

Of course, these two conceptions of Śaṅkara are caricatures. No scholar of any repute would actually purport to follow either as I have outlined them. However, in my opinion, it is the more liberal model that is closer to the actual historical situation. One wonders sometimes to what extent the verses passed down to us are the systematic exposition of an Indian philosopher or merely a collection of sayings from different periods of the author's teaching career. How many redactors, editors, compilers, and thinkers have been involved in the transmission of a text from its original author(s) to us today? This poses a further problem for the scholar dealing with an ancient religious text, i.e. to what extent do scholars impose a level of doctrinal unanimity and systematization upon what may be composite material? Such hermeneutical problems in the final analysis tend to be unresolvable in the absence of any substantial historical information. Consequently, we cannot know for sure what historical and personal circumstances lead to the composition of the *Gauḍapādīya-kārikā* or its commentary. An awareness of this fact, however, should temper any over-confident conclusions on these issues.

In our enthusiasm to understand and label the doctrines of various philosophers it is easy to fall into overly simplistic categories. No system of thought can be completely autonomous and it is important to recognize that in India, as much as anywhere else, the dynamic interplay between differing religious and philosophical traditions is a major factor in the development of any given system of thought.

In the early stages of any new movement, there must be some interaction with what may later become an opposing tradition. This much is clear from an analysis of the major texts of Indian philosophy. This reflects the fact that *darśanas* are structured in opposition to rival points of view or perspectives. It is a common feature of philosophical *śāstras* to find the views of an opponent put forward first, the *pūrvapakṣin*, and then refuted on the way to one's final position (*siddhānta*). In the early stages of a developing philosophy there is little or no option but to adopt some of the concepts and linguistic forms current at the time. This combined with the "new insight" forms the basis for the new religious or philosophical movement. It should not be surprising then to find much evidence of Buddhist influence upon the *Gauḍapādīya-kārikā*, which is an example of a philosophical school (i.e. Advaita Vedānta) in an early stage of formation. What has surprised many, however, is the extent of the Buddhist influence upon what is clearly a Vedāntic text.

As the only available example of an uncompromising *Advaita-vāda* before the Śaṅkara school, the *Gauḍapādīya-kārikā* is of unparalleled importance for an understanding of the roots of Advaita Vedānta, the school which since Śaṅkara's time has been the predominant orthodox interpretation of *śruti*. Surprisingly, little work has been carried out on the *Gauḍapādīya-kārikā*. Most scholars who have looked at the text have done so as a means to an end, that is in order to gain a better understanding of the thought of Śaṅkara, considered the major figure, if not the "founding father," of Advaita Vedānta. In general, there appears to have been an undue emphasis placed upon the works of Śaṅkara as representative of the "quintessence of Advaita philosophy."

Consequently, there has been a lack of interest in the *Gauḍapādīya-kārikā*, a text which remains the only major example of a pre-Śaṅkarite formulation of Advaita.

Recent Work on the *Gauḍapādīya-kārikā*

There have been little more than a handful of works exclusively devoted to an appraisal of Gauḍapādian thought. Surendranath Dasgupta devotes a mere nine pages to the GK, despite spending over three hundred pages on the Śaṅkarite school of Vedānta in his five volume work, *The History of Indian Philosophy*.[1] In 1981, volume III of the *Encyclopaedia of Indian Philosophies*, a 635 page study devoted to "Advaita Vedānta up to Śaṁkara and his pupils," was published with only twelve pages devoted to an examination of "Gauḍapāda."[2] Until the 1980s, only four books and one unpublished Ph.D. dissertation, had been written in the West which dealt specifically with the *Gauḍapādīya-kārikā* as its central topic.[3] More recently there have been signs that this situation is being rectified with a number of new works appearing on the subject.

The first work to incorporate a critical edition (in roman script), an English translation, and a brief commentary on the text was Vidhushekara Bhattacharya's (1943), *The Āgamaśāstra of Gauḍapāda* (University of Calcutta Press). Bhattacharya's thesis is that the text of the GK is composite in nature, comprising of four separate works, all of which have been heavily influenced by Buddhism, especially the fourth *prakaraṇa*. Bhattacharya's commentary is not so much an explanation of the *kārikās* as a collection of mainly Buddhist references, cited to support his thesis of Buddhist influence on the *kārikās*. The sheer weight of evidence provided by Bhattacharya should be enough to convince even the most partisan reader of the GK's reliance upon Buddhist philosophical texts. Little time is spent, however, discussing the complexity of the Buddhist and Vedāntic philosophical traditions. The book lacks any attempt at a critical appraisal of the GK in its own terms and from within the Vedāntic tradition with which it aligns itself, despite the Buddhist terminology. There is no detailed exposition or discussion of the philosophy of the text itself, nor is any attempt made to place the GK in historical perspective. Nevertheless, Bhattacharya's work is a pioneering and innovative study.

It was only a matter of time before Bhattacharya's view of the Buddhist content of the GK came under attack. This situation occurred with the appearance of T. M. P. Mahadevan's (1952), *Gauḍapāda: A*

Study in Early Advaita (University of Madras Press). Mahadevan's study is written largely as a response to the arguments of Bhattacharya. Thus, Mahadevan argues on behalf of the Vedānta tradition that the GK is in fact a unitary text written by Gauḍapāda, identified as Śaṅkara's *paramaguru*. Much of the text is devoted to refuting Bhattacharya's claim of the Buddhist content of the GK. Of course, Mahadevan does not deny that the GK is influenced by Buddhist arguments; his point, however, is that Gauḍapāda's ideas are firmly established within the *Upaniṣads* themselves and are a rebuttal of Buddhist views. Thus, Mahadevan argues, one need not look toward Buddhist texts to find the fundamental sources of Gauḍapādian thought. In general, Mahadevan has provided us with a good, balanced summary of the traditional Vedāntic conception of the *Gauḍapādīya-kārikā*. The book also contains a reasonably accurate exposition of the philosophical views contained within the text. The problem with Mahadevan's study, however, is that it is too concerned with supporting the traditional Vedāntic view, at times to the detriment of objective scholarly acumen. Mahadevan denies that the GK is substantially influenced by Buddhism (although he accepts that the form of the GK's arguments are often taken from Buddhist sources), but Mahadevan's own conception of Buddhism is ill-informed and today appears rather dated. Virtually no time is spent discussing and explaining Buddhist philosophical ideas on their own terms, and when Buddhism is mentioned, it is invariably misunderstood and dismissed out of hand. For instance, in a discussion of the Buddha's silence Mahadevan suggests that:

> Two ways of understanding their [Buddhist] statements are possible, the absolutistic and the nihilistic. The absolutistic interpretation is that silence is the genuine teaching about the ultimate Reality, because the Absolute is beyond the scope of speech and thought. This is indistinguishable from the Upaniṣadic conception; and Mahāyānism received from the Upaniṣads. The other interpretation is that since nothing is real, the Buddha and what he said are also unreal. This is the logic of nihilism carried to its conclusion. Nihilism itself is *śūnya*.[4]

This statement shows no awareness of the subtlety of Buddhist thought, the complexity of Buddhist discussion of the Buddha's silence, or of the Buddhist claim to be following a middle path between absolutism and nihilism. Mahadevan is also guilty of interpreting the GK through Śaṅkarite eyes, thus detracting from the originality of the text and over-simplifying the relationship between Śaṅkara and the author(s) of the GK. As a result, we find the author suggesting that:

"Doctrinally there is no difference whatsoever between what is taught by Gauḍapāda in the *Kārikā* and what is expounded by Śaṅkara in his extensive works."[5]

R. D. Karmarkar's (1953), *The Gauḍapādakārikā* (Govt. Oriental Series Class B, No. 9, Bhandarkar Oriental Research Institute, Poona), was also written to counter Bhattacharya's thesis of Buddhist influence upon the *kārikās*. His study provides a Sanskrit edition, translation, and explanatory commentary on the text. Karmarkar's entire thesis is written as a response to Bhattacharya and involves the citation of Vedāntic and Brahmanical sources to counter the Buddhist citations found in Bhattacharya's study. Gauḍapāda, Karmarkar suggests, is the author of the entire text; he is a thorough-going Vedāntin with an interest in Buddhist ideas. The GK, however, is written with the intention of establishing Vedāntic ideas and constrasting them with prevailing (mostly Buddhist) views. Karmarkar, like Mahadevan, is an upholder of Vedāntic orthodoxy. His work is useful as something of a corrective to the exclusively Buddhist interests of Bhattacharya. No attempt is made, however, to confront the underlying philosophical problem involved in an examination of Gauḍapādian thought, namely the question of the actual nature of Buddhist and Vedāntic philosophy. What do the cardinal philosophical texts of the two traditions actually say and how are we to understand their relationship in the light of their mutual occurrence in the GK? Throwing rival citations at one another, while useful in establishing something of the philosophical and textual sources of the GK, will not answer these fundamental questions.

In more recent times a number of studies have been written which attempt to deal with these issues more fully. Caterina Conio's (1971), *The Philosophy of the Māṇḍūkya Kārikā* (Arun Press, Varanasi), is an attempt to provide a systematic analysis of Gauḍapādian thought, but again no real time is devoted to a consideration of the philosophical heritage on which the GK is dependent. Conio provides some interesting discussion of the authenticity of the Śaṅkara *bhāṣya* on the GK, that she seems to accept as authentic,[6] and incorporates the interpretations of other commentaries on the text (Kūranārāyaṇa, Madhva, Puruṣottama). In general, however, the study fails to be wide-ranging enough to make any real impact and makes no substantial improvement in our understanding of the nature of the GK's philosophy and its relationship to Buddhism.

Sangamlal Pandey's (1974), *Pre-Śaṁkara Advaita Philosophy* (Allahabad: Darshan Pith), provides a further example of an Indian scholar thoroughly versed in the Brahmanical background of the GK but sadly deficient in his understanding of the Buddhist tradition.

Pandey provides some useful and insightful discussion of the Brahmanical sources of early Advaita and the Vedāntic precursors of Gauḍapāda. His discussion, however, shows no real grasp of the questions of multiple authorship and his polemical attitude towards the Buddhist schools and their potential influence on the GK marrs an already ill-informed discussion about the nature of Buddhism and its relationship to the GK.

With Alexander Hixon's (1976), *Mahāyāna Buddhist influence on the Gauḍa school of Advaya Vedānta* (unpublished Ph.D. thesis, University of Columbia), one finds the first real attempt to discuss the relationship of the GK with Mahāyāna Buddhist philosophy. Hixon suggests that the GK is a composite text (with GK IV being the earliest of the four *prakaraṇas*), representing a number of historical stages of development of a Bengali school of Advaya Vedānta in existence before the time of Śaṅkara. The author has something of a piecemeal approach to the text, dividing it up into eleven fragments.[7] This is textual criticism taken to an extreme degree. Such an analysis is dependent not only upon a shrewd understanding of the differences between Vedāntic and Mahāyāna Buddhist philosophy, but also upon the somewhat shaky methodological premise that the use of a different technical term points to separate authorship.[8] Hixon also differentiates between many fragments on the basis of the degree to which they display ''Vedāntic'' or ''Buddhist'' orientation. This differentation requires a thorough-going analysis of both traditions—something that Hixon neither carries out nor displays in his own discussion of the *kārikās*. Consequently the discussion of Mahāyāna influence upon the GK is superficial, overly simplistic, and far too definitive in its conclusions. Hixon does, however, provide a useful review of the major scholarly work on the GK up to that point, aligning himself with what he calls the ''liberal'' tradition of interpretation represented by Surendranath Dasgupta, Vidhuskekhara Bhattacharya, and T. R. V. Murti. Hixon's own work, however, is rather too dependent upon the work of Bhattacharya and provides little in the way of an improvement of our understanding of the nature of the GK. A running discussion is provided of each *kārikās*, but the author does not deal with Mahāyāna Buddhist ideas in sufficient depth to establish the precise philosophical relationship of the GK to them.

Tilmann Vetter's article ''Die Gauḍapādīya-kārikās: Zur Entstehung und zur Bedeutung Von (A)dvaita'' in *Wiener Zeitschrift für die Kunde Süd-Und Ostasiens* 22 (1978, pp. 95–131), remains the best textual study of the GK to date. Vetter suggests, in agreement with Hixon, that historically the GK was composed in reverse order, GK IV being the earliest of the *prakaraṇas* and GK I the latest. The reason for this, Vetter argues, is that the discussion of the non-origination of the *ātman* in GK I, II, and III presupposes the development of this doctrine with regard to the *dharmas* which are the focus of discussion in GK IV (p. 105). He points to the philosophical and hermeneutical problems which the Śaṅkarite commentator has with the term "*dharma*" and suggests that the author of the GK was initially interested in Mahāyāna Buddhist ideas but then gradually became more Vedāntic in orientation. The development of Gauḍapāda's thought, therefore, can be chronologically seen in the composition of the third, second, and first *prakaraṇas*. Our discussion of the date and authorship of the GK occurs in the first chapter and so we shall consider Vetter's views more fully therein. Vetter, however, has presumed too much. His argument merely points to the Gauḍapādian reliance upon the Mahāyāna non-origination of *dharmas*. This in itself does not entail that the fourth *prakaraṇa*, which discusses this doctrine, was necessarily the earliest composition.

Despite the detailed discussion of the text, there are many aspects and features of Gauḍapādian thought that Vetter does not consider. His discussion of the Mahāyāna Buddhist background of the GK is minimal and it is not made clear to what extent the author is indebted to Mahāyāna doctrines other than *ajātivāda*, nor on what grounds Gauḍapāda and his Buddhist sources can be philosophically differentiated. It is perhaps asking too much for this to be achieved in a single article. Nevertheless, Vetter does not follow up his textual analysis with further studies of Gauḍapādian thought and philosophical sources. Vetter does, however, progress from his philological analysis of the GK to a study of the influence of the *Gauḍapādīya-kārikā* on the early thought of Śaṅkara (1979, *Studien zur Lehre und Entwicklung Śaṅkaras*, Wien, esp. pp. 27–74). Sadly though, further consideration of the sources and origins of the GK itself are not forthcoming.

Colin Cole's (1982), *Asparśayoga: The Māṇḍūkya-Kārikā of Gauḍapāda*, aims at providing a definitive exposition of Gauḍapādian thought. No discussion is made of textual questions concerning the date and authorship of the text, which Cole treats as a single text. Cole's exposition of Gauḍapādian philosophy, however, is hampered by an inadequate and insufficient consideration of Buddhist philosophy. Thus,

> The arguments which Gauḍapāda uses in his explanation are reminiscent of Buddhist Vijñānavāda theory. But he is not a "subjective idealist." Rather he is an "Absolute Idealist" in that he posits a basis for all experience.[9]

Vijñānavāda, at least in the form that the author(s) of the GK would have been aware of it, was not a form of subjective idealism as

Cole implies, nor is it wholly unproblematic to describe Gauḍapāda as an "Absolute Idealist." This will become clearer in chapter 5, where I shall argue that neither the Yogācāra school which preceded the GK, nor the Vedāntic text itself, can be simplistically described as "idealistic." Failure to discuss the nature of (what Cole calls) "*Vijñānavāda*" thought leaves the GK floating in a philosophical vacuum, giving the reader no conception of the text's place in the history of Indian thought. Cole's work also shows little awareness of the differences between the doctrines of the GK and those of the later Advaita tradition.[10] No attempt is made to place the GK in historical or philosophical context. The reader, therefore, is left floundering if he or she wishes to grasp the relevance of the GK and its place in Indian philosophical thought.

Stephen Kaplan's (1987) *Hermeneutics, Holography, and Indian Idealism* provides us with the first work to acknowledge the inherent limitations of the use of the Western philosophical term "idealism" when discussing Indian philosophical texts such as the GK. Recent work in Yogācāra studies in the West has drawn attention to this particularly knotty problem,[11] and it was only a matter of time before such considerations would carry over into the philosophical analysis of Hindu philosophical schools. Karl Potter first expressed reservations about the validity of describing the philosophy expounded in the GK as "idealistic,"[12] and Kaplan continues this reappraisal of the GK by providing what he describes as a "phenomenological interpretation" of the text. Kaplan, to his credit, does not deny that the GK upholds a non-dualistic ontological position. He does, however, suggest that many of the *kārikās* expound a "phenomenological" theory of perception. Thus, when the GK states that the mind "does not touch an external object" (GK IV.26) it is not putting forward an idealistic doctrine (that the world is the creation of the mind), rather it is stating the fact that the mind deals with the experience or appearance of objects and not objects in themselves. Such an analysis is innovative and agrees in many respects with my own analysis of the text, which also draws attention to the problem of "idealism" (see chapter 5). Kaplan, however, spends no time considering the Buddhist philosophical background to Gauḍapādian thought, and much of the discussion is taken up with a comparison of the Gauḍapādian theory of perception with modern holographic theories of mind. The commonalities between these two widely disparate fields seem to center around an epistemology where the mind projects itself outward in perception. In this sense, holographic epistemological theory certainly has some sort of similarity with certain Indian theories of projection where the *antaḥkaraṇa* projects itself outward, thereby taking on the form (*vṛtti*) of the object, but it is debatable as to how far this has improved our understanding of Gauḍapādian thought (although it may help the westerner, interested in modern holographic theory, to appreciate the text more). Kaplan, however, consistently fails to note that the traditional Indian epistemology of the outward-going *antaḥkaraṇa* is a realist view of perception. This is not the view of perception outlined in the GK, although it is the theory which predominated in the Śaṅkarite school of Vedānta. Indeed the realist epistemologies of the classical Advaita Vedānta school ignore the fundamental features of Gauḍapādian epistemology, which do not tend towards epistemological realism.

Andrew O. Fort (1990), *The Self and its States: A States of Consciousness Doctrine in Advaita Vedānta* (Motilal Banarsidass) provides us with a good literal translation of the *Māṇḍūkya Upaniṣad*, chapter one of the *Gauḍapādīya-kārikā*, and Śaṅkara's (?) commentary upon both (with Sanskrit text).[13] The scope of Fort's book is not the *Gauḍapādīya-kārikā* as such, but an analysis of the development of the Vedāntic doctrine of the four states of experience (*catuṣpād*) from the early *Upaniṣads* to the thought of contemporary Advaitins in India. The study also includes a brief comparison of the doctrine with the modern western movement known as "transpersonal psychology." Fort's work is an example of sound textual analysis characterized by a careful delineation and explanation of Advaita terms coupled with a keen awareness of their historical context. Fort rightly emphasizes the importance of the notion of an unchanging substratum as the subjacent ground for the fluctuating states of mind of waking, dreaming, and deep sleep. *Turīya*, as such, is the pure consciousness which simultaneously supports and transcends the other three states.

From the point of view of an analysis of Gauḍapādian thought, however, a number of criticisms must be noted. Fort, while acknowledging the differences between Gauḍapāda and Śaṅkara with regard to the relationship of the waking and dream states, fails to discuss the underlying reasons for this. Like Kaplan, there is an insufficient acknowledgment of the underlying epistemological differences between the two thinkers. The book provides a good historical discussion of the notion of *turīya*, but token gestures to the place of the Yoga and Buddhist schools in the development of this concept provide no real insight into their possible influences upon the notion of *turīya*. It should be noted, however, that Fort does not intend to provide a definitive examination of the GK and as such there is no discussion of the second, third or fourth *prakaraṇas*, all of which ignore the *catuṣpād* doctrine. The book constitutes a useful primer on an important doctrinal theme within the Vedānta tradition.

Thomas Wood's (1990), ***The Māṇḍūkya Upaniṣad and the Āgama-śāstra: An Investigation into the Meaning of the Vedānta***, (University of Hawaii Press), includes the text (in Roman script) and a reasonable translation of the GK. The main focus of Wood's analysis is the dating of the GK, its authorship, and the authorship of the commentary written upon it (traditionally attributed to Śaṅkara.) Wood disagrees with virtually every aspect of the traditional, Vedāntic conception of the GK. First, he suggests that the text is composite, being the work of a number of different authors. While accepting that most of GK I, II, and III are pre-Śaṅkarite, he argues that GK IV is a very late text (perhaps as late as the twelfth century Common Era). Not surprisingly, Wood also rejects the traditional ascription of the commentary to Śaṅkara. All of these views are supported by well documented evidence and the work provides an interesting discussion of the date and relationship of the four *prakaraṇas* to each other.

Wood, however, provides more than a simple discussion of the date and authorship of tht text. He argues (quite convincingly) that the *Māṇḍūkya Upaniṣad* (MU) upholds a broadly "theistic" interpretation of *turīya* in that the reference to the "lord of all" (*sarveśvara*) in MU 6 is to be associated with the description of *turīya* in MU 7 and not with the deep sleep state discussed in MU 5. This interpretation, of course, is at variance with the traditional Advaitic understanding of the *Upaniṣads*. Wood supports his own interpretation of the MU with evidence from the early *Upaniṣads* and late mediaeval Advaitins. He also argues that the first *prakaraṇa* of the GK conforms to the positive theism of the MU. Wood's entire discussion of philosophical issues, however, is marred by his simplistic view of Advaita Vedānta, which, on his interpretation, unqualifiably denies the existence of the world. The universe is a complete illusion in the most simplistic sense. This as we shall see is a misleading interpretation of Advaita Vedānta. No acknowledgment is given to the subtlety of the two-truths doctrine which prevents the Advaitin from making a simple denial of the world's existence. Consequently, Wood's understanding of Mahāyāna Buddhism suffers from the same simplistic analysis. Despite this, the author does acknowledge that the Advaitin and the Mahāyānist say what they do for different reasons and for this we must be grateful. Wood is critical of the Advaitin's *māyāvāda* which he sees as a simple form of "world-illusionism." His conception of Advaita Vedānta and Mahāyāna Buddhism as totally world-negating is too superficial and misrepresents both traditions.

The most recent monograph to discuss the *Gauḍapādīya-kārikā* to date is Douglas A. Fox's (1993), *Dispelling Illusion: Gauḍapāda's Alātaśānti* (State University of New York Press). This work contains a useful introduction, summarizing some of the main issues surrounding the text, followed by a translation of, and commentary upon, the fourth *prakaraṇa*. The book meets its aims well insofar as it provides a readable introduction both to "Gauḍapāda" and to the issues surrounding the text in general. The monograph remains rather brief, however, with a total of 146 pages. The book is to be commended as a readable introduction to early Advaita for the uninitiated reader and also as a reminder to the Indologist of the central issues and importance of Gauḍapāda in the history of Advaita Vedānta. Overall, however, the most redeeming feature of Fox's work is at the same time its weakest feature, namely its popular approach. The book makes very scant reference to Sanskrit originals (no original verses from the GK are given) and the entire work contains only forty-four end notes. Consequently, Fox completely omits references to the work of Pandey, Hixon, Vetter, Kaplan, and Wood etc., and indeed to any work published after 1986, including my own! There is also no discussion of the question of multiple authorship of the text, a feature which reflects the author's apparent decision to sacrifice incisive analysis for clarity of exposition. Despite a general lack of academic depth and acknowledgment of work in this area, Fox provides a very accessible introduction to Gauḍapāda that functions as a useful primer for undergraduates and non-Advaita specialists. However, the work cannot really be said to significantly contribute to our understanding of the *Gauḍapādīya-kārikā* or the context in which it developed.

Outline of the Monograph

A proper understanding of Gauḍapādian thought requires not only a basic grasp of the nature of early Vedānta philosophy, but also a *comprehensive* grasp of the philosophical texts of Mahāyāna Buddhism. This reflects not only the fact that the GK often uses Buddhist terminology as its *lingua franca*, but also that the development of the early Advaita perspective (*darśana*) of the GK is structured according to Mahāyāna philosophical paradigms. Without a grasp of the philosophical dependence of the GK upon Mahāyāna ideas, an assessment of the originality of the text would be impossible to achieve. As yet, no one has provided a study of the *Gauḍapādīya-kārikā* that displays anything like an adequate consideration of the Mahāyāna philosophical context to which the GK is undoubtedly indebted. Consequently, their assessment of Gauḍapādian thought has been sadly deficient. The time is ripe then for a reappraisal of the nature of early (i.e. pre-Śaṅkarite) Advaita Vedānta, as espoused in the *Gauḍapādīya-kārikā*, in the light of the philosophies of the Mahāyāna Buddhist tradition which form a conceptual backdrop to the philosophical position of the text. Only then can one hope to evaluate the innovations of the GK and establish the importance of the text in the history of Indian philosophy.

Most of the emphasis of this study will be upon the Mahāyāna traditions of Buddhism and their philosophical relationship with Gauḍapādian thought. The Vedānta school, however, cannot be properly understood without some awareness of its philosophical and religious heritage in the *Upaniṣads*. Therefore, chapter 2 provides a brief overview of the philosophical heritage of pre-Śaṅkarite Vedānta. It is my opinion that Advaita Vedānta (particularly in the early phase of development under consideration in this study), cannot be properly understood without a basic understanding of the pre-Gauḍapādian Mahāyāna philosophy that influenced its early formation. Focusing this study upon the *Gauḍapādīya-kārikā* has also enabled a restriction of the subject matter to those aspects of Indian Buddhism that may have exhibited an influence (either directly or indirectly through other schools) upon the doctrines of the GK. The conclusions drawn concerning the date and authorship of the text (chapter 1) therefore provide the current investigation with a suitable *terminus ad quem* for material to be considered.

In the context of the Mahāyāna :: Advaita Vedānta philosophical interaction in classical India the focus for the debate appears to have centered upon the applicability (or not) of the concept of a self (*ātman*) to ultimate reality. Advaita Vedānta, I suggest, can be philosophically differentiated from the mainstream position(s) of the two central schools of Indian Mahāyāna (i.e. the Madhyamaka and the Yogācāra) insofar as it postulates the existence of an Absolute (i.e. Brahman). The view that the Mahāyāna schools are not forms of absolutism is, of course, accepted by many scholars today; little or no time, however, has been spent discussing the sense in which both the Advaita Vedānta and the Mahāyāna schools propound a doctrine of non-origination (*ajātivāda*) given this fundamental philosophical divergence. Differentiation of the meaning of non-origination in the Advaita and Mahayana traditions is necessary in order to fully appreciate the distinction between the Buddhist philosophical rejection of absolutism and the absolutism of the GK. Too many scholars in the past have been unaware of this distinction and so have been unable to distinguish the GK's absolutistic interpretation of Buddhism from the Buddhist tradition itself.

As far as the *Gauḍapādīya-kārikā* is concerned, this study will emphasize the fact that the questions of date and authorship of the text are complex and inter-related. It is suggested as a working hypothesis that the GK is in fact a composite text. It is also argued that the fourth (and longest) *prakaraṇa* was originally a separate text in its own right, composed by a member of the same philosophical lineage as the author(s) of the early *prakaraṇas*. GK I has certain problematic features that are suggestive of separate authorship, but there is nothing in the first *prakaraṇa* that *cannot* be reconciled with the others. In terms of the dating of the text, a consideration of the GK and Bhāvaviveka's *Madhyamakahṛdayakārikā* suggests that the relationship between these two texts is a complex one.

Furthermore, it is suggested that the fourth *prakaraṇa* of the GK is written with a purpose which differs from that of the other three. First, it is a treatise examining the nature of experience in the light of the doctrine of non-origination (*ajātivāda*) and, second, it attempts to facillitate a *rapprochement* between the Vedāntic and Mahāyāna traditions. The author of GK IV shows a keen awareness of internal Mahāyāna controversies but misinterprets the mainstream Mahāyāna doctrine of the non-origination of *dharmas* as a form of absolutism akin to his own.

The central themes of the GK are the twin concepts of *ajātivāda* and *asparśayoga*. Both are philosophically dependent upon the Madhyamaka and Yogācāra schools. Our analysis of the early Yogācāra with which the author(s) of the GK would have been acquainted and the text's own philosophical position casts doubt upon the traditional designation of both as "idealistic," stressing the need for an appreciation of the meditative background and ontology of these systems of thought. It is argued that one cannot appreciate the final position (*siddhānta*) of an Indian philosophical school such as the Yogācāra without a recognition of the distinction between mundane awareness (*vijñāna*) and ultimate gnosis (*jñāna*). The Gauḍapādian doctrine of non-origination is dependent upon Madhyamaka sources and involves an inversion of the latter school's basic position—taking what is in fact a criticism of others as a wholesale endorsement of the GK's own (absolutistic) view. The Gauḍapādian belief that its own absolutism does not conflict with any other views (*avirodhavāda*) is shown to be dependent upon the implications of Nāgārjuna's critique of all views (*dṛṣṭi*). This is exposed via a comparison of Nāgārjuna's *MūlaMadhyamakakārikā* and the *Gauḍapādīya-kārikā*.

With regard to the Mahāyāna, however, one should acknowledge the very real possibility that certain "trends" within the tradition seem close to upholding a form of absolutism akin to that of the Advaita Vedānta school. In this context we shall consider those texts which utilize the notion of the *tathāgatagarbha* and occasionally even the usually censured *ātman* terminology (e.g the *Mahāparinirvāṇasūtra* and to a certain extent the *Śrīmālādevīsiṃhanādasūtra* and the *Ratnagotravibhāgaśāstra*) in considering the scope of Mahāyāna influence upon the *Gauḍapādīya-kārikā*.

CHAPTER 1

The Date and Authorship of the *Gauḍapādīya-kārikā*

The *Gauḍapādīya-kārikā* may very well represent the earliest available record of an uncompromising non-dualistic doctrine (*advaita-vāda*) in the Vedānta school.[1] The text itself comprises of 215 verses traditionally divided into four *prakaraṇas*. The first *prakaraṇa* is traditionally interspersed between the prose of the *Māṇḍūkya Upaniṣad*,[2] and is said to be an exposition of its main themes, although Vidhushekhara Bhattacharya has suggested that the *Upaniṣad* is actually later than the *prakaraṇa*.[3] Because of this association, the text is often called the *Māṇḍūkyakārikā* or as Bhattacharya preferred, the *Āgama-śāstra*. However, the remaining three *prakaraṇas* show little or no connection with the actual text of the *Māṇḍūkya Upaniṣad*, although there is a degree of doctrinal overlap. Nevertheless, each *prakaraṇa* has evidence of Buddhist influence in its language and arguments. The propensity for Buddhist ideas reaches such a degree in the fourth *prakaraṇa*, that some have suggested that it is actually a separate Buddhist work in its own right.[4]

The Identity and Date of Gauḍapāda

According to the Vedāntic tradition, Gauḍapāda is the teacher of Govinda, Śaṅkara's own teacher. Śaṅkara twice quotes the *Gauḍapādīya-kārikā* in his *Brahmasūtrabhāṣya* (BSBh). In BSBh II.1.9 Śaṅkara cites GK I.16, referring to its source as "the teacher(s?) who know the meaning of the Vedānta tradition" (*atroktaṃ Vedāntārtha saṃpradāya vidbhirācāryaiḥ*). In BSBh I.4.14, GK III.15 is quoted and attributed to "those who know the tradition of the Vedānta" (*tathā ca saṃpradāyavido vadanti*). In his commentary on *Chāndogya Upaniṣad* 8.12.1, Śaṅkara also appears to refer to "the most revered follower of the school of Prajāpati," whose views are to be found in the four *prakaraṇas*. Again in *Upadeśasāhasrī* 2.18.2 Śaṅkara pays homage to his "teacher's teacher" (*guror garīyase*). Recently, however, Thomas Wood has cast doubt upon this evidence, pointing out that the phrase "*guror-garīyase*" can be taken to mean "extremely great teacher," "he who is greater than a (mere guru)," or even "highly venerable guru."[5] Wood argues that there is nothing in this section of the *Upadeśasāhasrī* which would link the reference in 2.18.2 either to Gauḍapāda or to the *Gauḍapādīya-kārikā*. As for the evidence from the *Chāndogya Upaniṣadbhāṣya*, he suggests that the phrase '*prakaraṇa-catuṣṭaya*' is a reference to the four instructions given by Prajāpati to Indra regarding the nature of the self in CU 8.7–12 and not to the four *prakaraṇas* of the *Gauḍapādīya-kārikā*.[6] Nevertheless, it is equally likely that Śaṅkara is here referring to the author of the four *prakaraṇas* (of the GK) and stating that they conform to the "school of Prajāpati" insofar as they deal with the doctrine of the four states of the self outlined by Prajāpati in the text of *Chāndogya Upaniṣad* (CU) 8.7-12. Enough doubt, however, has been cast on the import of these references to treat them with some caution.

In the commentary on the *Gauḍapādīya-kārikā*, which may or may not be by Śaṅkara, the author of the text is referred to as the *bhāṣyakāra's* "grand (or supreme) teacher" (*paramaguru*, GKBh IV.100.) The ambiguity of the term "*paramaguru*" however should be noted. The term may be used to denote a "grand-teacher" (that is the teacher of one's own teacher) or may be used in a more figurative sense where it merely implies the primary source of one's inspiration. In the latter sense, the term does not imply membership of the same *saṃpradāya* or lineage of teachers. One cannot be certain, then, that the traditional view that Gauḍapāda is the teacher of Śaṅkara's teacher is in fact an accurate interpretation of the textual evidence available.

Whatever the precise relationship between the author(s) of the GK and Śaṅkara, one cannot doubt the esteem with which the *kārikās* and the author to whom they are ascribed were held. This much is clear from the references to the knower(s) of the Vedānta tradition when quoting GK III.15 and I.16 in BSBh I.4.14 and II.1.9. Despite this we know little more about the figure of "Gauḍa" or "Gauḍapāda" other than a number of mythological legends accepted by the post-Śaṅkara Vedānta tradition.[7] Information about the life and precise identity of "Gauḍapāda" is lost in the same hazy mists that shroud our knowledge of the early Vedānta school in India.

There has been a suggestion that the verses are the handbook of an early school of Vedānta, established in Bengal.[8] This is based upon the fact that part of northern Bengal was once called Gauḍadeśa. "Gauḍapāda" then, would mean the "summary verses from Bengal," and would not be the name of an individual at all. This of course, goes against all of the traditional interpretation of the evidence that we have before us in the works of Śaṅkara and his successors. On this point, however, it is interesting to note that Sureśvara, one of Śaṅkara immediate disciples, quotes the *Gauḍapādīya-kārikā* and Śaṅkara's *Upadeśasāhasrī*, describing the two authors of these texts as "Gauḍas" and "Draviḍas" respectively (*Naiṣkarmyasiddhi* IV.44–46).

Sureśvara appears to be contrasting the two authors by referring to their places of geographical origin, Śaṅkara in the south of India (Draviḍas), and the author of the *Gauḍapādīya-kārikā* in the north (Gauḍas). Certainly, if the tradition is correct in describing Gauḍapāda as a *samnyāsī* he would have renounced his own family name. It would not have been inappropriate for him to have been known according to his connection with the Gauḍadeśa region, in which case "*pāda*" would be an honorific title like "*ācārya*." This is, in fact, how Sureśvara understands the name as he alternates between "Gauḍas," "Gauḍapāda," and "Gauḍācārya."[9] If this is a correct appraisal of the situation, the reason why Gauḍapāda's place of origin was so important to his identity is still an unanswered question. Perhaps he became famous in a region distant from his own native area and so, as a "foreigner," was named after his birthplace; alternatively, Gauḍapāda may represent the name of the foremost teacher of an early (i.e. pre-Śaṅkarite) school of non-dualistic Vedānta founded in Bengal.[10]

The GK makes no obvious reference to the *Brahmasūtra* and its concomitant traditions,[11] yet references are made to the "established doctrines of the Vedānta" and to the Upaniṣadic literature in the first three *prakaraṇas*. In the GK all Vedāntic texts, of course, are said to reflect the text's own radically non-dualistic position and not the realism of the difference-non-difference (*bhedābheda*) school usually associated with pre-Śaṅkara Vedānta.[12] Do we have here the work of an alternative Vedānta tradition, running counter-current to the realistic (*pariṇāma*) tradition of the *Brahmasūtra*, or are we just witnessing the age old technique of reading one's own views into the traditions of the past? There is no firm evidence that might substantiate the hypothesis that there was a separate strand of early Vedānta philosophy displaying a form of radical non-dualism similar to that of the Śaṅkarite school. Nevertheless, we must acknowledge that historical evidence concerning the roots of the Vedānta-*darśāna* is shrouded in mystery and that there is still much that remains undiscovered.

If one accepts the *prima facie* evidence that Śaṅkara's *Chāndogya Upaniṣadbhāṣya* refers to the four *prakaraṇas* of the GK (and, as we have seen, Wood's arguments suggest that this is by no means the only interpretation of the evidence), then it is clear that the GK must have been established as a composite work of the Vedānta school by the eighth century CE (Common Era). This is apart from the fact that we have a commentary on the GK which may well prove to be by Śaṅkara himself. Śaṅkara's near contemporary, the Buddhist Śāntarakṣita, in the midst of discussing the views of the "*aupaniṣadas*," cites at least thirteen verses from GK II and III in his *Madhyamakālaṅkārakārikā*.[13] Citations by Śaṅkara, Sureśvara, and Śāntarakṣita together firmly establish the existence of the first, second, and third *prakaraṇas* by the eighth century CE. Let us summarize the evidence of citations of the GK prior to the ninth century CE.

1. Śaṅkara (c. eighth century CE) cites GK I.16 and III.15 in his commentary on the *Brahmasūtra*. Both times he refers to their source as the knower(s) or teacher(s) of the Vedānta *saṃpradāya*.
2. Śaṅkara's pupil Sureśvara cites GK I.11 and 15 in *Naiṣkarmya-siddhi* (NS) IV.41-42, attributing the verses to "Gauḍas" (see NS IV.44). In his *Bṛhadāraṇyaka Upaniṣadvārttika* (BUV), Sureśvara quotes GK III.15 (BUV II.1.386), which he attributes to "Gauḍācārya." In BUV IV.8.886 and 888, Sureśvara quotes GK II.38 and III.46 referring to them as the "*ślokas* of Gauḍapāda." Finally in BUV I.4.389 three words from GK II.17 are quoted as "*Gauḍapādīya vacas*."

Other verses from the GK are also quoted by Sureśvara but without any specific attribution. BUV I.4.744 quotes GK I.3 as "*āgama-śāsana*"; BUV I.4.712 quotes GK I.11 without attribution (although in the NS Sureśvara attributes this *kārikā* to "Gauḍas.") In BUV 1.4.615, the author cites GK I.14, referring to it as "the well-established view of the Vedānta."

3. Maṇḍana-miśra (c. seventh-eighth century CE) cites GK I.11 in *Brahmasiddhi* III.171a (150) in his discussion of Vedic testimony with the words "Thus it is said" (*tad uktam*).
4. The Buddhist philosopher Śāntarakṣita (c. eighth century CE) cites *kārikās* 17–20, 31–32, and 35 of the second *prakaraṇa*

and *kārikās* 4, 6, 8, and 30–32 of the third *prakaraṇa* in a discussion of the views of the "*aupaniṣadas*" in his autocommentary to *śloka* 93 of his *Madhyamakālaṅkārakārikā*.

This evidence establishes beyond any reasonable doubt that GK I, II, and III were established texts of the Vedānta school by the eighth century. From the evidence of citations and attributions in the works of Sureśvara, we can establish that there was a link of authorship in the verses quoted, establishing an early acceptance of the common authorship of the first, second, and third *prakaraṇas*. The common source of these verses is said by Sureśvara to be known as "Gauḍas," "Gauḍapāda," or "Gauḍācārya." Note, however, that no author, not even the Buddhist Śāntarakṣita (who quotes copiously from the GK), makes any reference to the fourth *prakaraṇa* in spite of the fact that it amounts to nearly half of the entire text which we now have before us.

Citations from later authors also reflect an omission of *kārikās* from the fourth *prakaraṇa*. It is not, however, merely the fourth *prakaraṇa* that is conspicuous by its absence. Commentators from rival Vedānta schools refer to the first *prakaraṇa*, but in most cases, the remaining three are surprisingly ignored. Rāmānuja (1055–1137 CE) quotes GK I.16 in the introduction to his commentary on the *Brahmasūtra*, describing it as *śruti*. Kūranārāyaṇa, a member of Rāmānuja's own lineage, wrote a commentary on MU and GK I, referring to both as *śruti*. No mention is made in either case of any other *prakaraṇas*. The dualistic Vedāntin Madhva (1199–1278 CE) also wrote a commentary on MU and GK I, which he also refers to as *śruti*. Again, there is no suggestion that there are any other verses to be commented upon. This brings up two important issues. Why do these writers and commentators seem to think that GK I is *śruti* and why do they not mention the other *prakaraṇas*? It is certainly strange to write a commentary on a text and then to stop after the first chapter. Puruṣottama the seventeenth century Śuddhādvaitin wrote a commentary on the first and second *prakaraṇas* and according to Conio intended to comment on the third.[14]

Why is there no mention of GK IV in any text prior to the *Gauḍapādīyakārikābhāśya* (GKBh) itself? If the GKBh is not an authentic work of Śaṅkara then the author of that text may have lived as late as the twelth century CE since it is not until Ānandagiri (c.1300 CE), the author of the *Gauḍapādīyakārikābhāśyavyākhya*, that the commentary is first mentioned (and attributed to Śaṅkara). Kūranārāyaṇa, Madhva, and Puruṣottama, all make no reference to a fourth *prakaraṇa* despite writing a commentary on the first *prakaraṇa* (and in the case of Puruṣottama, on the second and probably the third *prakaraṇas* also).

This is all highly surprising since we know for sure that GK I, II, III and IV and the *bhāṣya* upon them must have been composed before the time of Ānandagiri (late thirteenth century CE). The *bhāṣyakāra* differs in many respects from the views of the original *kārikās* themselves, and this in itself suggests that the four *prakaraṇas* are sufficiently separated from the commentator in time for their meaning to be unclear. In the fifteenth century, we find Sadānanda quoting GK III.44, 45 with the words "*tad uktam*" (Thus it is said). However, the crucial point is that we find Vedāntic and Buddhist scholars writing in a time after Ānandagiri (and hence after the establishment of the four *prakaraṇas* as a single text and the composition of a *bhāṣya* upon them), who ignore the existence of certain *prakaraṇas*, especially the fourth. One cannot doubt that these *prakaraṇas* (especially the first three) were in existence at this time, nor can one doubt that they were considered by some to constitute a single text. The fact, however, that there were established traditions which took the first *prakaraṇa* to be *śruti* along with the *Māṇḍūkya Upaniṣad* to which it is appended, suggest that the identity of the four *prakaraṇas* was not a universally accepted view even perhaps as late as the seventeenth century (if we assume that Puruṣottama did not intend to write a commentary on GK IV also).

What we find, in fact, are authors who clearly post-date GK IV ignoring the fourth *prakaraṇa*, perhaps because they were not aware of it or because they did not consider it a text which belonged with the other three. Surely Rāmānuja and Kūranārāyaṇa (Viśiṣṭādvaita), Madhva (Dvaita), and Puruṣottama (Śuddhādvaita), as critics of the "*māyāvāda*" of Śaṅkara's Advaita school, would have jumped at the chance to further substantiate the charge that the Advaitin is a crypto-Buddhist by referring to the Buddhist terminology and arguments of GK IV. Yet none of these authors even go as far as to criticize the more Buddhistic aspects of any of the *prakaraṇas* on which they do comment. In fact, all appear to have an extremely reverential view of the *kārikās*, (in many cases GK I being ascribed the status of *śruti*). Madhva in his dualistic commentary on the first *prakaraṇa* interprets all references to "*advaita*" as "free from impurities and imperfections." Clearly, this is not what the author of the first *prakaraṇa* seems to have intended when he used the term. That Madhva felt a need to comment on such a markedly non-dualistic text is perhaps a testimony to its authority within Vedāntic circles in general.

Authorship of the *Gauḍapādīya-kārikā*

The Relationship Between the First and Second Prakaraṇas

As with many Indian works, the attempt to piece together the historical background of the texts composition is fraught with theoretical and practical difficulties. The first *prakaraṇa* is in many respects different from the other three, not least because of its intimate connection with the prose of the *Māṇḍūkya Upaniṣad*. The content of GK I consists of a discussion of various creation theories, an exposition of the doctrine of the four states of experience and an explanation and exhortation to meditate upon the syllable Om. Although a refutation of creation theories remains a central feature of all four *prakaraṇas*, both the doctrine of the four states of experience and meditation on the syllable Om are absent from the remaining three *prakaraṇas* despite great emphasis on the analysis of experience and on the practice of *yoga*.

This discrepancy could be explained in a number of ways. One might suggest that repetition of major themes is unlikely in the GK since it is a collection of terse and brief *kārikās* rather than a lengthy and verbose exposition of Advaita philosophy. Be that as it may, the centrality of these doctrines in GK I belies the silence of the later *prakaraṇas*. Many themes (and indeed even entire arguments and verses) are in fact repeated throughout the GK, and one would expect the psychological analysis of experience in GK I to be referred to again, particularly in the discussion of the nature of perception in GK IV. Nor can the centrality of meditation on the syllable Om be questioned. GK I.24, for instance, even goes as far to suggest that having concentrated the mind upon the syllable Om, "one should meditate upon nothing else whatsoever." Why in the 186 verses contained in the remaining three *prakaraṇas* does such a central practice go unmentioned? It is not because of lack of interest for GK III and IV spend much time discussing the nature and consequences of *asparśa-yoga*, the "*yoga* of no-contact." In response, one might point to the fact that GK I is an exposition of the central themes of the MU and that this necessarily restricts the author to a discussion of those ideas found in the *Upaniṣad* itself; in later chapters there is no such obstacle to free discussion. This is a possibility, but GK I is not a strict commentary (*bhāṣya*) on the MU, merely an exposition of some of the central themes of the *Upaniṣad*. The first *prakaraṇa* makes no real attempt to systematically explain the *Māṇḍūkya* prose as one might expect in a straightforwardly commentarial text. This feature of GK I led Vidhushekhara Bhattacharya to suggest that the *prakaraṇa* pre-dates the MU; a conclusion that seems unwarranted given that GK I is not in fact a *bhāṣya* but a *prakaraṇa*. Its purpose then is not to provide a comprehensive explanation of the words and phrases used in the MU, but rather to discuss some of its main themes.

Other aspects of GK I, however, seem to conflict with verses in the later *prakaraṇas*. GK I.6 introduces the discussion of various creation theories with an unannounced statement which seems to support the idea of creation.

> I.6: *prabhavaḥ sarvabhāvānāṃ satām iti viniścayaḥ.*
> *sarvam janayati prāṇaś ceto' ṃśūn puruṣaḥ pṛthak.*
> It is the firm conclusion [of sages] that there is an origin of all existing entities. *Prāṇa* creates the universe, *Puruṣa* creates each separate ray of consciousness.

Having already introduced the idea that it is the entirety of human experience that should be examined in an evaluation of reality and not just the experiences of our waking state (GK I.3d), various metaphysical theories explaining the nature of creation are put forward for consideration. *Prāṇa* as the vital breath brings life to things (i.e. causes them to come into being), and *Puruṣa* diversifies consciousness into living beings (*jīvas*). Karmarkar argues that the account of creation given in this verse cannot be Gauḍapāda's since he upholds *ajātivāda*;[15] however, there is no evidence from the text itself to substantiate Karmarkar's view. The *Vaitathyaprakaraṇa* (GK II) gives the following account of the world's appearance,

> II.16: *jīvaṃ kalpayate pūrvaṃ tato bhāvān pṛthagvidhān,*
> *bāhyān ādhyātmikāṃś caiva yathāvidyas tathāsmṛtiḥ.*
> [The *ātman*] first imagines the *jīva* (individual soul), and then different things, external and internal (objective and subjective); as one knows so does one recollect.

It should be noted, however, that GK I.6 and II.16 are not *necessarily* incompatible. I.6 can be interpreted as a description of a *vivarta*-type transformation where the individualization of consciousness into separate *jīvas* is merely imagined or "apparently-constructed" (*kalpita*).[16] Perhaps we are to assume that the theory propounded in GK I.6 is not the author's position, although it is the view of those convinced (*viniścaya*) about such things. Nevertheless, it seems most plausible to interpret the verse, along with Bhattacharya, as a reference to the views of wise men. The term *viniścaya* occurs nowhere else in the GK, although similar terms such as *viniścita* (GK I.8), *niścita* (GK I.14, 22; II.17, 18; III.23), *suniścita* (GK IV.92, 95), and *niścaya* (GK II.12) occur throughout the text.[17] One should note, however, that these terms are generally used in a positive manner, endorsing or supporting the view put forward, except perhaps for *viniścita* in GK I.8. That the latter is used to refer to the views of others may be significant in this instance since it occurs two verses after the *kārikā* currently under discussion.

The next three verses discuss various other cosmogonic theories. GK I.7 attributes the view that creation is "like a dream and an illusion" (*svapna/māyā-vat*) to "others"—it does not appear to be the author's own view (although GK I.16 accepts the concept of "beginningless *māyā*.")

> I.7: *vibhūtiṃ prasavaṃ tv anye manyante sṛṣṭicintakāḥ,*
> *svapnamāyāsvarūpeti sṛṣṭir anyair vikalpitā.*
> Some creation-theorists, however, think of creation as an outflowing (emanation). Creation is imagined by others as having the same form as dream and illusion (*māyā*).[18]

In the first line of this verse we find the term "*vibhūti*," the quality of all-pervasiveness. Thus for some thinkers creation is an emanation, an overflowing of the "pleroma." The second line describes a view that is hard to distinguish from the author's own. The natural interpretation of the reference to the *māyā* theory of creation in GK I.7cd is that it is the view of a rival school. Placing one's own view in the midst of discussion of the views of others would seem to be a peculiar juxtaposition to say the least. However, in GK II.31 that same doctrine is said to be the established view of the Vedānta. What are we to make of this?

Karmarkar takes GK I.7cd to be a reference to the doctrines of the *Laṅkāvatārasūtra*.[19] Certainly it is problematic to accept Bhattacharya's assertion that "[t]his view is held by some Vedāntists including our teacher."[20] Hixon suggests that the author's quarrel with this view is that it mistakenly accepts creation in the first place.[21] This is an attractive interpretation. In the *Vaitathyaprakaraṇa* (GK II) we find criticisms to the effect that our common sense notions of "normality" should not be derived purely from our waking experience and then extrapolated to stand for all facets of our experience (II.8). Thus, it would be absurd to talk of creation as having the form of a dream or an illusion for these can only be defined according to a dualistic creation scheme. It would be like explaining a flower by saying that it is like a lotus. Dreams and illusions constitute a (relatively) minor aspect of the so-called "created" realm. Be that as it may, this does not explain the attribution of this view to others given its adoption by the author at a later point.

Thomas Wood argues that GK I.7cd cannot be a reference to the author's own view since it occurs in the midst of a list of the views of others.[22] Despite this, in GK I.16 we find a reference to the enlightened *jīva* awakening to a non-dual reality which was previously masked by beginningless *māyā*.

> I.16: *anādimāyayā supto yadā jīvaḥ prabudhyate,*
> *ajam anidram asvapnam advaitaṃ budhyate tadā.*
> *When the jīva*, asleep due to beginningless *māyā*, is awakened, it then realizes the unborn, sleepless, dreamless non-duality.

How are we to reconcile the author's adoption of this term with his attribution of it to "others" in GK I.7? Wood suggests that *māyā* is used in GK I.16 in a 'non-illusionistic'' sense, that is in a manner which is more conducive to the earlier (realist) meanings of *māyā* as found in the various *Saṃhitās* and *Upaniṣads*.

> Note that this verse refers to the individual who awakens from the illusion of difference and of individuality. It does not say that the world itself is unreal, but only that duality is an illusion. This is compatible, of course, with the view that the world is unreal, but is also compatible with the view that the world is real but also non dual.[23]

For Wood in fact this verse

> does not necessarily mean that the world as such disappears. A more natural and much less problematic way of reading the *kārikā* is to say that when the true nature of things is realized, the world—which is a manifestation of brahman—is realized to be non-dual and non-different from *brahman*. In other words, when a person attains Self-realization, it is not the world as such but his misapprehension and misperception of the nature of the world that is sublated.[24]

This interpretation of GK I.16 is interesting since it is not incompatible with the *māyā* doctrine as it is actually found in the Advaita Vedānta school (although it would be on Wood's interpretation of Advaita). One way of stating the Advaita position is to say that the world exists insofar as it partakes of the reality of Brahman. This is not to deny that the world exists but merely to qualify the nature of that existence, so as to emphasize its total dependence upon the substrate Brahman. The problem with Wood's analysis of the GK is that his discussion of Advaita Vedānta is hampered by an overly-simplistic and one-sided interpretation of the *māyā* doctrine, which he takes to be an assertion of the complete unreality of the world. Wood wishes to suggest not only that GK I does not uphold such a view but also that such a view is philosophically more problematic than the realistic metaphysics of the *Upaniṣads* and early Vedānta. Thus,

> A Vedantist who adhered strictly to the *Upaniṣads* would treat the conclusion that world is unreal as absurd, and conclude that the argument shows that the no-substance (*adravya, niḥsvabhāva*) view of the Buddhist is untenable.[25]

The view that the world is an unreal illusion is attributed not only to Advaita Vedānta by Wood but, as the above quote suggests, to the various schools of Buddhism also. Thus, "according to the Mahāyāna, the world is not the manifestation of an absolute at all: it is simply unreal."[26] Of course, there is a sense in which "the world is unreal" is a kind of shorthand for the Mahāyāna notion of emptiness (*śūnyatā*) and the Advaitic notion of *māyā*; however, given the importance of the two-truths doctrine in both the Mahāyāna and Advaita, it is never the case that the world is *simply* unreal.[27] There is nothing simple or simplistic about the Advaitic denial of the ultimate reality of the dualistic world. The matter is a highly complex issue involving the utilization of a number of different analogies to explain the (ultimately) inexplicable (*anirvacanīya, acintya*) relationship that exists between Brahman and the universe. While the author of the GK pre-dates the adoption of the *anirvacanīya* explanation of *māyā*, it is misleading to suggest, as Wood does, that the GK, the Advaita Vedānta school and the schools of Mahāyāna Buddhism all *simply* deny that the world is real. As we shall see when we come to consider the meaning(s) of the term "*māyā*" in the GK, there are verses which could be taken to imply that the world is completely unreal only if read out of context. However, there are many others that refute this interpretation of *māyā* (e.g. GK III.28, IV.52, 53.) Wood, in his understanding of Advaita as a wholesale denial of the reality of the world is attributing to the school what GK IV.83 sees as an extreme view which "forever covers the Lord (*bhagavān*)" from sight, namely the nihilistic view that "it does not exist."

> I.8. *icchāmātraṃ prabhoḥ sṛṣṭir iti sṛṣṭau viniścitāḥ,*
> *kālāt prasūtiṃ bhūtānāṃ manyante kālacintakāḥ.*

Creation is merely the will of the Lord so [think others who have] a firm conviction about creation and those who speculate about time consider the creation of beings [to be] from time.

Prabhu, the "powerful one" is used in GK I.8 giving the view discussed a distinctively theistic connotation. Kūranārāyaṇa in his commentary suggests that creation by the Lord's volition is the view of the *aupaniṣadas*. Thus he takes this to be the author's final position (*siddhānta*). This is difficult to accept given the position of the view, embedded within a list of opponent's doctrines, and its apparent incompatibility with *ajātivāda*. In the commentary, the *bhāṣya-kāra* (Śaṅkara?) says that in this view the Lord is seen as a potter. As such his pots are manifestations of his creative will and are neither external nor unrelated to such will. The *Kālācintakās* are those who think about time, they accept that time is the great dispenser.[28]

Consider also GK I.9 the final verse of the creationist section of GK I, and so one might expect, some indication of the author's own position.

bhogārthaṃ sṛṣṭir ity anye krīḍārtham iti cāpare,
devasyaiṣasvabhāvo' yam āptakāmasya kā spṛhā.[29]
Creation is for the sake of enjoyment (or experience)—so say some. Others say it is for the sake of sport. This again is the lordly own-nature of the divine, for what desire is there for the one who has obtained all wishes?[30]

Two teleological theories are put forward to account for the purpose or aim of creation. This is an odd topic to consider given that the author of the *Gauḍapādīya-kārikā* upholds the doctrine of non-origination (*ajātivāda*), which denies that creation has even occurred in the first place. Discussion of the purpose or aim of creation then would seem to be philosophically irrelevant and superfluous to the author. However, it would appear that the GK is addressing "those who are convinced that there is an origin of all existent entities" (mentioned at the outset of this discussion in GK I.6). The first theory outlined in GK I.9 is that the purpose of creation is for the divine being to have experiences. This is the import of various Upaniṣadic verses, where the divine being creates because of a desire for duality.[31]

The second theory considered is that diversity is for the sake of God's sport or diversion. The author's response to these views is not without ambiguity. "This again is the lordly own-nature of the divine, for what desire is there for the one who has obtained all wishes?" Wood suggests that:

It is possible that the *siddhānta* is given by the doctrine of self-nature (*svabhāva-vāda*) of AP 9c-d only (so that the view that creation is the object of enjoyment or play is also rejected), but it seems more likely that the second half of the *kārikā* simply makes explicit what is implicit in the doctrine that creation is merely the play or sport of *īśvara*, i.e. that there can be no purpose or motive (*prayojana*) in creation, for the Lord is by definition beyond all desires. This is the view of the Brahma-sūtras.[32]

If the doctrine that creation occurs in comformity to the intrinsic nature (*svabhāva*) of the divine being (GK I.9cd) is the author's own view, as Wood suggests, then this appears to contradict GK II.34.

II.34: *nātmabhāvena nānedaṃ na svenāpi kathañcana,*
na pṛthan nāpṛthak kiñcid iti tattvavido viduḥ.
The universe is manifold neither through the nature of *ātman*, nor through its own nature. Nothing whatsoever is either separate or non-separate—this the knowers of reality know.

Wood acknowledges, however, (in the aformentioned quote) that there is another interpretation of GK I.9cd. On this view, I.9cd is an explanation of the form creation must take if it is to be said to occur at all. The author suggests that creation must conform to the nature of the divine being from which it stems. How then can a purpose be found for the creation of the universe given that the basic nature (*svabhāva*) of the divine (*deva*, literally "the shining one") is free from all unfulfilled desires? Here is a compact yet devastating attack upon attempts to formulate a cosmogonic theory applicable to the notion of an omniscient and omnipotent God. While the *līla* concept is used to overcome this philosophical problem in the *Brahmasūtra*, it is not immediately clear that the author accepts the validity of this conception himself. One might suggest that if Brahman has all of its desires fulfilled, then it will also have no desire to indulge in sport either.

While it seems likely that GK I.9cd corresponds to the author's own position, it is not immediately obvious that the same can be said for GK I.9ab. It should be noted that GK I.9 approaches the question of creation from a different angle than the views outlined in the previous *kārikās*. Previously, the author discussed theories about the nature of creation. In I.9, the purpose of creation is discussed (a topic that presupposes creation itself). The author then appears to be summing up his discussion of creation theories with the statement that, whatever one's view, creation must always conform to the intrinsic-nature of its creator. This does not commit the author of the GK to this view but is rather a summarizing statement to the effect that "if you have a theory about creation—you must accept that creation conforms to the nature of the divine [creator]." Given that Brahman is free from all desires, how then is the creation-theorist to explain the purpose of creation? The answer is, of course, that he cannot. This leaves the whole question of explaining the real nature of creation unresolved, which is not surprising since for the author of the GK, creation is only appearance (*māyāmātra*).[33]

Consider also GK I.17 and 18:

> I.17: *prapañco 'yadi vidyeta nivarteta na saṃśayaḥ,*
> *māyāmātram idaṃ dvaitam advaitaṃ paramārthataḥ.*[34]
> There is no doubt that if the multiplicity (*prapañca*) were existing, it would cease to be [upon enlightenment]. This duality is only *māyā*, in ultimate reality there is only non-duality.

I.17 states that *prapañca* does not disappear because it does not in fact exist in the first place. Wood suggests that GK I. 17 and 18 are philosophically untenable since the unreality of the world cannot account for the fact that we perceive the world. How can the unreal even appear?[35] Again we are confronted with Wood's misunderstanding of the Advaita position. In GK II and IV in particular we find most of the *kārikās* therein devoted to a discussion of the nature of perception in order to explain precisely what is going on when we perceive a world of diverse objects. Wood makes no effort to consider this doctrine on its own terms.[36] He suggests in fact that GK I.17ab

> commits the logical fallacy of negating the antecedent of a counterfactual. The valid argument (*modus tollendo tollens*) would negate the disappearance of the world, from which the nonexistence of the world would be inferred.[37]

The argument of GK I.17, however can be understood in a manner which is logically consistent. GK I.17ab suggests that:

a. If *prapañca* existed it would be able to disappear
b. *Prapañca* does not exist.
c. Therefore, *prapañca* cannot disappear.

I.17 is difficult to understand if taken out of context, but it makes perfect sense following on from the previous verse (GK I.16) which describes the realisation of *turīya*. If this world really existed then it would vanish with the experience of non-duality, but it remains precisely because it is duality and is to be taken as merely illusion (*māyāmātra*). The mistake is in thinking that duality even exists in the first place.[38]

> I.18: *vikalpo vinivarteta kalpito yadi kenacit,*
> *upadeśād ayaṃ vādo jñāte dvaitaṃ na vidyate.*
> [Upon enlightenment] wrong-interpretation (*vikalpa*) would disappear if it were imagined (or constructed) by someone. This way of speaking is for the sake of instruction; when it is known, duality is not found.

GK I.18 is an attempt to circumvent one of the greatest paradoxes of a non-dualistic soteriology—if duality is an illusion how is it that the dream is not broken by the first enlightened being? This presents no real problem for the *Gauḍapādīya-kārikā* for the following reasons:

1. Duality as *māyā* is not in conflict with non-duality as the ultimate reality (*paramārtha*) since the former is merely an appearance of the latter (see GK III.17, 18; IV.4, 5).
2. The idea of a liberated individual is an erroneous one, no *jīva* is ever liberated, since no *jīva* has ever entered bondage (i.e. *ajātivāda*, see GK II.32; III.48).

This verse is also as clear a denial as one is likely to find of subjective idealism.

We noted in I.7 that the author of the *prakaraṇa* seems to be critical of the view that creation is "in the form of dream and illusion" (*svapnamāyāsvarūpeti*). We also noted Hixon's point that this objection may itself be grounded in the denial of origination in that the use of an analogy from the dualistic realm (i.e., dreams and illusions) to explain that dualistic schema is problematic. The analogy may also have been objectionable on the grounds that describing the world as a dream can lead to the acceptance of some form of subjective idealism or solipsism where the individual "I" is given supreme status. Egocentricity is at the root of the ignorance of attachment to difference (*bheda*) (see GK II.16). The ineffable, non-conceptual nature of reality is developed further by the explicit utilization of Buddhist dialectic in the fourth *prakaraṇa*.

Here in I.17 and 18 we find the first usage of two very important terms in the Gaudapadian exposition of *advaita-vāda*, i.e. *prapañca* and *vikalpa*. *Prapañca* primarily denotes the idea of plurality (literally "fiveness" or *pañca*). It is a common Buddhist technical term denoting the empty "conceptual proliferation" characteristic of all (false) views, as is the other term which is used alongside it in the GK, the term *vikalpa*—the "conceptually-constructed," (and hence the "imagined"). Clearly these are to be taken as corollaries of each other. Just as ultimate reality is *nirvikalpa*—without conceptualization, so is it *prapañcopaśama* "the stilling of the multiplicity."

The purpose of the inclusion of verses 17 and 18 in the GK appears to have been to explain how it is that the liberation of an individual does not cause the dissipation of duality for everyone else. The objection the author appears to have in mind is one often stated by Sāṃkhyans in particular, namely that if there is only one *ātman*; salvation for one is salvation for all. The simple response to this is to point out that while there is in fact only the non-dual supreme self (*paramātman*) there are in fact many empirical selves (*jīvātman*). The author of the GK does not respond this way since it is his view that in fact there has been no origination of any empirical selves (*jīvātman*, see GK II.32; III.13, 48). The response that is given to such an objection therefore amounts to a denial that the problem exists. This duality was never there in the first place, and, as part of that duality, the individual is also not real. One should not be lead into the error of thinking that the world is merely a mental construction of the individual; to do so is to assume the reality of an individualized ego and this is precisely the type of "egocentricity" that causes the proliferation (*prapañca*) of duality.

GK I.18, however, appears to contradict II.12, 13, and 18:

> II.12: *kalpayaty ātmanātmānam ātma devaḥ svamāyayā,*
> *sa eva budhyate bhedān iti vedāntaniścayaḥ.*
> The divine *ātman* imagines itself through itself by means of its own *māyā*. It alone is aware of diverse things. This is the conclusion of the Vedānta.
>
> II.13: *vikaroty aparān bhāvān antaś citte vyavasthitān,*
> *niyatāṃś ca bahiś citta evaṃ kalpayate prabhuḥ.*
> It diversifies those objects existing within consciousness, and [those] fixed ones external to consciousness. In this manner does the Lord imagine.
>
> II.18: *niścitāyāṃ yathā rajjvāṃ vikalpo vinivartate,*
> *rajjur eveti cādvaitaṃ tadvad ātmaviniścayaḥ.*
> When the rope is clearly seen wrong-interpretation (*vikalpa*) disappears and there is non-duality of the rope alone; likewise is the clearly seen *ātman*.

There are, however, a couple of ways in which this apparent contradiction may be resolved. First, one could draw attention to I.18cd which suggests that verses discussing the imagining (*kalpita*) of anything are in fact provisional in the sense that they are put forward for the sake of teaching others. Thus, the rope-snake analogy of II.18 is not to be taken too seriously—it is, after all, only an analogy. In fact, both I.18 and II.18 agree in their final summation that in fact there is only non-duality (*advaita*) and nothing else. It is also possible to overcome the apparent contradictoriness of these verses by suggesting that they are discussing different topics. I.18 denies that any individual person (*jīva*) could have imagined the world. This is a denial of subjective idealism (*dṛṣṭisṛṣṭivāda*, "the doctrine that seeing-is-creating") and solipsism (*ekajīvavāda*). This does not conflict with the idea that a divine *ātman* (*ātmā devāḥ*) in fact does the imagining (*kalpayate*). (Even Wood acknowledges that the distinction between *jīvātman* and *ātman* is sometimes to be presumed—see his discussion of GK I.16 on p.119, quoted earlier.) That this is the author's intention can be elicited from the fact that verses such as GK II.12 and 13 use the "theistic" terms "*deva*" and "*prabhu*" to describe the *ātma*n that imagines (*kalpayate*) the universe. It seems beyond any reasonable doubt that these terms are included to differentiate the author's own view from the view explicitly denied in I.18. In GK II.12 and 13 it is clearly not the *jīvātman* that is the cause of the world's appearance.[39]

The Relationship of GK II, III, and IV

There are a number of instances of repetition of verses from the second and third *prakaraṇas* in the fourth (e.g. II.6–7 :: IV.31–32; III.20–22 :: IV.6–8; III.29–30 :: IV.61–62; III.48 :: IV.71). Occasionally minor terminological changes occur (e.g. GK IV often has the term "*dharma*" (Buddhist?) instead of the "*bhāva*" of GK II and III) (see chapter 5). This is an example of the more obvious adoption of Buddhistic terminology in the fourth *prakaraṇa*. Despite this change, there are no inconsistencies between the views propounded in GK II, III, and IV. GK II.32 could be seen to be contradicted by IV.73, but upon closer analysis it is clear that IV.73 is simply a clarification of II.32 (in the same way that II.34 is), establishing the sense in which it is correct to talk about origination and cessation. Such a clarification would have been inappropriate in GK II since it does not devote any *kārikās* explicitly to the two-truths doctrine, although it clearly presupposes such a distinction.

Other evidence, however, is suggestive of the separate authorship of the fourth *prakaraṇa*. The invocation (*maṅgalācaraṇa*) at the beginning of GK IV (possibly to the Buddha) implies that it is an independent work. Clearly the fourth *prakaraṇa* is a new departure, dealing with the topics of the previous *prakaraṇas* but from a slightly different perspective. This in itself does not necessitate separate authorship since the author of GK IV clearly endorses the views expounded in the second and third *prakaraṇas* (GK I as we have seen is more problematic). It should be noted, however, that GK IV is clearly the most philosophically sophisticated of the four *prakaraṇas*. Again this should not surprise us since the chapter constitutes nearly half of the entire text and so has more time to spend on the issues which it discusses. The degree of sophistication of GK IV implies that Vetter[40] and Hixon[41] are unlikely to be correct in their belief that GK IV is the earliest of the four *prakaraṇas* to be composed. Vetter argues that the doctrine of the non-origination of *ātman* propounded in the first three *prakaraṇas* presupposes the non-arising of *dharmas* as discussed in GK IV. Vetter, of course, is correct to argue that the Gauḍapādian conception of non-origination is dependent upon the Mahāyāna conception of *dharma*. This will become clearer as we come to consider these ideas in subsequent chapters. Such philosophical dependence, however, does not in itself prove that the GK's discussion of *dharmas* in the fourth *prakaraṇa* was thereby the first text to be composed. All four *prakaraṇas* presuppose Mahāyāna philosophical notions; GK IV is an explicit discussion of that dependence. This does not necessitate that it was written first. On the contrary, the sophistication of the fourth *prakaraṇa*, and its awareness of Mahāyāna scholastic controversies suggests that it is a supplement, openly infused with the technical vocabulary of Buddhist scholasticism, and designed to elaborate upon the issues discussed in the first three *prakaraṇas*.

Philological evidence in fact does not definitively resolve the matter of the chronological composition of the four *prakaraṇas*, nor does the silence of Buddhist and Vedāntic authors with regard to the fourth *prakaraṇa*. As we have seen, Vetter suggests that the four chapters are separate works connected to each other insofar as they reflect the development of thought of the author of the GK as a whole.[42] If Vetter and Hixon are correct in the establishment of GK IV as the earliest of the four *prakaraṇas*, then what we have in the GK is a textual crystallization of the process whereby Buddhist philosophy became increasingly "Brahmanized" and incorporated into the Vedānta tradition. Thus GK IV would represent the early thought of the Buddhist-inspired Gauḍapāda, while GK II, III, and I (probably composed in that order given their relative Brahmanical content) would represent later stages in the "Vedānticization" of Gauḍapādian thought.

Perhaps GK IV was explicitly written to show that even Buddhism has a great deal of affinity with Vedāntic doctrines. This, of course, would imply that Buddhism is worth considering. We can assume, therefore, that GK IV was composed with the intention of either "wooing" Buddhists toward Vedānta, or establishing the validity of Vedāntic ideas within a context of Buddhist philosophical hegemony. Both possibilities suggest a pre-Śaṅkarite date for the fourth *prakaraṇa*. Buddhism was in the beginning of its decline in India around the eighth and ninth centuries CE and there would have been little reason for justifying the (established) doctrines of Vedānta along Buddhist lines.

Upon examination it becomes clear that GK IV deals with two main philosophical themes. First, it spends a considerable amount of time discussing the nature of experience, developing a phenomenology of perception, that has most often been described as "idealistic." We shall have reason to cast doubt upon such unqualified characterization in due course. Nevertheless, this analysis of experience is not a significantly new departure for the GK, being little more than a rendering explicit of the implicit epistemological presuppositions of GK II. The second theme discussed in GK IV is the central tenet of the *Gauḍapādīya-kārikā* as a whole, i.e. the doctrine of non-origination. Together these two themes constitute the fundamental lynchpins of Gauḍapādian thought.

The originality of the fourth *prakaraṇa*, however, should not be over-emphasized. Both the third and fourth *prakaraṇas* accept the "consciousness-vibration" (*cittaspandita*) theory of perception and use the term "*māyā*" in a phenomenological-experiential context. GK III introduces the reader to the concept of "*asparśa-yoga*"—a term also discussed in the fourth *prakaraṇa*.[43] GK III is thoroughly Vedāntic in its style, form, and content and yet still shows clear signs of Buddhist influence.[44]

The philosophical unanimity of GK II, III, and IV can be illustrated by a brief consideration of their textual inter-relatedness. *Kārikās* 1–10 and 14–15 of GK II correspond to GK IV.32–41 in their elucidation of the doctrine that the world is like a dream (*svapna*) and an appearance (*māyā*.) Nevertheless, this does not mean that *kārikās* 11–13, 16–31, 33 and 35–38 of the second *prakaraṇa* are incompatible with GK IV, only that the content of these verses concerns specifically Vedāntic themes that are not considered in the fourth *prakaraṇa*. Thus those verses which do not find direct philosophical connections with the fourth *prakaraṇa* can be linked up with GK III.1–19 and 23–27, which deals with the same basic themes from the same philosophical perspective. The discussion of the many different ways in which the *ātman* is wrongly conceived (*vi-kḷp*) as many different things (GK II.20–30) is intimately connected with the author's underlying belief that *ajātivāda* does not conflict with any other doctrines (*avirodhavāda*). The explicit elucidation of this claim, however, is not to be found in the second *prakaraṇa* itself, but in GK III.17, 18, and IV.4, 5. Likewise GK III.20–22 and 27–48 expound views identical to those found in GK IV.

To sum up the relationship of the texts, GK III appears to be an important bridging text between GK II and GK IV. The second *prakaraṇa* functions as a basic outline of the GK's philosophical position (GK I being a discussion of the MU). GK III is a "theological" justification of this position through an examination of various Vedāntic sources and "great sayings" (*mahāvākya*). GK IV functions as a further exposition of the topics introduced in the second and third *prakaraṇas* using the philosophically sophisticated terminology of the Buddhists.

Philological analysis also points to further similiarities between GK III and IV. In particular the use of the phrase "*ajātisamatā*" in GK III.2 and 38 is unique to the GK and is paralleled by the conjunction of "*aja*" and "*samya*" in GK IV.93, 95, and 100. The philosophical and linguistic similarities between GK III and IV suggests common authorship or at least common lineage (perhaps the author of one was the teacher of the other). It is likely, however, that GK IV was originally a separate text in its own right (hence the invocation at GK IV.1). The purpose of GK IV, apart from its playfully Buddhistic pretensions, appears to have been to provide an exposition of the "*ajātisamatādvaita*" doctrines of the first three *prakaraṇas* through a philosophical analysis of the nature of experience. GK IV, then, is primarily a phenomenological treatise written with the intention of refuting the claim that the doctrine of non-origination contradicts experience. That the fourth *prakaraṇa* is a separate text, however, does not necessitate that it is the work of a different author.

The question of the chronological order of the four chapters, however, is not an easy one to answer definitively. It could be argued that the discussion of the similarity of the waking and dream states in the second *prakaraṇa* presupposes the "idealistic" epistemology elucidated in the fourth. This might imply that the fourth is the earlier of the two. However, it might also be argued that the fourth is merely an unpacking of the presuppositions of the second. The length of the fourth *prakaraṇa* makes it all the more likely that it will clarify points raised in the other *prakaraṇas*. The greater sophistication of the fourth *prakaraṇa* may be taken as evidence of an early date (based upon the argument that the other *prakaraṇas* presume its existence) or a later date (based upon the argument that GK IV is a development of the previous *prakaraṇas*). Let us consider this question in the light of external references to the GK.

The *Gauḍapādīya-kārikā* and Bhāvaviveka

The earliest reference to a "*Vedānta-vāda*" or "*Vedānta-darśana*" can be found in the work of the Mādhyamika Bhāvaviveka. An entire chapter (chapter III) is devoted to the views of the Vedānta in his *Madhyamakahṛdayakārikā* (MHK) and the commentary upon it (the *Tarkajvālā*). Although much of the ensuing discussion deals with a form of Vedānta more akin to the perspective of the *Brahmasūtra* than that of the *kārikās*, Bhāvaviveka does quote three verses that substantially resemble verses in the *Gauḍapādīya-kārikā*, and a fourth reference which is virtually identical with verse five of the third *prakaraṇa*.[45]

During his discussion of Vedānta philosophy, Bhāvaviveka deals with a doctrine which likens the relationship between the supreme and the individual self with that which exists between space and the space enclosed in pots. The supreme *ātman* is to be compared to the space in general, while the embodied self is like the confined space within the pot. While pots are made and destroyed, the space which exists within them is neither produced nor destroyed, but is eternal, singular, and omnipresent. The unique *ātman* likewise is divided in the same manner as space is divided in pots. All of this bears a remarkable resemblance to the discussion found at the beginning of the third *prakaraṇa* of the *Gauḍapādīya-kārikā*. What makes the evidence all the more convincing is the fact that Bhāvaviveka quotes a verse that appears to be taken directly from the third *prakaraṇa*.

MHK 8.13: *ghaṭākāśe yathaikasmin rajodhūmādibhir vṛte,*
tadvattā na hi sarveṣāṃ sukhāder na tathātmanaḥ.
Just as when the space enclosed in a jar is polluted by dust and smoke etc., not all are in fact affected, so is the *ātman* with regard to happiness etc.

GK III.5: *yathaikasmin ghaṭākāśe rajodhūmādibhir yute,*
na sarve saṃprayujyante tadvaj jīvāḥ sukhādibhiḥ.
Just as when the space enclosed in a jar is mixed up with dust and smoke etc., not all are associated with them, so are the *jīvas* with regard to happiness etc.

Although these verses are not verbatim (as Walleser[46] and Bhattacharya[47] mistakenly thought) their resemblance is too remarkable to go unnoticed. Most scholars place Bhāvaviveka sometime in the sixth century of the Common Era.[48] If the MHK is quoting directly from the *Gauḍapādīya-kārikā*, then this would seem to place the author of GK III.5 somewhere in the early sixth century at the latest. This creates problems for the traditional view which identifies Gauḍapāda as the teacher of Śaṅkara's teacher since today most scholars would place Śaṅkara in the eighth century.

However, the Bhāvavivekan evidence is not nearly as conclusive as some would have us assume. Bhāvaviveka may have been aware of some early form of Vedānta, pre-dating Śaṅkara, but this does not prove that the quoted verses originated in the *Gauḍapādīya-kārikā*. It is clear from the veiled allusions and frequent half-quotations of Buddhist and Upaniṣadic texts that the author(s?) of the *kārikās* were not afraid to acknowledge their debt to their own philosophical environment. There is no reason to believe that the "space in pots" analogy was a peculiar invention of the GK; indeed, there had already been a long tradition of associating the supreme Brahman with space (*ākāśa*), as well as traditional analogies based upon the status of clay pots in relation to the clay which they are made out of.[49] Such an analogy then would not have been out of place in the Upaniṣadic literature itself, nor indeed is it ignored by the Mahāyāna.[50] Three viable possibilities therefore present themselves. First, that Bhāvaviveka is here reliant upon GK III and is directly quoting from it. Second, that GK III.5 is in fact dependent upon Bhāvaviveka's MHK. A third possibility is that both texts are quoting from a common source. B. N. Krishnamurti Sharma suggested as long ago as 1931 that GK III.5 is "plagiarized" by its author, being in fact a verse from the *Viṣṇu Purāṇa*.[51] Sharma points out that Vijñānabhikṣu (second half of sixteenth century?)[52] in his *bhāṣya* on *Sāṁkhyapravacanasūtra* I.152 cites two verses which appear in the GK.[53] One of these verses is ascribed to the *Viṣṇu Purāṇa*. The verse reads:

yathaikasmin ghaṭākāśe rajodhūmādibhir vṛte,
na ca sarve prayujyante eva jīvāḥ sukhādibhiḥ.

Not only is this virtually identical to GK III.5, but the first line of the verse conforms almost exactly to MHK 8.13ab (the slight difference being in word order). The "*yute*" of GK III.5b differs from the "*vṛte*" found in both MHK 8.13b and the verse quoted by Vijñānabhikṣu. It would seem that Bhāvaviveka is quoting from the *Viṣṇu Purāṇa* and not from GK III.5 after all. This interpretation is confirmed by the fact that MHK 8.13ab conforms to the verse quoted by Vijñānabhikṣu more than it does to GK III.5ab in that it ends with "*vṛte*" and not "*yute*." However, as Sangamlal Pandey notes, this is simply a case of a mistaken attribution by Vijñānabhikṣu.[54] Thus, Vijñānabhikṣu notwithstanding, some form of relationship between the MHK and GK III remains a strong possibility.

GK III spends verses 3–7 outlining the analogy of the space in clay pots. This analogy occurs in the context of a wider discussion of the relationship between *ātman* and the many individual *jīvas*. Other analogies are also utilized and there is nothing to suggest that GK III.5 is an isolated verse quoted from another context. Also one should note that GK III.5 is discussing the relationship between an individual self, denoted by the use of the term "*jīva*," and the supreme self, referred to by the term "*ātman*." The verse as it appears in MHK 8.12 makes no explicit distinction between terms, referring simply to the self as "*ātman*." The greater sophistication of GK III could be seen as a further refinement of the verse as it occurs in the MHK. Certainly Bhāvaviveka makes no use of the term "*jīva*," referring instead to the plurality of bodies (*deha*) in contrast to the unity of the *ātman*. The most likely explanation, however, is that Bhāvaviveka is here adapting GK III.5 to fit the context of his own discussion—the verse being used by the Buddhist philosopher to illustrate the sense in which there is only one self (*ātman*) and yet a plurality of embodied selves (*śarīrin, dehin*). That this is Bhāvaviveka's intention is clear from verse 23 where he attributes the view that there are two forms of the self—embodied and liberated, to the Vedāntavādins. After elucidating the pot-space analogy (MHK, vv. 10–13) Bhāvaviveka has the Vedāntin declare that:

> *dehasaṃstho 'py asaṅgatvād bhuñjāno nopalipyate,*
> *rājavat kāmacārīca pāpenānaparādhy asau.*
>
> Although He resides in the body, he is not defiled when He enjoys [objects], since He is not attached; just like a king (*rāja*) who behaves according to his pleasure (*kāma*), that (*Puruṣa*) remains innocent of evil deeds.[55]

This view is attacked in verse 71 on the grounds that an unchanging (*avikāritva*) self cannot at the same time be an embodied enjoyer of experience. It seems likely then that Bhāvaviveka has adapted GK III.5 to fit his own discussion (and subsequent refutation) of Vedānta philosophy.

However, this is not the only evidence of a relationship existing between the GK and Bhāvaviveka's *Madhyamakahṛdayakārikā*. Chapter five of this work (the *Yogācāratattvaviniścaya*, vv.1–113) is devoted to the exposition and refutation of the Yogācāra school, and includes within itself quotations, in the *pūrvapakṣa*, of various texts of the Yogācāra school. MHK 5.6 is of particular interest to us since it reads:

> *prajñapteḥ sanimittatvād anyathā dvayanāśataḥ,*
> *saṁkleśasyopalabdheś ca paratantrāstitā matā.*

This is virtually identical to *Gauḍapādīya-kārikā* IV.24:

> *prajñapteḥ sanimittatvam anyathā dvayanāśataḥ,*
> *saṁkleśasyopalabdheś ca paratantrāstitā matā.*

The correspondence between these two verses in terms of terminology and word-order is so exact that coincidence can be quite confidently ruled out. From the context of the verse in the *Gauḍapādīya-kārikā*, it would also seem to be the view of a *pūrvapakṣin* and is not the author's own view since in the immediately succeeding verse there is a refutation of the idea that *prajñapti* (designation) can have a *nimitta* (objective referent, literally a "mark"). There can be little doubt, therefore, that the author of GK IV is here quoting either directly or indirectly from a Yogācāra text.

Lindtner has also noted the similarity between MHK 5.6 and GK IV.24, and pinpoints the quotation as a verse from the voluminous *Xiǎn-yáng-sheng-jiao-lun*, (reconstructed as * *Vikhyāpana*), a Chinese text ascribed to Asaṅga and a major source of Yogācāra ideas for Bhāvaviveka.[56] Lindtner himself suggests that

> [I]t is certainly most likely that GK is quoting from MHK rather than *vice versa*, not only because the appendix to the *Prajñāpradīpa* . . . leaves no doubt whatsoever that Bhavya in several places had the * *Vikhyāpana* before him when referring to Yogācāra, and thus knew it from autopsy, but also, if I am not wrong, because there are otherwise no references at all to the * *Vikhyāpana* in the GK. It thus seems likely that the quotation in the GK is a second-hand one.[57]

The philosophical position of *kārikā* 24 is clearly that of the Yogācāra school and is an attempt to establish the existence of the "dependency" realm (*paratantrāstitā*). Bhāvaviveka criticizes the *trisvabhāva* scheme in his appendix to chapter XXV of the

Prajñāpradīpa, and again in his critique of the Yogācāra in chapter five of the MHK. The status of the *paratantra-svabhāva* is in fact the main bone of contention in the scholastic controversy between the Madhyamaka and Yogācāra schools in the sixth century CE, reflecting as it does the paradigmatic distinction between their respective (developed) philosophies.[59] The author of GK IV is clearly aware of the debate between the Madhyamaka and Yogācāra schools over this issue and in this instance is in agreement with Bhāvaviveka in suggesting that ultimately the objective reference to be found in the dependency realm is itself lacking in any objectivity (*animittatva*) of its own.[60]

The author of GK IV (at least), therefore, is remarkably well informed concerning an issue which was, after all, an internal Mahāyāna controversy between Buddhist scholasts of the fifth and sixth centuries CE. This in itself shows a considerable awareness and depth of understanding of the Madhyamaka and Yogācāra positions. Influence from Mahāyāna *śāstras* is one thing, but for the author of an apparently Vedāntic text to feel the need to discuss a doctrinal issue that is largely internal to the Mahāyāna scholastic tradition is an astounding feature to find in an apparently non-Mahayana text. This aspect of the *Gauḍapādīya-kārikā* (and in particular the fourth *prakaraṇa*) will be considered further in a later chapter.

Let us consider the possible implications of this evidence. If it is in fact the case that the author of the fourth *prakaraṇa* is dependent upon the works of Bhāvaviveka rather than the other way around, as is usually suggested, then this would place GK IV historically later than the sixth century CE. This late date for the authorship of GK IV would provide some vindication for the Vedānta tradition which places Gauḍapāda some two generations before Śaṅkara (who lived c. eighth century CE). Our attention should be drawn, however, to the problem of multiple authorship. If GK III is pre-Bhāvavivekan (since Bhāvaviveka appears to quote from it), GK IV might still be post-Bhāvavivekan. To safeguard single authorship one might suggest that GK III.5 is in fact dependent upon Bhāvaviveka rather than the other way around. On this view GK III and IV would both be dependent upon Bhāvaviveka's MHK. Nevertheless, the question remains—why would the Vedāntic author of the third *prakaraṇa* rely upon a Buddhist scholastic summary (and critique) of Vedāntic philosophy, given that he is already considerably versed in the relevant texts and traditions themselves?

As we have seen Bhāvaviveka cites a verse which is virtually identical to *Gauḍapādīya-kārikā* III.5. Given that the verse is quoted in the context of a chapter on Vedānta philosophy and appears to be adapted to fit the context of Bhāvaviveka's discussion, it seems unlikely that GK III is dependent upon the MHK in this instance. The GK as a whole shows great familiarity with Upaniṣadic ideas and doctrines, and as a Vedāntic text in its own right would hardly need to refer to a Buddhist text to supplement the interpretation of its own tradition. Why then does Bhāvaviveka appear to ignore GK IV in his account of Vedānta philosophy? There are two possible explanations. First, he may not have been aware of its existence, which implies that it was not yet written or at least that it was a separate text in its own right. An alternative explanation is that Bhāvaviveka ignored the fourth *prakaraṇa* of the GK because of its unquestionably Buddhist content. This argument, however, is weak since Bhāvaviveka would surely have cited *kārikās* from GK IV to substantiate his claim that the Vedānta school is a ''completely heterogenous'' mixture (*atyantātulyajātīya*) of the doctrines of other schools (including Buddhism). GK IV, more than any other *prakaraṇa* adapts Buddhist terminology and arguments so as to conform to its own Vedāntic position. In verse 86 of the MHK chapter on the Vedānta Bhāvaviveka states that:

> Being convinced that this infallible system of the Tathagata is a good one (*śubha*), here [in the Vedānta system] the heterodox sectarians (*tīrthika*), being desirous (*spṛhā*) of [that doctrine], have therefore [even] made it their own, . . .[61]

No citation or reference to the fourth *prakaraṇa*, however, can be found in the text which might have substantiated this position.

As we have seen, the view that GK IV is later than Bhāvaviveka is supported by the fact that both MHK and GK IV.24 quote a verse from the *Vikhyāpana* of Asaṅga. Bhāvaviveka quotes other verses from this same text in his other works and so it would seem that GK IV.24 is itself dependent upon chapter five of the MHK as a source of Yogācāra ideas, or at least on the general Bhāvavivekan critique of the Yogācāra position. (This seem particularly apt when we note that GK IV.25 agrees with Bhāvaviveka in refuting the verse in question). Now, if Bhāvaviveka had GK III before him when he wrote his chapter on the Vedānta (MHK 8), this would seem to suggest separate authorship of GK III and IV, in that the former would be prior and the latter posterior to Bhāvaviveka.

However, silence with regard to the fourth *prakaraṇa* does not definitively prove that the text was not in existence at this time, or even that Bhāvaviveka was not aware of it. We know nothing of the status of the GK in Indian philosophical circles at this time. The fourth *prakaraṇa* may have been dismissed by the Buddhists for the obvious "plagiarized distortion" that it would seem to be in their eyes. Equally, one might argue that GK IV is in mind when Bhāvaviveka criticizes Vedānta for plagiarizing the teachings of the Buddha (MHK 8.86). This view is supported if one considers the views which Bhāvaviveka actually attributes to the Vedānta in his discussion of the school. Most of the doctrines mentioned show little similarity or dependence upon fundamental Buddhist views. The critique of the Vedānta school as a syncretistic amalgam of other schools (including Buddhism) therefore seems somewhat out of place given the evidence which Bhāvaviveka himself provides. Indeed, Bhāvaviveka seems to be basing his syncretistic view of the Vedānta on his knowledge of the *Gauḍapādīya-kārikā* in particular. Note, for instance, that cries of plagiarism are made immediately after verses criticizing the doctrines of non-origination (*ajātivāda*, 8.81,82), non-dualism (*advaita*, 8.83), and the concept of the "self-identity of non-origination" (*ajātisamatā*, 8.78-83). That Bhāvaviveka is here referring to the cardinal doctrines and concepts of the GK is therefore beyond any reasonable doubt.

Lindtner has suggested that the phrase "*ajātisamatām gatam*" (III.2 and III.38) is "a term almost showing the 'fingerprint' of Gauḍapāda."[62] This Gauḍapādian "technical term" found in GK III has clear parallels in GK IV (*ajaṃ sāmyaṃ*, IV.93, IV.100; *aje sāmye*, IV.95), a factor which is suggestive of single authorship of the two *prakaraṇas*. As already noted, Bhāvaviveka uses the compound "*ajātisamatā*" in MHK 8.78, 79 (79 and 80 in Qvarnström's edition) in his discussion of the Vedānta and Lindtner suggests that MHK 80cd (Qvarnström 81cd) is either a direct reference to the views expressed in GK III.38, or "to some passage virtually identical with this in word and thought." This would establish that Bhāvaviveka is indeed indebted to GK III. The concept of *ajātisamatā* is unique to the GK and consequently it is likely that the critique of the concept in MHK 8.78–84 (not present in the Tibetan manuscripts)[63] is a direct critique of the philosophical position of the GK.[64] Qvarnström notes that:

> As far as the "pot-space" simile is concerned, it is most likely that Bhavya in the VTV [*Vedāntatattvaviniścaya*] draws on GK. Gauḍapāda is, as far as we know, the one who introduced this simile into the Vedānta tradition, perhaps under Buddhist influence. Bhavya's criticism of the **ajātisamatāvāda* (the doctrine of the self-identity of non-origination) of GK, found in VTV, further strengthens this assumption. However, this does not mean that the *Vedāntadarśana*, presented by Bhavya, is in complete agreement with GK or even comes from the same tradition as GK.[65]

It is pertinent to note that Bhāvaviveka's description of Vedānta doctrines (MHK 8.1–17) makes no mention of the terms *avidyā* or *māyā*. The self is frequently referred to by the term "*puruṣa*," and in MHK 8.4ab Bhāvaviveka says that this "person" (*puruṣa*) is regarded by the Vedāntins as "whatever is past (*bhūta*), present (*bhavat*) and future (*bhaviṣyat*)."[66] Verse 5 adopts the analogy of the spider and its thread to explain the manifestation of the universe.[67] The self (*ātman*) is described as the world cause (*jagatkāraṇatā*, 8.19), and the agent (*kartṛ*) and enjoyer (*bhoktṛ*) of experience (8.3, 4, 14, 25–35; ad. 8.14). Liberation from *saṁsāra* is attained through the practice of *yoga* (8.16; ad. 8.3; ad. 8.5). This is the realization that the *ātman* is all-pervasive (*sarvagata*) eternal (*nitya*) and one (*eka*) (8.16). Being beyond the scope of words (*vācām agocara*), some, however, apply names to the *ātman* if "their minds are misled by difference" (*bhedāpahṛtabuddhi*, 8.17). While there is little here which directly corresponds to the perspective of the *Gauḍapādīya-kārikā*, there is also little which explicitly contradicts it. It would seem from the contents of MHK 8 that Bhāvaviveka has a number of different Vedāntic texts before him when writing the MHK.[68]

We have already noted that Bhāvaviveka criticizes the notion of the self-identity of non-origination (*ajātisamatā*), a phrase peculiar to GK III. MHK 8.73 is a refutation of the oneness of the self (*ekatva*), on the grounds that oneness requires a relationship and presupposes a duality (of other numbers). This criticism, however, is not relevant to the radical non-dualism (*advaita-vāda*) of the GK which avoids the pitfalls of a simplistic monism (*ekatva-vāda*). In MHK 8.79, however, Bhāvaviveka attacks the notion that one can have knowledge (*jñāna*) of the "self-identity of non-origination" without presupposing a duality between the knowledge (*jñāna*) and the thing known (*jñeya*). This seems to be a critique of the view propounded in GK III.33 and 38 (and possibly, though less securely, IV.95, 96). Bhāvaviveka also attacks the Vedānta school for its understanding of the fact that non-origination is the intrinsic nature (*svabhāva*) of entities (MHK 8.89–104). This amounts to a direct assault upon the Gauḍapādian conception of reality, which precisely establishes its philosophical position in terms of the concept of an unchanging intrinsic nature (*svabhāva*), see chapter 4. This combined with the citation of a verse almost verbatim to GK III.5 suggests that there can be little doubt that Bhāvaviveka had (at least) the third *prakaraṇa* of the GK before him when he wrote his *Madhyamakahṛdayakārikā*. This places the third *prakaraṇa* in a period earlier than the sixth century CE. It is conceivable (although not so assured) that other *prakaraṇas* can be assigned to that date also given their philosophical and linguistic coherence with GK III. But to what date are we to assign the fourth *prakaraṇa*?

The Author of the Fourth *Prakaraṇa* and Buddhist Scholasticism

The Buddhist University of Nālandā appears to have been founded at the beginning of the fifth century CE by the Gupta royal household.[69] Paul Williams notes that the University seems to have "taught not only Buddhism but Hindu thought and other disciplines such as medicine."[70] By the sixth century, Nālandā had become an important center for the study of Mahāyāna, and in particular Yogācāra, philosophy. Dharmapāla was active there from 530–561 CE, and it was under his pupil Śīlabhadra that Hsüan-tsang is said to have studied and founded the Chinese *Vijñānavāda* school (*Fa-hsiang*) in 633 or 637 CE, (as explicated in his *Tch'eng wei che louen*). Consequently, Chinese Yogācāra incorporated many of the doctrinal idiosyncracies of Dharmapāla and the Nālandā school.

In contrast to the Nālandā understanding of Yogācāra, there also existed a rival sub-school of the Yogācāra represented by Sthiramati. This sub-school was established at the University of Valabhī, founded in the sixth century by Sthiramati's teacher Guṇamati on his departure from the Nālandā institute.[71] Richard Robinson suggests that,

> Buddhist Tantra especially prospered from the eighth century on, under the Pāla dynasty of Bengal (circa 750–1150 CE). At Nālandā, the great center of Buddhism at that time, Perfection of Wisdom ideas combined with Tantra, uniting metaphysics with ritual, magical practices.[72]

I-Tsing, who visited Nālandā circa 700 CE, remarked that the two schools remained in their own vicinity and did not become embroiled in disputes with one another.[73] He further noted that there were some ten thousand monks studying Hīnayāna, Mahāyāna, logic, maths, medicine, etc. at Nālandā. The university, however, is thought to have been destroyed in the Islamic invasions of the twelfth or thirteenth century. Nevertheless, it is clear that the two universities at Nālandā and Valabhī flourished around the time to which we have assigned the composition of the *prakaraṇas* of the *Gauḍapādīya-kārikā* and, as we have seen, the author of the fourth *prakaraṇa* of that text seems to be acutely aware of the nature of the ensuing debate between the Mādhyamikas (represented by Bhāvaviveka in chapter XXV of his

Prajñāpradīpa, and chapter III of his MHK, and later by Candrakīrti in his *Madhyamakāvatāra*) and the Yogācārins (represented by Dharmapāla at Nālandā and Sthiramati at Valabhī). One should not discount the possibility that the author of the fourth *prakaraṇa* (at least) may have spent some time at one of these (or related) institutions. The depth of knowledge of Buddhist ideas and terminology is considerable and it is inconceivable that the fourth *prakaraṇa* could have been written without a substantial grounding in Buddhist philosophy and its internal controversies. Our assessment of the doctrine of the *Alātaśāntiprakaraṇa* (GK IV) is that it rejects the Yogācāra's assessment of the dependency realm as existent (*paratantrāstitā*) (see GK IV.24 and 25) on the grounds that the dependency realm itself has no independent or objective basis for its existence. As such, the fourth *prakaraṇa* displays a greater affinity with the Madhyamaka point of view, although this does not preclude the acceptance of a Yogācāra-style analysis of experience.

Thus, the fourth *prakaraṇa* shows a highly developed Madhyamaka-Yogācāra syncretism. The *prakaraṇas* of the GK adopt arguments rejecting common-sense notions of causality from the Madhyamaka school and a phenomenological analysis of experience from the Yogācāra school. This is remarkable for a number of reasons. First, because it may well precede (or at least be contemporaneous with) the Mahāyāna's own syncretism of the two schools in the works of Vimuktisena (sixth century CE) and Śāntarakṣita (seventh century CE), and second, because it is performed by a Vedāntin and not by a Buddhist. The sophistication of the syncretism of Buddhist philosophical schools in the fourth *prakaraṇa* in particular implies a later date for GK IV in comparison with the other *prakaraṇas*, as would the author's awareness of the sixth century Mahāyāna controversy over the status of the *paratantra-svabhāva*. If we follow Tibetan sources in assigning the earliest attempted syncretism of the Madhyamaka and Yogācāra to the sixth century Mahāyānist Vimuktisena, the juxtaposition of Yogācāra and Madhyamaka ideas in GK IV does not seem so odd.[74] In fact, one might suggest that the author of the fourth *prakaraṇa* was a sixth century Vedāntin stimulated by the Madhyamaka-Yogācāra discussions of his day. One should acknowledge, however, that the first three *prakaraṇas* contain the views of a non-dualistic lineage (*saṃpradāya*) to which the author of the fourth *prakaraṇa* belonged.

It seems undeniable that the fourth *prakaraṇa* of the GK is a separate treatise in its own right (hence the *maṅgalācaraṇa* at the beginning of the text). The author of GK IV writes with a different purpose than the other three—namely to establish the sense in which *ajātivāda* does not contradict our experience of the world. To achieve this end GK IV openly adopts Mahāyāna arguments, drawing upon Buddhist scholastic debates concerning the analysis of experience into *dharmas*. Taking a broadly Yogācāran position, though adapted to suit a Vedāntic ontology, GK IV is an attempt to explain the dualistic nature of our experience in the light of the doctrine of non-origination (*ajātivāda*). It is in this context that the dynamic notion of *asparśayoga* is introduced as the soteriological (meditative), and theoretical focus of GK IV.

Bhāvaviveka criticizes a number of different Vedāntic systems in the MHK. One of those systems appears to have established its philosophical position around the notion of "*ajātisamatā*," a term which Bhāvaviveka takes to be a technical term of the Vedānta school. Given that this concept appears in no Vedāntic text before or after GK III, it would seem that it is this to which Bhāvaviveka is referring. The linguistic commonalities of GK III and IV, however, suggest a close link between the two.

Conclusion

Our analysis has brought forward the following conclusions with regard to the nature of the text known as the *Gauḍapādīya-kārikā*. They are:

A. GK IV is composed by an author influenced by GK III, perhaps even a member of the same lineage (*saṃpradāya*). The Gauḍapādian conception of Vedānta centers upon the doctrine of the self-identity of non-origination (*ajātisamatā-vāda*), a central concept of GK III and IV. The points of departure for GK III and GK IV, however, fundamentally differ. The third *prakaraṇa* approaches the question of non-origination from an ontological and broadly speaking Vedāntic perspective, though Buddhist influence is still obvious. In contrast to this GK IV spends much of its time discussing the phenomenology of experience, openly using a carefully selected but wide-range of Buddhist concepts taken from the Madhyamaka and Yogācāra philosophical traditions.

B. By the eighth century of the Common Era the first, second, and third *prakaraṇas* of the GK were linked and attributed by the

Śaṅkarite tradition to a figure (or figures—the references are often ambiguous) known as "Gauḍa," "Gauḍācārya," or "Gauḍapāda."

C. *Gauḍapādīya-kārikā* IV.24 is a quotation from the *Vikhyāpana* of Asaṅga. The author of the fourth *prakaraṇa* may not be directly indebted to Bhāvaviveka here, but the refutation which follows in GK IV.25 would appear to suggest that the author flourished in a time when the Madhyamaka-Yogācāra controversy over the status of the *paratantra-svabhāva* was apparent. Since Bhāvaviveka appears to have been the main Mādhyamika protagonist in this particular inter-scholastic debate, one can assume that GK IV was in fact composed with his work in mind. This would appear to place the author of the fourth *prakaraṇa* in the mid-to late sixth century CE at the earliest.

D. Historically speaking, it can only be stated with absolute certainty that GK IV is first acknowledged (and at the same time specifically connected with GK I, II and III) by the author of the *Gauḍapādīya-kārikā-bhāṣya*. It seems likely that GK IV was initially a separate treatise discussing a different (but related) area and perhaps even written for a different audience, a Buddhist one perhaps. Whatever the status of the four *prakaraṇas* as a single text, all four (and in particular II, III, and IV) uphold the same fundamental view with regard to the equality of dream and waking states, and the non-origination of the *ātman*, etc. It is likely therefore, that the chapters are the work of an early tradition (*saṃpradāya*) of Bengali (Gauḍadeśa) Advaitins flourishing in the pre-Śaṅkarite era. GK I is more problematic, but not irreconcilable with the other *prakaraṇas*. Clearly by the eighth century CE it is linked with the figure(s) of "Gauḍa" and the second and third *prakaraṇas*.

The problem of assiging a fixed date to the compositon of the fourth *prakaraṇa*, however, remains. Why does GK IV (in particular) go unmentioned in Vedānta and Buddhist texts until the composition of the *Gauḍapādīya-kārikābhāṣya*? Wood suggests that this is because GK IV is a comparatively late post-Śaṅkarite text.[75] This hypothesis, however, does not explain:

1. The Buddhist nature of the language. Buddhism was not a viable force in post-Śaṅkarite India. There would have been no reason

for the adoption of Buddhist terminology and arguments since Advaita Vedānta had already formulated its own distinctive approach and terminology.

2. The fourth *prakaraṇa* is relatively unsophisticated in comparison with other Vedāntic works of the post-Śaṅkarite period. The text shows no grasp of the concept of *anirvacanīya*, etc. nor is there any evidence of an awareness of rival interpretations such as the Viśiṣṭādvaita. While the fourth *prakaraṇa* deals with the issues it discusses in a more sophisticated manner than the other *prakaraṇas*, nowhere can one find evidence that would date the sources of the text to a period later than the sixth century of the Common Era.

The most likely explanation, therefore, is that GK IV is a comparatively early text of the Vedānta school written before the time of Śaṅkara and before the decline of Buddhism in India. Perhaps the figure of "Gauḍapāda," traditionally Śaṅkara's *paramaguru*, was indeed a seventh century Advaitin. This figure might then be the author of the fourth *prakaraṇa* and editor of the other three. One discrepancy remains in this theory however. In the few citations of the GK that can be unquestionably demonstrated to be from the early tradition of Śaṅkara and his immediate disciples, references to the fourth *prakaraṇa* are conspicuous by their absence. However, this can be accounted for if we consider the problematic nature of the text for the Advaita Vedānta school. Not only does the fourth *prakaraṇa* show an unmistakable reliance upon Buddhist logic and terminology, it also appears to endorse an epistemological "idealism" which was frankly unacceptable to Śaṅkara and his disciples (the question of the GK's "idealism" will be discussed in a later chapter). It would seem that in the period between the composition of the fourth *prakaraṇa* and the works of Śaṅkara (eighth century CE), the Vedānta tradition closed ranks, and entered into a more antagonistic and aggressive relationship with the Buddhist traditions of India.

The fourth *prakaraṇa* of the GK causes immense problems for the Advaita school because of its free-flowing adoption of Buddhist ideas, arguments and terminology. Consequently, no mention of GK IV is found within the cardinal texts of Vedānta, even amongst those which must have been writing after Ānandagiri's *vyākhya* on the *Gauḍapādīya-kārikābhāṣya*. This fact in itself is astounding and should be kept in mind when attempting to assign a firm date to the composition of GK IV. Certain commentators on the first *prakaraṇa* (and in the case of Puruṣottama the second *prakaraṇa* as well) would have seized upon GK IV as evidence of the crypto-Buddhism of Advaita Vedānta. That this did not occur can only be explained by the fact that these authors were unaware of the fourth *prakaraṇa* or at least that they did not link it with the text upon which they were commenting.[76] This omission is despite the fact that all four *prakaraṇas* had been commented upon as if a single text (possibly by Śaṅkara himself)[77] and that Ānandagiri had written a *vyākhya* to that commentary c.1300 CE.

If the Advaita tradition avoids referring to GK IV at all costs, then this would also explain the silence of the Buddhist sources—they simply were not made aware of it. Bhāvaviveka (early sixth century) and Śāntarakṣita (early eighth century) quote from the second and third *prakaraṇas* but not from the fourth. Surely neither would have missed the opportunity of pointing out the Buddhistic leanings of the fourth *prakaraṇa* if given the chance. As we have seen, GK IV shows an awareness of the Madhyamaka-Yogācāra debate between Bhāvaviveka and Dharmapāla concerning the status of the *paratantra-svabhāva*. While GK IV appears to be later than both GK II and III, it is not sufficiently late to be considered a post-Śaṅkarite text, for if it were, its author would appear to have lived in an intellectual vacuum for some two hundred years or more. We should note that GK IV has doctrinal and philological affinities with GK III (as well as GK II one might add). It is likely, therefore, that the three *prakaraṇas* are written by members of the same lineage. The same assurance, however, cannot be given concerning their relationship to the first *prakaraṇa*, which contains a number of doctrinal discrepancies, which, while reconcilable with the rest of the GK, sit uncomfortably together. Nevertheless GK I, in its present form at least, upholds the doctrines of non-dualism (*advaita*) and non-origination (*ajātivāda*) and is likely to have had some historical connection with the tradition represented by the other three *prakaraṇas*. It is unlikely, however, that GK I is from the same source as GK II, III or IV.

Despite the composite nature of the *Gauḍapādīya-kārikā*, continuity of thought in the text as a whole can be generally established, though this may reflect the work of an editor. Nevertheless, insofar as the four *prakaraṇas* of the GK are indisputably linked, both philologically and philosophically, one can assign a single, coherent philosophical position to the text as a whole. This philosophical position, which can be labeled "Gauḍapādian" for the sake of discussion, may be that of the texts' editor, who in all likelihood is also the author of the fourth *prakaraṇa*. The central philosophical conceptions of "Gauḍapādian" thought (as represented by the four *prakaraṇas*) are the non-origination of *ātman* (*ajātivāda*) and *asparśayoga* and its concomitant epistemological themes. Both of these concepts reflect influence from the Madhyamaka and Yogācāra schools of thought.

CHAPTER

2

The Vedāntic Heritage of the *Gauḍapādīya-kārikā*

The Three Foundations (*Prasthānatraya*) of the Vedānta-*Darśana*

The classical (i.e. post-Śaṅkara) Vedānta *darśana* accepts three textual foundations (*prasthānatraya*) upon which its doctrines are reputably based. These three are the *Upaniṣads* (usually but not exclusively the eleven classical *Upaniṣads*), the *Brahmasūtra*, and the *Bhagavadgītā*. The establishment of the "three foundations" became a permanent feature of all Vedānta schools only sometime after the time of Śaṅkara. The classical *Upaniṣads* are usually those which are said to have been commented upon by Śaṅkara. Critics of the non-dualistic (*advaita*) school of Vedānta often quote from other *Upaniṣads* that are not considered authoritative by Śaṅkara's followers. Rāmānuja for instance, often quotes from such texts as the *Garbha Upaniṣad* when it suits his theological purpose. The *Bhagavadgītā*, as part of chapter six of the *Mahābhārata*, is actually part of the *smṛti* ("remembered") tradition and is, strictly speaking, not necessarily an example of non-human revelation (*śruti*), not being part of the Vedas.[1] However, both Śaṅkara and Rāmānuja felt that the text warranted further explanation through the writing of a commentary. The acceptance of the *Gītā* as a scriptural authority by these great Vedāntins (itself no doubt influenced by the *Gītā*'s popularity) resulted in the establishment of the *Gītā* as a text of pre-eminent status for the Vedānta school, being placed alongside the *Upaniṣads* and the *Brahmasūtra* as a foundational text (*prasthāna*).

The purpose of this chapter, however, is not to give a comprehensive analysis of the various sub-schools of the Vedānta and their complex inter-relationships, but rather to give some brief flavor of the philosophical (or perhaps theological) tradition with which the GK aligns itself. As we have seen from the first chapter (dealing with the textual questions such as the date and authorship of the GK), the status of the early Vedānta as a philosophical school (*darśana*) and the precise nature of its doctrines are somewhat unclear. This is largely due to the fact that our best source of knowledge on such matters are not Vedāntic texts themselves but the work of Buddhist scholars such as Bhāvaviveka, the author of the earliest known compendium of Indian philosophies, the *Madhyamakahṛdayakārikā*. Nevertheless, by the time of the composition of the *Gauḍapādīya-kārikā* those texts which later became established as fundamental (i.e. the *prasthānatraya*) seem already to have been in existence. A short introduction to the Vedāntic tradition which preceded the formation of the GK then requires some consideration of the philosophical ideas found in these texts and how they might relate to the doctrines and practices propounded in the *Gauḍapādīya-kārikā*.

The Upaniṣadic Heritage of the *Gauḍapādīya-kārikā*

Since the term "Vedānta" denotes the final portion of Vedic scripture, that is the *Upaniṣads*, the early history of the Vedānta school is nothing more than the early history of the Upaniṣadic texts themselves.[2] There are roughly four historical layers to the development of the Upaniṣadic ideas, i.e. early, middle, late, and new *Upaniṣads*. It is generally accepted that the earliest stratum contains the *Bṛhadāraṇyaka* and *Chāndogya Upaniṣads*. These are said to contain material that is pre-Buddhist, placing them at some time before the fifth century (before the Common Era) BCE. The middle period covers such *Upaniṣads* as the *Aitareya*, the *Kauṣītaki*, the *Taittirīya*, the *Kāṭhaka*, the *Muṇḍaka*, the *Praśna*, and the *Śvetāsvatāra Upaniṣads*, which show evidence of Buddhist influences, and must therefore have been compiled after the fifth century BCE.[3] The late *Upaniṣads*, dating from the first two centuries of the Common Era are the *Kena*, the *Īśa*, the *Māṇḍūkya*, and lastly the *Maitrayāṇīya* (or *Maitri*) *Upaniṣad*.[4] Of the new *Upaniṣads* (which are not usually accepted as valid by the Advaita Vedānta school), nine are pure Vedānta texts, eleven are *yoga upaniṣads*, seven are *saṃnyāsa upaniṣads*, and twelve are sectarian (five *Śaiva* and seven *Vaiṣṇava*).[5] This list is by no means definitive, but the important point for our purposes is the acknowledgment of the fact that the Vedānta-*darśana* developed out of the speculations of the early, middle, and late *Upaniṣads*.[6]

It is important to note the following wise words from P. T. Raju,

> what is called the philosophy of the *Upaniṣads* is not a system of philosophy, but several philosophical doctrines brought together, some of which are even mutually conflicting. For example, the statement "Everything is the Brahman" (*sarvaṃ khalu idaṃ brahma*), is manifestly opposed to the statement, this is not the Brahman (*neti neti*), and a system of philosophy is needed to reconcile the two. The *Upaniṣads* do not belong to the same time or place, neither are they composed by the same authors. . .The *Upaniṣads* do not use the same method, and often their method is not what is strictly called logical. They use in their explanations and demonstrations myths, etymologies, dialogues, etc., which are not really logical proofs.[7]

There is no definitive Upaniṣadic view. The various Upaniṣadic texts do not present a unified religious or philosophical system despite many later attempts to impose a systematic and definitive philosophical position upon them. This makes it particularly difficult to attempt to summarize the immense variety of views and approaches in the short space that is available here. Not only do the *Upaniṣads* contain a plethora of diverse perspectives within them, they are also largely unsystematic compositions, using parables and mythological modes of expression rather than the strict logical forms that we shall encounter when we come to deal with the GK and philosophical Buddhism. This inevitably makes any attempt to summarize or appraise Upaniṣadic thought a difficult one to undertake. Our concern, however, is not to provide a comprehensive examination of Upaniṣadic thought, but rather to consider some of the main speculative trends that run through the Upaniṣadic literature as a whole and that appear to have influenced the distinctive perspective of the *Gauḍapādīya-kārikā*.

An important feature of the Upaniṣadic literature and indeed of post-Vedic religion in general, (that is Brahmanical and non-Brahmanical religion), is the centrality of the doctrine of rebirth (*saṃsāra*) and its corollary, *karman*—action which leads to rebirth. By the time of the composition of the early *Upaniṣads* and the rise of Buddhism around the fifth century BCE, belief in rebirth seems to have become so prevalent as to remain philosophically beyond question in many schools of thought (only movements such as the deterministic *Ājivīkas*, the materialistic *Cārvakas*, and sceptical agnostics such as Sañjaya Belaṭṭhiputta seem to have found any fault with the doctrine). Given the resounding silence of the *Saṃhitās* on this belief, one wonders to what extent belief in rebirth was a religious feature originally found outside the mainstream Vedic religion in the *śramaṇa* communities from which Buddhism and Jainism sprang, only influencing Brahmanical circles during the formative period of Upaniṣadic thought.

Generally speaking, in the *Brāhmaṇas* and *Āraṇyakas* one can see a gradual change in interest from an elaboration of the precise technicalities of the performance of the sacrificial ritual to the meaning and purpose (*artha*) behind the ritual. As time went on, the significance of ritual came to be understood in an increasingly symbolic sense. This attitude is exemplified well by the following passage taken from the beginning of the *Bṛhadāraṇyaka Upaniṣad* (I.1.1)

> Truly, the dawn is the head of the sacrificial horse; the sun, his eye; the wind, his breath; the universal fire his open mouth. The year is the body (*ātman*) of the sacrificial horse; the sky his back; the atmosphere his stomach,. . . the stars his bones, the clouds his flesh . . .

The consequence of this re-interpretation of the sacrifice is that the entire creation, subsistence, and destruction of the universe is seen in terms of the primordiality of the sacrificial act. In the *Puruṣasūkta* (*Ṛg Veda* X.90), the universe is said to have been created through the self-dismemberment of the *Puruṣa*. Here in the *Upaniṣads* we find an extension of this style of universalizing the importance of the sacrifice, through symbolic re-interpretations. This is achieved by means of the discovery of great parallels and correspondences (*bandhu*) between the macrocosmic and microcosmic realms of existence.

Eventually, it became clear that the important aspect of the ritual was the mental state of the agent carrying it out. The sacrificer was therefore raised in importance to that of the sacrifice itself. This development led to further speculation in the *Upaniṣads*, with regard to the intrinsic relationship between the individual as sacrificer and the universe as the actualization of the sacrifice itself. In the *Upaniṣads* it became increasingly clear that if the ritual performer was as important as the sacrifice itself, then in a very basic sense he was the sacrifice. This idea clearly links up well with the *Puruṣasūkta*. The sacrifice, therefore, is relevant in some deeply symbolic sense to our understanding of our place in the universe. In this sense, the idea of sacrifice was applicable not just to the performance of the ritual itself but to the agent's entire life.

This attitude led many Upaniṣadic thinkers to dwell upon the question of the nature of the individual self. The term which came to prominence in this context was *ātman*. *Ātman*, the *Upaniṣads* agree, is the true self of each living being, that which constitutes its real essence. But what was the precise nature of this essence?

The notion of a transmigrating agent (*saṃsārin*) emphasized the fact that the true self (*ātman*) of a person was not just the person embodied in the present lifetime. The self has experienced a myriad of different existences in different bodies and in different circumstances. This reincarnating self constitutes the permanent essence, the intrinsic nature of each individual. As such our bodies are merely vehicles or chariots,[8] and it is only through ignorance that the individual continues to spend his or her life wrongly associating their true self (*ātman*) with the ephemeral embodied self (*śarīrātman*).[9]

Salvation is thus achieved not so much through the external performance of the ritual as through its internal performance through the practice of certain forms of asceticism or ''self-sacrifice.'' Such activities lead the individual away from the slavery of following the passions and desires of his transient human lifetime and would eventually precipitate an intuitive realization of one's true nature as *ātman*, the permanent self that lies behind the many lives experienced during the cycle of rebirths.

Here we have a clear change of emphasis in relation to the earlier Vedic cult of the sacrifice. It is not action (*karman*) which leads to salvation. Action leads to a corresponding re-action in this world. In the *Upaniṣads* this is not usually seen as a desirable consequence. The goal is the attainment of knowledge, a mystical gnosis of one's true self, the permanent essence of conscious existence—beyond the incessant round of rebirths. It is in the *Upaniṣads*, then, that we find the establishment of a new spiritual goal, that of *mokṣa*—liberation or salvation from rebirth. Salvation no longer consisted in being established in a heavenly realm somewhat similar to life on earth, but in an awareness that one's own true nature is beyond the fluctuations of rebirth. Liberation (*mokṣa*) is the realization of Truth (*satya*), truth being that which is (*sat*), was and forever will be. This reflects the cosmogonic interest of the Vedānta scriptures. Reality is that which always is, i.e. that which exists before, during, and after the created realm of names and forms (*nāma-rūpa*).

Thus, it is soon established in the *Upaniṣads* that there were two ''states of being'' or ''modes of existence''—*saṃsāra*, ''the common flowing,'' that is the endless cycle of rebirths, and *mokṣa*, liberation from that cycle. This is sometimes expressed in the idea that the fate of the deceased can follow two distinct paths, the path of the gods (*devayāna*) or the path of the ancestors (*pitṛyāna*). It is the latter which eventually leads to a future rebirth (ie. continued participation in *saṃsāra*).[10]

Cosmogonic Speculation in the Upaniṣads

> How many gods are there Yājñavalkya?. . .Three hundred and three and three thousand and three. . .Thirty-three. . .Six. . .Three. . .Two. . .One and a half. . .One.[11]

The *Upaniṣads* develop their ideas from the speculations of some Vedic hymns concerning the nature of the creation of the universe. Certain hymns display an implicit monism in the sense that they envisage the creation of the multiplicity as a derivative of a pre-existent unity. The Upaniṣadic thinkers were interested in establishing what truly and fundamentally exists. This involved answering such questions as "where did the universe come from?" and "what is it made up of?" The most important question, however, concerned the nature of ultimate reality: "what is it that exists both before the creation and after the dissolution of the universe?" In hymns such as the *Puruṣa-Sūkta* (*Ṛg Veda* X.90) there is a pre-figuring of a number of important Upaniṣadic themes and this in itself is not surprising for the *Upaniṣads* are largely an outgrowth of the same Brahmanical world-view. It also seems fair to note that insofar as the *Puruṣa-Sūkta* is a relatively late hymn of the *Ṛg Veda*, it is more likely to be closer to the age of the *Upaniṣads* than other (earlier) parts of the *Saṃhitā* corpus of hymns.

Interest in the pre-cosmic state is evident throughout the Upaniṣadic texts and included a variety of speculations, often within the same *Upaniṣad*. The *Chāndogya Upaniṣad*, for instance, outlines a variety of cosmogonies. In III.19 the creation of the universe is said to arise from non-being in the form of a cosmic egg. However, later in the same text (VI.1–2) one finds the following,

> "In the beginning, my dear, this world was just Being (*sat*), one only, without a second. To be sure, some people say: 'In the beginning this world was just Non-being (*a-sat*), one only, without a second; from that Non-being Being was produced.' But verily, my dear, whence could this be?" said he. "How from Non-being could Being be produced?"[12]

In *Taittirīya Upaniṣad* II.6 , the primeval being desires to be many and procreates via the practice of austerities (*tapas*).

> Having performed austerity he created this whole world, whatever there is here. Having created it, into it, indeed, he entered. Having entered it, he became both the actual (*sat*) and the yon (*tya*), both the defined (*nirukta*) and the undefined, both the based and the non-based, both the conscious (*vijñāna*) and the unconscious, both the real (*satya*) and

the false (*anṛta*). As the real, he became whatever there is here. That is what they call the real.[13]

Similar themes can be found in *Aitareya Upaniṣad* I.1, *Praśna Upaniṣad* I.3, and 4 etc. The strong Upaniṣadic interest in cosmogony lead to further speculation about the nature of the fundamental support (*ādhāra*) of the universe. In the *Bṛhadāraṇyaka Upaniṣad* (III.6), the sage Yājñavalkya is asked by Gārgī, the daughter of Vacaknu, a series of penetrating questions concerning the fundamental substratum of the universe. After a long list of questions and answers Yājñavalkya retorts,

> "Do not, O Gārgī, push your inquiry too far, lest your head should fall off. You are questioning about a deity that should not be reasoned about."[14]

Yājñavalkya, however, is not always so reticent in the *Bṛhadāraṇyaka*. In BU V.1 Brahman is said to be the plenitude (*pūrṇakta*) which remains full even when emptied. Throughout the *Upaniṣads* there are frequent statements which characterize Brahman as the underlying essence of all things:

> Verily, this whole world is Brahma. Tranquil, let one worship It as that from which he came forth, as that into which he will be dissolved, as that into which he breathes. . . .Containing all works, containing all desires, containing all tastes, encompassing this whole world, the unspeaking, the unconcerned—this is the Soul of mine within the heart, this is Brahma. Into him I shall enter on departing hence.[15]

Indeed, one of the great sayings (*mahā-vākya*) of the Vedānta, appearing in a number of *upaniṣads*, states that,

> "That which is the finest essence—this whole world has that as its soul. That is Reality. That is *Ātman* (Soul). That art thou, Śvetaketu."[16]

At other times, however, it is the term "*brahman*" and not "*ātman*" which is emphasized as the source of all. The *Muṇḍaka Upaniṣad* for instance begins with the declaration that Brahman is the creator of the entire universe (*kartāviśvasya*), and the protector of the world (*goptābhuvanasya*). (*Muṇḍaka Upaniṣad* I.i.1) Brahman's status as universal source is again reiterated in II.i.1:

> As from a fire, fully ablaze, fly off sparks, in their thousands, that are akin to the fire, similarly O good-looking one, from the Immutable (*akṣara*) originate different kinds of creatures and into It again they merge.

The ambiguity of some of these statements reflects the fact that the *Upaniṣads* do not have a definitive point of view, even within the same *Upaniṣad*. GK III.23 notes for instance that the *śruti* equally upholds the view that creation occurs from a pre-existent being (*sat*) and that it proceeds from non-existence. Creation is most frequently understood to be a transformation (*pariṇāma*) or an emanation from a pre-existent reality. Creation from non-being (*asat*), however, is put forward as a possibility in *Chāndogya Upaniṣad* III.19 and *Taittirīya Upaniṣad* II.7. This is not necessarily a *creatio ex nihilo*, but in all likelihood denotes an emergence of being from the pregnant and undifferentiated chaos known as non-being (*asat*). Nevertheless, the equating of non-being with nothingness may have been intended and it is certainly criticized on those grounds in *Chāndogya Upaniṣad* VI.2. The predominant Brahmanical creation theme, however, describes an emanation from or transformation of "*sat*," whether envisaged as an abstract impersonal reality as in *Taittirīya Upaniṣad* II.i, or from a personal creator, as in *Praśna Upaniṣad* I.4. Here we can see the roots of the later philosophical theory of *satkāryavāda*—the doctrine that the effect (in this case the universe) is a modification (*pariṇāma::vikāra*) of the pre-existent cause (Brahman).

Brahman is the ground and support of the entire universe. The overwhelming trend in the *Upaniṣads* suggests that Brahman is not a personal god of some sort; rather it is impersonal (or perhaps suprapersonal) and essentially beyond description. Brahman is basically the source of everything, including the gods themselves. It is the conscious and intelligent principle which created the universe *in illo tempore*. Thus we find the *Upaniṣads* frequently stating that: "Truly, in the beginning this universe was Brahman, one alone by itself."

Psychology in the Upaniṣads

One consequence of the doctrines of *karman* and *saṃsāra* or rebirth was the fact that personal destiny was now firmly placed in the hands of the individual. The *Bṛhadāraṇyaka-Upaniṣad* states that:

> According to how one acts, according to how one conducts oneself, so does one become. The doer of good becomes good, the doer of evil becomes evil. . .[17]

However, the text continues:

> . . . But, it is said that 'a person is made [not by his acts but] by his desires alone.' As is his desire so is his resolve, as is his resolve, such is the action (*karman*) that he performs.

Since it is our desires (*kāma*) which motivate our actions, it is the underlying desire and not the act itself which is the root cause of birth and its perpetuation in *saṃsāra*. The source of our continued sorrow (*duḥkha*), the perpetuation of the lifecycle, is our desire (*kāma*) for sense-objects and pleasures. This is the beginnings of the ethicizing of the concept of *karman*, that is its transformation from an external theory of causation to an intrinsic moral theory based upon the motives behind our actions.[18]

These features are aptly displayed in the *Kaṭha Upaniṣad* in the story of Naciketas, the son of a Brahmin priest.[19] In a moment of rage Naciketas is sent to Death (Yama) as a sacrifice by his father. However, upon his arrival there is no attendant to greet him. Three days elapse before Yama, the god of the dead finds Naciketas alone (Yama in fact, in Vedic mythology was the first man to die. He it is therefore who prepares the rest of mankind upon their death). Yama is dismayed for "this is no way to treat a Brahmin!," and so offers Naciketas three boons. The first is for Naciketas to return to his now remorseful father, and Yama agrees that this should be granted. Second, Naciketas requests to know the secret meaning of the sacrificial fire (*agni*) and how it ascends to the heavens. This is also granted by Yama. Third, Naciketas asks to know if there is an after-life, and if so, the path to immortality. Yama is reluctant to impart this information, saying that it is extremely profound and that even the gods do not know of its precise nature. Instead he offers riches and kingdoms beyond compare. But Naciketas is undeterred—these are ephemeral, he says, they do not lead to lasting salvation; they are but temporary distractions. Finally, Yama relents and tells Naciketas the path to the "deathless state" (*amṛta*).[20]

In many ways, in fact, Naciketas already knows the answer Yama is to give him since he has already declared that the pleasures of the world are inadequate and superficial. Liberation from the repeated cycle of birth and death is to be attained through the restraint of our faculties. This is to be achieved by the practice of *yoga*. Thence follows the analogy of the chariot, in which the following comparisons are made:

> Know the (individual) Self (*ātman*) as the master of the chariot, and the body (*śarīra*) as the chariot. Know the intellect (*buddhi*) as the charioteer, and the mind (*manas*) as verily the bridle.
>
> They call the senses (*indriya*) the horses; the senses having been imagined as horses, (know) the objects (*viṣaya*) as the ways. The discriminating people (*manīṣiṇa*) call that Self the enjoyer (*bhoktṛ*), when it is associated with the body, senses, and mind.[21]

Thus, the body is likened to a chariot, and the mind to the reins of that chariot. *Ātman*, our true self, is the lord of the chariot, that is the person traveling within it. Liberation is achieved by controlling the mind-body complex (here said to be made up of the material body, the sense-organs, the intellect, and the mind,) and the realization that the true essence of existence is not this ephemeral complex, but rather the *ātman* which travels within it. Rather than roaming around searching for ephemeral satisfactions like a chariot without a master controlling its reins, one should endeavor to control the "vehicle" of one's experiences. Likewise, just as a person travels in various chariots at different times, so does the *ātman* transmigrate from body to body. The goal then is to gain control of our saṃsāric vehicles through the yogic control of the senses. One should endeavor to realize one's status as "Lord of the chariot" (*rathin*).

The belief that one should restrain all misguided hedonistic tendencies probably reflects external influence upon Upaniṣadic thought from the communities of wandering ascetics (*śramaṇa*) from which the heterodox movements of Buddhism and Jainism first sprang. Buddhist influence on the middle and late *Upaniṣads* is beyond reasonable dispute. The focus of the earliest (pre-Buddhist) *Upaniṣads*, however, had also been on the intuitive apprehension of *ātman*, the innermost essence of all living beings. These texts thus represent a tradition aiming at an intuitive knowledge of the innermost nature of all sentient beings—the very source of conscious existence. In this respect the primacy of the *Upaniṣads* in post-Vedic "orthodoxy" reflects the establishment of a religious movement within mainstream Brahmanism which emphasizes the importance of gnosis (*vidyā*) for the attainment of liberation (*mokṣa*). In classical times this aspect contributed to the separation (at least intellectually) between the path of ritual action (*karma-mārga*) and the path of knowledge (*jñāna-mārga*), the respective emphases of the (Pūrva)-Karma-Mīmāṃsā and the Vedānta (Uttara-Mīmāṃsā) schools. An early example of the supreme importance attached to the discovery of the indwelling (*antaryāmin*) self (*ātman*) can be seen from Yājñavalkya's final teaching to his wife Maitreyī in *Bṛhadāraṇyaka Upaniṣad* II.4. Here Yājñavalkya declares that everything that is valued is so treasured not because of itself but because of the *ātman* within. This establishes the enquiry into the interior nature of the self as the most important to undertake.[22]

In the *Bṛhadāraṇyaka Upaniṣad* the individual self is analyzed in terms of the sense-faculties fighting for supremacy. The greatest of these faculties is *prāṇa*—the life-force, the breath which sustains all conscious existence.[23] This is polytheism in a psychological context—

the individual like the rest of the universe is made up of a number of conflicting powers or *devas*. Indeed in some instances the term "*deva*" is used to denote the sense-faculties.[24] Nevertheless, the competition between the senses ends upon sleep when there is a unity (*ekadhā*) of the various faculties.[25]

Just as cosmogonically speaking the one Brahman becomes the many in creation, and the return to oneness at universal dissolution, the one *prāṇa*, identified with the animating consciousness-self (*prajñātman*), divides itself up into the various bodily faculties during the day and becomes one at the end of the day. These correspond on a cosmogonic level to what have been called "the day and night of Brahmā." Taking this correspondence to the extreme, one might suggest that the individual creates the world of his experience (*dṛṣṭisṛṣṭivāda*) just as Brahman creates the universe. Nevertheless, this step is not taken by the *Upaniṣads*, nor is it made by classical Advaita Vedānta.[26] All Advaitins, however, acknowledge that a significant aspect of an individual's experience (or at least the form in which it is experienced) is the product of that individual's own activity. This, however, is little more than a re-statement of the centrality of the *karman* doctrine.[27] Advaita Vedānta, in common with virtually the entirety of Indian philosophical speculation, tended to accept the *karman* doctrine as axiomatic.

The Four States of Experience

There are three "normative" states of consciousness—waking, dream, and deep sleep. In the *Bṛhadāraṇyaka Upaniṣad* Yājñavalkya is asked by King Janaka "what is the light of man?" After a series of answers and further questions establishing a progressive dialectic, the final irreducible source of light is said to be the *ātman*.[28] This is reminiscent of certain Indian theories of perception where the inner organ (*antaḥkāraṇa*) proceeds outward and illuminates the dark insentient world (like beams of light emitted from the eyes). Here the point of the discussion is that sentient experience is impossible without the *ātman* as the conscious support of experience. This allows Yājñavalkya to draw a distinction between dream and waking experiences. In waking experience one is dependent upon the natural light of the sun as well as the inner (consciousness-giving) light of the *ātman*, while in dreams one only requires the self-illuminating light of the *ātman*.[29] The dream state, however, is an intermediatory place existing at the boundary between this world and another (*paraloka*). In dreams, the person has the freedom and creativity to construct his own world based upon his insight into the waking world and the world beyond. As a free agent (*kartṛ*), the person constructs chariots, roads etc. experiencing great joy and sadness. This state does not last, however, and the agent is said to be like a fish forever swimming between the two shores of waking and dream states.[30] Finally the weary traveler reaches the end of his sojourn in a state beyond desire or fear. Here the self resides in blissful rest (*samprasāda*) where there are absolutely no distinctions. The text is not without ambiguity on this issue, but it would seem that at this stage no explicit distinction has yet been made between the blissful non-distinction of deep sleep and the insightful non-dual awareness of a fourth state of experience.

Nevertheless, in the *Bṛhadāraṇyaka Upaniṣad* we find a hierarchy of experience which is something of a reversal of the common-sensical attitude. Dreams provide a greater degree of insight into the nature of the self when compared to waking experience since in the former only the inner light of the self is involved. Moreover, in deep sleep even the fantasies and mental fabrications of dreams cease (if only temporarily) and one experiences a blissful state of quiescence (*samprasāda*) beyond all desires, fears, and distinctions. The unmediated awareness of the *ātman* then is closest to the experience of deep sleep since it is here that one may find a clearer apprehension of the self, devoid of all external and internal distraction.[31] Thus Yājñavalkya declares

> As a lump of salt is without interior or exterior, entire, and purely saline in taste, even so is the Self without interior or exterior, entire, and Pure Intelligence (*prajñāna*) alone. The (self) comes out (as a separate entity) from these elements, and (this separateness) is destroyed with them. After attaining (this oneness) it has no more (particular) consciousness (*saṃjñā*).[32]

In the *Chāndogya Upaniṣad* sleep is more clearly distinguished from the attainment of mystical knowledge of the *ātman*. This much is clear from the teaching Prajāpati gives to Indra in *Chāndogya Upaniṣad* VIII.7-12. Sleep in fact is not a state of bliss, Indra suggests, but an annihilation of consciousness.[33] Prajāpati thus teaches Indra that the true self is beyond the state of the embodied, the dream, and the serenity of deep sleep. The body is merely the locus (*adhiṣṭhāna*) of the supreme person (*uttamapuruṣa*) which in fact is neither embodied nor touched by pleasure and pain.[34] Having risen beyond bodily form and ascended toward the highest light (*paraṃ jyotir*), "one goes around laughing, sporting, having enjoyment with women, or friends, not remembering the appendage of this body."[35]

In the *Gauḍapādīya-kārikā* waking and dream experience are conflated. Sleep is temporary and, following Indra in the *Chāndogya Upaniṣad*, is said to lack any awareness whatsoever. As such it is a non-apprehension of reality (*tattva-agrahaṇa*).[36] The explanation of the similarity of the waking and dream states in GK II, however, is dependent upon the *Bṛhadāraṇyaka* analysis. Both states are dependent upon the light of the indwelling *ātman*.[37] In fact the GK's view that both states are non-veridical is based upon the fact that they are impermanent and sublated by each other. This is the point made in *Bṛhadāraṇyaka Upaniṣad* IV.iii.18 with the analogy of the fish swimming between the two shores. Thus, the emphasis in the GK is placed upon the fourth state (*turīya*), which is a permanent insight into reality (unlike the absence of awareness in deep sleep), but without the distractions of an inner world (as in dream and waking experience) and an outer world (as in the waking state, but also implicitly in the dream state).[38]

The conjunction of cosmological and psychological speculation in the *Upaniṣads* was achieved by way of the *bandhutā* homology,[39] that is the scheme whereby great correspondences and parallels were envisaged between different realms of existence. The complementarity between the cosmic and the individual can be illustrated if we consider the Vedic notion of desire (*kāma*). As we have seen, the Upaniṣadic acceptance of the doctrines of *karman* and rebirth (*saṃsāra*) and the early recognition that the karmic power of an action lay in the intention or desire motivating it rather than in the act itself stressed the importance of desire in the perpetuation of rebirth.[40] There are a number of instances in the *Saṃhitās*, however, where desire (*kāma*) is specifically associated with the creation of the universe.[41] What the intentional view of *karman* suggests is that just as the *kāma* of the divine being creates the macrocosm, the *kāma* of the individual self perpetuates rebirth and thus in one sense creates the microcosmic universe of personal experience. In the *Upaniṣads* the macrocosmic and the microcosmic are identified. Brahman is the mysterious support of everything, the universal and transcendent substratum.[42] This Brahman is *Ātman* the (immanent) inner-controller (*antaryāmin*) of all things.[43]

In terms of the Upaniṣadic sources which influenced the rise of Advaita Vedānta we should note that the *Upaniṣads* were already moving in the direction of postulating an eternal and unchanging essence to man. This was *ātman*, the self that existed through a succession of lives. Speculation from the cosmological angle had also established that there was a basic underlying principle which supported the entire universe, i.e. Brahman, the totality of existence, pure Being itself. This two-pronged investigation of ultimate reality, the one interested in finding an underlying cosmic principle supporting the universe, and the other searching for the underlying essence of the individual person culminated in their eventual identification:

> *ātman* as the innermost essence or soul of man, and
> Brahman as the innermost essence and support of the universe.

The goal of the *Upaniṣads* then can be seen in terms of a return to one's origins, a realization that the individual self and the universe are created, supported, controlled, and thoroughly pervaded by Brahman, the mysterious source of everything. "That One" (*tad ekam*) is what all created things emerged from, and "That One" is what they shall return to. Brahman is the source of the universe as well as its inner controller (*antaryāmin*). Thus we can see in the *Upaniṣads* a tendency towards a convergence of microcosm and macrocosm, culminating in the equating of *ātman* with Brahman. The scheme of hidden correspondences already firmly established in the pre-Upaniṣadic literature and the monistic speculations of some of the Vedic *Saṃhitās* contributed to an investigative attitude and an interest in fundamental principles. The prevailing monism of the *Upaniṣads* was developed by the Advaita Vedānta to its ultimate extreme. This is not to suggest that the Upaniṣadic texts support the Advaita point of view, nor is it to deny that there are verses and statements which are amenable to such an interpretation. There is no systematic philosophy expounded in the *Upaniṣads*; rather these texts represent a number of speculative trends intertwined and interspersed with one another. The various schools of Vedānta philosophy which subsequently developed in response to the unsystematic nature of Upaniṣadic monism reflect the cryptic nature of the Upaniṣadic texts. The rich complexity of the Upaniṣadic source material made such texts amenable to a variety of sophisticated interpretations and philosophical accretions. Indeed our own analysis has highlighted the difficulty in making any general statement about the *Upaniṣads* without running the risk of misrepresentation and over-systematization.

Like the *Upaniṣads*, the GK approaches similar issues from two basic directions. Throughout the text we find a psychological analysis of states of consciousness, culminating in a non-dualistic (*advaya*) theory of perception (the theoretical basis for the practice of *asparśayoga*). In addition to this the GK also provides an ontological analysis of the nature of cosmogonic theories, culminating in the doctrines of non-origination (*ajātivāda*) and non-dualism (*advaita*). The Upaniṣadic texts to which the GK seems most indebted are the *Bṛhadāraṇyaka* and *Māṇḍūkya Upaniṣad*. We have briefly considered the former. Given the connection of GK I with the latter it would seem appropriate to consider the MU also.

The Māṇḍūkya Upaniṣad

The *Māṇḍūkya Upaniṣad* provides the focus for the exposition of Vedāntic philosophy in the first *prakaraṇa* of the GK. The text is important for its concise development of various Upaniṣadic themes, notably the symbolism and meditation upon the syllable Om and the doctrine of the four states of experience (*catuṣpād*). The text is short and is given below in full:[44]

1. This syllable Om is all this. Its further explanation is: All that was, is, and shall be is merely the syllable OM. Whatever else there is, beyond the three periods of time, that too is only OM.
2. Indeed, all this is Brahman; The self (*Ātman*) is Brahman. This same self has four quarters.
3. The first quarter is *Vaiśvānara*, conscious of an external [world], in the waking state, having seven limbs and nineteen mouths; [it is] the enjoyer of gross objects.
4. The second quarter is *Taijasa*—The Radiant, conscious of an internal [world], in the dream state, having seven limbs and nineteen mouths; [it is] the enjoyer of subtle objects.
5. When sleeping, "one desires no pleasure whatsoever and sees no dream,"[45] that is deep sleep. The third quarter is *Prājña*, just a unified mass of cognition, consisting of bliss, in the state of deep sleep; indeed, [it is] the enjoyer of bliss and the aperture of cognition.
6. This is the Lord of all; this is the knower of all, the inner controller. This is the womb of all, for it is the beginning and end of beings.
7. Not conscious of an "internal," not conscious of an "external," not conscious of both [together], not a mass of cognition, neither cognitive nor non-cognitive, unseen, unrelated, incomprehensible, indefinable, unthinkable,

undesignated, the essence of the unity of the self, the cessation of plurality, the quiescent, appeased non-duality—as such do the wise ones consider the fourth. This is *Ātman* (the Self). This is the known.

8. This *Ātman*, in terms [of the syllable], is OM. In terms of the portions [of the syllable], the portions are the quarters [of *ātman*] and vice versa, i.e. [the letters] A, U, and M.

9. In the waking state, *Vaiśvānara* is the letter A—the first portion, either from "Acquiring" ("*āpt'i*" literally "obtaining"), or from "Archetypal" ("*ādimatva*," literally "being the first"). Indeed, he who knows this acquires all desires and also becomes the Archetype (lit. "first") [for others to follow].

10. In the dream state, *Taijasa* is the letter U—the second portion, from "Upliftment" ("*utkarṣa*") or from "Unbiasedness" ("*ubhayatva*" literally "bothness"). Indeed, he who uplifts the constancy of his knowledge, becomes equal; there is no one ignorant of Brahman in his family for the one who knows this.

11. In the state of deep sleep, *Prājña* is the letter M—the third portion, from "Measuring" ("*miti*," literally "constructing") or from "Mergence" ("*apītiḥ*" from "*mi, minat'i*"). Indeed, he who knows this measures out (*minoti*) this entire world and becomes its mergence.

12. The fourth is portionless [and] unrelated, [it is] the cessation of plurality, the appeased non-duality. This syllable OM is the self. For the one who knows this, he enters the *Ātman* by means of itself.

Thus, the MU states that there are four states of experience. The waking state is given the epithet "Universal" or "Common to all" (*vaiśvānara*) since it is the sphere of public experience. Here one experiences gross (*sthūla*) objects.[46] In the dream state one experiences subtle objects (*pravivikta*). This state is known as "radiant" (*taijasa*), presumably because in dreams the *ātman* is its own light.[47] In deep sleep one experiences pure bliss. This state is named "cognition" (*prājña*) since it consists of an undifferentiated mass of cognition (*prajñāna-ghana*).

MU 6 is interesting for a number of reasons. The introduction of theistic and cosmogonic concepts into a discussion of psychological states of experience is an example of the Upaniṣadic acceptance of wide-ranging correspondences (*bandhu*) between the microcosmic and macrocosmic realms. Traditionally, the prose of MU 6 has been taken to be a further elaboration of the description of the deep sleep state in MU 5. Thomas Wood, however, suggests that this interpretation of MU 6 is in fact mistaken. Drawing our attention to the teachings concerning the nature of the deep sleep state in *Chāndogya Upaniṣad* VI.8, VIII.6, and VIII.11–12, Wood argues that:

> [It] would appear to make no sense to associate the state in which one "does not know himself" and in which one has "gone to destruction" with the omniscient, omnipotent *īśvara* which is described in Maṇḍ. 6. The Chāndogyopaniṣad shows very clearly that the Vedāntists were no more inclined than we are to associate the concept of *īśvara* with the state of deep sleep. . .[48]

In Wood's view, MU 6 is to be associated with MU 7 and is thus a description of the fourth state (*caturtha* in the MU, although more commonly known by the term "*turīya*") To support this interpretation Wood cites the first *prakaraṇa* of the GK, which he takes to be a separate work in its own right. In GK I.10, for instance, *turīya* is described as the ordainer (*īśāna*), the lord (*prabhu*), the non-dual (*advaita*) and all-pervading (*vibhu*) god (*deva*) of all beings. Again in GK I.12, the lack of awareness characteristic of the deep sleep state is sharply contrasted with *turīya*, which is described as omniscient. Thus Wood suggests that "The only natural way of reading this is to link it with Maṇḍ. 6, which says that *īśvara* is omniscient."[49] Wood also points to evidence from post-Śaṅkarite commentarial literature which also appears to endorse his interpretation of MU 6.[50]

Nevertheless, such hermeneutical issues need not detain us. We need merely note the importance of the MU in the establishment of a number of central themes to be developed upon in the *Gauḍapādīya-kārikā* and the subsequent Advaita Vedānta tradition. Firstly, in MU 2 we find the simultaneous declaration of three cardinal doctrines of the Vedānta—that the universe is Brahman, that the self is Brahman, and that there are four states of experience pertainable to that self. Meditation upon the syllable Om is elaborated further in GK I, but this did not become a central feature of the Vedāntic tradition as such.[51] Finally, one should note the negative theology of MU 7 and the first occurrence of the term "*advaita*" in a Vedāntic context.

The *Bhagavadgītā* and the *Gauḍapādīya-kārikā*

The main proponents of the view that the GK is dependent upon the *Bhagavadgītā* have been Raghunath Damodar Karmarkar (1953)[52] and Sangamlal Pandey (1974).[53] Both the *Gītā* and GK I for instance mention the yogic practice of meditation upon the syllable Om (GK I.19–29 :: BG VIII.13; XVII.23–24.) Such meditation, however, is a widespread Indian practice and does not provide evidence of a connection between the two texts. Both texts also adopt the absolutist principle that something can only be real if it exists absolutely (in the beginning, middle and end), (GK II.6–7; IV.31–32 :: BG II.14, 28; V.22). However, it is likely that the *Gauḍapādīya-kārikā* adapts this from similar statements found in the *Mūla-Madhyamaka-kārikā* (MMK) of Nāgārjuna (see chapter 4).

Certainly there are verses and phrases used in the GK which echo the words of the *Gītā*. GK IV.92d echoes BG II.15d with an identical reference to "attaining the state of deathlessness" (*so'mṛtatvāya kalpate*). The context differs radically however, the GK referring to the immortal nature of *dharmas* and the *Gītā* referring to the state attained by sages (*muni*) who have gone beyond pleasure and pain. GK I.28 states that the Lord is "established in the heart of all" (*sarvasya hṛdi saṃsthitam*). This is similar to statements made in BG XIII.17 and XVIII.61. The former, however, is a reference to Brahman, while in the *Gītā* it is Kṛṣṇa who is the Lord of all. As with meditation upon the syllable Om, there are many such references to Brahman, *Ātman* or *Puruṣa* dwelling in the heart of all to be found in the *Upaniṣads*.[54] Indeed GK I.28 uses the phrase "*matvā dhīro no śocati*" which is taken from the *Kāṭha Upaniṣad*.[55] Thus one need not turn to the BG as a source for this and other phrases. Again GK II.35ab echoes BG II.56 and IV.10 in its reference to the wise men (*dhīr*) who are devoid of passion, fear, and anger (*vīta rāga bhaya krodha*). While this may be a veiled allusion to the *Gītā* there is nothing else which might substantiate this hypothesis. The fact that the *Gītā* uses the compound more than once suggests that it is a stock phrase for describing the state of the wise man and perhaps not unique to the text itself. We should note that the GK makes no obvious reference to any views which might connect it specifically with the *Gītā*.

In the second *prakaraṇa* of the GK a list of (mis-)conceptions (*vikalpa*) of the non-dual *ātman* are given. This list is commented upon with a concluding statement to the effect that the *ātman* appears to the individual in a manner conducive to the expectations of the individual, that is according to one's preconceived views (GK II.29).

This allows the author of the GK to argue in the third and fourth *prakaraṇas* that his view does not conflict (*avirodha*) with the dualistic views of others since all are apprehending the same thing, i.e. the non-dual *ātman*. The problem for the non-dualist of course is that they apprehend the *ātman* wrongly! A similar syncretistic view is propounded in the *Bhagavadgītā*.[56] Later Advaitins (such as Madhusūdana Sarasvatī (1540–1647) in his *Prasthānabheda*) explain this inclusivist acceptance of all views on the grounds that *ātman* appears according to the qualifications of the seeker (*adhikāribheda*). However, as we shall see, it is likely that the author(s) of the GK developed their view by way of an adaptation of Mahāyāna ideas, in particular an absolutistic reading of chapter XXIV of the MMK.

A clear philosophical similarity between the GK and the *Bhagavadgītā* can be found in the absolutism of both texts. The *Gauḍapādīya-kārikā* argues that the mortal cannot change into the immortal (III.21; IV.7), that which exists must exist in the beginning, the middle and the end (II.6; IV.31) and that the *ātman* is unoriginated—no *jīva* has ever been born or undergone any change (I.16; II.32; III.48; IV.22; IV.71 etc.) All of these views are paralleled by the doctrines expounded in the *Gītā*. As early as chapter two we find Kṛṣṇa telling Arjuna that the non-existent cannot arise (because it is non-existent), and the existent cannot cease (because it is existent) (BG II.16–17).[57] This is a concise exposition of the absolutist view endorsed by the GK. Consequently, Kṛṣṇa continues, the self can neither slay nor be slain—it is immortal and eternally existent.

> II.20: *na jāyate mriyate vā kadācin n'āyaṁ bhūtvā bhavitā vā na bhūyaḥ, ajo nityaḥ śāśvato 'yam purāṇo na hanyate hanyamāne śarīre.* Never is it born, nor does it die; never did it come into being, nor will it ever cease to be. It is unborn, permanent, eternal and primeval. It is not slain when the body is slain.

This verse, however, is not likely to originate from the *Gītā* since it is also found in *Kaṭha Upaniṣad* I.ii.18. One cannot, therefore use this as evidence of the dependence of the GK upon the BG. Indeed, one should note that despite the absolutistic parallels between the GK and the *Gītā*, the two texts have little else in common. The *Gītā* is a poetic work endorsing a form of devotional worship (*bhakti*) of the Supra-Personal Kṛṣṇa.[58] This sharply contrasts with the philosophical and scholastic orientation of the GK. The former, whilst endorsing the logic of non-origination (and in fact using it to explain to Arjuna how it is that he will not really kill his fellow warriors in battle), subsumes the static and impersonal Brahman under the Supra-personal Kṛṣṇa. Thus, in BG XIV.27 Kṛṣṇa states that "I am the base supporting Brahman, immortal [Brahman] which knows no change. . ." (*brahmaṇo hi pratiṣṭhā 'ham amṛtasy'āvyayasya*). The *Gītā* in fact suggests that Kṛṣṇa has a higher and a lower nature (*prakṛti*).[59] The "fixed, still state of Brahman" (*brāhmī sthitiḥ*, BG II.72) is merely the lower nature (*prakṛti*) of Kṛṣṇa. Thus,

> XIV.3: *mama yonir mahad brahma tasmin garbhaṁ dadhyām aham, saṁbhavaḥ sarva-bhūtānāṃ tato bhavati. . .*
> Great Brahman is to me a womb,[60] in it I plant the seed: from this derives the origin of all contingent beings.

This view radically differs from the philosophy expounded in the *Gauḍapādīya-kārikā*. The *Bhagavadgītā*'s relegation of Brahman to a position inferior to that of Kṛṣṇa, the utilization of Sāṃkhyan procreative imagery (male—*Puruṣa*/Kṛṣṇa :: female—*prakṛti*/Brahman) to explain creation, and the very acceptance that there has been a creation in the first place, all point to the contrasting perspectives of the two texts under consideration. Neither Pandey nor Karmarkar provide any concrete evidence for the view that the GK is reliant in any significant way upon the *Bhagavadgītā*. Given the philosophical divergence between the two texts one can perhaps see why.

The Brahmasūtra

The *Brahmasūtra* is said to be the logical beginning or foundation (*nyāya-prasthāna*) of Vedānta. *Bhagavadgītā* 13.4 refers to aphoristic verses concerning Brahman (*Brahmasūtra-pāda*), but Śaṅkara, author of the oldest extant commentary on the text, understands this to be a reference to the *Upaniṣads*. Traditionally, Bādarāyaṇa is said to be the author of the *Brahmasūtra*. Śaṅkara refers to the author of the text as "*bhagavān sūtrakāraḥ*," and simply as *ācārya*,[61] without mentioning his name. However, in the commentary to the final *sūtra*, Śaṅkara refers to its author as "*bhagavān bādarāyaṇa ācāryaḥ*." On the other hand, in the *Upadeśasāhasrī*,[62] Śaṅkara mentions Vyāsa as the supreme Vedāntic authority, and while not referring to this figure as author of the *Brahmasūtra*, the identification is likely to be implied. The term "*vyāsa*," however, means compiler and may be an epithet rather than a personal name. It is likely that the text of the *Brahmasūtra* has undergone some redaction (for instance there are divergent readings between the various commentators). The possibility remains therefore that Bādarāyaṇa may have been editor (*vyāsa*) of the text, and not its original author.

The thinker whose ideas are most often referred to is Jaimini, the traditional author of the *Mīmāṁsā Sūtra*. However, authorship of this text is also considered to be spurious. First, Jaimini is referred to by name in the *Mīmāṁsā Sūtra* five times. It is an odd occurrence for the author of a text to refer so obviously to himself by name. Second, in *Mīmāṁsā Sūtra* 6.3.4. Jaimini's opinion is quoted in the *pūrvapakṣa* and then subsequently rejected. It is unlikely then, that Jaimini is the author of this text, despite Sangamlal Pandey's suggestion that Jaimini is here modifying his own opinion.[63] From the evidence deduced from the *Brahmasūtra*, it is clear that Jaimini, as well as being a *Mīmāṃsaka*, was also a great Vedāntin. His views are clearly addressed eleven times in the *Brahmasūtra*, making him by far the most quoted thinker.[64] However, Jaimini's views are not always endorsed, in fact Nakamura goes as far as to suggest that Bādarāyaṇa "considered his chief task to be to criticize the theories of Jaimini. Whenever his theories are quoted, the theories of Jaimini are always listed as the object of his criticism."[65]

However, the *Brahmasūtra* does not accept all of Bādarāyaṇa's views as its final position (*siddhānta*). Thus, Nakamura notes that Bādarāyaṇa believes in the ideal of the renunciate (*saṃnyasin*), while the *Sūtra* encourages the actions of the ritual performing householder who contemplates Brahman.[66] Again, Bādarāyaṇa seems to distinguish between two types of Brahman, but this is not found in the *Sūtra* itself. Indeed, in 4.4.5–7, Bādarāyaṇa's view is listed among various heterodox opinions. Nevertheless, of all the thinkers quoted in the text (including Jaimini) Bādarāyaṇa's thought seems closest to that of the text's actual author.

The text appears to have been compiled for two main reasons. First and foremost, it is an attempt to establish a definitive exegesis of the *Upaniṣads*, thereby circumventing the apparent contradictoriness of various Upaniṣadic statements. Thus, its motive and method is more akin to Western theology than philosophy. The second purpose behind the *Sūtra*'s composition appears to be the criticism of what it considers to be non-Upaniṣadic points of view (mainly Sāṃkhya, but also Vaiśeṣika, various Buddhist schools etc.) Nakamura places the development of the *Brahmasūtra* into three historical stages:

1. A synopsis of Upaniṣadic doctrine, based mainly upon the *Chāndogya Upaniṣad*, and probably originating from a school of the Sāma Veda (to which the *Chāndogya Upaniṣad*, Jaimini, and Bādarāyaṇa belonged).

2. Enlargement of the text, incorporation of theories from other *Upaniṣads*, and general adoption by Vedic schools in general as a synopsis of Upaniṣadic ideas.
3. Revision of the *Sūtra* and incorporation of logical disputation aimed particularly at the rival schools of Indian thought.[67]

This seems a useful model of development to accept. However, it is doubtful to what extent it can be either verified or falsified, and thus it can be accepted only as an heuristic and provisional starting point. It seem likely that the *Brahmasūtra* incorporated critiques of the Sāṃkhya school at a much earlier stage in its development, since proto-Sāṃkhya-style doctrines are archaic, and thus must have represented a threat to the Brahmanical monism of the *Sūtra*. Nevertheless, it seems beyond any reasonable doubt that the *Brahmasūtra* has gone through a number of developmental stages, and that it reached its final form around the fifth century CE (this is clear from its critique of the Yogācāra theories in BS II.2.28–32). However, the greater part of the *Sūtra* must have existed long before this time, and with the undoubted antiquity of the *Chāndogya*, its foundational text, the earliest parts of the text may be very old indeed. Nakamura notes that the thinkers referred to in the BS lived before the Common Era (BCE)[68] which implies that the bulk of the text was compiled at least some four to five hundred years before the sections which attack Mahāyāna Buddhist philosophy.

Doctrines of the Brahmasūtra

The BS is a highly orthodox text from the Brahmanical point of view, since it restricts access to its doctrines to the upper three *varṇa*, as does the *Mīmāṁsā Sutra*. It also presupposes the Brahmanical form of life (*varṇāśrama* etc.)

The definitive Vedāntic position is espoused in direct contrast to the doctrines of the Sāṃkhya school. Sāṃkhya is said to be based upon traditional thought (*smārta*, 4.2.21), as opposed to the revelatory word (*śabda*) of the Vedic scriptures. The school utilizes inference (*anumāna*) and does not rely upon scriptural foundations (*śruti*, literally "that which is heard") alone for its theories. The *Brahmasūtra* accepts the validity of *smṛti*, but only when it accords to *śruti* (3.3.31). This position is expressed as early as BS 1.1.3, 4, where scripture is said to be the source or womb (*yoni*) of all knowledge. The Vedas are eternal (*nitya*, 1.3.29,30). The theories of the Vedānta school, thus are based upon the revelatory word (*śabdamūla*, 2.1.27). The Vedas, of course, are believed to derive from a non-human (*apauruṣeya*) origin. The text places the revealed text above all other sources of authoritative knowledge. Thus, whereas *śruti* is direct perception (*pratyakṣa*), *smṛti* is inference (*anumāna*), based upon that direct knowledge (see BS 1.3.28; 3.2.24; 4.4.20).

However, this will not convince those who do not accept the revelatory status of the Vedas. Therefore, the *Brahmasūtra* also endorses the utilization of logic based upon the insights of the scriptures (2.1.18). Thus, we find two types of argument in the *Brahmasūtra*, the hermeneutical type—based upon the harmonization of Upaniṣadic ideas, and the apologetic—based upon the refutation of rival points of view. Thus, the BS utilizes *reductio ad absurdum* (*prasaṅga*) arguments to refute other doctrines. In fact the term *prasaṅga* is used several times in the BS (2.1.1; 8, 11, 12, and 26; 2.3.32). However, there is often little in the way of conscious effort to substantiate the *Brahmasūtra*'s own position through the use of logical arguments, and philosophical problems are often circumvented via the use of parables and references to the infallibility of scripture. This is not surprising given the *Brahmasūtra*'s essentially theological approach, and foundational regard for the Vedas. As a means of persuading one's philosophical opponents, however, it remains highly unsatisfactory.

Pūrva and *Uttara Mīmāṃsā*

The *Brahmasūtra* begins with a statement of its intentions: "Now, for the enquiry into Brahman." Commentarial debate concerned the reason for the occurrence of the term "*atha*"—"Now." Does the text presuppose any other enquiry before the enquiry into Brahman?[69] It seems likely that this is a self-conscious reference to the status of the Vedānta, as the "end of the Vedas." Thus, the text is expressing its concern for the doctrines of the *Upaniṣads* and not that of the *Saṃhitā*s and *Brāhmaṇa*s which have "gone before." The division between the initial exegesis (*pūrvamīmāṃsā*) and the final exegesis (*uttaramīmāṃsā*, or Vedānta) is an early distinction which seems clearly to pre-date Śaṅkara. The former, envisaging the performance of rituals as the goal of man (*puruṣārtha*) was laid down in the *Mīmāṃsā-Sūtra*, that became the fundamental text of the *Mīmāṃsā darśana*. The latter, establishing liberation (*mokṣa*) as the ultimate goal, placed more emphasis upon knowledge (*vidyā*) than action (*karman*) (e.g., see *Brahmasūtra*, 3.4.1–8). This trend within Brahmanical thought developed into the Vedānta *darsána*.

The ancient Brahmins saw *vidyā* as the knowledge of the correct performance of the ritual. However, as the exegesis (*mīmāṃsa*) of ritual practices became more sophisticated, this knowledge also came to refer to the contemplative worship (*upāsanā*) of the deity.[70] This process developed within Upaniṣadic circles through the interiorization of the *agnihotra* ritual (*prāṇāgnihotra-vāda*). Thus, *upāsanā* came to denote an inner contemplation of the object or meaning (*artha*) of the ritual act. Thus, for the renunciate, there was no longer any need to perform the *agnihotra* ritual (BS 3.4.25), since his aim is liberation (*mokṣa*) through the attainment of knowledge (3.4.17).

The establishment of a fourth goal, *mokṣa*, as well as duty (*dharma*), wealth (*artha*), and pleasure (*kāma*), and of a fourth stage of life, that of the renunciate (*saṃnyasin*) reveals a tension within Brahmanical thought between the lifestyle and goals of the householder (*gṛhastha*) and those of the retired forest-dweller (*vānaprastha*). As such, the incorporation of the renunciate as a Brahmanical ideal constitutes an attempt by Brahmanical ortholoxy to assimilate the tradition of wandering renunciates (*śramaṇas*), out of which the Buddhist and Jaina movements developed. The importance of the forest-dweller (*vānaprastha*) to the early Upaniṣadic movement, and subsequently to the later development of the Vedānta school, cannot and should not be underestimated in the "Brahminization" of the ideal of the *saṃnyasī*.

The *Brahmasūtra* explicitly subordinates the efficacy of the ritual to that of knowledge (*vidyā*) of Brahman (see 3.4.17). This marks the major departure of the Vedānta's understanding of the meaning behind Vedic utterances and injunctions. The scriptures are the means whereby one can attain true knowledge of Brahman (1.1.4). Thus, for the early Vedāntin what is important is the grounding of his or her doctrines in the Upaniṣadic literature, and the reconciliation of differing doctrines and statements within that same literature. However, the *Brahmasūtra* does not thereby reject the efficacy of ritualistic practices. Rituals themselves are necessary for the correct acquisition of knowledge (3.4.26), and the practice of the *agnihotra* ceremony, for instance, is said to be conducive to liberation (4.1.16). Nevertheless, even the householder must practice contemplation of Brahman as well as performing the rituals if he is to secure his own liberation. This displays the synthetic method of the *Sūtrakāra*, never rejecting an orthodox view where it can be assimilated at some (albeit inferior) level. The Vedānta stands upon its acceptance of knowledge of Brahman as the supreme means to liberation. Both the means and the goal display an internal movement away from the traditional goals of the *Pūrva Mīmāṃsa*. Nevertheless, at this stage, the performance of rituals is an indispensable means to salvation itself. It is from this religious and theological background that the Vedāntin establishes his position.

Yoga in the *Brahmasūtra*

The practice of contemplation on Brahman (*upāsanā*) clearly involves some form of yogic practice. Nakamura lists the following terms as synonyms of meditation in the *Brahmasūtra*: reverence (*upāsanā*), cognition (*vijñāna*), knowledge (*vidyā*), concentration (*dhyāna* 4.1.8; *dhī*, 3.3.33), seeing (*dṛṣṭi*, 4.1.5), and awareness (*buddhi*, 3.2.33).[71] Such contemplation is counter-current to the "normal," extrovertive flow of consciousness because of its essentially introspective nature. The development from the external worshipping of a deity to the interiorized worshipping of the divine within oneself, was undoubtedly a major contributory factor in the development of the Vedānta's interest in the relationship between the divine and the inner self (*ādhyātma*). Thus, Brahman is to be realized in a state of meditative concentration (*saṁrādhana*, 3.2.24). This is an experience of effulgence (*prakāśa*, 3.2.25), a description which no doubt confirms the *Sūtra*'s equating of Brahman with light (*jyoṭis*, 1.1.24; 1.3.40).

The *Brahmasūtra* allows for the renunciation of ritual activity by the *saṃnyasī* (e.g., see BS 4.4.25). However, the renunciate is required to perform certain prescribed auxilliary practices (*aṅga*) in order to attain liberation, as laid down in *Bṛhadāraṇyaka Upaniṣad*. 4.4.23. These prerequisites include the cultivation of calmness (*śama*), self-control (*dama*), repose (*uparati*), patience (*titikṣā*), concentration (*samādhi*), and faith (*śraddhā*) (3.4.27). One should also practice silent meditation (*mauna*) which is equally conducive (*sahakārin*) to the attainment of knowledge (*vidyā*, 3.4.47), and should observe a strict diet at all times unless in danger of starvation (3.4.28). In order to meditate successfully one must be in a sitting posture (*āsīna*, 4.1.7). As a result of the concentration produced one is able to remain motionless in mind and body (4.1.9). This practice can be undertaken in any place, so long as it is conducive to the one-pointedness of mind (*ekāgratā*, 4.1.11). Such practices are to be consistently carried out until one's death (4.1.12). The result of constant meditation is the attainment of non-attachment and the destruction of succeeding and previous sins (4.1.13). However, liberation as such can occur only upon death (4.1.15; 4.1.19).

The *Sūtra* appears to accept the contemplation of various symbolic forms but only insofar as they do not become identified with the object of meditation itself (4.1.4). Thus, all symbols are temporary objects of contemplation (*pratīka*), Brahman being the object of all meditation as taught in the *Upaniṣads* (3.3.1). The aspirant may choose (*vikalpa*) one of the numerous meditative techniques found in these texts and practice that one alone, since the result does not differ from one technique to another (3.3.59). However, those techniques designed for goals other than liberation (such as meditation on the Udgītha etc., which is practiced in order to eradicate obstacles (*apratibandha*) to the correct performance of the ritual, see 3.3.42 and 4.1.18), can be practiced either singly or with other techniques since their goal is the attainment of worldly pleasures (3.3.60).

The Nature of Brahman in the *Brahmasūtra*

The *Brahmasūtra* presupposes that there is an intrinsic relationship between Brahman and the self (*ātman*).[72] This presupposition is a legacy of the *Sūtra*'s upaniṣadic background. Brahman as such is understood by the *Sūtra* to be the supreme self (*paramātman*), and the inner controller (*antaryāmin*). Brahman is also described as the supreme Lord (*parameśvara*) and the intelligent self (*prājña*, 1.4.5; 2.3.29). The most common epithet, however, is "*paraḥ*," "the supreme one," (is the masculine gender significant)? There is no evidence in the text, though, to support Śaṅkaras distinction between the lower Brahman (*aparam/saguṇa brahma*, i.e., *Īśvara*) and Brahman in itself (*param/nirguṇa brahma*). Thus, BS 3.2.11 states that Brahman does not possess a two-fold characteristic (*liṅga*).

Brahman is defined in BS 1.1.2, as "that from which the origin, subsistence and dissolution of this [universe occurs]." Thus, Brahman is established as the cause (*kāraṇa*) and support (*adhiṣṭhāna*) of the world's manifestation and subsequent dissolution. This would appear to be the most basic definition of Brahman, the term deriving from the root "*bṛh*," meaning "to expand," "grow," or "develop."[73] Brahman in actual fact is "Being" itself (*sat*, BS 2.3.9). It is also the principle of intelligence (I.1.5; 1.1.9; 1.1.10; 3.2.16). The *Brahmasūtra* thus, describes Brahman as unbound (*ayama*), omnipresent (*sarvagata*, 3.2.37), endless (*ananta*, 3.2.26); the plenitude (*bhūman*, 1.3.8). It is partless (*niravayava*, 2.1.26), and without form (*arūpavad*, 3.2.13). As the eternal and undifferentiated (3.2.11) principle of existence it is imperishable (*akṣara*, 1.3.10; 3.3.33; a term which also denotes "syllable," or more specifically the syllable "Om.")

Brahman can only be described negatively (3.2.12). Nevertheless, it is light (*jyotis*, 1.1.24; 1.3.40). As such, Brahman is self-illuminating (*svaprakāśa*), and its essence is bliss (*ānanda*, 3.3.11,13); it is the source of all happiness (*sukha*, 1.1.14; alluded to in 1.2.15) in the world. It is only Brahman which has the fulfillment of all desires (*satya-saṃkalpatva*, 1.2.2).[74] Thus, in contrast to Śaṅkara, Brahman is felt to possess qualities (*guṇa*) in a pre-eminent sense. This would appear to contradict the earlier statement that Brahman can only be spoken of apophatically, but this is not necessarily so, since the idea seems to be that all worldly experiences of pleasure are imperfect realizations of the bliss (*ānanda*) of Brahman. This follows from Brahman's fundamental status as creator and sustainer of the universe, and our experiences within it. As such, any attempt to understand Brahman in terms of our own worldly based pleasures will be wholly inadequate, since Brahman is in fact the source of those characteristics (*pradhāna*, 3.3.11.)[75] Thus Brahman's pre-eminent qualities are best approached from an oblique angle through the negation of all worldly categories. While the post-Śaṅkarite formula of *sac-cid-ānanda* (Being-Consciousness-Bliss) is not openly endorsed, one can clearly see the roots of the later Vedāntic definition of Brahman in the text.

Brahman as the cause of the world's manifestation is described in the *Brahmasūtra* as the womb (*yoni*) of the universe (1.4.27). Allied with the *Sūtrakara*'s equation of Brahman with intelligence (*prājña* //*jña*), one can see that this view has developed in contrast to the views of the Sāṃkhya school where the material cause of the world is primordial, insentient matter (*pradhāna*). It is likely that this distinctive feature of the *Brahmasūtra*'s theology was developed specifically in response to Sāṃkhya doctrines. Indeed, much of the *Brahmasūtra* appears to have been written to refute the perspective of the Sāṃkhya school.[76] This point should not be overlooked, for the historical and philosophical roots of early Vedānta are intrinsically bound up with the Sāṃkhya movement. Thus, Nakamura notes that:

> The Sāṃkhya system had an intimate connection with the Vedānta school from ancient times. The seeds of the theory of the three qualities (*triguṇa*) of Sāṃkhya are found in the older *Upaniṣads* of the initial period (Chand. Up. VI). And Sāṃkhya ideas and expressions are clearly evident in the older *Upaniṣads* of the middle and later periods. In the great epic, the Mahābhārata, and the Code of Manu, Sāṃkhya philosophy, having the characteristic of Vedāntic ideas, is taught. . .the Sāṃkhya system maintained intimate relationships with the Vedānta schools, and they claimed orthodox Brahmanical authority to rival the Vedāntic claims.[77]

Indeed from the evidence of Buddhist texts, the early Vedānta school seems to have resembled the Sāṃkhya school in a number of doctrinal respects.[78] For evidence of this one need only look at the Sāṃkhya-cum-Vedānta doctrines to be found in chapter XII of the *Mahābhārata*.

The *Brahmasūtra* accepts Brahman as both the material cause (*upādāna*, 1.4.23; 2.1.19–20) of the universe, and its creator (*kartṛ*, 1.4.6).[79] Brahman, however, is not a personal being (*puruṣa*), a conception commonly ascribed to the Vedānta of this period by Jain and Buddhist scholars,[80] being essentially without organs (*karaṇa*, 2.1.31). Nevertheless, the *Brahmasūtra* clearly sees Brahman as a dynamic force, in contrast to the advaitic view of Brahman as the essentially static and unchanging reality. Thus, the position adopted in the *Brahmasūtra*, in regard to the nature of the creative act, is that of *brahma-pariṇāma-vāda* (e.g. see BS 1.4.26), that is, the doctrine of the transformation of Brahman [into the world], as opposed to the *prakṛti-pariṇāma-vāda* of the Sāṃkhya school, which maintains that it is primordial matter (*prakṛti* // *pradhāna*) which is transformed into the world (via the conscious intervention of the *Puruṣa*).

Both Sāṃkhya and the Vedānta of the *Brahmasūtra* base their understandings of the process of creation, or rather "transformation" (*pariṇāma*, for there is no "*creatio ex nihilo*" for these schools, see BS 2.2.26) on a causal theory known as *satkāryavāda*, or the doctrine that the effect exists [within the cause], (BS 2.1.7). Thus, the world exists *in potentia* within its material base prior to the creative act (2.1.16). Brahman as world-cause and the world itself as the effect are non-different (*ananya*, 2.1.14). The doctrine as expressed through the notion of *pariṇāma* ("transformation" or "change") is unacceptable to the Advaitin, for as we shall see it is a fundamental presupposition of the Advaita school that change cannot occur.

An objection is raised in BS 2.1.26 that the *brahma-pariṇāma* theory cannot be maintained because:

1. If the whole of Brahman transforms, it becomes another, rendering Brahman non-existent. and yet,
2. If only a part of Brahman is transformed, this contradicts the unity and partlessness of Brahman.

The author of the *Sūtra*, however, makes no attempt to answer these problems, asserting that the student of the Vedānta must accept the views of the scriptures regardless of logical problems and apparent philosophical inconsistencies (2.1.27). There has been much written subsequently by opponents and supporters of the *pariṇāma* doctrine both within the Vedānta school, and in the context of Indian philosophy in general on this important question. Indeed, questions of causality remain central to the philosophers of classical India. Nevertheless, this is not the place to further indulge in the debate, suffice it to say that the problem of change encountered in BS 1.2.26 is one that has been encountered by philosophers in the East and the West since philosophizing first began.[81]

As to the reason behind the creative act, 1.3.7 states that Brahman abides (*sthiti*) within the created world and assimilates experiences (*adanāmyām*: literally "eats"). The apparent imperfections and injustices (*vaiṣamya*) of the world are not attributable to Brahman, since they are based upon "other factors," i.e. the individual conditions which are dependent (*apekṣā*) upon the actions (*prayatna*) of the individual self (2.1.34; 2.3.42). These actions are clearly those performed by individual selves (*jīvātman*) in previous creations; they provide the structural basis for Brahman's world-creation, which is here envisaged as a process for the working out of each individual's karmic residue. The objection that the individual selves cannot be responsible for their conditions since they did not exist before creation is dismissed by the *Sūtra* on the grounds that *saṃsāra* is beginningless (2.1.35–36). Whether this is an adequate philosophical response is a moot point. Nakamura notes that:

> Judging from the above reply, there must have been a view prevalent that some part of the karma committed by the individual self before absorption in Brahman resulted in effects in the next kalpa or world creation . . . At the same time the Highest God was not an absolutely free personal god, because he is dependent upon external factors for world creation. Since he merely allocates the karmic effect appropriate to the individual, his function was that of an automaton.[82]

It seems that a similar conception of creation is presupposed in *Gauḍapādīya-kārikā* II.16.

> *jīvaṃ kalpayate pūrvaṃ tato bhāvān pṛthagvidhān,*
> *bāhyān ādhyātmikaṃś caiva yathāvidyas tathāsmṛtiḥ.*
> [The *ātman*] first imagines the *jīva* (individual soul), and then different things, external and internal (objective and subjective); as one knows so does one recollect.

Of course, for the *Gauḍapādīya-kārikā*, creation is an imaginary event (*kalpita*). Nevertheless, it appears to follow a carefully prescribed sequential order, comprising firstly of the creation of individual selves (*jīvas*), and then of various known objects, based upon the memory traces (*smṛti*) of past experience (*vidyā*) pertaining to the various individual selves. Note also that this may have been in the background of Śaṅkara's later notion of *adhyāsa* as the superimposition of past, remembered qualities of what is not-self onto the *Ātman*.

We should not underestimate the importance that may be attached to the philosophical problems of this notion of Brahman, as outlined by Nakamura above. The quest for philosophical systematization may have lead to a rejection of all theories attempting to explain creation. This certainly occurred in the case of the author of the first *prakaraṇa* of the *Gauḍapādīya-kārikā*, who argues in verse 9 that

> *bhogārthaṃ sṛṣṭir ity anye krīḍārtham iti cāpare,*
> *devasyaiṣa svabhāvo 'yam āptakāmasya kā spṛhā.*
> Creation is for the sake of enjoyment (or experience), so say some. Others say it is for the sake of sport. This again is the lordly nature of the divine, for what desire is there for the one who has obtained all wishes?

The *pūrvapakṣin* in BS 2.1.32 argues in a similar vein that there can be no purpose behind creation since Brahman can have no motive. This is dismissed in 2.1.33 since creation is merely the "sport" or "play" (*līlā*) of Brahman. So the creative act has no actual purpose, but is merely an overflowing of Brahman's essential fullness (*bhūman*). The conclusion drawn in the *Brahmasūtra*, then, is actually not that different from the one found in GK I.9. Both texts accept that Brahman can have no motive (BS 1.2.2; GK I.9), and to that extent creation can have no purpose. What is interesting about I.9 of the GK is that it does not necessarily imply that creation is therefore a false event; creation occurs in conformity with the intrinsic nature (*svabhāva*) of the divine being (i.e. Brahman). This concluding statement says nothing that the author of the *Brahmasūtra* would find disagreeable. Nevertheless, as we suggested in the previous chapter, GK I.9 can be understood to imply that even the notion of creation as play (*līlā*) is inadequate for precisely the reason that Brahman does not desire anything, not even the indulgence of sport. This difference in emphasis is important since it is based upon two different notions of Brahman, that of the *Brahmasūtra*, that allows for a dynamic and transformative reality, and that of the *Gauḍapādīya-kārikā*, that envisages Brahman as the static and essentially changeless ultimate reality (see for instance GK III.34, IV.80).

As the cause of the world and through its own transformation the world itself, Brahman is said to be the totality of all things (see I.1.23; cf. GK II.19). The *Brahmasūtra* upholds a thorough-going realism. The world of multiplicity exists, partaking of the "being" (*sat*) which is the essence of Brahman. The text does not uphold the theory of the merely-apparent nature of duality (*māyā-mātra*), as one finds in the GK and later Advaita Vedāntins. The term "*māyā*" occurs only once in the *Brahmasūtra*, and then in a discussion of the dream state, that is said to be "mere-illusion" or "*māyāmātra*," due to the fact that dream experiences do not reveal their true nature (3.2.3). Śaṅkara notes in his commentary that dreams are incomplete since "the space needed for a chariot etc. is not possible in dream; for within the narrow limits of the body, the chariot etc. cannot get sufficient room."[83] This argument seems to have originated from *Bṛhadāraṇyaka Upaniṣad* 4.3.10 (which Śaṅkara referred to earlier in BSBh 2.1.28), and is alluded to in GK II.3. It is likely that Śaṅkara got the idea through his reading of GK II.4 and GK IV.33 which are concise developments of this argument. Indeed, the *bhāṣya* on the GK (traditionally ascribed to Śaṅkara) also utilizes the argument from spatial limitation to the same effect. However, in that text the commentator follows the GK in denying the validity of waking experience also. This step is not taken by Śaṅkara in his *Brahmasūtrabhāṣya*,[84] and may be taken as strong evidence for doubting the GK-*bhāṣya*'s authenticity as a work of Śaṅkara. However, the difference of opinion with regard to the status of the waking state may reflect a development in Śaṅkara's thinking (away from Yogācāra Buddhist influences), or the fact that he is restricted by the realism expounded in the *Brahmasūtra* itself.

Nevertheless, the occurrence of the same argument in two supposedly Śaṅkarite texts may suggest that in commentating on BS 3.2.3, Śaṅkara is drawing upon the arguments of an Advaitic exegetical tradition of his own, deriving in all probability from the GK itself, and his (earlier) commentary upon it. The term "*māyāmātra*" can also be found in GK I.17, where it refers to the dualistic world of common experiences (that is the world experienced in the waking state), as well as dream experiences. For the author of the *Gauḍapādīya-kārikā*, both the waking and the dream states are *māyāmātra*, being self-contained (*saṃvṛti*, literally "enclosed") and therefore sublatable experiences.[85] For the early Vedānta of the *Brahmasūtra*, however, this was most certainly not the case. Our waking experiences correspond to a real external world brought into existence through the real transformation of Brahman. This much is clear from the *Brahmasūtra*'s critique of Yogācāra ideas in BS 2.2.28–30. The uncompromising realism of the *Brahmasūtra* is one of the most predominant features of early Brahmanical Vedānta, stemming as it does from the school's basic presupposition that the world is the transformation (*pariṇāma*) of Brahman.

The most striking philosophical feature of the Vedānta school is its basic presupposition that Brahman is the universal substratum for all things. This derives from a belief in the absolute divinity of Brahman, a clear indicator of the school's theological background in the various types of theism found in the Vedic scriptures. The *Brahmasūtra* thus, maintains that all things are dependent (*adhīna*, 1.4.3) upon Brahman for their existence. This much, of course, should be clear from the text's equating of Brahman with Being (*sat*) itself (2.3.9). Nothing is distinct (*avyatireka*) from Brahman (2.3.6), since Brahman is the substrate of all things up to space (*ambarāntadhṛti*, 1.3.10), and the common support of heaven, earth, and others (*dyu-bhv-ādy-āyatana*, 1.3.1). This substrative function is something to be found in Brahman alone, since it derives from His mighty rule (*praśāsana*, 2.3.11), and greatness (*mahiman*, 1.3.16). As universal support, Brahman is also that which resides within (*antarabhāva*) all things (3.2.20). Allied to this, in conformity with *Bṛhadāraṇyaka* 3.7.1., Brahman is described as the inner controller (*antaryāmin*, BS 1.2.18–20).

Brahman and the Individual Self (*jīvātman*) in the *Brahmasūtra*

The question of the precise relationship between Brahman and the individual self constitutes a major focal point of Vedāntic theorizing. The differences of opinion on this issue have largely been responsible for the formation of the various Vedānta schools (Dvaitādvaita, Advaita, Viśiṣṭādvaita, and Dvaita). According to the *Brahmasūtra*, the individual self is a part (*aṃśa*) of Brahman (2.3.43). Śaṅkara protests in his commentary that this statement is metaphorical since Brahman is essentially partless (*niravayava*, see BS 2.1.26). However, the *Brahmasūtra* specifically maintains that individual selves are parts of Brahman, because they are different (*nānā*) and yet not different (see 2.3.43). The text clearly divorces itself from the unqualified identity of *jīvātman* and *paramātman*. This is a "holistic" point of view—Brahman being more than the sum of its parts (thus, it is not pantheism—the doctrine of pure immanence). The individual self is atomic (2.3.23) whereas the supreme self is not (2.3.21). The two are non-distinct (*avaiśeṣya*, 3.2.25) and yet are not identical (*tadātmya*).

That the *Brahmasūtra* does not uphold the position of unqualified non-difference (*advaita-vāda* // *abheda-vāda*), as expounded in the *Gauḍapādīya-kārikā* and the *Brahmasūtra-bhāṣya* of Śaṅkara, is clear from BS 2.1.22, where the supreme self is said to be greater (*adhika*) than the individual self on account of their basic difference. Thus, the *Brahmasūtra* also makes a differentiation (*vaiśeṣya*) between Brahman and *jīvātman* on the grounds that Brahman is not subject to the pains and pleasures of experience (BS 1.2.8, 2.1.13, 2.3.46). It is the supreme self that is responsible for the very possibility of action on the part of the individual self (2.3.41), and while Brahman is the world-creator, the individual self never acquires such a position (1.1.16), not even in liberation (*mokṣa*), which is said to be union (*yoga*) with Brahman (1.1.19; 1.1.7), since this is dependent upon the *Īśvara* (4.4.17,18). In fact both bondage and liberation originate from Brahman (3.2.5). The liberated self is only equal to Brahman in its enjoyment (*bhoga-mātra*, 4.4.21). The result of this is that it is possible to talk of two selves (*ātmānau*, 1.2.11), although, we should note that they are not two distinct entities, since the individual self is only an atomic part (*aṃśa*) of Brahman.

The philosophical position of the *Brahmasūtra* in regard to the relationship between Brahman and the individual self is technically known as the doctrine of difference-non-difference (*bhedābheda-vāda*). There are many forms in which this doctrine can occur,[86] but in the case of the *Brahmasūtra*, it is based upon the notion of Brahman as the plenitude (*bhūman*) which transcends the sum of its parts, and yet inheres fully within them (*ādhyātma, antarabhāva*, 3.2.20) as their inner controller (*antaryāmin*). This is possible since Brahman is essentially a spiritual or intelligent principle (1.1.5; 1.1.9; 1.1.10; 3.2.16). Thus, it is not subject to any spatial or temporal limitations (3.2.37; 3.2.26; 1.3.10; 3.3.33), and is essentially formless (*arūpavad*, 3.2.13). As such, spatial notions such as size or quantitative partition (*avayava*) are inappropriate (since Brahman has no parts, *niravayava*, BS 2.1.26). Thus, Brahman resides in its entirety within the smallest particle imaginable (*aṃśa*), i.e. the individual self and yet remain the receptacle (*āyatana*, 1.3.1) or totality (*bhūman*) which transcends the sum of these parts. Nevertheless, the individual selves are permanent and unoriginated (2.3.17; 2.2.42). It is likely that the self remains imperishable (*akṣara*) only insofar as it is non-different from Brahman, and also "atomic" (*aṃśa*) (thereby being irreducible).

Because of the uniqueness of Brahman (Brahman being "one without a second," *Chāndogya Upaniṣad* 6.2.1, see Śaṅkara's BSBh 3.2.32), analogies are always hopelessly inadequate. Nevertheless, the *Brahmasūtra* utilizes a number of analogies to explain the relationship between Brahman and the individual self. Thus, it is like that of a torch as the source of light, and the light which it emits (*prakāśa*, 3.2.25, 28, 2.3.46). The relationship is also similar to that existing between the sun and its image reflected upon the water (3.2.18, see also 2.3.50), and that between a snake and its coils (3.2.27).

The analogy of a snake and its coils is particularly interesting since it can be extended to describe the nature of the creative act. Thus, at some times the snake is outstretched while at other times it is recoiled. The analogy can thereby be seen as envisaging the creation of the world in terms of the "rolling out" (evolving, Latin "*e-volvere*": literally "to roll outward") of Brahman. Thus, in the *Brahmasūtra*, creation is said to be nothing more than the self-development or self-unfoldment of Brahman (literally, "self-making," *ātmakṛti*, 1.4.26, cf. GK II.12.)

It is clear that the earliest usage of the term "*vivarta*," (understood in post-Śaṅkarite Vedānta as a technical term for the illusoriness of the creative act), was to denote the "rolling out" or "unfolding" of creation. Thus, it had none of the "illusionistic" connotations that were later attributed to it. This is how the term was used by Śaṅkara himself[87] and conforms to the understanding of the term "*viparivartate*" as it occurs in *Bhagavadgītā* 9.10, and Śaṅkara's commentary upon it. It is only in the post-Śaṅkarite works of Advaita Vedānta that we find the term "*vivarta*" used in the specific sense of "apparent" as opposed to "real" (*pariṇāma*) transformation. The term does not occur in this sense in the works of Śaṅkara and is not to be found in the *Gauḍapādīya-kārikā*, although Śaṅkara's contemporary Maṇḍana-miśra does appear to have used it in distinction to *pariṇāma*.[88] Pre-Śaṅkarite Vedānta, therefore, seems unaware of the *vivarta :: pariṇāma* dichotomy. This in all likelihood reflects the fact that the early Vedānta school was overwhelmingly realistic in its approach to the created world of duality. It is important to note, however, that the development of the doctrine of creation as an illusory transformation of Brahman occurs in the *Gauḍapādīya-kārikā*, without recourse to the "*vivarta*" terminology.

Nevertheless, we should note that the notion of "unfoldment" does not imply any change in the thing that is being unfolded (in this case the unfoldment of Brahman at creation). Perhaps the best translation of the term "*vivarta*," (one which remains etymologically similar and semantically appropriate), is that of "distortion." *Vi-varta* then is a *distortion* in two basic respects. On the one hand such a rendering reflects the basically negative attitude of (particularly, but not exclusively) later Vedānta towards the realm of *saṃsāra*. The created realm is a "disfigurement" of Brahman's essential non-duality. It is this evaluative depreciation of the material world of multiplicity that is emphasized in so much of the post-Buddhistic formulations of Vedānta. On the other hand, the notion of "distortion" implies that what appears is not what actually is. This latter sense of the term is one that is particularly emphasized in Advaita Vedānta. The world appears as if it is real, but it is really nothing but a distortion, a false apprehension, of the all-encompassing unity of Brahman. Just as in the dark a rope can be distorted so as to appear as a snake, so is Brahman distorted so as to appear as the dualistic world of *saṃsāra*. This particular aspect of the term *vivarta* is that which is most clearly brought into prominence in the Vedānta of Śaṅkara's successors.

It is easy to see then how the term *vivarta* could be used by later Vedāntins to support the principle of the immutability of reality. Creation is apparent insofar as Brahman is only unfolding what is essentially there already. This is orthodox Vedāntic realism in that it is an expression of *satkāryavāda* (the doctrine of the existence of the effect in the cause); where it differs, however, is in the refusal of the Advaitin thereby to accept the reality of the effect as something other than the cause. It is easy to see how early Vedāntic *bhedābheda-vāda* could be transformed into non-dualism (*advaita-vāda // abheda-vāda*) through a subtle change in emphasis. Such a change seems to have occurred as a result of the school's adoption of the two-truths scheme. Indeed, Bhartṛhari seems to have been the earliest (and indeed the only pre-Maṇḍana) philosopher to utilize the term *vivarta* in anything like its later technical sense, and it is interesting to note that one can also find the analogy of the snake and its folded coils in his *Vākyapadīya*.[89]

Liberation (*Mokṣa*) and Bondage (*Saṃsāra*) in the *Brahmasūtra*

Liberation is said by the *Brahmasūtra* to be union (*yoga*) with Brahman (1.1.19; 1.1.7), and occurs upon death (4.1.15; 4.1.19). Death is the dissolution of bodily functions and the merging of each one of the senses (*prāṇa*) into Brahman (4.2.15). The fate of the liberated individual, however, differs from that of the self in bondage insofar as the former follows the path of the gods (4.2.7) upon death, and becoming indistinguishable (*avibhāga*, 4.2.16; 4.4.4) from Brahman. However, it is important to note that Brahman and the individual self are not totally identical since the latter cannot be the world-creator (4.4.17). Despite this, the liberated self acquires various divine powers as a result of its knowledge, notable attributes being the ability to inhabit multiple bodies simultaneously (4.4.15), and actualize desires through thought alone (*saṃkalpād eva*, 4.4.8; cf. GK II.30). Such a one has no master (*adhipati*, 4.4.9). Liberation is final, there being no return to bondage for the liberated self (4.4.22).

The *Brahmasūtra* also describes liberation as the manifestation (*āvirbhāva*) of one's real nature (*āvirbhūta svarūpa*, 1.3.19; 4.4.1).[90] This statement is fascinating, for it opens up the possibility of denying the ontological reality of the state of bondage (*saṃsāra*), which is here understood as a consequence of one's ignorance. This conclusion is never actually drawn by the author of the *Brahmasūtra*, although he does acknowledge that in *saṃsāra*, certain things are obscured (*tirohita*, 3.2.5–6). The denial of ultimate reality to the realm of transmigration, however, became an important feature of the fully-blown absolutism of Advaita Vedānta. The development of such a radically acosmic (i.e. "no created realm") view is the result of the emphasis upon knowledge (*vidyā*) as the sole means to liberation, since this view changes the status of *saṃsāra* from that of an ontological realm to that of an epistemological (*pramāṇa* // *avidyā*) error.[91] This is also the function performed by the idea that creation is a "distortion" (*vivarta*) of Brahman—the appearance of a multiplicity has become an error of apprehension and not a reality in itself.

This brief overview of the Vedāntic heritage of the *Gauḍapādīya-kārikā* has highlighted the fact that the authors of this text are conversant and reliant upon Upaniṣadic ideas in a number of significant areas. The first three *prakaraṇas* are particularly dependent upon the *Bṛhadāraṇyaka Upaniṣad* but show clear evidence of influences from the *Chāndogya, Taittirīya*, and *Kaṭha Upaniṣads*. There is no evidence of a direct relationship between the GK and the *Bhagavadgītā*, nor of direct influence from the *Brahmasūtra*. These texts are considered, however, since they are representative of (at least aspects of) pre-Śaṅkarite Vedānta. Their importance for post-Śaṅkarite Vedānta, of course, can hardly be overestimated. Their inclusion in this study, however, is warranted since one cannot hope to appreciate the innovations of the GK without an awareness of the philosophical positions embodied in these cardinal texts of the early Vedānta tradition.

CHAPTER

3

The Abhidharma Context of Non-Origination (*Ajātivāda*)

The Non-Origination of Dharmas—Absolutism and the *Svabhāva* Debate in Buddhism

"Absolutism" has become a common designation of the Mahāyāna and Advaita systems of thought in modern Western scholarship. It is a technical philosophical term that has a strong tradition in Western philosophical thought, in particular one thinks of the systems of Hegel and Bradley. As such its use in an Indian philosophical context requires some justification. The term "absolute" itself derives from the Latin *absolutus*, to "be alone" or "cut off from," thus it is that which displays no relations, the "non-relative." As a result the term is often used with a capital letter and pre-fixed by the definite article—"the Absolute." Here it is clearly being used to denote the conception of an unconditioned and all encompassing reality. Understood in this sense it would seem permissible to describe Advaita Vedānta as a form of absolutism since Brahman is said to exhibit precisely these characteristics.[1] Brahman is the ground of all being (*sat*), the unchanging substratum and source of the created universe. With regard to the Mahāyāna tradition however, the designation of its philosophy as "absolutistic" is problematic to say the least. Whereas the Advaitin sees Brahman as the supreme self (*paramātman*), "mainstream" Mahāyāna Buddhism, in conformity with the traditional position of the non-Mahāyāna Buddhist schools, denies that a substantial self can be found in any *dharmas*, whether compounded (*saṃskṛta*) or uncompounded (*asaṃskṛta*). Thus the one concept that might have been described as an "absolute" within the Buddhist tradition, i.e. *nirvāṇa*, is equally lacking any self-hood, being accepted as an uncompounded *dharma* by all schools of Buddhism. Within the Buddhist tradition, therefore, accepting some form of absolutism is often seen as the extreme view of eternalism (*śāsvata-vāda*). With the possible exception of some Mahāyāna texts utilizing the notion of the "*tathāgatagarbha*" (see chapter 7), the Mahāyāna tradition cannot be described as absolutistic in the sense in which it is used in most Western scholarship. Nevertheless, it is important to consider the reasons why the absolutistic intepretation of Mahāyāna Buddhism has gained currency in western scholastic circles, for the consequences have been a blurring of the distinctions between the Advaita Vedānta and Mahāyāna world views. It is important for our purposes, therefore, to attempt to clear up some of the problems in evaluating the philosophical relationship between Mahāyāna Buddhism and Advaita Vedānta. Such a consideration will inevitably involve discussion of the question of absolutism in the respective traditions.

In the history of Vedāntic thought it has become a standard criticism of the Śaṅkarite school that Advaita Vedānta is really a form of crypto-Buddhism. Many modern scholars have ventured to substantiate this claim by an analysis of the doctrines of Śaṅkara's purported *paramaguru* Gauḍapāda, traditionally held to be the author of the *Gauḍapādīya-kārikā*. As we have seen, this text appears to exemplify not only the earliest formulation of *advaita-vāda* within the Vedānta school but also a great propensity for Buddhist ideas (particularly in the fourth chapter, the *Alātaśāntiprakaraṇa*). Any attempt to delineate the philosophical relationship between Mahāyāna Buddhism and Advaita Vedānta must take the question of "absolutism" very seriously indeed. An examination of the philosophical standpoints of the "foundational texts" (*mūlaśāstra*) of Madhyamaka Buddhism and Advaita Vedānta, i.e. the *MūlaMadhyamakakārikā* of Nāgārjuna and the *Gauḍapādīya-kārikā* should enable us to consider this question more fully.

In the previous chapter we considered the Vedāntic background of the *Gauḍapādīya-kārikā*. It is clear that this text is also dependent upon philosophical insights and arguments taken from the Buddhist tradition. For instance, in the fourth *prakaraṇa* of the GK we find the frequent use of the term "*dharma*" to denote an "object of thought," or more generally an "occurrence." There can be no doubt that this important term derives from the author's acquaintance with Buddhist philosophy. There are many apparent similarities between the doctrines espoused in the GK and the central philosophical themes of the Mahāyāna Buddhist tradition in India. In particular, the Gauḍapādian doctrine of non-origination (*ajātivāda*) shows evidence of Mahāyāna influence insofar as the Prajñāpāramitā *sūtras* and Madhyamaka *śāstras* themselves expound the non-arising (*anutpāda*) nature of all *dharmas*. Consider for instance the following verse,

> GK IV.93: All *dharmas* indeed are quiescent from the very beginning (*ādiśānta*). By their very nature they are unoriginated, nirvāṇic, homogenous, non-separate, fearless, and unoriginated sameness.

It is inconceivable that verses such as the above could have been composed without some acquaintance with this central Mahāyāna theme.

It is widely known that the notion of "*svabhāva*," otherwise known as "own (or self) nature," "own being," "intrinsic nature" etc. is of supreme importance for Nāgārjuna's exposition of *śūnyatā*. The actual term and its related notions (i.e. *niḥsvabhāva*) occur in thirty-four of the verses in the *MūlaMadhyamakakārikā*, but the notion itself constitutes the main point of focus of the Nāgārjunian critique. It is because of this that emptiness (*śūnyatā*) is often said to be synonymous with the quality of lacking an intrinsic-nature (*niḥsvabhāvatā*). It is almost universally accepted that the GK has been influenced, at least in terms of his argumentation, by the philosophy of Nāgārjuna. However, no one, to my knowledge, has attempted to delineate the relationship between these two thinkers in terms of their respective attitudes towards the question of "intrinsic nature." This is surprising given that Nāgārjuna was the philosopher primarily responsible for replacing the traditional *ātman—anātman* debate of the Vedāntic and Buddhist traditions with the wider notions of *svabhāva—niḥsvabhāva* and that, in so doing, he provided a new philosophical framework within which the debate could be structured.

The movement from the debate about "self" to one of "intrinsic nature" shifts the angle of the Buddhist critique from the Abhidharma denial of a personal self (*pudgala nairātmya*), to the Madhyamaka denial of self pertaining to all factors (*dharma nairātmya*). The author of the GK, as a post-Nāgārjunian thinker, as a potential crypto-Buddhist and as a philosopher quite clearly steeped in (and indeed deeply influenced by) Mahāyāna arguments, surely must have taken the *svabhāva—niḥsvabhāva* debate very seriously indeed. All four of the *prakaraṇas* of the *Gauḍapādīya-kārikā* address the problem of "intrinsic nature" or "own being."[3] Of the four, the last has by far the most references to *svabhāva* and its related notions. This is hardly surprising given that the fourth *prakaraṇa* has the most overtly Buddhist tone to it, and constitutes virtually half of the entire text.

Nevertheless, the more "Vedāntic" *prakaraṇas* do not ignore the notion. In its critique of "creation" theories, the first *prakaraṇa* concludes in *kārikā* nine that

> *bhogārthaṃ sṛṣṭir ity anye krīdārtham iti cāpare, devasyaiṣa svabhāvo 'yam āptakāmasya kā spṛhā.*
> Creation [is] for the sake of enjoyment (or experience)—so say some. Others say it is for the sake of sport. This again is the lordly nature of the divine for what desire is there for the one who has obtained all wishes?

Svabhāva then, must be used in some sense in Gauḍapādian thought in an attempt to establish the doctrine of non-origination (*ajātivāda*). To see how this is achieved we must first understand the notion of *svabhāva* itself. Verses 7–10 of the fourth *prakaraṇa* are a discussion of this very issue. Thus, *kārikā* 9 states that:

> *sāṃsiddhikī svābhāvikī sahajāpy akṛtā ca yā, prakṛtiḥ seti vijñeyā svabhāvaṃ na jahāti yā.*
> That should be known as nature which is permanently established, intrinsic, innate, not produced, [and] that which does not abandon its own nature.

This sets the tone for a proper evaluation of the notion of *svabhāva*, it is that which is "intrinsic" to a thing. In this context the term is virtually synonymous with *svalakṣaṇa* (own characteristic) since it is the *svabhāva* of a thing which demarcates it from all other things. The notion then is philosophically linked to the epistemological question of how one differentiates between one factor and another. It is hardly surprising, then, that an early text of the Advaita Vedānta school should find the problem of *svabhāva* so interesting, given that *advaita-vāda* is a basic denial of differences. It is clear that the primary connotation of *svabhāva* is "characteristic mark" or "essential" nature. It is this "essence" which is disputed by Nāgārjuna and the Madhyamaka school.

Thus, to fully understand the nature of Gauḍapādian Advaita and its historical significance requires a grasp of those Mahāyāna philosophical ideas to which the text is itself indebted. Equally one cannot hope to appreciate the innovatory aspects of the GK unless one is aware of the extent of that debt. This will become clearer when we compare the doctrines of the GK with those of the Mahāyāna schools. First, however, it is necessary to provide some background analysis of the relevant features of Buddhist philosophy on and in their own terms.

The Sarvāstivāda Abhidharma

The Abhidharma texts, constituting one of the three categories of the *Tripiṭaka* (the other two being the *Sutra piṭaka*, and the *Vinaya piṭaka*), appears to have developed from *Mātṛkās* (Pali : *mātikā*), numerical and nmemonic lists, that appear to have served as headings for doctrinal considerations.[4] These early lists constituted an attempt to formulate a compact abridgement of the Buddha's fundamental ideas, as found in the various dialogues of the *sūtras*.[5]

The schism that resulted in the emergence of the Sarvāstivāda as a separate Buddhist school seems to have occurred during Aśoka's reign, probably between 244 and 237 BCE (the latter being the year of Aśoka's "Schism Edict"). Most authorities accept that the split from the Vibhajyavādins was made official at the Council of Pāṭaliputra, called during the seventeenth year of Aśoka's reign.[6] Andre Bareau sees this council as the one that separated the Sarvāstivāda from the Theravāda.[7] The Theravāda do not record this event as a schism, referring to it as the expulsion of non-Buddhists from the community. This attitude perhaps reflects the Theravāda's awareness of the similarities between the Sarvāstivāda, Vaiśeṣika, and Sāṃkhya lists of "ultimates" (*dharmas*, *guṇas*, and *tattvas* respectively), and a firm belief that the eternality of these ultimates contravened the basic Buddhist doctrines of no-self and universal impermanence. That the group expelled was the Sarvāstivāda school (or at least an early precursor of it), is clear from the *Kathāvatthu*, the traditional Theravāda record of that council, which refers to the disputants as "*Sabbathivādins*."

Those who opposed the Sarvāstivāda were called the Vibhajyavādins, "those who make distinctions." The question of the historical relationship between this movement and the latter-day Sinhalese Buddhists (Theravādins) is still a matter of considerable dispute; nevertheless, the name need not denote a particular school, and may simply highlight a specific attitude. The tenets of the Sarvāstivāda appear to have developed as an attempt to distinguish themselves from the Vibhajyas. The council records the affair "as the expulsion of persons who were not Buddhists, followers of other sects who had joined the favored community. They were expelled not for reasons of discipline but for holding false (non-Buddhist) opinions about metaphysical questions."[8] Interestingly, both schools maintain that Majjhantika (Sanskrit/Sarvāstivāda : Madhyāntika) as the propagator of Buddhism in India (their own particular form of Buddhism, of course)!

From approximately 200 BCE onwards, the Sarvāstivāda became the dominant Sanskrit, non-Mahāyāna Buddhist tradition on the Indian subcontinent.[9] The Sarvāstivāda became active in Mathurā, Gandhāra, Kashmir, Kashgar, Udyāna, the Northern frontier, Kanoj, Rājagṛha, Persia, parts of East India, Sumatra, Java, Champa, and Cochin China.[10] This dominance reached such a height that whenever later writers refer to the Abhidharma, they invariably mean the Sarvāstivāda (or more specifically the Vaibhāṣikas).

In Kashmir, the Sarvāstivāda became elaborated in a system known as the Vaibhāṣika. The texts so established were:

1. *Jñānaprasthāna*, attributed to Ārya Katyāyanīputra. This is the major "body" of Sarvāstivāda ideas (*śarīra*), of which the remaining six (numbers 2–7), are the feet (*pāda*) or appendages.
2. *Prakaraṇapāda*, attributed to Sthavira Vasumitra.
3. *Vijñānakāya,* attributed to Sthavira-Devaśarma.
4. *Dharmaskandha*, attributed to Ārya Śāriputra.
5. *Prajñāptiśāstra*, attributed to Ārya Maudgalyāyana.
6. *Dhātukāya*, attributed to Pūrna.
7. *Saṅgītiparyāya*, attributed to Mahā Kauṣṭhila.

Warder and Takakusu place their composition c. 200 BCE.[11] Dutt defers judgement and gives dates of translation into Chinese,[12] which range from the fourth to the eleventh century CE.[13] Finally, we have the composition of the *Mahāvibhāṣa*, the "Book of Great Options," a huge commentary on the *Jñānaprasthāna* and the culmination of Sarvāstivāda philosophy. Compiled around 200 CE, by five hundred *ārhats* in Kashmir,[14] the *Vibhāṣa* accepts Vasumitra's theory that the difference between past, present, and future events lies in their causal efficacy. Past and future *dharmas* can only be apprehended by mental consciousness, while *dharmas* in the present have complete efficacy, being graspable by the appropriate sense-consciousness. The Sarvāstivāda became more and more associated with the school that took its name from this voluminous text, the Vaibhāṣika. The predominance of the Kashmirian Sarvāstivāda reached such heights that, as Murti notes "the only Hīnayāna Abhidharma Piṭaka which we can prove to be known to the Buddhists of North India was that of the Sarvāstivādins."[15]

The Sarvāstivādins derive canonical evidence for their realist interpretation of the Abhidharmic analysis of experience ("*sarva asti," all [dharmas*] exist,) from declarations attributed to the Buddha in such texts as the *Mahāniddeśa*. Here, in a discussion with the *Ājīvakas*, the Buddha declares that "everything exists." When pressed as to his meaning, the Buddha states that the "twelve *āyatanas* exist." This, of course, is precisely what the Sarvāstivādins implied in their own distinctive formulation of the Buddha's message,[16] and is not to be found in the Pali canon. The import of this text differs radically from such texts as the *Cūlasuññatasutta* where insight into the six sense-fields is said to bring about a realization of emptiness (*suññata*).

Murti notes that,

> In the *Dhammasaṅgani* and other treatises we are treated to interminable lists and classifications of *dharmas* undertaken mostly from the ethical point of view. The underlying metaphysical principles are hardly stressed; they can be elicited only by implication. There is little attempt at argument and no *a priori* deduction of the categories is made.[17]

In fact, we find that in the *Dhammasaṅgani* several lists of *dhammas* remain incomplete and end by stating "and whatever others occur." This suggests that the original purpose of this text was not to establish a strict ontological classification of "ultimates." Murti, however, believes that this and other texts uphold a pluralistic realism.[18] Even today, there is still dispute among Theravādins as to whether the lists are ontological or not. The widespread use of abhidharmas in different schools may perhaps point to their underlying ontological neutrality or at least their open-endedness.

That the Abhidharma is basically soteriological in motive is established by Vasubandhu in his *Abhidharmakośa*, which is widely regarded as the authoritative account of the Sanskrit Abhidharma tradition. Thus, in *Kośa* I.3 it states that:

> Whereas the world erroneously falls into the flood of becoming by reason of defilement (*kleśa*), and, whereas there is no access to the taming of defilement, without the discernment of *dharmas*, therefore for the purpose of discerning the *dharmas* it is said that the Abhidharma was declared by the teacher (The Buddha).[19]

Thus, one can see that the primary motivation behind Buddhist scholasticism is soteriological. In this context, this refers primarily to the idea of the "purification" of the mind or "life-stream" (*cittasaṃtāna*) resulting in its subsequent "blowing out" (*nirvṛti*) with the attainment of *nirvāṇa*. This goal is strived for through the practice of the discernment (*pravicaya*) of the ultimate constituents of experience (*dharmas*), which itself is dependent upon the cultivation of meditative insight (*vipaśyanā/prajñā*).

The preoccupation with final and complete classification meant that, as the Abhidharma schools developed, no door could be left unopened in the quest for universal applicability. Thus, one of the specific features of Abhidharmic lists is precisely their comprehensiveness. This is at once both their redeeming feature (being applicable to the entirety of human and non-human experience), and the source of the utmost frustration (being interminably long-winded and hair-splittingly fastidious). It is precisely the comprehensiveness of the Abhidharmic lists that made it possible for the Abhidharmic schools to claim that their conceptual system was as close as one could get to an ultimate description of experience, since it could be argued that all possible cases were included within it. This may account for the category known as *cittaviprayuktasaṃskāra*, which denotes those dharmic compounds that are not experienced by consciousness (and so are by definition outside of our experience). The claim to universality was probably the primary factor in the Sarvāstivāda claim that these *dharmas* were ultimate and irreducible elements of our experience.

The Sarvāstivāda seem to have caused the schism resulting from the Pāṭaliputra council by arguing that past, present, and future events are real. Though momentary in the present, *dharmas* have a real, durable essence (*svabhāva*). The problem for the Sarvāstivāda was how to reconcile this notion to the Buddhist doctrine of impermanence (*anitya*). This necessitated the development of the notion of "*prāpti*" or possession. This is an essentially impersonal force which holds an element within a given stream of consciousness. The attainment of *nirvāṇa*, an *asaṃskṛta dharma*, was also understood in this manner, being the influence of insight (*prajñā*) during the following of the path. "Where there is no cognition of it (i.e. *nirvāṇa*) *dharmas* arise; where there is [cognition] they absolutely do not arise."[20] Notice that *nirvāṇa* is here expressed in contradistinction to "*dharma*," an important "confusion" which allows for the Sarvāstivāda to circumvent some of the problems of the "*sarva anātmāḥ dharmāḥ*" formula.

Ontological theorizing, however, is by no means absent from the texts of the Theravāda school. Here there is also the utilization of the doctrine of *svabhāva*. This is certainly a late notion, not found in their *Abhidharma piṭaka*, in which, unlike the Sarvāstivāda, the question of ontological status remains a moot point. "*Sabhāva*" (Sanskrit : *svabhāva*) appears in the post-canonical *Peṭakopadeśa*, which is concerned mainly with scholastic methodology. The cause is the *svabhāva* of a thing and the condition is the *parabhāva* (other-nature) of it. Warder, however, suggests that this is rather a casual reference.[21] Nevertheless, it is developed explicitly in the *Patisambhidhamagga*, which forms a supplement to the *Vibhaṅga* and may be regarded as a record of discussions with the Sarvāstivāda. Here it says that "a *dharma's svabhāva* is its individual essence." The commentarial literature is unequivocal, yet appears to represent quite old compositions (c. first century BCE to first century CE, and said by the Theravādins to be based upon commentaries brought to Śri Lanka, when Buddhism arrived c. 240 BCE).

The *Aṭṭhāsalinī* defines *dhammas* in the following manner (II.10):

> *attano pana sabhāvaṃ dhārentī ti dhammā, dhāriyanti vā paccayehi, dhāriyanti vā yathāsabhāvato ti dhammā.*
> *Dharmas* bear their intrinsic nature, or they are supported by conditions, or they are supported according to their intrinsic nature.[22]

The practice of insight itself came to be seen as penetration into the *svabhāva* of *dharmas*. In the Pali formulations, *svabhāva* (*sabhāva*) was elucidated with regard to the momentariness of *dharmas*. Despite their evanescence, *dharmas* were real entities each defined by their own characteristics (*svalakṣaṇa*). The development of the notion of *svabhāva* displays a movement beyond that of the original Abhidharma formulations, that nevertheless paved the way for these developments in their quest for scholastic precision and meditative appropriateness.

It should be noted in passing that a dharmic analysis of conventional "entities" need not imply any existent or ontologically real "ultimate." One could conceive of an abhidharma system which "reduced away" the need for any attribution of an ontological substantiality to the "given." Certainly, this was the case in the Mahāyāna understanding of the notion of "*dharma*." Thus, for instance, Asaṅga argues that the developed Abhidharma categories of the Hīnayāna schools are illegitimate in an ultimate sense,[23] while at the same time accepting the given as "present" (though not existent in any recognizable sense of the term, i.e., as an independent, self-subsisting entity). This may well have been the early understanding of "*dharma*" in pre-scholastic Buddhism., (i.e. before the formation of the Sarvāstivāda etc. views about *dharmas*). However, the precise nature of early Buddhist doctrines is outside the scope of this study, and so cannot be dealt with here.

Piatigorsky argues that the denial of the applicability of the notions of "being" (*bhāva*) and "non-being" (*abhāva*) to *dharmas* is in fact a feature of the "Abhidharma," (although what precisely "Abhidharma" denotes for Piatigorsky is unclear). Thus,

> *dharmas* cannot be, but are what and as they are (i.e., in the sense of *yathābhūtatā*). . . .Therefore, in the sense of "being" in general, *dharmas* are not, while in the sense of their own being they cannot be classified even into *saṃskṛta* and *asaṃskṛta*, being, in fact, the same. Their classification is very conventional and relative, that is, they may be classified in one way or another, but always with intimation that in classifying them one always thinks or meditates on them as related to something which, at this given moment at least, is not a *dharma*; or, . . . is not a "dharmic object."[24]

It seems appropriate at this point to note a distinction between two uses of the verb "to be," found in both ordinary and philosophical discourse, that is the distinction between predicative and existential usage. In most cases of course, the existential "is," (x exists), is implicitly assumed in predicative usages of the verb "to be" (x is blue). This is the "ontologically affirming" or reifying nature of language, frequently decried by Buddhists (of varying persuasions). Buddhism in general has shown a marked tendency to deny the validity of the existential or ontological function of language, de-constructing many of the "entities" believed to be ultimately existing, linguistic referents. In the "process-dynamism" of the Abhidharma, *dharmas* cannot strictly speaking be said to "exist" in the usual ontological/existential and "common-sense" meaning of the term, that is, in the conventional sense of the "existence" of tables and chairs etc. For the Abhidharmist, all such "entities" are conglomerations (*saṅghāta*) of various evanescent *dharmas*, which, appearing and then disappearing in quick succession, create the illusion of a permanent and singular entity (cf. GK III.3). Such existence is secondary, being based upon conceptual and linguistic forms (*prajñāptisat*). The "existential" function of language is a subtle confutation of meaning, showing, as the Buddhists argue, that language is bound up within an "ontologically-affirming" frame of reference. The Buddhist sees this as the false-attribution of *svabhāva* to an empty (*śūnya*) and ego-less (*anātma*) "entity." It is this that Venkata Ramanan aptly calls the "fallacy of misplaced absolutism" (*sasvabhāva-vāda*).[25]

As a result of the confusion of existential and predicative uses of the verb "to be," terms such as "*yathābhūta*" ("things as they are"), are often misconstrued as evidence of Buddhist "realism," or, to put it another way, such terms are often taken to show that Buddhism affirms the existence of some "ultimate reality" or absolute behind appearances. This is a misleading approach, since Buddhist philosophy is grounded in the conception of process without a processed or a processor. With such a conception, conventional language is often misleading and should not be relied upon in the context of the "true nature of things." One should note that terms such as "*yathābhūta*" are primarily used descriptively, that is they pinpoint the "true nature of things" without necessarily making ontological assertions about the existence of those "things." It is clear that the "predicative" usage of "*bhūta*" is the primary usage of this term in such a context, and (in the context of Mahāyāna philosophy) the only usage of the term. It does not necessarily imply any form of substantial real.[26]

Broadly speaking, the refusal to become embroiled in an ontological debate is the position of the various Mahāyāna schools in general, and the Madhyamaka in particular. The Mahāyāna utilized the Sarvāstivāda Abhidharma in their own literature but criticized the Sarvāstivādins for their attachment to these same categories as ultimate. Consequently, for the Mahāyāna schools, no doctrinal formulation is acceptable in the ultimate sense (*paramārtha*), the Mahayanist having no statement (*pratijñā*) to put forward, or view to establish (*dṛṣṭi, siddhānta*). Thus, the Mādhyamika walks the tightrope of a middle path in that he or she refuses to accept the non-existence of the "given" that constitutes our experiences, while at the same time disputing the ontological status that is ascribed to that "given." As we shall see, this is also fundamentally the position of the classical Yogācārin, (the main dispute between the schools being the problem of accounting for the peculiar status of the "given"). This is also the import of the Prajñāpāramitā statements which state that: "form is emptiness, and emptiness is form."

Mahāyāna Buddhist philosophy rejects the entire system of ontological bi-polarity that exhibits itself in all discursive activities; language is "ontologically affirming," whereas for the Mahayanist no "thing" can be said "to exist," nor "to not exist." Thus, we find Nāgārjuna stating that one should neither proclaim the empty (*śūnya*) nor the non-empty (*aśūnya*).[27] This idea was developed by the Yogācārins, who argued that both poles of the debate are hopelessly entangled in misleading ontological categories and the inherent problems of attribution (*samāropa*) and negation (*apavāda*) that exhibit a necessary function and quality of language. One can only speculate as to the similarities between this and the perspectives of the early Abhidharmists. Certainly the "*sabbe dhammā anattā*" formula is an archaic one, and the possibility remains that some early Buddhists may have understood this in the sense that it is utilized by the Mahāyāna. It would have been remarkable indeed if all early Buddhists had generally understood the formula exclusively in terms of the Sarvāstivāda perspective, that upholds the ontological reality of *dharmas*. Piatigorsky suggests that the early Abhidharma theories are neither ontological nor epistemological.

> It would be an utter mistake to say that the Buddhist Masters of old conceived the world as being or consisting of *dharmas*. . . .There was neither a dharmic ontology, or a mere dharmic epistemology there. . . .*dharmas* do not carry any information about the world or the psychology of men, because *dharmas* are not specific. On the contrary, they are as unspecific as one could imagine.[28]

Moreover, he suggests that it is only in the late and modern Abhidharma, despite the protestations of some modern Theravāda scholars, that *dharmas* take on a specifically ontological rather than purely psychological aspect.[29] With respect to the Theravāda attitude towards the *dharmas*, Etienne Lamotte maintains that,

> The Theravādins did not expatiate upon the transcendental nature of a *dharma*. They accepted the fact as it was presented to them, without attempting to seek further, or dispute the degree of its reality. . .the Theravādins confined themselves to distinctions which earned them, among others, the epithet of Vibhajyavādins.[30]

However, it would seem that there was no definitive Theravāda position as to whether the *dharma*-categories were ontological or not, and Guenther notes[31] that among the definitive works of this school, Buddhaghoṣa accepts the existence-theory of the Sarvāstivādins,[32] while the author of the *Aṭṭhāsalinī* clearly endorses the Sautrāntika understanding of *asaṃskṛta* as non-existence (*abhāva*).[33]

The notion of *svabhāva* is central to the Sarvāstivāda conception of a *dharma*. It is this notion which comes under such stringent attack in Mahāyāna scholastic works because of its perceived eternalist or absolutistic consequences. As we shall see in the fourth *prakaraṇa* of the *Gauḍapādīya-kārikā* the notion of *svabhāva* is utilized in an attempt to reconcile Mahāyāna philosophy with the Vedāntic absolutism of the author.

The Nature of Saṃskṛta and Asaṃskṛta Dharmas

As we have seen, for the Sarvāstivāda *dharmas* are the ultimate, substantial constituents of reality (*paramārtha/dravya sat*). In total, the Sarvāstivāda accepts the existence of seventy-five of these "ultimate" categories. Three of these ultimates are *asaṃskṛta*—

uncompounded or unconditioned, i.e., space and two forms of liberation. *Ākāśa* is *asaṃskṛta* because it is unchanged by the modifications occurring within it, and also because it is the locus for the manifestation of the seventy-two *saṃskṛta dharmas*. The other two *asaṃskṛta dharmas—apratisaṃkhyā nirodha* (the cessation of *saṃskṛta dharmas* not through discriminative knowledge), and *pratisaṃkhyā nirodha* (the cessation of *saṃskṛta dharmas* through discriminative knowledge) denote two forms of cessation, the former based upon the non-occurrence of causal factors leading to its manifestation, and the latter on the cessation of formative forces (*saṃskāras*) through the exercise of discriminative knowledge. *Apratisaṃkhyānirodha*, for instance, denotes the cessation of a formation due to the non-occurrence of the factors causing its manifestation. Takasaki argues that:

> It is beyond our powers of conception to visualize such a situation in concrete terms, but it is at least theoretically conceivable, and that being the case, it was probably felt necessary to add it to the list of elements. Generally speaking, although the theories of the Sarvastivādins and the doctrines of the *Abhidharmakośabhāṣya* did have their origins in the sphere of spiritual cultivation, practice and experience, there was a strong tendency to give priority to theoretical consistency. That is why this school of thought became transformed into an abstruse and complex body of speculative doctrine.[34]

The scholastic precision with which these dharmic lists were drawn up is plain to see. The remaining seventy-two *dharmas* are all compounded (*saṃskṛta*). As such they are causally conditioned, non-eternal (*anitya*), momentary (*kṣaṇika*), mundane (*laukika*), and predominantly impure (*āsrava*). These compounded factors are often classified in terms of further categories, for example as the five *skandhas*, the twelve *āyatanas* ("bases of cognition"), or the eighteen *dhātus* (element-groups—the six sensory-organs, their corresponding sense-objects, and the consciousnesses of each). In contradistinction to the compounded factors, *asaṃskṛta dharma* are unchanging, eternal (*nitya*), and always pure (*anāsrava*).

The more radical ramifications of the Sarvāstivāda position were somewhat circumvented by the schools tendency to conflate "*dharma*" with "*saṃskāra*" ("formative force") and "*saṃskṛta*" (compounded), which nevertheless constitutes a wholly different level of "existence" (*prajñapti sat*), being a momentary compound and thus, capable of further reduction. This, of course, allowed the Sarvāstivādin to argue that all *dharmas* (in fact, all *saṃskṛta dharmas*) are impermanent. Piatigorsky makes the following illuminating distinctions between "*dharma*" ("constituent element"), and "*saṃskāra*" (formative force):

> If then we try to conceive all *dharmas* as separate and of all things as complex or composite, we will clearly see that each individual object has its existence which is dharmic, and its individuality which is samskaric, . . .Therefore, when we read here about the separateness of objects we must understand it as the secondary separateness, i.e. derived from that of *dharmas* which are discrete par excellence, . . . it is *dharmas* that cause objects to be dharmic, but it is *saṃskāras* that cause the very existence of objects. . . . *saṃskāras* do not have their own existence, while *dharmas* do have it, though only with respect to and in comparison [to] objects.[35]

Dharmas are said to come in and out of "being" insofar as they have the power (*karaṇaśakti*) or causal functionality to manifest in a given formation (*saṃskāra*). Formations are, of course, momentary (*kṣaṇika*) and impermanent (*anitya*), yet the *dharmas* that make up these compounds are ultimate (*paramārtha/dravya sat*) and forever possess their own-dharmic-nature (*svabhāva*). The Sarvāstivādins maintain that this does not subvert the notion of impermanence since the manifestation and causal functionality of *dharmas* (in formations) are momentary; this of course is their understanding of the formula—"all formations are impermanent" (not all *dharmas*)! *Dharmas* in themselves possess a *svabhāva* and hence an ultimately immutable nature. The distinction between the impermanence of a *saṃskṛta dharma* and the immutability of its own-nature (*svabhāva*) is an aspect of Sarvāstivāda philosophy that has often been overlooked. The significance of the possessive nature of the statement—that all *dharmas* *have* an own-nature (*sasvabhāva*), rather than are an own-nature is an important point to note.

The svabhāvic quality of a *dharma* is immutable in the sense that it refers to the "tenseless" or atemporal "persistence" of that *dharma* in distinction to the temporal manifestation of that same *dharma* in a functional or causal setting (in a formation or "*saṃskāra*"). This atemporality establishes the impossibility of change since something that is outside the temporal field cannot be subject to the fluctuating conditions of its passage. There are similarities that can be drawn between this "two tier" system of existence (temporal, i.e. causally functional, and atemporal, i.e. "essential" (*svabhāva*) and the philosophy of time propounded by the philosopher James McTaggart, but discussion of this would be beyond the scope of this work. For the Sarvāstivādins, *dharmas* are impermanent in their manifestation, but not in their own-natures (*svabhāva*), which exist throughout the three temporal spheres of past, present, and future. This philosophical position was developed by the Sarvāstivādins to account for the problem of the time lapse between action and its karmic fruition. Thus, *dharmas* persist *in potentia* in the intervening spatio-temporal gulf between cause and effect. This view was also necessitated by the Sarvāstivāda insistence upon the ultimate and substantial existence (*dravya sat*) of these *dharmas* as ultimate realities; these *dharmas* were, strictly speaking, beyond causal conditions.

Moreover, not only is change impossible for an *asaṃskṛta dharma*, the same can also be said for a *saṃskṛta dharma* (or *saṃskāra*) since it is momentary (*kṣaṇika*) and therefore cannot "persist" through a change in quality. Thus, in the *Abhidharmakośa* the Vaibhāṣikas (Sarvāstivādins) argue that motion is not possible for a compounded thing since all compounded things are momentary. A compounded thing cannot undergo alteration (*anyathībhūta*), since loss of character is not valid for a momentary state and would in fact amount to the arising of a new and different state. Thus, Vasubandhu notes in *Abhidharmakośabhāṣya* IV.2 that:

> Since all that is compounded does not exist after it has attained identity, it is destroyed in the same place where it was produced. Transference to another place (*deśāntarasaṃkrāntiḥ*) is not valid for it.[36]

According to the Buddhist doctrine of selflessness (*anātma-vāda*), a given object (x) cannot continue to "persist" if there is a change in any of its qualities. The reason for this is, of course, that a change in quality would mean that x would no longer be identifiable as itself. Rather what we perceive as the single, persisting object x is in reality a series of similar, but nevertheless discrete *dharmas*, which may be appropriately denoted x^1, x^2, x^3, x^4, etc. according to their sequence in temporal succession. It is interesting to note that, despite the "realism" of the Sarvāstivāda Abhidharma, the "*anātma*" analysis of change actually disposes of the realist distinction between "things" (the "bearers" of properties) and "properties" (that which "inheres" within a "thing"). The dharmic analysis of the world from this perspective is explainable in terms of a pure stream of *qualia* or "percepts" and involves no ontological attribution whatsover, based as it is upon the notion of "qualities" without a "qualified." Thus, as Anacker notes,

> A change in characteristic is always a change in things : there are in fact no underlying entities which have characteristics—there is only whatever is presented to the consciousnesses themselves.[37]

Consequently, one must draw the conclusion that the Buddhist deconstruction of everyday objects into final, immutable, and wholly discrete moments, has in effect completely eradicated the notion of "change" as we commonly understand it. Compounded *dharmas* are only momentary and so cannot undergo change (since on this view change is the destruction of one moment and the arising of the next); uncompounded *dharmas* also cannot undergo change since the very notion of "*asaṃskṛta*" implies permanence (*nitya*) and immutability (*na anyathābhāva*). It is the inapplicability of the notion of "change" that is pounced upon so decisively by the Mādhyamikas and by the author of the GK, following the lead established by Nāgārjuna in his MMK and other works (see chapter 4).

The *Abhidharmakośa* of Vasubandhu is the definitive statement of the Vaibhāṣika position. *Kośa* V.25ab puts forward a summation of four arguments which together constitute the main thrust of the Sarvāstivāda position.

> *sarvakālāstitā, uktatvād dvayāt sadviṣayāt phalāt*
> [*Dharmas*] exist at all times because
>
> 1. it is said so (by the Buddha?)
> 2. [consciousness (*vijñāna*) arises] out of the duality [of sense-organ and sense-object],
> 3. [consciousness] takes an existing thing as its object,
> 4. [past actions] have a result.

The first argument can be interpreted in two ways. First, it may be an argument that *dharmas* exists because one can refer to them in speech (*uktatva*). Alternatively, the verse may be suggesting that *dharmas* exist because the Buddha says so. On this interpretation it is not, strictly speaking, a philosophical argument, but is based upon the acceptance of the authority of the canonical texts as authentic records of the Buddha's teachings. The second argument bases itself upon the realist assumption that consciousness depends upon a substratum (*āśraya*), and an objective-support (*ālambana*). If this were not so, argues the Sarvāstivādin, what would be the need of the two in the first place? Equally there could be no *nirvaṇa*, for consciousness would always arise, there being no objective means to differentiate between perception and non-perception. The third argument is closely connected to the second and presupposes an intentional view of consciousness, i.e. the idea that consciousness must be a consciousness of something (which is then also assumed to be existent). Thus, *Abhidharmakośabhāṣya* V.25 states that:

> Consciousness arises if a sense-object exists, and not otherwise. If past and future times did not exist then consciousness would have a non-existent objective-support. Thus, consciousness would not exist owing to the non-existence of its objective-support. . . If the past does not exist then how could there be the future fruition of good and bad actions? In fact, at the time that the effect arises the present cause of its fruition does not exist. For these reasons, the Vaibhāṣikas maintain that the past and the future exist.[38]

Sarvāstivāda reasoning runs along the following lines: Consciousness is so called because it is conscious of an object (*vijñeya*); if there were no object there could be no consciousness. If there is consciousness of a non-existent, how can you say that it is conscious of anything at all (the "intentional" view of consciousness)? Again if one could be conscious of a non-existent one would be unable to doubt it since doubt can only arise when there is an object of knowledge (*jñeya*). The bottom-line for the Sarvāstivādin is the belief that knowledge presupposes existence, since you cannot have knowledge of nothing (that is, something that does not exist). Thus, as Williams notes,

> Philosophically the Sarvāstivāda doctrine was essentially built on the intentionality of consciousness, the theory that all consciousness must be conscious of something, combined with the *apriori* assumption that therefore the intentional object must exist.[39]

The fourth and final argument for the Sarvāstivāda position, as outlined in *Abhidharmakośa* V.25ab, concerns the possibility of explaining the karmic process. For the Sarvāstivādin the continued existence of a *dharma*, albeit in a state of latency or potentiality, was required to account for the temporal gulf between action and fruition. Past actions have a result in the present and in the future—therefore those *dharmas* must in some sense "be" (in a latent and non-functioning form). This argument was attacked by Vasubandhu, who argues, from the Sautrāntika point of view, that to exist is to be causally efficient (*karaṇabhāva, śakti*). For Vasubandhu, then, to "exist" is to function, thus, a *dharma* cannot be said to exist outside its own phenomenal manifestation. *Karman* is explained in terms of the transformation of a given consciousness stream rather than as the actualization of an existent but previously latent cause.

The Mahāyāna attacks the Sarvāstivāda from the same point of view, i.e. that you cannot extrapolate a *dharma's* existence beyond the realms of its functional given-ness (*vastumātra*). This position, ostensibly deriving from the Sautrāntika critique, is extended further to refer even to the "present" existence of a *dharma*, which is still accepted by the Sautrāntika school. For the Mahāyāna critic of the Sarvāstivāda, the latter's view involves the hypostatization of *dharmas*, which may be said to be causally efficient but not substantially existent. To argue contrary to this (as the Sarvāstivāda and the Sautrāntika schools do) is, according to the Mahāyāna, to extrapolate a *dharma's* given-ness (its "*dharma*-ness" if you like) beyond the parameters of its own evanescent and experiential manifestation.

The Sautrāntika Position: *Asaṃskṛta-Nairātmya*

It is clear that the development of the Sarvāstivāda philosophy would inevitably precipitate a reaction to the ultimate finality of their dharmic classification. The two main centres of Sarvāstivāda doctrine were at Kashmir and Gandhāra. The former, as we have seen, became known as the Vaibhāṣikas. The Sarvāstivādins at Gandhāra, however, were the more progressive, and it is from here that the Sautrāntikas appear to have developed initially as a splinter group of the Sarvāstivāda. Warder refers to the *Samuktābhidharmahṛdaya*, a text compiled by Dharmatrāta some time after 50 CE, which denies ultimate status to many of the *dharmas* then being proclaimed by the Sarvāstivāda school.[40] He regards "this assembly as that which rejected the Sautrāntika revisions, as a result of which the revisionists formed themselves into a new schismatic school."[41] At this council, the particular explanation of "*sarvāsti*" attributed to Vasumitra (II) was accepted by the Sarvāstivāda, and systematized in the *Mahāvibhāṣa*. Henceforth, all Buddhists who accepted the authority of this text were called the Vaibhāṣikas, which became the epithet of orthodox Sarvāstivāda as it established itself in Kashmir, which subsequently became the undisputed centre of Sarvāstivāda thought.

The Sautrāntikas denied primary existence (*dravya sat*) to many of the *dharmas* postulated in the Sarvāstivāda's Abhidharmic classification. The *cittaviprayuktasaṃskāras*, apparently first formulated in Vasumitra's *Prakaraṇapāda*, was one such refuted category. For the Sautrāntikas this was a designation (*prajñapti*), having no reality as a substance (*dravya*). The same opinion was held with regard to the existence of past and future *dharmas*, for the simple reason that these *dharmas* have either ceased to be or are yet to arise. The main reason why these *dharmas* had originally been postulated as existents by the Sarvāstivāda scholars was in an attempt to explain causal continuity between an action at one moment and its subsequent fruition at a later date. This was deemed necessary not only to safeguard Buddhist ethical philosophy but also the concept of causality itself. It can be seen as an early attempt by Buddhist scholastics to come to terms with the idea of different "types" of existence. The Sautrāntikas also attacked the legitimacy of the *avijñāptirūpa*, the *cittaviprayukta-saṃskāra*, and the *rūpaviprayuktasaṃskāra* categories, as well as the Vaibhāṣika interpretation of shape (*saṃsthāna*) as a substantial entity (*dravya sat*).

As the name of the school suggests, the Sautrāntikas accepted the *sūtras* (or rather in this case the Sanskrit *Āgamas*) as their ultimate authority. The Sautrāntika did not deny the validity of *abhidharma* analysis, their point being that the Buddha's own *abhidharma* can be found in the canonical *Āgamas* themselves. The various Abhidharma texts of the Sarvāstivādins and others, however, are not the authentic words of the Buddha. Thus, if the Abhidharma texts utilized terms that were not to be found in the *āgamas*, then they were considered to be invalid. This did not mean that the Sautrāntikas totally rejected the Sarvāstivāda abhidharmic analysis, far from it, the school in fact accepted much of the Vaibhāṣika dharmic classification (at least those aspects that they felt were legitimate elaborations of the Buddha's teachings). This can be seen from Vasubandhu's *bhāṣya* on *Abhidharmakośa* I.3, that is written from the Sautrāntika perspective.

> Whereas the world erroneously falls into the flood of becoming by reason of defilement (*kleśa*), and, whereas there is no access to the taming of defilement, without the discernment of *dharmas*, therefore for the purpose of discerning the *dharmas* it is said that the Abhidharma was declared by the teacher (The Buddha).[42]

Vasubandhu (as a Sautrāntika) does not deny I.3 of the *Kośa*, accepting the necessity of a discernment of *dharmas* (*dharma-pravicaya*). However, where his commentary disagrees with the Vaibhāṣika position outlined in the *Kośa* is in his denial that this abhidharmic analysis was taught by the Buddha. Consequently, the Sautrāntika does not accept the scholastic attempts to define these *dharmas* with any degree of finality. The Abhidharma is accepted, but only insofar as it is grounded in the words of the Buddha, i.e. the *Āgamas*, (whether these accurately reflect the words of the Buddha is another question altogether).

While criticizing the postulation of various *dharmas*, Vasubandhu is in agreement with the Vaibhāṣika as to the general categories of *dharmas* into which substantial *dharmas* (*dravya*) can be classified, with the exception of the *citta* and *rūpaviprayuktasaṃskāras*.[43] These last two categories include those *dharmas* called *prāpti* and *aprāpti*, "possession" and "non-possession." These were postulated by the Vaibhāṣika to account for the presence of a non-functioning *dharma* in a given stream of consciousness in any given moment. The Vaibhāṣikas evidently felt that this was the only way in which they could account for the connection between successive thoughts, words and deeds, and their karmic consequences. Presence or absence of a given *dharma* is thus due to *prāpti* or *aprāpti* respectively. This also allowed the Vaibhāṣika to differentiate between an *Ārya* and the average person (*pṛthagjana*), since the Noble One has the *prāptis* of certain natures resulting from meditative attainment, which the average person does not. These "possessions" however, cannot be connected with conscious thought processes (i.e. they must be *cittaviprayukta*) since when the Noble One is having mundane thoughts he is still distinguishable from the average person by virtue of his previous attainments. However, *prāpti* and *aprāpti* cannot be classified along with the *rūpasaṃskāras*, since "possession" and "non-possession" are not material or "formal" in any respect, thus they are also *rūpaviprayukta*. For the Vaibhāṣika *prāpti* is the cause that originates (*utpattihetu*) specific natures in a given consciousness-stream and is also the cause which differentiates (*vyavasthāhetu*) the Noble One from the average person.[44]

Vasubandhu criticizes the postulation of *prāpti*, arguing that differentiation between the two is merely the state of having destroyed or not destroyed the defilements. This is the characteristic feature of the Sautrāntika's dharmic taxonomy, being something of a critical abridgement of the Sarvāstivāda classification. Thus, for the Sautrāntika *nirvāṇa* is merely the name (*prajñapti*) for the non-existence (*abhāva*) or cessation (*nirodha*) of the *saṃskṛta dharmas* and is not to be misconstrued as another entity. Dowling notes that,

> The tendency to reify or attribute substantial being to their theoretical entities is characteristic of the Vaibhāṣika school as it is portrayed in the *Abhidharmakośa*. A return to the more skeletal system of theoretical entities found in the canonical *sūtras* characterizes the Sautrāntika school as it is portrayed in the same text.[45]

In their persistent refusal to hypostatize *asaṃskṛta dharmas*, as in their idea that *nirvāṇa* and *ākāśa* are merely the absence (*abhāva*) of *saṃskṛta dharmas*, the Sautrāntikas can be seen to occupy a transitional position in the development from (Sarvāstivāda) Abhidharma to Prajñāpāramitā. Given that all *dharmas* (as ultimates) were necessarily *asaṃskṛta* in their essential-nature (*svabhāva*), all *dharmas*, from the Sautrāntika perspective, are empty (*abhāva:* literally "non-existent") since this is what the term *asaṃskṛta* seems to amount to for this school. Of course, in the strictest sense "non-existence" (*abhāva*) is an extreme position, unless understood to be shorthand for the denial of all alternatives (the *catuṣkoṭi*). This expansion of Sautrāntika ideas, of course, would have been unacceptable to the Sautrāntika school itself since this would in effect lead it towards the emptiness doctrine of the Mahāyāna Prajñāpāramitā movement.[46]

The Sautrāntikas, then, can be characterized by a "metaphysics of economy." In certain respects this can be seen as a transitional precursor of the Madhyamaka denial of the validity of all metaphysical categories. However, the school does appear to have upheld a subtle transmigrating consciousness (*vijñāna*), perhaps a precursor of the Yogācāra's *ālayavijñāna*. This is not to be taken to be the acceptance of a persisting personal self in the *saṃskāras* but was again postulated in an attempt to establish some form of causal continuity between the actions and consequences of one rebirth and another in a given stream of consciousness. Consciousness (*vijñāna*) is in a constant state of transformation (*pariṇāma*) and thus can never be said to constitute a persisting individual entity (*pudgala*); rather it is the succession of discrete, yet causally connected, mental states.

The Sautrāntika school is in agreement with the position of the Madhyamaka in its refusal to hypostasize uncompounded *dharmas*, but in the acceptance of the (impersonal) reality of compounded *dharmas* the Sautrāntikas still accept the finality of a (somewhat dove-tailed) version of the Sarvāstivāda classification. This is clearly not the position of the Madhyamaka school, which reduces all *dharmas* to the level of nominal existents (*prajñaptisat*). The Sautrāntika interpretation allows for the "reality" of the *skandhas* themselves, which nevertheless do not constitute a unified and persisting personality (*pudgala*), while at the same time avoiding the Sarvāstivāda hypostatization of their eventual cessation. This is still *pudgala nairātmya*.[47]

It has often been said that the Sautrāntika school was something of a transitional school in the development of Yogācāra ideas.[48] It is not impossible that the Sautrāntika school could have been in the background of the development of Prajñāpāramitā thought, for it is clear that the Sautrāntika reaction to the Sarvāstivāda is one step closer to the *dharma nairātmya* of the Prajñāpāramitā *sūtras*. Nevertheless, it is beyond the scope of this study to speculate about the relationship between Sautrāntika ideas and the early Prajñāpāramitā movement. The *vaipulya sūtras* of the developing Mahāyāna must have seemed scriptural "anathema" to the Sautrāntikas who adhered closely to the canonical *sūtras* in all matters (hence the school's name). Warder has suggested that Nāgārjuna, as author of the MMK, may not have been a Mahāyāna Buddhist.[49] Nevertheless, ideas that are traditionally seen as exclusively Mahāyāna (in this case *dharma nairātmya*) were not confined purely to the Mahāyāna schools.[50]

Our discussion of Abhidharma ideas has highlighted the centrality of the notions of *dharma* and *svabhāva* to Indian Buddhist philosophy in the period preceding the composition of the Vedāntic *Gauḍa-pādīya-kārikā*. The GK itself shows no evidence of direct influence from the Abhidharma schools of the Sautrāntika and Sarvāstivāda. Nevertheless, it has been necessary to consider these schools since the GK frequently utilizes the terms *dharma* and *svabhāva* and, as we shall see, bases its doctrine of non-origination on a particular understanding of these concepts. An appreciation of the meaning and importance of these terms, therefore, requires a consideration of the Abhidharma endeavor. However, one should not make the error of attributing a necessary and direct connection between Abhidharma and Gauḍa-pādian thought. In the *Gauḍapādīya-kārikā* it is the Mahāyāna understanding of these central terms which has been influential in the development of the Gauḍapādian philosophical position. Thus, before we proceed further a brief consideration of the Mahāyāna use and understanding of the terms "*dharma*" and "*svabhāva*" is necessary.

The Unique Particularity of Dharmas—A Mahāyāna Critique

From a Mahāyāna perspective the Abhidharmic belief in the finality of its dharmic classification results in a number of philosophical problems, focusing mainly around the unique particularity of the *dharmas* as ultimate and irreducible factors of existence. In particular such a conception leads to the following problems:

A. ultimate discreteness—the impossibility of continuity.

B. ultimate ineffability—the impossibility of classification.

A. As we have seen, a "*dharma*" in the Abhidharma context is an ultimate and unique particular. As such, it cannot be defined or described in any "common sense" (*saṃvṛti*) manner, in that there are no common "meanings" or "senses" that could possibly be attributed to a unique entity.[51] This point was noted for instance, by the later Buddhist logician Dignāga (fifth-sixth century CE), who argued that perception (*pratyakṣa*) was necessarily non-conceptual (*nirvikalpa*) since it can only apprehend the unique particular (*svalakṣaṇa*). Concepts (*vikalpa*) only became applicable in the realm of common qualities (*sāmānyalakṣaṇa*), which is the result of mental activity subsequent to the initial pre-conceptual perception. The distinction between *svalakṣaṇa* and *sāmānyalakṣaṇa*, is thus similar in scope to the Abhidharmic distinction between substance (*dravya*) and designation (*prajñapti*) in that the *svalakṣaṇa* is a unique and truly existent substance, while the *sāmānyalakṣaṇa* is a mental construct through which we understand and classify the *svalakṣaṇa*.

As a unique moment or "particular," indescribable in any but the most exclusively unique (and tautological) terms, it becomes impossible, strictly speaking, to pinpoint any similarity between one *dharma* and the next, since similarity requires a common attribute, and *dharmas* have already been established, by definition, to be "unique particulars." As a general principle of the Abhidharma exercise, it can be said that "if two momentary particulars have anything in common then the particulars must be composite and therefore cannot be primary existents (*dravya sat*)."[52]

Thus, the possibility of continuity between one *dharma* and the next becomes a logical impossibility since each unique *dharma*, as a self-contained absolute (after all that is what a *dharma* amounts to in the Abhidharma systems), must be "wholly distinct" from another (since this is the implication of a *dharma* "having a *svabhāva*"). This suggests that from one moment (*kṣaṇa*) to the next there can be no possibility of similarity, continuity, or connection between distinct *dharmas* for the reasons given above, i.e. that a *dharma* is a unique particular and must therefore in its "*dharma*-ness" (*dharmatā*), be essentially (*svabhāva*), "wholly discrete" and distinguishable from every other unique particular. Any similarity between one *dharma* and the next would mean that they were not non-composite, and would contradict their fundamental uniqueness.

B. The other upshot of the unique particularity of a given *dharma*, is its ultimate indescribability, since language is based upon commonly accepted definitions and designational forms, and *dharmas* as unique moments cannot be so classified by definition. The Abhidharma schools clearly believed that it was possible to construct a technical language that encompassed the entirety of possible existents. This is sharply criticized by the Mahāyāna, not only because of the inherent inadequacies of language itself, but also because, on Abhidharma presuppositions, *dharmas* were uniquely existent substances (*dravya sat*) that were thereby essentially beyond designation (*prajñapti*). In particular this notion of *dharmas* as ultimately irreducible elements was attacked by the Madhyamaka and Satyasiddhi schools.[53]

The Non-arising (Anutpāda) *and Immutability of Dharmas*

Those aspects of the Mahāyāna tradition which have been influenced by the Prajñāpāramitā *sūtras* emphasize the non-arising (*anutpāda*) of *dharmas* in the first place, (a theme that is also a central aspect of the *Gauḍapādīya-kārikā*). This doctrine stems from a particular understanding of the nature of "dharmic existence" and a rejection of the notion of an immutable inherent nature (*svabhāva*).

According to Abhidharmic theories of causation, *dharmas* are the ultimate, momentary (*kṣaṇika*) "building blocks" of the fluctuating causal continuum. In fact, the Abhidharmic reduction of composite entities makes the common sense notion of change largely redundant. An entity undergoing some form of change is for the Abhidharmist merely the arising and ceasing of a flow of momentary, but nevertheless, discrete factors (*dharmas*), which, by following each other in quick succession, provide the appearance of a subsisting and unified entity where there is none. Thus, as the supporting factors (*dhṛ: dharma*) of the causal continuum, *dharmas* must be in some sense, immutable. As ultimate units, *dharmas* are themselves incapable of being broken down or reduced to any further degree. The philosophical result of this, however, is that *dharmas* are immutable and uncompounded (*asaṃskṛta*), even, it would seem, the Sarvāstivādas seventy-two *saṃskṛta dharmas*. This appears to be a necessary consequence of their ultimacy (*paramārtha sat / dravya sat*). Thus, the ultimacy of *dharmas* necessitates that they are all in some sense uncompounded, being incapable of change.[54]

In a recent study of the *dharma* theories of the Buddhists, Piatigorsky suggests in a footnote that:

> . . . in the final analysis it can be said of all *dharmas* (i.e., both *saṃskṛta* and *asaṃskṛta*) that they are *asaṃskṛta dharmas*. . . However paradoxical it might sound, but that is to what the Prajñāpāramitā theory of *dharmas* seems to be tantamount.[55]

However, if this were the case then the Prajñāpāramitā *sūtras* would uphold a form of absolutism akin to that found in the GK. This in fact does not appear to be the case. It would be more correct to say that from the Prajñāpāramitā perspective, the unconditioned (*asaṃskṛta*) nature of all *dharmas* is the conclusion to be drawn from the Abhidharmic postulation of an own-being (*svabhāva*) to *dharmas*. Thus, it is not the Prajñāpāramitā position that all *dharmas* are ultimate and uncompounded (*asaṃskṛta*), but the derived conclusion (*siddhānta*) of the Abhidharma schools *as interpreted* by the Prajñāpāramitā. The mistaken attribution of absolutism to the Prajñāpāramitā (and Madhyamaka) movements is common in modern scholarship and, as we shall see, also appears to be the view of the author of the fourth *prakaraṇa* of the GK with regard to the Buddhist tradition.

According to the Prajñāpāramitā analysis, Abhidharma doctrines lead to the inevitable conclusion that all *dharmas* are uncompounded (*asaṃskṛta*). This, however, is not the Prajñāpāramitā position, since these texts view such a conclusion as unacceptable. The view that all *dharmas* are *asaṃskṛta* is, in fact, (from the Prajñāpāramitā perspective) the logical conclusion of the Sarvāstivāda position. This view is to be rejected since it contradicts the impermanence (*anitya*) and selflessness (*anātmatā*) of all *dharmas*. The Prajñāpāramitā critique then is not an attempt to establish a rival doctrinal position (such as the *asaṃskṛta* of all *dharmas*); rather, it is a rejection of the Abhidharmic attempt to establish an ultimate classification of reality. Thus, *dharmas* are neither *saṃskṛta* nor *asaṃskṛta*. This rejection occurs in a number of different spheres. First, there is the philosophical rejection of Abhidharma ideas, based upon the establishment of certain unfavorable conclusions from central Abhidharmic premises. Alongside this, however, is the methodological rejection of the Abhidharma practice of reviewing *dharmas*, on the grounds that this technique leads to attachment to self, (that is attachment to the "selfness" of *dharmas*.)[56] Thus, the *Vajracchedika-prajñāpāramitāsūtra* states that:

> If Subhūti, these *Bodhisattvas* should have a perception of either a *dharma*, or a no-*dharma*, they would thereby seize on a self, a being, a soul, or a person. And why? Because a *Bodhisattva* should not seize on either a *dharma* nor a no-*dharma*. Therefore this saying has been taught by the *Tathāgata* with a hidden meaning : "Those who know the discourse on *dharma* as like unto a raft, should forsake *dharmas*, still more no-*dharmas*."[57]

However, the Prajñāpāramitā movement does appear to have accepted the Abhidharma technique of reductionism, that is the "deconstruction" of entities based upon their complexity and reducibility into more basic constituents. The main difference here is that the Abhidharmists have constructed a technical meta-language which they believe to be a coherent and representative classification of the way things really are (*yathābhūta*). The reductionism, therefore, stops at the level of the fundamental *dharma*-types of that particular system (seventy-five in the case of the Sarvāstivāda). For the Prajñāpāramitā texts however, there is no level at which the reductionist process can conceivably end. Thus the correct position, both philosophically and soteriologically (in that it does not lead to attachment and subsequent bondage), is no position at all. All conceptual frameworks are ultimately inadequate. This does not of course preclude the Prajñāpāramitā from making conventional statements as indicators (*prajñapti*) to the "wisdom that has gone beyond" (Prajñāpāramitā), but it does exclude the possibility of taking any of those statements in anything other than a "liberative," "therapeutic" or propadeutical sense. Thus, Conze suggests that,

> The thousands of lines of the Prajñāpāramitā can be summed up in the following two sentences : 1) One should become a *Bodhisattva* (or Buddha-to-be), i.e., one who is content with nothing less than all-knowledge attained through the perfection of wisdom for the sake of all beings. 2) There is no such thing as a *Bodhisattva*, or as all-knowledge, or as "being," or as the perfection of wisdom, or as attainment. To accept both these contradictory facts is to be perfect.[58]

This is an example of the use of paradox as a means to liberation from intellectual ratiocination. More specifically, paradox within the Prajñāpāramitā framework is a didactic or pedagogic technique of switching from ultimate (*paramārtha*) to conventional (*saṃvṛti*) levels of expression so as to liberate the individual from his or her own fundamental presuppositions (although Williams suggests that this is not paradoxical in itself, it should be noted that the mode of expression involves the juxtaposition of *apparently* contradictory statements. This, as far as I can see, is what a paradox is)![59] At a comparatively early stage (although perhaps not in the earliest stages) of the Prajñāpāramitā movement, the conceptual presuppositions and categories which are most directly criticized, (and by implication the presuppositions that much of scholastic Buddhism must have been working with), appear to be those of the Abhidharma schools. Thus the Prajñāpāramitā literature continually subverts the basic distinction between *saṃskṛta* and *asaṃskṛta*, thereby rendering such conceptual divisions ultimately inconsequential, (such classifications do however remain conventionally valid).[60] The Prajñāpāramitā critique by implication is to be extended to all conceptual systems, not just those of the Abhidharma schools.

There is, of course, a tendency in the Prajñāpāramitā texts to describe *dharmas* as essentially "blown out" (*nirvṛti*), or "nirvāṇized." This could be said to be a declaration that all *dharmas* are essentially "unconditioned," since *nirvāṇa* itself is an uncompounded (*asaṃskṛta*) *dharma*. It is equally apparent that one of the important features of the Prajñāpāramitā position is that of the non-arising (*anutpāda*) of *dharmas*. While it is clear that an unconditioned entity (*asaṃskṛta*) is also unoriginated (*anutpāda*) by definition, it would be misleading to understand the Prajñāpāramitā texts as postulating some form of unconditioned reality (*asaṃskṛta*), for this is not their fundamental purpose. In the Prajñāpāramitā sense *dharmas* do not arise (*an-utpāda*) because, in actual fact, they do not ultimately exist. This should not be (mis)understood to be a statement of pure nihilism, since there are three levels of logic at work in the Prajñāpāramitā literature. Basically they are:

1. x does not exist.
2. x neither exists nor does not exist.
3. the four-fold negation or tetralemma (*catuṣkoṭi*).

Prajñāpāramitā dialectic is a spiraling series of negations—each time a position is established it is then negated from a higher point of view. Doctrinal argument in these texts are "pointers" (*prajñapti*) to liberation, rafts to be relinquished once the goal is attained. The frequent statements that "x does not exist," therefore, should not be taken as the establishment of a nihilistic doctrine, but rather as shorthand for the negation of all possible classifications of reality. Without an awareness of this fact the Prajñāpāramitā texts will forever appear nonsensical and inconsistent.

> "Śāriputra : For what reason are all *dharmas* unborn and do not go forth?
> Subhūti : Form is empty of the own-being of form; one cannot apprehend any birth or going-forth with regard to it. And so for all *dharmas*, up to : the Reality limit."[61]

The distinctive philosophy of the Prajñāpāramitā literature is established through a critique of the entire Abhidharmic enterprise of defining and classifying *dharmas*. Such an attack upon the finality of the dharmic taxonomy is a pointed refusal to accept the ontological implications of the Abhidharma position, implications which, on Prajñāpāramitā arguments, would be equally unacceptable to the Abhidharmists themselves. Thus, even *nirvāṇa* is denied any ultimate ontological validity.[62] Having all possible rugs pulled from beneath one's mind (*citta*), it is then said to be "non-residing" or "unsupported" (*apratiṣṭha*). This is the perfection of wisdom (*prajñāpāramitā*).[63]

The difference between the conclusions derived from a rival system (in this case, that all *dharmas* are uncompounded realities (*asaṃskṛta*), and therefore, do not arise (*anutpāda*) and those accepted by the critics themselves (i.e., that all *dharmas* are empty [either as *saṃskṛta* or *asaṃskṛta*], and therefore do not arise (*an-utpāda*), is subtle and easily overlooked. Indeed, as we shall see, the author of GK IV seems unaware of the distinction and consequently interprets the Mahāyāna tradition in terms of his own (Vedānta-based) absolutism.

To further elucidate the distinction between one's own position and the "derived-position" of another, perhaps it would be useful to consider an example. Take, for instance, the frequent Mahāyāna suggestion that *dharmas* are like space (*ākāśa*). From a Sarvāstivāda point of view, space is an *asaṃskṛta dharma*, since it is the locus (*āśraya*) for the manifestation of other *dharmas*, and is itself unaffected by their transformation. From the Sarvāstivāda perspective, then, the Mahāyāna declaration that "all *dharmas* are like space," amounts to an affirmation that all *dharmas* are *asaṃskṛta*. This seems to be what the author of the GK is implying when he makes a similar statement in GK IV.1. For the Prajñāpāramitā (but not necessarily for the entire Mahāyāna movement as we shall see when we come to consider certain texts utilizing the notion of a "*tathāgatagarbha*"), this position is "un-Buddhist" since it denies the basic Buddhist orientation toward the notions of impermanence and selflessness. Why then is the analogy so prevalent in Prajñāpāramitā texts? The comparison is useful since both space and *dharmas* are said to be:

1. ungraspable,
2. having no beginning or end limits (*koṭi*),[54] and
3. having no foundation or support.

This understanding of *dharmas* is remarkable since, if there are no beginning or end points to any *dharmas*, then they can have no distinguishing marks (*svalakṣaṇa*), or fundamental boundaries. Consequently, one can never hope to pinpoint when (or where) one *dharma* ends and another begins. Of course, having no own-marks or characteristic features, *dharmas* are indistinguishable. *Dharmas* have no essences of their own (*svabhāva*) and are to that extent equal (*samatā*). The importance of the third attribute, that of being without a support, should not be underestimated. We noted earlier that the etymology of the term "*dharma*," establishes it as a derivative of the root *dhṛ*, "to sustain" or "support." In the Abhidharma schools *dharmas* were taken to be the ultimate supports of experience. The Prajñāpāramitā movement, however, subverted this basic position by denying the very possibility of pinpointing *dharmas* by suggesting that they too were without a support, having no essential-being (*svabhāva*) of their own.

It should be noted at this point that there are (at least) two different ways in which the concept of emptiness (*śūnyatā*) can be "unpacked."[65] First, there is the notion of emptiness as it tends to be explicated in the scholastic texts of the Madhyamaka school (and as it is espoused in the previous paragraph). Here, the "emptiness of all *dharmas*" means that they are essentially indistinguishable, having no own-being or nature of their own (*niḥsvabhāvatā*). This understanding of emptiness gives rise to an apophatic language (*via negativa*). However, the lack of boundary between one *dharma* and another can also give rise to a cataphatic language (*via positiva*) based upon the idea that if all *dharmas* are empty then all *dharmas* can equally be described as "sublime," "wholesome," "unconditioned" etc. This is a major feature of many Mahāyāna texts. Gadjin Nagao sees this as a result of the identity of emptiness (*śūnyatā*) with dependent-origination (*pratītyasamutpāda*). This identity can be approached from the direction of emptiness or from the direction of causal inter-dependence. Thus,

> On the one hand, dependent co-arising means that all beings are not independent (*svātantrika*) and self-existing (*ātman*) things, but only transient beings brought about by the constellation of a cluster of causes. This no-self and absence of any independent self underlying transient

> being is the emptiness of things. . .On the other hand, this emptying and negating of things does not mean that things do not exist at all; non-being is not nothingness. Emptiness signifies only the absence of essence. The evolving, changing world understood through insight into emptiness is not meant to be negated. Beings that exist in emptiness exist just as they are. . .This restored and purified second dimension of dependent co-arising is indeed wondrous (*āścarya*). Because of emptiness, the existence of beings together with their causes is ineffable (*avācya*) and inconceivable (*acintya*). In truth, the phenomenal world is first and foremost a beautiful world, and phenomenal being is a being wondrous and enjoyable beyond description. But this is not the beauty or joy of the one-dimensional birth-death cycle, which consists in unlimited suffering. The wonder, beauty and joy of the dependently co-arising world is entirely due to its being free of essence and empty.[66]

Nagao has made a salient point here. Emptiness language can be developed in two axiological directions. If everything is empty, then nothing is *essentially* real! On the other hand, if everything is empty then anything is possible! The clearest example of the cataphatic development of the concept of emptiness is the idea of the mutual interpenetration of *dharmas* (as found for instance in the *Avataṃsakasūtra*, and the Chinese Hua-Yen school which is based upon it), and perhaps the notion of emptiness found in certain texts which utilize the notion of a "*tathāgatagarbha*." In the latter both types of language appear to be used: *saṃskṛta dharmas* are ultimately "non-existent" in the usual scholastic sense of the term, and yet *asaṃskṛta dharmas* are "amazing," unrestricted, and unconditioned (see chapter 7).

In the *śāstras* of Nāgārjuna we find the development of a philosophical system, based upon the Prajñāpāramitā insight into the non-ultimacy of all conceptual classifications. Here also the familiar Abhidharmic distinctions are continually subverted.[67] Thus, in the *Vigrahavyāvartanī* (VV) (verse 54), Nāgārjuna states that if one accepts the wholesome own-nature of *dharmas* (*kuśalaḥ svabhāvo dharmānāṃ*) there would be no state of spiritual purification (*syād vāso na brahmacaryasya*). Not only that but in the following verse Nāgārjuna states that,

> *nādharmo dharmo vā saṃvyavahārāś ca laukikā na syuḥ,*
> *nityāś ca sasvabhāvāḥ syur nityatvād ahetumataḥ.*
> There would be neither vice nor virtue, and worldly practicalities would not be possible. Self-existent entities would be eternally existent due to the permanence of that which is causeless.

Nāgārjuna then proceeds to attack the Abhidharma distinction between unwholesome (*akuśala*), "liberative" (*nairghāṇika*), and undefined (*avyākṛta*) *dharmas*, since, having accepted that *dharmas* have an intrinsic-nature (*svabhāva*), "therefore, all compounded entities would exist as uncompounded." (*tasmāt sarvaṃ saṃskṛtam asaṃkṛtam te bhavaty eva*, VV.56).

For Nāgārjuna the Abhidharma view, as he presents it, is inappro-riate since it subverts the Buddhist notions of no-self and imperma-ence. The primacy of these notions within the Buddhist tradition is shown by the fact that all schools of Buddhism have felt the need to reconcile their own specific interpretations of the Buddha's teaching in terms of these basic conceptions. Nāgārjuna bases much of his critique upon the primacy of impermanence (*anityatā*). Thus, in MMK 21.4 he states that "impermanence always occurs (literally, 'never does not occur') in entities." This position is further expressed in the *Mahāprajñāpāramitāsūtra-upadeśa*, a text attributed (probably falsely) to Nāgārjuna, which states that the "notion of impermanence" (*anitya-saṃjñā*, Chinese : *pu-ch'ang hsiang*) is "merely a synonym for the noble path itself."[68] Impermanence and change, in fact, are only possible because everything is essentially empty (*svabhāva-śūnya*). Thus, Nāgārjuna states in *Vigrahavyāvartanī*, verse 70 that

> *prabhavati ca śūnyateyaṃ yasya prabhavanti tasya sarvārthāḥ,*
> *prabhavati na tasya kiṃ cin na prabhavati śūnyatā yasya.*
> All things are possible for the one for whom emptiness is possible; nothing whatsoever is possible for the one for whom emptiness is not possible.

Again, note that emptiness eradicates all boundaries, so anything is possible if everything is empty. This is an important point to realize because it provides a philosophical justification for the grandiose metaphysical speculations of many texts and the catholicity of the Mahāyāna movement. Aligned with the notion of skillful-means (*upāya-kauśalya*), it seems that from a Mahāyāna point of view anything can be postulated as long as one remains mindful of its essential emptiness!

In a scholastic context the primary insight of the Madhyamaka analysis is that conditioned arising (*pratītya-sam-utpāda*) is no arising (*an-utpāda*), since a causally conditioned factor is an empty and ultimately unreal factor. *Dharmas* are conventionally real (*saṃvṛti sat*) and the ultimate meaning of their existence (*paramārtha sat*) amounts to that very fact. Again, Paul Williams has expressed this point well,

> The situation is one of *prajñaptisat* entities producing *prajñaptisat* entities in a play which has only empirical significance. Thus, the system is closed in upon itself and cannot seek outside itself for ontological justification since this would give the system an ultimate, albeit derivative, status which it lacks. Like dream entities causing other dream entities, the entire stream, Candrakīrti observes, has only phenomenal existence where questions of ontological justification are completely out of place. Ultimately, of course, there is no foundation for a *prajñaptisat* entity—but then ultimately there is no such entity.[69]

The primary Mahāyāna critique of the Abhidharma model, represented particularly by the Sarvāstivāda, is that it leads to a form of pluralistic absolutism, in that *dharmas* are established as self-sufficient (*svabhāva*), immutable (*na anyathābhāva*), and unoriginated absolutes. This is an unacceptable conclusion for the Abhidharmist, for whom it is hoped such an insight will lead to the realization that even this dharmic classification is merely *prajñapti sat* and purely conventional (*saṃvṛti*).

To sum up the basic Prajñāpāramitā critique of the Sarvāstivāda Abhidharma, one might suggest the following. To assert the primary existence (*dravya sat*) over and above the functional manifestation of that factor (*dharma*) is to abstract that factor from its actual occurrence. For the Mahāyāna this proliferation of abstractions (*prapañca*) leads one to imagine that factor as somehow separable from its given manifestational and causal environment. Such a view contravenes the causally-co-dependent (*pratītyasamutpanna*) nature of that factor. Thus, to assert that a *dharma* has a primary (*dravya / paramārtha sat*), and therefore unchanging (*asaṃskṛta*) essence (*svabhāva*), is not only to extrapolate beyond the realms of the "given," it is also blatantly to contradict it, since we experience the cessation (*nirodha*) of a *dharma* almost immediately upon its initial origination (*utpāda*). Thus, an appeal can be made to our experience of change and impermanence (*anitya*) as evidence for the inappropriateness of the attribution of an "essence" (*svabhāva*) to a *dharma*. All instances of the attribution of *svabhāva* therefore result in the fallacy of misplaced absolutism since there is no factor of our experience that can be said to transcend its own occurrence as a causally-dependent factor. For the Prajñāpāramitā this is the universality of *dharmaśūnyatā*.

CHAPTER

4

Non-Origination in the *Gauḍapādīya-kārikā*: Early Vedāntic Ontology and Madhyamaka Buddhism

Mahāyāna Buddhism and the Fourth *Prakaraṇa* of the GK

The fourth *prakaraṇa* of the *Gauḍapādīya-kārikā* shows a keen interest and involvement in the central doctrinal themes of the Mahāyāna Buddhist tradition. Consider for instances the following verses:

> IV.42: *upalambhāt samācārād astivastutvavādinām, jātis tu deśitā buddhair ajātes trasatāṃ sadā.* Origination has been taught by the Buddhas for those whom, due to perception and common consent, maintain that objectivity exists (*astivastutvavādin*) and are afraid of non-origination.

> IV.44: *upalambhāt samācārān māyāhastī yathocyate, upalambhāt samācārād asti vastu tathocyate.* As the illusory elephant is said to exist owing to the perception [of it] and common consent, likewise it is said that an object (*vastu*) exists on account of [its] perception and common consent.

In these verses the author suggests that the conception of origination is based upon perception and common consent (i.e. conventional truth). Therefore, in order to understand the truth of non-origination one needs to grasp the nature of conventional truth on the one hand and the nature of perception on the other. Both subjects are dealt with in great detail by the Madhyamaka and Yogācāra schools of philosophy.

The Two Truths in the Mahāyāna Tradition: the Nature of Saṃvṛti

The distinction between conventional (*saṃvṛti*) and ultimate truth (*paramārtha satya*) is central to Mahāyāna Buddhist philosophy. The implicit antecedents of the distinction between the two truths can be traced back to the *sūtras* of the *Tripiṭaka*.[1] The idea, for instance, is already implicit in the conception of the Buddha as a "healing physician."[2] The Buddha teaches according to the propensity of the student. This is apparent from a number of occasions where the Buddha responds differently to the same question, the criterion for determining an answer being the level of understanding and intent of the questioner.[3] In fact the Buddhist teaching of no-self (*anātman*) requires that some form of distinction be made between conventional discourse which involves the frequent use of personal pronouns such as "she" or "he," and theoretical discourse which necessitates strict scholastic precision.

The distinction between conventional and ultimate, however, seems to have been explicitly drawn for the first time by Buddhist scholars in an attempt to reconcile conflicting statements within the canon.[4] In this context, statements made by the Buddha were divided into two categories—texts of final import (*nītārtha*) and texts of secondary import (*neyārtha*). The scholastic precision of the teaching of no-self was further developed by Abhidharma scholars. As we have seen, the Buddha proclaimed a doctrine of no-self and yet continued to use personal pronouns in everyday discourse. The reason for this is clear: the Buddha denied the efficacy of terminology presupposing a "self" only in contexts where he was being precise and definitive and *not* in conventional language. The refusal to adopt the "personalist" language of conventional discourse would have made coherent discourse (and teaching) virtually impossible. Developing upon this distinction Abhidharmists distinguished between nominal existence (*prajñapti sat*) and substantial existence (*dravya sat*). The classical definition of the distinction between the two is found in the *Abhidharmakośa*.

> If the awareness of something does not operate after that thing is physically broken up or separated by the mind into other things, it exists conventionally like a pot or water; others exist ultimately.[5]

The distinction between nominal existence (*prajñapti sat*) and substantial existence (*dravya sat*) is crucial to the development of the Madhyamaka perspective, that amounts to a further deconstruction of the level of substantial entities (*dravya sat*), so as to render all factors (*dharmas*) nominal in their existence (*prajñapti sat*).[6] The distinction between ultimate and conventional, however, remains crucial to Madhyamaka in that it circumvents the threat of an encroaching nihilism. Emptiness is not mere nothingness!

The *MūlaMadhyamakakārikās* (MMK) stresses the importance of the distinction between conventional truth (*saṃvṛtisatya*) and the ultimate import (*paramārtha*) of the Buddha's message. Thus MMK 24.8–10 reads:

> The teaching of the *dharma* by the Buddhas rests upon the two truths: worldly conventional truth and truth in the ultimate sense. Those who do not discern the distinction between these two truths do not discern the profound truth (*tattva*) in the teaching of the Buddha. Without relying upon the practical, the ultimate is not taught. Without understanding the ultimate, one cannot attain *nirvāṇa*.[7]

Mervyn Sprung maintains that,

> Though the notion of two truths (*satyadvaya*) is implicit in Buddhism from the beginning, as it is in Vedānta and, indeed, in any philosophy or religion that holds to a norm distinct from the everyday, Mādhyamika alone makes the distinction into its crucial thought.[8]

Nevertheless, in the context of the Madhyamaka, it would be a mistake to take *satyadvaya* as anything other than a distinction between "levels of meaning" (*artha*). The "two truths" must not be seen in terms of two specific "levels of reality," for to do this would be to undermine Nāgārjuna's denial of a difference between *saṃsāra* and *nirvāṇa* (MMK 25.19–20). *Saṃvṛtisatya* is the conventional and "concealing" level of meaning, while *paramārthasatya* is the supreme or "ultimate meaning" (*parama-artha*). In contradistinction to the conception of two truths found in the Sarvāstivāda school, the Madhyamaka distinction between the two truths is semantic and not ontological.

Nāgārjuna accepted the practical distinction between ultimate and conventional truth, but this is essentially pragmatic and derives from his analysis of all *dharmas* as essentially nominal entities (*prajñapti sat*); it should not be taken to be a distinction between two independently existent realms. The emphasis upon *satyadvaya* as an ontological distinction in Nāgārjuna's corpus of works has only perpetuated an understanding of *śūnyatā* as some form of absolute reality "behind" appearances, when in fact his entire philosophy is an attack upon the acceptance of any distinctions whatsoever as absolute. This is understandable in the West given its philosophical background in the absolutisms of Hegel and Bradley etc., but that does not make it any more excusable.

When we come to consider the later works of the Indian Mahāyāna schools it is important to note that there are, in fact, two Sanskrit versions of the Buddhist term for "conventional truth." On the one hand, we find "*saṃvṛti*," from the root *vṛ* meaning to "cover, screen, veil, conceal, hide, surround or obstruct."[9] On the other hand, one sometimes find the term "*saṃvṛtti*," from the root *vṛt* meaning "to turn, turn around, proceed or advance," and "to take place, occur, or exist."[10] "*Saṃvṛti*," as its etymology suggests, points to that truth which conceals or obscures (*saṃvṛti-satya*) ultimate reality. The primary connotation of "*saṃvṛtti*," however, suggests that *saṃvṛtti-satya* is the truth which "comes about" or "arises within the world" itself.[11]

Candrakīrti gives three etymological meanings of the term conventional truth (*saṃvṛti/saṃvṛtti*) in his *Prasannapadā* (24.8/492.10–12). They are:

1. A "masking on all sides" (*samantād varaṇam*). *Saṃvṛti* is not knowing (*ajñāna*) caused by the veil of ignorance (*avidyā*) common to all.[12]
2. "Inter-dependent existence" (*paraspara-saṃbhavana*). Here the world of *saṃvṛti* (or does Candrakīrti imply *saṃvṛtti* from the root *vṛt* in this context?), is said to occur due to the "mutual support" (*anyonya-samāśrayeṇa*) of its component factors.
3. "Symbolic and worldly discourse" (*saṃketo loka-vyavahāraḥ*). *Saṃvṛti* is the set of conventions set up through linguistic symbols, social discourse, and custom.

In his *Madhyamakāvatāra* (MĀ) Candrakīrti further describes *saṃvṛti-satya* as that which is revealed through false perception (*mṛṣādṛś*).[13] As such it is "the delusion (*moha*) which obstructs the intrinsic-nature (*svabhāvāvaraṇād*) of things."[14] The fundamental connotation of *saṃvṛti* for Candrakīrti then seems to be that of a veil obscuring the ultimate truth. Exclusive emphasis upon this conception of conventional truth, however, drives a wedge between conventional and ultimate that would seem to make it impossible to establish a relationship between the two. If this were the case how could the ultimate truth of the Buddha's doctrine ever be conveyed by means of the conventional? For, as Nāgārjuna notes,

> Without relying upon the practical, the ultimate is not taught. Without understanding the ultimate, one cannot attain *nirvāṇa*.[15]

Thus, it is necessary to emphasize the fact that conventional truth is not simply "erronous perception" or the "delusion which hides reality," since there would then be no legitimate grounds for describing *saṃvṛti* as truth (*satya*) in any meaningful sense. Such a simplistic analysis of *saṃvṛti* as simply delusory would be a distinction not between two truths but between truth and falsehood. Therefore, there must be a meaningful sense in which *saṃvṛti* is veridical, or at least a sense in which it can convey something of the import of ultimate truth. Bhāvaviveka's distinction between false worldly convention (*mithyāsaṃvṛti*) and true worldly convention (*tathyasaṃvṛti*) was clearly an attempt to express the fundamental ambivalence of the notion of *saṃvṛti*—that is the polarity between worldly convention as a veil covering ultimate truth on the one hand and worldly convention as the conceptual "vehicle" or means whereby the ultimate is expressed on the other. The more positive aspects of the term *saṃvṛti* are conveyed by Candrakīrti in his explanations of the term as "the dependently-existent" and "conventional discourse." That Candrakīrti generally envisages *saṃvṛti* in the sense of occlusion can be seen from his usage of the term and from his use of the term "*saṃvṛti-mātra*," convention-only, a compound that implies a negative appraisal of conventional truth and an implicit contrasting of it with ultimate truth.

It is clear that the Madhyamaka distinction between *saṃvṛti* and *paramārtha* is open to abuse and misunderstanding. Sthiramati in his *Madhyāntavibhāgaṭīkā* gives an alternative analysis of conventional truth (*saṃvṛti-satya*) in conformity to the Yogācāra conception of the three own-beings (*trisvabhāva*), which is itself an attempt to clarify the nature of the two truths.[16] Thus Sthiramati suggests that *saṃvṛti* can be understood as,

1. "Designation" (*prajñapti*). This is the establishment of names (*nāmābhilāpa*) and the positing of substantial existence (*vyavasthāna*) based upon those names. This conforms to the *parikalpita* aspect of conscious activity and is roughly equivalent to Candrakīrti's notion of *saṃvṛti* as "symbolic discourse" (Candrakīrti 3).
2. "Ascertainment" (*pratipatti*). Sthiramati explains this as "attachment to an object (*arthābhiniveśa*), despite its non-existence."[17] This is conventional truth functioning as the actual operation of conceptualization (*vikalpa*) and conforms to the *paratantra* aspect of conscious activity.
3. "Manifestation" (*udbhāvanā*). Here language functions as the vehicle for the appearance (*saṃdarśana*) of ultimate truth. This

is the fulfilled or perfected (*parinişpanna*) aspect of conventional truth. Here linguistic conventions are used to describe things "just as they are" (*yathābhūta*).

The *pratipatti* mode of conventional truth (Sthiramati 2) represents the actual process whereby *saṃvṛti-satya* operates, that is in a relationship of mutual dependence (cf. Candrakīrti 2). *Prajñapti* denotes the everyday and unenlightened mode (*avasara*) of conventional truth, where names and designations (*prajñapti*) are (mistakenly) taken to be sounds corresponding directly to independently existent entities. The *udbhāvanā* mode of conventional truth is that which is embodied in the Mahāyāna teachings; it is the correct application (*prayojana*) of conventional language for the manifestation of ultimate truth (*paramārtha-satya*). The interesting feature of Sthiramati's analysis is the suggestion that words describing the ultimate (such as *śūnyatā*) are in actual fact still a part of the conventional (*saṃvṛti*) realm. Nevertheless, such concepts, if utilized correctly (*prayojana*) may still function as pointers (*prajñapti*) to the ultimate truth. Insofar as they perform this function, concepts do indeed allow for the manifestation (*udbhāvanā*) of ultimate truth in conventional discourse.

The Two Truths in the Gauḍapādīya-kārikā

The GK also upholds the doctrine of two truths, though this is less explicitly developed in the first three *prakaraṇas.* In the Buddhistic fourth *prakaraṇa* one can discern different shades of meaning with regard to ultimate and conventional truth.

In GK IV.97 we find the use of the term "*āvaraṇa*"—denoting the veil which masks ultimate reality. This conforms to the understanding of conventional truth as universal ignorance or occlusion (Candrakīrti 1). In GK IV.44 and 45, however, we find the occurrence of "*samācārād*," expressing the idea that conventional truth is dependent upon "common consent," as well as perception (*upalambha*). This clearly corresponds to Candrakīrti's conception of *saṃvṛti* as "symbolic discourse" (*saṃketa*, Candrakīrti 3).

In GK IV 73 and 74 a distinction is made within the conventional realm between that which is *kalpita-saṃvṛtyā* and that which is *paratantra-abhisaṃvṛti.*

> IV.73: *yo'sti kalpitasaṃvṛtyā paramārthena nāsty asau, paratantrābhisaṃvṛtyā syān nāsti paramārthataḥ.*

That which exists according to the imagined conventional [reality] (*kalpita-saṃvṛti*) does not exist in ultimate reality. It may exist in the relative aspect (*paratantra*) of conventional [reality], [but it] does not exist in ultimate reality.

IV.74: *ajaḥ kalpitasaṃvṛtyā paramārthena nāpy ajaḥ, paratantrābhiniṣpattyā saṃvṛtyā jāyate tu saḥ.*
What is even unoriginated in the imaginary conventional [reality] is not even unoriginated in ultimate reality. But that is originated with the relative aspect of *saṃvṛti* as its cause.

This distinction would seem to be dependent upon the Yogācāra conception of three own-beings. The point being that one can distinguish between that which is merely fabricated (*kalpita*) and that which has some form of relative existence, dependent upon causal conditions and worldly consensus (*paratantro 'bhihsaṃvṛtyā*). On this view "*kalpitasaṃvṛti*" conforms to the conventional truth as designation (*prajñapti*) and occlusion (*āvaraṇa*) (Sthiramati 1 and Candrakīrti 1). The use of *paratantra* in IV.74, therefore, would seem to conform to "ascertainment" (*pratipatti*, Sthiramati 2) and "interdependent existence" (*paraspara-saṃbhavana*, Candrakīrti 2). While one cannot deduce from this that the author of GK IV was aware of the works of Candrakīrti and Sthiramati, one can establish that GK IV accepts the validity of a relative or dependently-existent category (*paratantra*) within the conventional realm. This distinction, however, is wholly contained within the conventional realm, for the author of GK IV clearly believes that even a relative existent does not exist on an ultimate level.[18]

The Gauḍapādian tradition, however, adds yet another shade to the various meanings of the term "*saṃvṛti*. In GK II.1, 4, and IV.33 we find the terms "*saṃvṛtatvam*" and "*saṃvṛtā*"—meaning "to be enclosed." Here these terms are used in the context of an analysis of states of consciousness in order to show that so-called "normative" (i.e. unenlightened) experience is "state-bound." All such experience is "located within" (*antaḥsthāna*) the fluctuating mind. This conception has clearly been influenced by the Yogācāra analysis of the nature of waking and dream experience. The application of the term *saṃvṛti* to an analysis of the nature of perceptual experience, however, seems to be a particular innovation of GK, despite the fact that the theoretical background for this move was initiated by the Yogācārins.

As we have seen there is a concern within the Buddhist tradition to avoid the extremes of eternalism and nihilism. This concern, however, does not apply outside the Buddhist tradition where the basic premises upon which the Buddhist Middle Path is based are not accepted. Nevertheless, the author of the fourth *prakaraṇa* of the GK is equally keen to avoid the charges of eternalism and nihilism, as the following verses confirm.

> IV.57: *saṃvṛtyā jāyate sarvaṃ śāsvataṃ tena nāsti vai, sadbhāvena hy ajaṃ sarvam ucchedas tena nāsti vai.*
> All is born according to the conventional; therefore, in fact there is no eternal. In terms of reality, all is unborn; thus, there is no annihilated.
>
> IV.58: *dharmā ya iti jāyante saṃvṛtyā te na tattvataḥ, janma māyopamaṃ teṣāṃ sā ca māyā na vidyate.*
> Those *dharmas* said to be born by convention are not born in reality. Their birth is like *māyā*, and that *māyā* itself does not exist.
>
> IV.59: *yathā māyāmayād bījāj jāyate tanmayo 'ṅkuraḥ, nāsau nityo na cocchedī tadvad dharmeṣu yojanā.*
> Like a *māyā*-made seed, a sprout of the same nature is born. It is neither permanent nor destructible; so likewise is it for *dharmas*.
>
> IV.60: *nājeṣu sarvadharmeṣu śāsvatāśāsvatābhidhā, yatra varṇā na vartante vivekas tatra nocyate.*
> The terms "eternal" and "non-eternal" do not apply to all the unoriginated *dharmas*. Where words do not function (lit. exist) discrimination (*viveka*) is not spoken of.

If the author of GK IV is not an adherent of the Buddhist tradition, why is there so much concern to avoid Buddhist heterodoxical positions?[19] To answer this question properly requires a further investigation of the relationship between the GK and the cardinal philosophical texts of the Mahāyāna Buddhist tradition. With this in mind, let us consider the philosophical basis of the doctrine of non-origination (*ajātivāda*).

Foundations of Non-Origination: The Paradox of Change

Both the MMK and the GK use the analogies of dream and illusion to explain the world of change:

> *yathā māyā yathā svapno gandharvanagaraṃ yathā, tathotpādas tathā sthānaṃ tathā bhaṅga udāhṛtam.*

Like an illusion, like a dream, like a castle in the air, thus is origination, thus is duration, thus is destruction declared. (MMK XVIII.34)

svapnamāye yathā dṛṣṭe gandharvanagaraṃ yathā, tathā viśvam idaṃ dṛṣṭaṃ vedānteṣu vicakṣaṇaiḥ.
As are seen dream and illusion and a castle in the air, so also is this whole universe seen by those well-versed in the Vedāntas. (GK II.31)

The similarity between these two verses is further evidence that the author of the GK has "borrowed" from the MMK and certainly it is difficult for any but the most partisan scholar to deny the influence of the Madhyamaka upon the *Gauḍapādīya-kārikā* as a whole.

The *MūlaMadhyamakakārikā* (MMK) begins with a critical analysis of causal conditions (*pratyaya*). Nāgārjuna opens his work with an emphatic denial of the origination of beings. Thus the first verse states that:

na svato nāpi parato na dvābhyāṃ nāpy ahetutaḥ, utpannā jātu vidyante bhāvāḥ kvacana kecana.
No entities whatsoever are ever found originated from themselves, from another, from both nor causelessly.

The fourth *prakaraṇa* of the GK likewise states in *kārikā* 22,

svato vā parato vāpi na kiñcid vastu jāyate, sad asat sadasad vāpi na kiñcid vastu jāyate.
Nothing (*vastu*) whatsoever is originated either from itself or from something else; nothing whatsoever existent, non-existent, or both existent and non-existent is originated.

The similarity of these two statements has often been taken as evidence for the acceptance of some form of absolutism and as such both the MMK and the GK are said to uphold the doctrine of non-origination (*ajātivāda*). Vidhushekhara Bhattacharya maintains that "It is to be noted here that Gauḍapāda is a Vedāntist, and yet he accepts the doctrine of non-origination of the *Advayavādins* or Buddhists expressing his approval."[20] Mahadevan agrees, stating that "The doctrine of non-origination (*ajāti*) which Gauḍapāda advocates is essentially a Mādhyamika view."[21] S. S. Roy accepts this claiming that "Those who maintain that Gauḍapāda is a Buddhist derive strength from the position that Gauḍapāda has deliberately voted in favor of *ajātivāda*, which is entailed by *Advayavāda*."[22] Some scholars, however, have noted a difference between the doctrines in Buddhism and Advaita, albeit in the main to substantiate the traditional view that the GK is not reliant upon Buddhist ideas. Sangamlal Pandey states that "*Ajātivāda* which is common to both Advaita and Buddhism is not the same in the two systems." In Vedānta *ajātivāda* is "at once the negation of creation and assertion of the absolute reality. In Buddhism, however, it simply denotes the negation of creation."[23]

Although such an awareness of distinctions is admirable and while it is true that *ajātivāda* can be interpreted in various manners, the tendency for scholars to label Indian philosophers with Sanskrit terms ending in "*vādin*" can often be misleading. Pandey's interpretation of "*śūnyatā*" does a grave injustice to the Madhyamaka position which is not merely a nihilistic denial of the world. As we have seen, all Buddhists are keen to avoid the charge of nihilism which is seen as an extreme view advocated by some non-Buddhists. Unlike the author of the GK, however, Nāgārjuna does not uphold *ajātivāda*—the absolutistic doctrine of non-origination since the true import of *śūnyatā* is said to be a denial of all views including the absolutistic view that all things exist in some unoriginated form. To appreciate the differences between Madhyamaka and Gauḍapādian thought on this issue requires an examination of the philosophical roots of non-origination.

The philosophical basis of *ajātivāda* in the GK is elucidated in GK II.6 (and again in IV.31): *ādāv ante ca yan nāsti vartamāne 'pi tat tathā*, "That which does not exist in the beginning and the end is equally so in the present." This is precisely because (GK III.21):

> *na bhavaty amṛtam martyaṃ na martyam amṛtaṃ tathā, prakṛter anyathābhāvo na kathañcid bhaviṣyati.*
> The deathless cannot become subject to death, similarly that which is subject to death cannot become deathless. The becoming otherwise (i.e. change) of nature in no way occurs.[24]

This basic principle is shared by Nāgārjuna in his examination of own-being (*svabhāva*) and lies as the basis of the philosophies of both the MMK and the GK. Thus MMK XV.8 declares that:

> *yady astitvaṃ prakṛtyā syān na bhaved asya nāstitā, prakṛter anyathābhāvo na hi jatūpapadyate.*
> If there were existence by nature, then there would not be its non-existence, for a change of nature does not occur.

The primary target for Nāgārjuna's arguments in the MMK seem to have been the "substantialist" doctrines of the Abhidharma schools.

As we have seen previously, the abhidharmic doctrine of radical momentariness renders the common sense notion of change redundant. A compounded *dharma* lasts for a moment (*kṣaṇa*) and then ceases, to be replaced by another. No change of substance occurs, merely a succession of evanescent occurrences. As Richard Robinson suggests:

> If each moment has three sub-moments—arising, abiding, and ceasing—then each sub-moment has three sub-sub-moments of arising, abiding, and ceasing; arising has arising, abiding, and ceasing, abiding has arising, abiding, and ceasing, and ceasing has arising, abiding, and ceasing, and so on *ad infinitum*. . .The doctrine of momentariness (*kṣaṇikatva*) takes as axiomatic that no *dharma* occurs in two moments. Nāgārjuna shows that if each moment is segmentable into several sub-moments, then no *dharma* can occur at all.[25]

B. K. Matilal with characteristic breadth of vision explains the general principle of the argument with great clarity:

> Nāgārjuna uses the familiar paradox of causation, i.e. the paradox of change and permanence. This paradox, according to Nāgārjuna, shows that a thing cannot possess its own-nature; its essence. If a thing has its own-nature it cannot change, for that would go against the presumed unchangeability of own-nature; and if the thing does not have its own-nature then change cannot take place either, for "change" means transformation of the own-nature into something else.[26]

The problem of the apparent incompatibility of the notions of "intrinsic nature" and change is the primary impetus and starting point for both Nāgārjuna's philosophy and the many philosophies of absolutism both East and West.[27] Thus, the nineteenth century English Absolutist Francis Herbert Bradley explains the basic problem in the following manner:

> Something, A, changes, and therefore it cannot be permanent. On the other hand, if A is not permanent, what is it that changes? It will no longer be A, but something else. In other words, let A be free from change in time and it does not change. But let it contain change, and at once it becomes A^1, A^2, A^3. Then what becomes of A, and of its change, for we are left with something else? Again, we may put the problem thus. The diverse states of A must exist within one time; and yet they cannot, because they are successive. Thus, it is required that A must change; and, for this, two characters, not incompatible, must be present at once.[28]

However it would seem that change has to occur in A at some point; Bradley thus continues,

> . . . this is clearly impossible, for what could have altered it? Not any other thing, for you have taken the whole course of events. And, again, not itself, for you have got itself already without any change. In short, if the cause can endure unchanged for any [of] the very smallest piece of duration, then it must endure for ever. It cannot pass into the effect, and it therefore is not a cause at all.[29]

It is clear that the same perplexity spurred Nāgārjuna onto a denial of the reality of both "own-nature" (*svabhāva*) and "other-nature" (*parabhāva*)—"for if there is no 'own nature' how can there be an 'other nature'?"[30]

The dilemma seems to provide two possible responses.[31] On the one hand one could choose to deny the possibility of origination, and cessation (i.e. change), in which case one is left with an unoriginated and unchanging reality. On the other hand one could deny own-nature, which would deprive all factors of an essence. Nāgārjuna clearly opts for the latter since it allows for the possibility of origination and change. This much can be gleaned from a careful analysis of MMK XV.8. Nāgārjuna states that "If there were existence by nature there could not be its non-existence." He is pointing, therefore, to the absolutistic consequences of the belief that things have an intrinsic nature by which they exist. If this were the case, he suggests, they could never cease to exist. Clearly, Nāgārjuna wishes us to see the undesirability of such a consequence.

In the GK, however, we find the adoption of the alternative position, i.e. a radical absolutism which denies the existence and efficacy of change (origination, cessation etc.) in favor of an unoriginated ultimate reality. As seen above Nāgārjuna bases his ideas on the primacy of impermanence (*anityatā*), one of the three marks of existence according to the Buddhist. The contrast between these two views reflects their divergent, underlying paradigms. Both the MMK and the GK focus upon the inconsistencies of the common sense notions of duality and change. In the former case, however, this is because all is impermanent (*anitya*) and lacking in self-existence (*anātman*), while in the latter it is because change is not possible for something that exists (for the authors of the GK "to exist" is "to exist absolutely"!). Thus in the debate over the status of an object (A) and its various modes or states of manifestation (x^1, x^2, x^3 etc.) the Buddhist accepts the empirical efficacy of changes in states but does not accept the independent reality of the possessor of those states (A). This is the doctrine of no-self which rejects such notions as mentally fabricated reifications (*prapañca*). In Advaita Vedānta (A) is accepted and it is the manifested states that are denied ultimate reality since reality cannot change. Thus, both the Madhyamaka and Gauḍapādian Advaita derive their positions from the logical dichotomy between an entity and change.[32] The GK and the subsequent Advaita Vedānta school is fundamentally interested in upholding the unconditioned nature (the *ātman*) of an entity, while the Madhyamaka wishes to show the emptiness (or lack of an abiding self—*anātmatā*) of that same entity, given that it changes. Both as it were grasp separate "horns" of the dilemma. The consequence, however, is a denial of common sense notions of change and origination on both sides.

In a nutshell, then, the philosophical difference between the Mādhyamika and the absolutistic Advaitin is that while the former maintains that the self-contradictory nature of change points to the impossibility of a fixed nature to anything, the latter relegates "change" to the realm of appearance, declaring that reality is thereby the unchanging basis to these appearances.

So far we have established that the GK is dependent upon the philosophical ideas and arguments of the early Madhyamaka school (and in all likelihood the MMK itself) for its doctrine of non-origination. We have also suggested that the doctrine of non-origination as it occurs in the GK is absolutistic and is therefore to be distinguished from the Madhyamaka position which is fundamentally a rejection of absolutism. How then does the author of the GK derive absolutistic consequences from a text (the MMK) which is so vehemently anti-absolutistic? To begin to answer this question we must consider Nāgārjuna's refutation of absolutism (*svabhāva-vāda*) in the MMK more closely.

Nāgārjuna's Refutation of Absolutism (svabhāvavāda) *and the Gauḍapādian Response*

In MMK 24.1–6 Nāgārjuna gives objections to *śūnyatā* which seem to display an absolutistic interpretation of it. These objections are turned back upon the *pūrvapakṣin* (*svabhāva-vādin*) who is said to be guilty of "attributing your errors to us."[33] These objections are doubly important for they not only allow us to provide an appropriate appraisal of the non-absolutism of Nāgārjuna, they also allow us to further evaluate the *ajātivāda* of the GK that appears to bear a remarkable resemblance to the logical consequences of what Nāgārjuna calls the "non-empty" (*aśūnya*) or substance view of reality (*svabhāva-vāda*). Thus, MMK 24.20f. states that:

> If all this is non-empty, then there would be no arising and no ceasing. . . How can that which exists by its own being come into existence? Hence for him who rejects emptiness, there is no arising. If the path has own being, then its following is not appropriate, but if the path is followed, then your path with own-being is not found. When there is no suffering, origin and cessation, where will the path lead to through the cessation of [that] suffering? If incomplete knowledge [of suffering] is due to own being, how [will there be] complete knowledge? [It would seem that] own being is not fixed? As with knowledge [of suffering], so are [it's] elimination, realization and development not admissible, nor are the four fruits. To one who holds onto "own being," how could the fruits be obtained, already obtained through own being?. . . No one will ever do right or wrong. What action of the non-empty could be done, since own being does not act?. . . You contradict all worldly practicalities when you contradict the emptiness of dependent origination. . . According to "own being" the world would be unoriginated, unceased, unchanging, and free from varying conditions.[34]

Nāgārjuna maintains that the only way to account for change is to understand that there is no abiding self-nature or essence to any factor of our experience. One should understand that there is no *dharma* that can be pinpointed from the flux of experience since all *dharmas* arise inter-dependently. Therefore,

> *yaḥ pratītyasamutpādaṃ paśyatīdaṃ sa paśyati, duḥkhaṃ samudayaṃ caiva nirodhaṃ mārgam eva ca.*
> He who sees dependent origination sees suffering, [its] origin, [its] cessation and the Path.[35]

Attempts to see some form of *ajātivāda* akin to the Gauḍapādian doctrine in the *śūnyatā* concept of Nāgārjuna are guilty of misreading the emptiness of all *dharmas* as a form of absolutism when in fact the "no-view" of emptiness is precisely an attempt to liberate oneself from belief in any absolutes. Elwin Jones puts this particular point well:

> The prime target of Nāgārjuna's criticism seems to have been the predisposition, whether of common sense or of philosophical speculation, to view the existing as somehow absolutely existing. If, however, something exists absolutely or really, then it has to be permanent and unchanging, and so never nonexistent; otherwise, it cannot have a real nature of being existent.[36]

The consequences of a substantialist view of reality, far from being seen as criticisms, are accepted as logical facts in the GK. Thus in II.32 we read:

na nirodho na cotpattir na baddho na ca sādakaḥ. na mumukṣur na vai mukta ity eṣā paramārthatā.
There is neither cessation nor origination; no one in bondage, no one aspiring, no one desirous of liberation, no one who is emancipated. This is the highest truth.

The GK "inverts" the implications of *śūnyatā* by maintaining that reality must have an intrinsic-nature (*svabhāva*) if it is to be reality in any meaningful sense of the term. As such, one might say that the position of the GK is that of the archetypal *aśūnyavādin*; a view which on Nāgārjunian premises would be a radical form of absolutism. The GK re-examines our common sense notion of reality in the light of the MMK's arguments and maintains that for something to be real it must be unchanging. Contrary to Nāgārjuna and against the entire spirit of the MMK, it is argued that reality has *svabhāva* precisely because it **must** have a "nature" in order to be reality. *Ajātivāda* in the GK then is the assertion of a fixed ultimate reality based upon the principle that nature cannot change (*prakṛter na anyathābhāva*). This is something of a reversal of the Madhyamaka position.

Emptiness (Śūnyatā) *and Non-dualism* (Advaita)

The Madhyamaka denial of own-nature (*svabhāva*) is fundamentally based upon the realization of *dharma-nairātmya*—the selflessness or essencelessness (*niḥsvabhāvatā*) of all factors. As such it is a logical extension of the Buddha's exposition of the lack of abiding self (*anātman*), which was understood by the Sarvāstivādins as the denial of a personal self (*pudgala-nairātmya*). Although *dharma-nairātmya* is not exclusive to the Mahāyāna tradition, it is here that it is explicitly developed on a systematic basis. The doctrine of no-abiding-self (*anātmatā*) is thereby extended to refer to all *dharmas* (*dharma-nairātmya*) and not just the conception of a personal self (*pudgala*). Thus *śūnyatā* is little more than the *anātmatā* of all *dharmas*. Arguments in support of universal emptiness, therefore, are often directed towards attempts to codify and analyze these *dharmas*. Clearly this is an attack which reaches the heart of Abhidharmic speculations.

In his critique of the concept of own-nature (*svabhāva*), Nāgārjuna undermines the very idea that one can distinguish between one *dharma* and another. Universal emptiness necessitates a denial of "boundaries." In the context of scholastic Buddhism the most fundamental "boundary" is that between *saṃskṛta* (compounded) and *asaṃskṛta* (uncompounded) *dharmas.* To promote the universality of *śūnyatā,* Nāgārjuna subverts this fundamental abhidharmic distinction,

> *utpādasthitibhaṅgānām asiddher nāsti saṃskṛtam, saṃskṛtasyāprasiddhau ca kathaṃ setsaty asaṃskṛtaṃ.*
> With the non-establishment of origination, duration and destruction, the compounded does not exist; and if the compounded is not established, how will there be an uncompounded? (MMK 7.33)

Streng in fact suggests that,

> Nāgārjuna's denial of distinctions correlates with the Buddha's opposition to theoretical speculations. The distinctions, claims Nāgārjuna, are not conducive to the cessation of ignorance and craving because they suggest that what is distinguished has some kind of intrinsic reality which "marks" it off from something else. In practical life it is necessary to recognize that a chair is not a table, that a gold coin is not the same as clay, and that a merchant who cheats is not identical with one who does not. However, a person who does not slip into the error of regarding these practical distinctions as ultimate facts is able to see that there is indeed neither one absolute substance nor many individual substances.[37]

The declaration that all *dharmas* are empty is a universal application of *anātmatā.* Denying any notion of an abiding self or "nature" involves a denial of duality (*dvaita/dvaya*) and difference (*bheda*); if all *dharmas* are empty of self-nature, there can be no boundaries between one *dharma* and another. Thus, "What indeed is 'that', what is 'another'?" (*kiṃ tad eva kim anyat,* MMK 25.23). Even the fundamental distinction between bondage (*saṃsāra*) and liberation (*nirvāṇa*) is subverted:

> 25.19: *na saṃsārasya nirvāṇāt kiṃcid asti viśeṣaṇaṃ, na nirvāṇasya saṃsārāt kiṃcid asti viśeṣaṇaṃ.*
> Of *saṃsāra*, there exists no feature that distinguishes it from *nirvāṇa*. Of *nirvāṇa*, there exists no feature that distinguishes it from *saṃsāra*.

This is not an identity of the two realms, for Nāgārjuna has already been at pains to show that there is no *dharma* that can be identified to begin with. The stanza can perhaps best be seen in the context of the general denial of a distinction between *saṃskṛta* and *asaṃskṛta.* Thus, the next stanza describes the relationship between *saṃsāra* and *nirvāṇa* in terms of their "delimitating boundaries" or "limits" (*koṭi*),

nirvāṇasya ca yā koṭiḥ saṃsārasya ca, na tayor antaraṃ kiṃcit susūkṣmam api vidyate.
The extreme limit of *nirvāṇa* is also the extreme limit of *saṃsāra*; there is not even a subtle something between them.

At times this can appear reminiscent of the non-dualism of the Advaita Vedānta school. Certainly the tendency to interpret the Madhyamaka school as an absolutistic system has contributed to a confusion between the fundamental conceptions of these two traditions. Both Madhyamaka and Advaita Vedānta deny that ultimate reality can be understood in a dualistic manner. In the former this amounts to a subversion of the notion of separate self-sufficiency (*niḥsvabhāvatā*), while in the latter non-difference is a proclamation of the reality of the non-dual substratum underlying all appearances.

In an analysis and a rejection of the various theories of causality on offer Nāgārjuna argues that they all presuppose a substantialist (*svabhāvatā*) view of reality, in other words all views are guilty of what might be called the "fallacy of reification." This is the tendency of language and its users to "objectify" concepts (*vikalpa*), thereby creating the illusion that the world of our experience is made up of real, unitary, and self-sufficient substances (*bhāva*). The result is *prapañca*—the incessant proliferation of concepts. The experience of a manifold world made up of boundaries and distinctions is caused by our attachment to the idea of a fixed nature (*svabhāva*) to the internal world of one's own "self" and to the "external" world of objects and other people (*bahirdhādhyātma*). It is important to understand that *niḥsvabhāvatā* is a denial of self in both of these realms and not just a denial of a personal self. This is the import of the Mahāyāna doctrine of *dharma-nairātmya*. As such, the saṃsāric world of suffering exists for as long as there is an adherence to a view of "self" (both subjectively and objectively) and liberation is the cessation of all such conceptions (*vikalpa/prapañca*). Thus, MMK 18.4–5 states that,

mamety aham iti kṣīṇe bahirdhādhyātmam eva ca, nirudhyata upādānaṃ tat kṣayāj janmanaḥ kṣayaḥ. karmakleśakṣayān mokṣaḥ karmakleśā vikalpataḥ, te prapañcāt prapañcas tu śūnyatāyāṃ nirudhyate.
When "mine" and "I", whether pertaining to an outer or an inner self, have ceased, there is a relinquishment of grasping; with that cessation, there is the ceasing of birth. On the cessation of the karmic defilements, there is liberation. For the one who constructs (*vikalpataḥ*) the karmic defilements [exist] due to conceptual proliferation (*prapañca*), but this conceptual proliferation ceases with emptiness.[38]

Compare this with a similar acceptance of egocentricity as the root cause of the manifold world in *Gauḍapādīya-kārikā* (GK) II.16 and IV.55, and 56:

> *jīvaṃ kalpayate pūrvaṃ tato bhāvān pṛthagvidhān, bahyān ādhyātmikāṃś caiva yathāvidyas tathāsmṛtiḥ.*
> [The *ātman*] first imagines the *jīva* (individual soul), and then different things, external and internal (objective and subjective); as one knows so does one recollect.

> *yāvad hetuphalāveśas tāvad dhetuphalodbhavaḥ, kṣīṇe hetuphalāveśe nāsti hetuphalodbhavaḥ. yāvad dhetuphalāveśaḥ saṃsāras tāvad āyataḥ, kṣīṇe hetuphalāveśe saṃsāro na prapadyate.*
> As long as there is attachment to cause and effect, so long does it arise; when the attachment to cause and effect ceases there is no arising of cause and effect. As long as there is attachment to cause and effect, so long is *saṃsāra* spread out; when attachment to cause and effect ceases one does not attain to *saṃsāra.*

For Advaita Vedānta the primary cause of bondage to *saṃsāra* is ignorance (*avidyā*) of the basic non-difference of *ātman* and Brahman. Attachment to an individualized self (*jīvātman*) is a gross error for in reality the aspirant must realize that she or he is identical with the universal ground of being (*sat*). Thus, a substrative metaphysics (*sad-adhiṣṭhana-vāda*) is a fundamental presupposition of the school, rooted as it is in the acceptance of *ātman* as the non-dual reality. Debate within the Vedānta school concerned the status of Brahman as the efficient and material cause of the universe. For the Mahāyāna Buddhist, however, *saṃsāra* is not supported by anything other than the inter-dependence of its own constituent factors (i.e. *pratītyasamutpāda*). The introduction of a universal substratum would lead to the subversion of both the dynamics of inter-dependence (the *pratītyasamutpanna* of all *dharmas*) and the denial of own-being (*niḥsvabhāva*). MMK XXII.16 is quick to point out that:

> *tathāgato yatsvabhāvas tatsvabhāvam idaṃ jagat, tathāgato niḥsvabhāvo niḥsvabhāvam idaṃ jagat.*
> Whatever is the own being of the Tathāgata, that is also the own being of this world. The Tathāgata is without own being, this world is without own being.

The belief in some form of "self-sufficient" existent, in other words the adherence to some form of absolutism, is precisely the target of

Nāgārjuna's incisive arguments. Because the MMK is written with the purpose of exposing the absolutistic implications of all doctrines it is not surprising that the text seems preoccupied with the terminology of absolutism. It is this feature of the logical corpus of Nāgārjuna's literary output which has contributed more than any other factor to the misinterpretation of *śūnyatā* as a concept denoting a substantial and unconditioned reality.

Non-Origination and Emptiness: The Madhyamaka and Advaita Perspectives

We have seen that Nāgārjuna rejects all metaphysical speculation (including the assertion of any form of absolutism). We have also suggested that the designation of his thought as "*śūnyavāda*" or any other similar doctrinal epithet (such as *ajātivāda* for instance), strictly speaking, may not be applicable to the import of his message. As we have seen, Nāgārjuna denies that he has a thesis to propound (*pratijñā*); *śūnyatā* is not to be understood as a dogma. It is conventional-talk, a designation, useful merely as a indicator (*prajñaptir upadāya*).[39]

Although Nāgārjuna uses the term "*dṛṣṭi*" in the MMK when he states that *śūnyatā* is not a view, it would seem that "*vāda*" would have been just as problematic. The realization (*prajñā*) of emptiness is an insight beyond the disputations of the *vādin*. This point will become clearer when we come to deal with the theory of non-conflict (*avirodhavāda*) that is found in the *Gauḍapādīya-kārikā*. It is unlikely given the MMK's denial of the appropriateness of the terms "*śūnya*" and "*aśūnya*,"[40] that Nāgārjuna would have accepted the title of *śūnyavādin*, (unless etymologically understood to mean "one who declares all doctrines to be empty"), although this does not prevent him from viewing things from the "perspective of emptiness" (*śūnyatā-darśana*).[41] In this respect, it is even more misleading to call Nāgārjuna and his Mādhyamika followers "*ajātivādins*," as many scholars have, since it is clear that the school does not accept the existence of an "unborn" substratum underlying the world.

One of the most important themes in Buddhist thought is the traditions own conception of itself as the "Middle Path," a feature of Buddhism established in the Buddha's first sermon. The Middle Path has both a doctrinal and a practical aspect. On a practical level the path of moderation is between the extremes of asceticism (self-torture) and licentiousness (self-indulgence). This feature of the Buddhist path was established as early as the Buddha's first sermon at Sarnath near Benares.

The doctrinal aspect of the path involves an attempt to avoid what the Buddhist tradition sees as "extreme views." Indeed, it is clear that from a Buddhist point of view the practical extremes of asceticism and licentiousness are in fact dependent upon extreme (and false) conceptions of the self. Ascetic practices are based upon the belief that the self is somehow separate from the five *skandhas* (thus one must submit the *skandhas* to rigid control). Self-indulgent practices are based upon the belief that the self is somehow identical with or inherent to the *skandhas.* For the Buddhist, neither of these views are appropriate since there is no-abiding-self (*anātman*), either in the five *skandhas* or beyond them.

In all Buddhist philosophical schools, therefore, the doctrinal extremes of eternalism and nihilism are to be carefully avoided. Either interpretation of Madhyamaka philosophy then is tantamount to seeing the school (and its notion of emptiness) in terms of one of the extremes that it so expressly denies. It is not so much the case that the Madhyamaka school endorses *ajātivāda*, but that it refutes origination (*jāti*) and non-origination (*ajāti*) as appropriate designations of "things as they are" (*yathābhūta*).[42] All *dharmas* are empty of essential nature (*svabhāva-śūnya*) and as such are inter-dependently arisen (*pratītyasamutpanna*).

If it is remains legitimate to designate Madhyamaka thought as *ajātivāda*, as many scholars have suggested, it is certainly not in the absolutistic sense that it is found in the GK. The Madhyamaka does call into question the ideas of origination and causation but this is coupled with a consistent rebuttal of the charge that it is asserting a rival position of its own. In stark contrast, to this the author of the GK argues that his position (*ajātivāda*) is in fact the basis of all other views. The distinction between Madhyamaka and Vedānta on this issue reflect two different conceptions of negatives such as "*ajāti*." In English, this distinction is reflected in the following two statements,

1. "There is no birth." (Madhyamaka), and
2. "There is an Unborn." (Advaita Vedānta).[43]

The Madhyamaka understanding of non-origination (*anutpāda, ajāti*) is an example of the first ("intransitive"?) use of the term "*ajāti*" where all essences are denied and yet no alternative proposition is put forward. Philosophically, this negation is known as non-implicatory negation (*prasajya-pratiṣedha*) as opposed to implicatory negation (*paryudāsa-pratiṣedha*) that implies the contrary position.[44] The explicit distinction between these two types of negation seems to have been first introduced by Bhāvaviveka.[45] Consequently, Bhāvaviveka's position became known as "Svatantrika Madhyamaka" in order to distinguish it from that of Candrakīrti (Prāsaṅgika Madhyamaka).[46] The source of the distinction between Svatantrika and Prāsaṅgika seems to have been based upon the question of the validity of adopting independent logical arguments to substantiate the Madhyamaka point of view (*darśana*). Bhāvaviveka and his successors accepted the valid use of independent syllogisms whereas Candrakīrti and his followers did not. This difference of opinion seems to derive from their respective interpretations of the two-truths scheme. For Bhāvaviveka, conventional truth could be divided into false (*mithyā*) and true (*tathya*) convention (*saṃvṛti*). There is a legitimate sense, therefore, in which the ultimate import (*parama-artha*) of the Buddha's teaching can be expressed in conventional discourse and disputation. For Candrakīrti, however, no such distinction between the conventional realm is ever made explicit. Conventional truth exists in polar opposition to ultimate truth; it is the veil which obscures it from view. Consequently, for the latter conventional discourse and independent logical arguments can never be fully redeemed of their capacity to produce delusion (*moha*) and ignorance (*avidyā*). Therefore, the Prāsaṅgika Mādhyamika endeavors to establish *śūnyatā* on the basis of their refutation of all other points of view and not through the use of independent arguments.

It is clear, however, that even the early texts of the Madhyamaka school never considered their negation of origination to imply the existence of an unoriginated absolute. Indeed Nāgārjuna's statement that "I have no (rival) theory (*pratijñā*) to put forward" presupposes that one can criticize a view without necessarily accepting its opposite (i.e. non-implicatory negation, *prasajya-pratiṣedha*). This is the Madhyamaka conception of the Middle Path, clinging neither to the "positive" nor to the "negative" extreme. Whatever the nature of the later disputes between the Svātantrikas and the Prāsaṅgikas, Indian Madhyamaka has always shown a keen awareness of the pitfalls of absolutism. Thus in chapter eight of his MHK, we find Bhāvaviveka explaining the difference between the Madhyamaka and Vedānta conceptions of non-origination (*ajāti*) on the grounds that for the former

> "Non-origination (*ajāti*) is a phenomenon (*dharma*) which resembles origination (*jāti*), but it exists [only] as the non-existence [of origination]. It is [therefore] not at all (*nāpi na*) logical that [this phenomenon of non-origination] is identical with the Self or abiding in it."[47]

For Bhāvaviveka non-origination (*ajāti*) means "not originated" and does not imply an unoriginated absolute (MHK 8.91ab.) In the GK, however, it is clear that ontological implications are in fact drawn from the denial of a change in nature. "Reality is unoriginated!" Tentatively one might suggest that the authors of the GK understand the negation of origination to be of the implicatory kind (*paryudāsa-pratiṣedha*) since they wish to argue that the refutations of origination contained within the text imply the reality of an unoriginated absolute. Implicatory negation involves the implicit acceptance of an alternative point of view. Thus, the term "*ajāti*" in its denial of origination would in this case also imply the existence of the unoriginated.

The Gauḍapādian doctrine of non-origination (*ajātivāda*) is not just a denial of origination but a proclamation of the unoriginated nature of Brahman. This is clear from an analysis of the attitude of the *Gauḍapādīya-kārikā* to other doctrines. All doctrines are said to lead to *ajātivāda* (GK III.17–22). Refutation is seen as the establishment of non-origination as the basis for all ontological theories. By refuting each other, the disputants thereby proclaim non-origination (GK III.17).

The difference between these respective conclusions reflect the contrasting paradigmatic presuppositions of the Madhyamaka and Advaita Vedānta traditions. The authors of the GK are steeped in the "theism" of the Vedic and Upaniṣadic texts.[48] Even the author of the fourth *prakaraṇa* is an heir to the *ātman* tradition which upholds permanence and constancy as the fundamental nature of reality. For the GK as a whole the appearance of the world can only be adequately explained if there is some unchanging substratum supporting its manifestation. Reality must have an unchanging intrinsic nature or it could not be "reality." This is clearly a Vedāntic and not a Madhyamaka conception of reality, despite the GK's propensity for Buddhist arguments and terminology.

Conversely, the Mādhyamika is grounded in the Buddhist conception of the world as impermanent (*anitya*) and lacking an-abiding-self (*anātman*). Thus we find MMK 21.4 putting forward the following axiomatic statement: "For impermanence is never absent in entities." In fact, for the Mādhyamika the only way that change can be accounted for is to accept that there is no abiding self-nature or essence to any factor of our experience (*dharma-nairātmya*). All *dharmas* arise interdependently. Thus in MMK 24.40 Nāgārjuna maintains that "He who sees dependent origination sees suffering, [its] origin, [its] cessation and the Path."

CHAPTER

5

Asparśa-yoga in the *Gauḍapādīya-kārikā*

Having considered the Gauḍapādian doctrine of the non-origination (*ajāti*) of *ātman* in the light of Mahāyāna speculation concerning the non-origination of *dharmas*, we shall now turn to the other central theme of Gauḍapādian philosophy, i.e. the phenomenological analysis of experience outlined in the text. The conceptual focus for our discussion of this will be the notion of "*asparśa-yoga*" an idea as central to the Gauḍapādian conception of reality as the doctrine of non-origination. It is to "*asparśa-yoga*," therefore, that we shall now turn.

The term "*asparśa-yoga*" occurs only twice in the 215 verses of the *Gauḍapādīya-kārikā*, in the third and fourth *prakaraṇas* respectively.[1] Its importance, however, should not be underestimated for it is connected to a number of issues central to the distinctive position of the text as a whole. The notion of non-contact (*asparśa*) has a number of interesting connotations which place it in the forefront of early *advaita* philosophy. First, it can be seen as a negation of tactile experience. Touch (*sparśa*) is perhaps the most basic of the five sense-faculties (excluding the mind (*manas*), that is sometimes treated as a sixth sense-faculty in India, and with which we shall deal later). Arguably, one could lose any one of the other four senses and yet still grasp the idea of "externality." However, if one had no sense of touch it is doubtful that the boundary between "self" and "other" would have developed at all. Certainly the ability to make a distinction between oneself as subject and everything else as object seems to be based to a greater or lesser degree upon the concept of "externality"; a concept that we derive from our tactile experience of bodily boundaries. Equally, if there is no sense of touch, there can be no feeling of pain. Thus, "*asparśa*" is also connected to the soteriological aim of the cessation of suffering (*duḥkha*).[2]

As with the English terms "touch" and "contact," "*sparśa*" may also refer to sensory contact in general rather than specifically to tactile experience. The meditative practice of sensory withdrawal (*pratyāhāra*) is the prevention of contact between the sense-faculties and their respective objects.[3] The notion of contact also may be said to presuppose the notion of duality, for one cannot have contact without at least two participating principles. A denial of contact then may equally be said to be linked to a denial of duality (*dvaita*).[4]

The most obvious interpretation of "*asparśayoga*" is that it denotes a form of meditative practice culminating in the realization of a state of non-contact (*asparśa*). A second possibility is that it is a technical term for the intended goal of such practice, i.e. a description of a meditative state. In this case the term "*asparśa-yoga*" may be rendered in English by "isolated-union," a phrase denoting something akin to the idea of "*kevalādvaita*," the "non-dualism of the isolated," an epithet sometimes used to describe Śaṇkara's conception of *Advaita*. *Asparśa* is a term which also conveys the very nature of Brahman as the Absolute; Brahman is the non-relative, that which exhibits no relations, that which is unaffected by change. If we are to pinpoint precisely what the term "*asparśa-yoga*" denotes, we must consider both of the above mentioned possibilities.

The question of Buddhist influence on the *Gauḍapādīya-kārikā* has already been discussed with regard to the central doctrine of non-origination (*ajātivāda*) expounded in the text.[5] It is not my intention to spend too much time discussing the question of the origins of the GK's conception of yoga. This is for a number of reasons. First, we have comparatively little to go on in the text itself which would enable us to differentiate Gauḍapādian yoga from other forms of meditative practice current at the time. Second, it seems to me that the question of whether Gauḍapādian yoga is Buddhist or Vedāntic in origin is something of a pseudo-problem. Yoga is a pan-Indian phenomenon and similar techniques are adopted by different religious schools and traditions. In the Buddhist tradition for instance, one finds the simultaneous adoption of two forms of meditative technique; one involving techniques of concentration intended to promote a greater quiescence of the mind (*śamatha*), the other utilizing techniques leading to greater awareness and insight (*vipaśyanā*). The relationship between these two is complex and a matter of considerable debate within the Buddhist tradition itself. Nevertheless, the predominant view seems to be that insight-meditation (*vipaśyanā-yoga*) is the unique discovery of the Buddha. The various techniques for calming the mind (*śamatha*) are usually said to be pre-Buddhist meditative practices, utilized by the Buddha and his followers for the promotion of greater degrees of mental concentration (*samādhi*). In consonance with this, the Buddhist scheme of the *jhānas* are usually taken by the Buddhist to be part of the meditative practice of calming (*śamatha*). Knowledge, however, is only to be gained through the adoption of some form of "insight" (*prajñā/vipaśyanā*) meditation at certain appropriate points. Calming meditation (*śamatha*) practiced by itself is believed to lead to nothing more than a pacification of the mind.

Needless to say, this two-fold division of yogic technique is not accepted by the orthodox (*āstika*) systems of Hindu philosophy. In the *Upaniṣads*, for instance, *dhyāna* (cognate with Buddhist *jhāna* i.e. *śamatha* meditation), involves both mental pacification (Buddhist *śamatha*) and insight (Buddhist *prajñā*) into the nature of reality. Thus it would be rather presumptuous of us to take either Buddhist or Vedāntic conceptions of yoga in an *apriori* or definitive form, since there are clearly different senses attributed to certain important technical terms (such as *dhyāna* (*jhāna*)) in the different religious traditions of India. One should also note that no religious tradition develops in a cultural vacuum and so mutual influence and interaction would not have been uncommon.

Since the authors of the *Gauḍapādīya-kārikā* show such a propensity for Buddhist ideas, however, it would be useful to examine the notion of "*asparśa*" within the context of Buddhist thought in general. As is well known, the Buddhist analyzes the psycho-physical components of the individual into five groups: the five *skandhas* (i.e. *rūpa, vedanā, saṃjñā, saṃskāra,* and *vijñāna*). Sensation (*vedanā*) is impossible without contact between the two polar aspects of the *rūpa-skandha* (*i.e.* the five sense organs (*indriya*) and the five sense objects (*viṣaya*). *Saṃjñā*, requires not only contact between the sense organ and its object, but also the intervention of a reflective consciousness, a mind, in order to occur.[6] Vasubandhu notes in his *Abhidharmakośa* that "*sparśa*" is

> the encounter of the triad of consciousness (*vijñāna*), sense-organ (*prasādendriya*), and material object (*viṣayālambana*); by virtue of this contact there is sensation (*vedanā*) and perception (*saṃjñā*).[7]

Without this threefold contact, the whole system would fall apart, and there would be no possibility of the continuance of the five *skandhas.* Buddhaghoṣa says in his *Aṭṭhāsalinī* that:

> This contact is like a pillar in a palace being the firm support to the rest of the structure; and just as beams, cross-beams, wing-supports, roof-

> rafters, cross-rafters, and neck-pieces are fastened to the pillar, so also is contact a firm support to the simultaneous and associated events. It is like the pillar, the rest of the psychic events are like the other materials forming the structure.[8]

In the Buddhist scheme of *pratītyasamutpāda*, the twelve-fold chain of dependent origination, *sparśa* is the sixth link in the chain. It is interesting to note that the scheme can be divided into three parts:

(1) to (2) = past existences,
(3) to (10) = the present existence, and
(11) to (12) = future existences.

Sparśa is said by some to denote the moment of birth in the present life.[9] It is the moment when we first come into contact with an external world. Taking this at face value, we can then see how the notion of *asparśa* links up with the central doctrine of the *Gauḍapādīya-kārikā*, i.e. the doctrine of non-origination (*ajātivāda*), since this is precisely what *asparśa* amounts to when related to the Buddhist conception of dependent-origination.

Thus one could say, by implication, that for the Buddhist the realization of a state of non-contact (*asparśa*) amounts to the cessation of the perpetual chain of saṃsāric experiences. In this sense *asparśa* denotes liberation itself. Although the term is rarely if ever used in this context, a state of non-contact is the fundamental prerequisite for the attainment of the cessation of sensation and perception (*saṃjñā-vedayita-nirodha*), or *nirodhasamāpatti*, the ninth and supreme level of Buddhist meditative attainment. However, in the meditative context *asparśa* can be said to denote little more than the successful application of *pratyāhāra*, a technique adopted by Buddhist and non-Buddhist yogins alike.

Asparśayoga as a Meditative Technique

The most obvious usage of the term *asparśayoga* is as a specific name for a form of meditative practice aiming at complete detachment, that is non-contact in the strictest sense.[10] This is a familiar aspect of all forms of yoga to some extent and is inextricably bound up with the notion of *pratyāhāra*—the withdrawal of the sense-faculties.[11] The term "*yoga*" appears for the first time in the Upaniṣadic literature in *Taittirīya Upaniṣad* 2.4 where it is used in connection with the notion of a cognizing self (*vijñānamaya ātma*).[12] In *Kaṭha Upaniṣad* II.3.10–11 yoga is defined as the concentrated stability of the sense-organs (*sthirāṃ indriyadhāraṇāṃ*), based upon the practice of sense-withdrawal (*pratyāhāra*):

> When the five senses of knowledge (*pañca jñānāni*) come to rest together with the mind (*manas*), and the intellect (*buddhi*), too, does not function—that state they call the highest (*paramām gatim*). They consider that keeping of the senses steady as yoga. One becomes vigilant (*apramatta*) at that time, for yoga is subject to growth and decay.[13]

Again in the *Maitrāyaṇīya Upaniṣad* we find a sixfold path of yoga:

> The precept for effecting this [unity] is this: restraint of the breath (*prāṇāyāma*), withdrawal of the senses (*pratyāhāra*), meditation (*dhyāna*), concentration (*dhāranā*), contemplation (*tarka*), absorption (*samādhi*). Such is said to be the sixfold yoga. . .[14]

In the classical yoga of eight limbs (*aṣṭāṅga*) sense-withdrawal is the fifth external limb (*bahiraṅga*) and is a fundamental prerequisite for the attainment of the inner limbs (*antaraṅga*) of concentration (*dhāranā*), meditation (*dhyāna*), and enstasy (*samādhi*). In the *Bhagavadgītā* the relinquishing of all sensory contacts (*sparśa*) is described in the following terms:

> And when he draws in on every side his senses from their respective objects as a tortoise [draws in] its limbs, the wisdom (*prajñā*) of this one is firmly established (*pratiṣṭhitā*).
> His self detached from contacts with the outside world, in [him] self he finds his joy, [his] self in Brahman joined by yoga he finds unfailing joy. For the pleasures that men derive from contacts assuredly give rise to pain, having a beginning and an end. In these a wise man (*budha*) takes no delight.
> All contact with things outside he puts away, fixing his gaze between the eyebrows; inward and outward breaths he makes the same as they pass up and down the nostrils.[15]

At first sight then "*asparśa-yoga*" seems to be a reference to the meditative practice of sensory withdrawal (*pratyāhāra*). Such a technique inevitably leads to a state of consciousness devoid of sensory stimuli. This is a state of non-contact (*asparśa*) or disunion (*asaṃyoga*) between consciousness (*citta*) and sense-object (*viṣaya*). Perhaps it would be fruitful to examine the *Gauḍapādīya-kārikā's* distinctive philosophy of mind, since this clearly has a bearing upon the interpretation of the experience gained through the practice of sensory withdrawal.

The Four States of Experience in the Āgama-Prakaraṇa (*GK I*)

The first chapter of the *Gauḍapādīya-kārikā*, often called the *Āgamaprakaraṇa*,[16] is an exposition of the main themes found in the *Māṇḍūkya Upaniṣad* (MU).[17] The most important of these, as far as the GK's conception of yoga is concerned, is the analysis of experience into four levels or "states" (*pāda*) of consciousness. These states are waking (*jāgarita, viśva*), dreaming (*svapna, taijasa*), deep sleep (*suṣupta, prājña*), and *turīya*, the fourth indescribable state.

There is a gradation of increasingly more refined experience moving from the gross objects of waking experience, through the dream state to the lack of sense-object (*viṣaya*) in deep sleep. In deep sleep all that is experienced is bliss (*ānanda*). It is a mere "mass of cognition" (*prajñānaghana*) and does not apprehend anything.[18] It is our attachment to these experiences that causes the suffering (*duḥkha*) of transmigration.[19] However, if we understand the true nature of these states we will be uncontaminated by them.[20] In the last analysis *turīya* is the only real state. It is not really a fourth state but in fact *the only state.*

> Able to bring about the cessation of all suffering, powerful, immutable, and divine, the non-dual [essence] of all beings (*bhāva*); the all pervading one is traditionally known as *turīya* (the fourth).
>
> When the *jiva*, asleep due to beginningless *māyā*, is awakened, it then realizes the unborn, sleepless, dreamless, non-duality.[21]

The scene is set for an appraisal of the sole reality of *turīya*. One has to awaken from the other states of "normative" experience in order to understand the so-called "fourth" state. The description of it as unborn, sleepless, dreamless, and non-dual, provide a sharp contrast with the nature of the three other states. *Turīya* is untouched by the experiences of these states just as one is unaffected by the imagined experiences of a dream when one returns to the waking state. The implication of this idea is that *turīya* is the true state of experience—we are all "in" *turīya*; we are just unaware of that fact. Thus in a very real sense we are all already liberated, our mistake is merely in our failure to apprehend this basic fact of our experience.

Meditation on the Phoneme OM

Towards the end of the first *prakaraṇa* the text provides us with an exposition of the OM symbolism found in the *Māṇḍūkya Upaniṣad*; the letter "A" of "A-U-M" corresponds to the waking state of consciousness, "U" to the dream state, and "M" to the state of deep sleep. Meditation upon these letters and their intrinsic connection with the various states of consciousness will lead the aspirant to an understanding of the nature of their complex inter-relationship and the "fragmentary" view that these states provide. It is only upon realization of the whole, that is, OM or *turīya*, that reality can be properly understood. There can be no pathway to the "measureless" and "limitless" reality (*amātra*). It can only be attained by a dialectical analysis of the "limited." Strictly speaking, one cannot even talk of the attainment of *turīya* since it is the one and only, unchanging "state" of reality.

> One should fix the mind upon the syllable OM; OM is Brahman the fearless; for the one who is permanently fixed upon OM, there is no fear whatsoever to be found.

> OM indeed is the beginning, the middle, and likewise the end itself of all things. Having indeed known *Praṇava* thus, one attains to that [Brahman] immediately.[22]

This latter verse assimilates the OM symbolism with one of the standard "tenets" of Gauḍapādian philosophy, the assumption that for something to be real it must exist in the beginning, middle, and end.[23] This presupposition is based upon the immutability of nature (*prakṛter na anyathābhāva*, GK III.21, IV.7, and 29) and forms the fundamental logical framework for the development of the GK's radical absolutism.

The relationship between *turīya* and the other three states is analogous to the relationship between OM and the letters A, U, and M. Just as OM encompasses the entire range of syllables (from the opening of the mouth with "A" to the closing of it with "M"), *turīya* is the all encompassing ground of all diversity—as OM transcends its portions (*mātra*), so does *turīya* transcend the three states of experience. Our experience of diversity then, is firmly grounded in a perception of Brahman; as we perceive the experiential equivalents of A, U, or M, what we are actually perceiving ultimately is the non-dual Brahman itself.[24]

Asparśayoga as a Description of the Ultimate State

As we have seen the term "*asparśayoga*" is often taken to be a specific name for a form of meditative practice leading to a complete cessation of perceptual activity. As such it is usually rendered by the English "the yoga of no-contact." Some scholars, however, have argued that *asparśayoga* is a description of ultimate reality, a sort of *kaivalya*-type isolation. For instance, Hixon suggests that

> *asparśayoga* is more a path of insight into the nondual nature of mind and the birthlessness of the universe than it is a form of yogic meditation-exercise to control the mind. . . It is to this doctrine of emptiness or nonorigination which the term *asparśayoga* refers, because there is nothing to contact or touch when one knows that nothing has come into being, hence the term "free from touch" or *a-sparśa*.[25]

For Hixon *asparśayoga* refers to the specific philosophy of mind outlined in the *Gauḍapādīya-kārikā*, i.e. the idea that the mind never comes into contact (*asparśa*) with an external object.[26] This interpretation is given added strength once we realize that as far as the GK is concerned there is no real possibility of following a meditative path since nothing has ever come into existence in the first place. However, it must be noted that in various places the text does stress the need to control one's mind through the practice of meditation.[27] It may be the case that nothing has ever come into existence, but for us to be fully aware of that fact we need to practice some form of yoga.[28]

We noticed in the first *prakaraṇa* that we are urged to meditate upon the meaning and denotation of the syllable OM. This in itself is an exhortation to a certain form of meditative practice. In the third *prakaraṇa* we are again urged to control the flow of the mind in an attempt to realize our essential non-difference from Brahman. Vyāsa in his commentary on the *Yogasūtra* states that "Yoga is *samādhi*."[29] It would be a mistake to take this to mean that Vyāsa does not accept that there is such a thing as the practice of yoga—clearly he does. In this instance it is obviously an example of defining a practice in terms of its experiential goal, i.e. the attainment of *samādhi*. Likewise, despite the fact that the authors of the GK believe in non-origination, this does not necessarily exclude the possibility of following a specific religious path on the conventional (*saṃvṛti*) level. Ultimately, of course, the practice of yoga can be of no consequence since only Brahman is, but, strange as it might seem, if we do not practice yoga we will not realize this fact.

It is easy to become embroiled in such paradoxical problems as those found in the doctrine of non-origination, but in this instance I think it would be fruitless. Suffice it to say that, despite the fact that reality is unoriginated, the authors of the GK want us to realize this fact for ourselves in order that we may alleviate the suffering caused by our belief in a changing world of plurality. This suffering of course is ultimately an illusion, but that fact in itself does not help those who partake of the illusion. Some form of practice is necessary to liberate us from our own attachments and preconceptions. In fact, one could argue that the very paradoxicality of the *Gauḍapādīya-kārikā's* understanding of yoga is expressed in the name which the text applies to it: "*asparśayoga.*" The word is something of a contradiction in terms since one half of the compound denotes a state of separation, a state of no-contact, while the other half denotes an implicit act of union, the "joining" of "yoga." This paradox perhaps reflects the impossibility of describing the ultimate (*paramārtha*) and non-conceptual (*nirvikalpa*) in conventional (*saṃvṛti*) terms. To use one of Mircea Eliade's favorite terms, "*asparśa-yoga*" is an example of *coincidentia oppositorum*—the coincidence of opposites, a characteristic feature of many mystical philosophies.

The Attainment of Gnosis (Jñāna) *in the GK*

The four *prakaraṇas* of the *Gauḍapādīya-kārikā* do not appear to make any technical distinction between the terms *manas, citta,* and *vijñāna*, all of which are used in general to denote mundane "consciousness." The explicit goal of the practice of yoga in GK III and IV, however, is the cessation of mental activity or the state of no-mind (*amanastā*). This is interesting since there is no occurrence of any of the three terms used to denote mundane consciousness in the last twenty-three verses of the fourth *prakaraṇa*. Instead we find reference to *jñāna*, a term that clearly denotes a type of intuitive knowledge or gnosis. *Jñāna* differs from *vijñāna* insofar as it is devoid of the fluctuations of consciousness (*vijñāna/citta - cala/spanditā*).[30]

Earlier in the second *prakaraṇa*, embedded in a list of "entities" (*bhāva*) mistakenly thought to be the *ātman*, the text refers to those who believe that the self is mind (*manas*), intellect (*buddhi*), or consciousness (*citta*).[31] From this it would seem that even GK II does not accept the equation of *ātman* with ordinary consciousness except in the broader sense where, in actual fact, everything is to be equated with *ātman*. In the third and fourth *prakaraṇas*, the goal of yoga is specifically described as a state of no-mind (*amanastā*).

> This duality, comprising of the moveable and the immoveable is perceived by the mind; when the mind has become non-mind duality is not experienced.
>
> When by knowledge of the truth about *ātman*, [the mind] ceases to imagine, it is in the state of mindlessness; there is no perception in the absence of a perceptible [object].[32]

The denial of the ultimate reality of the mind is a blow to all who wish to read subjective idealism into the *Gauḍapādīya-kārikā*. Even in GK I.18 the view that the world is imagined by someone is expressly refuted. *Manas* is part of the phenomenal world of dualism and as such is not an ultimate reality (*paramārtha-satya*). The inappropriateness of equating the self (*ātman*) with the mind (*manas*) is established in many Upaniṣadic texts. In *Muṇḍaka Upanisad* II.1.2–3 for instance, the unborn *Puruṣa* is described as "without mind" (*amanas*)—being the originator and supporter of all things (including the mind), without thereby being qualifiable by them. In the *Taittirīya Upaniṣad* (itself referred to in GK III.11), one of the five sheaths (*kośa*) is the self made of mind (*manomaya*). This is not the deepest level of reality, since within this is the sheath of understanding (*vijñāna-mayakośa*) and the sheath of bliss (*ānandamayakośa*).

The type of non-dual awareness of the ultimate envisaged by the *Gauḍapādīya-kārikā* is similar in many respects to the views attributed to the sage Yājñavalkya in the *Bṛhadāraṇyaka Upaniṣad* (that the authors of the GK have been influenced by the *Bṛhadāraṇyaka Upaniṣad* is beyond question—*kārikās* 25 and 26 of GK III even quote from the text). Such a non-dualistic state is not devoid of awareness. On the contrary, it is a deep insight into the nature of reality. Nevertheless, "there are no notions (*saṃjñā*) here."[33] The cognizing self (*prajñātman*) knows no distinctions, continues Yājñavalkya, as in sexual intercourse.[34] One important difference between Yājñavalkya and the authors of the GK, however, is that the former accords the highest status to the experience of deep sleep, whereas the latter distinguish between the non-awareness of sleep (*suṣupti*) and the non-discursive awareness of *samādhi* (*turīya*). Nevertheless, it could be argued that the GK is merely expounding a more sophisticated blue-print of states of consciousness, developed from the ideas already found in such early texts as the *Bṛhadāraṇyaka Upaniṣad.* In the state of deep sleep, which Yājñavalkya suggests brings forth knowledge of the true nature of the self, no sensory contacts are experienced.

> That it does not touch in that state is because, though touching then, it does not touch; for the toucher's function of touching can never be lost, because it is imperishable. But there is not that second thing separate from it which it can touch.
>
> Because when there is a duality, as it were, there one sees something, one smells something, one tastes something, one hears something, one thinks something, one touches something, one knows something. But when to the knower of Brahman everything has become the Self. . . then what should one touch?. . .This self is that which has been described as "Not this, not this."[35]

As I have suggested, the GK seems to make an implicit distinction between "*vi-jñāna*," the state of an active and diversifying consciousness, and "*jñāna*," a state of gnostic realization beyond the range of mundane consciousness. *Jñāna* as such is the quiescence of all conscious activity. There is nothing strange in this idea; such a distinction can also be found in other philosophical texts[36] and is perhaps first pointed to in a Vedāntic context in *Chāndogya Upaniṣad* VII.7 where *dhyāna* (meditation) and *vijñāna* (understanding) are clearly differentiated.[37] This distinction should be kept in mind for it has implications for attempts to classify the philosophical position of the GK as "idealistic." In the GK the images of perceiver and perceived (*grāhya-grāhaka*) are merely vibrations of mundane consciousness (*vijñāna*) in its distracted (*vikṣipta*) aspect. Enlightenment (*jñānaloka*),[38] however, is a radically transformative state where the mind no longer functions.[39]

The third *prakaraṇa* describes the proper control of mental activity as "Brahman devoid of fear, with the illumination of *jñāna* all around."[40] In this condition:

> [There is] *samādhi*, devoid of all expression, risen above all thought, completely quiescent, ever effulgent, unmoving, and fearless.
>
> Where there is no thought, there is no grasping and no letting go. At that time *jñāna*, established in itself, attains unoriginated equanimity (*ajātisamatā*).
>
> This is [called] *asparśa-yoga* by name, [and] it is difficult for all yogins to attain it. In fact, the yogins are afraid of it, seeing fear where there is no fear.[41]

It would appear from this that *asparśayoga* is a description of the highest form of non-conceptual enstasy (*nirvikalpa samādhi*). This, in fact, is the opinion put forward by Vidhushekhara Bhattacharya, who suggested that *asparśayoga* was another name for the highest level of Buddhist meditative attainment—*nirodhasamāpatti*, the attainment of cessation.[42] However, as Griffiths notes in his discussion of the latter:

> The term, and its equivalent, "cessation of sensation and conceptualization" (*saṃjñāvedayitanirodha*) denote a specific very precisely defined altered state of consciousness, one which occurs as the direct result of specified meditative techniques.[43]

Consequently, the equation of *asparśayoga* with the Buddhist *nirodhasamāpatti* is not without some difficulties. What should be noted, however, is the possibility that *asparśayoga* refers not to a set of meditative practices but to a meditative state. Clearly, the author of GK III believes that for many yoga practitioners its realization is difficult to achieve. This would seem to imply that *asparśayoga* is a goal rather than a method.

Asparśayoga is again referred to by name at the beginning of the fourth *prakaraṇa*, where the author pays obeisance to it.

> I bow down to that which has been named the "Yoga of No-contact" for the happiness of all beings, beneficial, free from dispute and contradiction.[44]

The commentator remarks that,

> *Asparśayoga* is that yoga which has no contact or relationship with anything at any time; it is the very nature of Brahman. Thus, it is "indeed so named"; as *asparśayoga,* it is well-known to the knowers of Brahman.[45]

In the two instances where the *Gauḍapādīya-kārikā* explicitly uses the term "*asparśayoga*," particular attention is drawn to the fact that it is a specific, yet well known, designation.[46] The commentator also mentions this fact, as we have seen above, saying that the term is well-known to the knowers of Brahman. This perplexity has cast doubt on the authenticity of the commentary as one of Śaṇkara's works for the term "*asparśayoga*," far from being a well-known Vedāntic term, is not to be found in any of the classical *Upaniṣads*, nor, to my knowledge, can it be found explicitly in any work prior to the *Gauḍapādīya-kārikā*.

Asparśayoga: The Gauḍapādian Phenomenology of Perception

Perception is based upon the possibility of "contact" (*sparśa*) between a perceiver and a perceived object. An attack upon this notion then is fundamental to an attack upon all "realist" theories of perception. The *Nyāya sūtra*, for instance, defines perception (*pratyakṣa*) as "the determinate, unnamed, and unerring knowledge which arises from the contact of a sense organ with its object."[47] This is an inherently dualistic understanding of experience and as such is clearly unacceptable to the non-dualistic authors of the *Gauḍapādīya-kārikā*. An attack upon the notion of "contact" is fundamental to a thorough-going non-dual theory of perception. In fact, it is the GK's position that:

> Consciousness does not make contact with an object, nor even the appearance of an object. In fact, the object is unreal, and the appearance of the object is not different.[48]

The idea implicit in the Gauḍapādian analysis of perception is that in order to be aware or to experience something, one has to have that thing before the mind. If experience requires contact between the mind and its object, then that object cannot be separate from the mind in the sense that we believe that it is.[49] As such, "*asparśa*" is a corollary of the theory of the non-duality of consciousness (*advaya-vāda*), there being no possibility of contact in a non-dualistic (*advaya*) realm. As we shall see, the doctrine of the non-duality of consciousness (*vijñāna-advaya*) is endorsed by the *Gauḍapādīya-kārikā* in agreement with the Yogācārins.

Thus, upon analysis, "*sparśa*" must really be "contact" between two things already intimately connected. In effect "*sparśa*" becomes "*asparśa*" for it is the realization that one can only come into contact with that which one is already in contact with.

> Perceived by the mind of the waking one, [these things] do not exist apart from it. Similarly that which is perceived by it (i.e. the mind) alone is said to be the waking consciousness.[50]

Reality is non-dual (*advaita*), untouched (*asparśa*) and non-relational (*asaṅga*). This is the realization of *asparśayoga*, the goal of the GK's soteriological system. It is a state of non-contact, following on from the dissolution of all mental activity (*amanastā*). Thus, "when the mind has become no-mind, duality is not experienced."[51] In this enlightened state "there is no perception in the absence of a perceptible object."[52] Thus,

> When the mind is not asleep and is also not distracted, it is motionless and without image. Then it becomes Brahman.[53]

A proper analysis of the nature of perception reveals the fact that the mind never actually touches an object. The division of our experience into a "subject" and an "object" is nothing more than a vibration of consciousness. This consciousness is said to be permanently unrelated to an object.[54] In reality, all is Brahman. Thus, the GK's final position on things is that there is

> Neither cessation nor origination, neither one bound, nor one practicing spiritual discipline, neither one aspiring for liberation nor one who is liberated. This is the ultimate truth.[55]

Non-contact (Asparśa) *and Representation-Only* (Vijñapti-mātra)

The extent of Mahāyāna influence on the doctrines of the *Gauḍapādīya-kārikā* is not restricted to the Prajñāpāramita *sūtras* and the works of Nāgārjuna. The author's equation of the waking and dream states, the doctrine of the non-duality of perception (*advaya*) and the concept of *asparśa-yoga*, all show a reliance upon the ideas espoused by the early Yogācāra school of Mahāyāna Buddhism. This will become apparent from our analysis of Gauḍapādian epistemology. First, however, it is necessary to consider the nature and perspective of the early Yogācāra school in an attempt to distinguish it from the subsequent adoption and adaptation of its ideas in the *Gauḍapādīya-kārikā*.

As the second important philosophical school to develop in Indian Mahāyāna Buddhism, the Yogācāra school seems to have developed the distinctive features of its philosophy from a comprehensive analysis of meditative experience (hence the name "Yogācāra"—the "practice of yoga.") The term "*yogācāra*" is here used in preference to the terms "*Vijñaptimātratā*" and "*vijñānavāda*" because of its wider scope of denotation, and independence from certain specific theoretical positions. This is important when dealing particularly with the early stages of development of the school. It should be noted, however, that the term "*Vijñaptimātratā*" (Cognitive-Representation-Only) is applicable with regard to the perspective of the early Yogācāra (Maitreya, Asaṅga, and Vasubandhu all utilize the term), but the term "*Vijñāna-vāda*" (the doctrine that "consciousness [alone] exists") is not, since the early Yogācārins did not accept the ultimate reality of subjective consciousness (*vijñāna*).[56]

Asparśayoga, as a critique of correspondence theories of perception, appears to be the *Gauḍapādīya-kārikā's* own "Vedāntic" version of the fundamental insight of the Yogācāra tradition—the realization of *Vijñaptimātratā* or "Representation-only." This is the idea that what we perceive as objects is in actual fact only the representation of objects in the mind. Thus, the *Madhyānta-vibhāga* I.7 states that

> Depending upon perception, there arises non-perception, and depending upon non-perception, there arises non-perception.[57]

Vasubandhu explains this rather obscure verse in the following manner:

> Depending upon the perception that there are only Representations, there arises the non-perception of objects. Depending upon the non-perception of objects, there arises the non-perception of mere-representations (*vijñaptimātra*) as well. Thus, one understands the definition of the non-existence of the perceived and the perceiver.[58]

This idea is repeated in Vasubandhu's *Trisvabhāvanirdeśa*,

> Through the perception that there is only thought (*citta-mātra*), there arises the non-perception of knowable things, through the non-perception of knowable things, there arises the non-perception of thought as well.[59]

The insight into the fact that we only experience representations of objects, and not the objects themselves leads to the realization that the presence of an external object is not a prerequisite for its perception by us. This is evident from the fact that every night in a dream we have a whole host of experiences and representations of objects without any corresponding objects "out there." On this point Vasubandhu notes elsewhere that

> Perception can occur as in a dream, etc. At the time when that occurs an object is not seen. How then, can one speak of its perception?[60]

The argument from dream experience is one of the characteristic features of Yogācāra thought.[61] What we perceive in actual fact, according to the Yogācārins is nothing more than the mind itself (*cittamātra*).

In the third and fourth *prakaraṇas*, the nature of dream and waking experiences (declared to be one (*eka*) and false (*vitathā*) in the second *prakaraṇa*) are re-considered. Thus,

> As through *māyā*, the mind in dream vibrates with the image of two, so through *māyā*, the mind in the waking state vibrates with the image of two.[62]

The author of the fourth *prakaraṇa* of the GK grounds his epistemology in the notion of *advaya* (literally, "not two").[63] The term "*advaya*," although not a uniquely Buddhist term, has a clear technical background in the Mahāyāna schools. In general, there appears to be two senses in which it is used. First, it is used as a designation of the Buddha's Middle Path. In this context it refers to the fact that the Buddhist Path is an avoidance of the two poles of extreme views. While this usage is not ignored by the author of GK IV,[64] "*advaya*" is predominantly used in the form that became particularly associated with the Yogācāra school, that is "not two" in the sense of the "non-duality of consciousness." The duality rejected in this context is the duality of perceived and perceiver (*grāhya-grāhaka*) apparent in everyday perception. Our fundamental error is that we take this dichotomy to be a characteristic of "things as they are" (*yathābhūta*) and not of "things as they appear" (*yathābhāsa*). The use of specific terms from the Yogācāra school in the exposition of *advaya-vāda* makes Buddhist influence upon these *kārikās* beyond doubt.

The world appears as it does because of our attachment to the unreal (*abhūtābhiniveśa*).[65] For the GK the realization that the subject-object distinction does not hold is the realization that reality is essentially non-dual. Only Brahman is. Our mistake is in allowing the mind to bifurcate into perceiver and perceived in the first place. The dissolution of the mind is the attainment of Brahman and the quiescence of all constructed ideality (*vikalpa*).

> This duality, comprising of the moveable and the immoveable, is perceived by the mind; when the mind has become non-mind, duality is not experienced.
>
> When by knowledge of the truth about *ātman*, [the mind] ceases to imagine, it is in the state of mindlessness; there is no grasping in the absence of a graspable.[66]

Nevertheless, it is important to keep in the mind the fact that for the authors of the GK one can only attain that which already is. Liberation and bondage are convenient fictions.[67] To this extent it becomes difficult to uphold any methodology whatsoever, given that there is actually nothing to do. This refers us back to an earlier observation, that the term *asparśayoga* is a paradoxical one. This points to the dialectical tension found throughout the GK's rich, integrative, and innovative thought.

In the fourth *prakaraṇa*,[68] rather poetically entitled the "Peace of the Firebrand" (*alātaśānti*), we find a detailed exposition of *advaya-vāda*. There are no occurrences of the terms "*dvaita*" or "*advaita*" in this *prakaraṇa*, but this in itself is not necessarily evidence of separate authorship.[69] In GK IV the terms "*advaya*" and "*dvaya*" generally refers to the dualistic perceived-perceiver complex (*grāhya-grāhaka*) and "*advaita*" and "*dvaita*" to the metaphysical doctrine of non-dualism. In the main, the Gauḍapādian philosophy of perception has been neglected by the later tradition of Advaita Vedānta. Śaṇkara and his immediate disciples favored a correspondence theory of perception whereby the psyche (*antaḥkaraṇa*) takes on the form (*vṛtti*) of an external object. Kaplan (1987, *passim*.) suggests that this is a development of the Gauḍapādian theory of perception, but this is clearly not the case for the GK conflates waking and dream experiences, while Śaṇkara and his followers tend towards epistemological realism. While these two epistemological theories are not totally irreconcilable, it is clear that the Śaṇkarite school implicitly accepted the reality of external objects, and differentiated between the waking and dreaming states accordingly. In this respect, the authors of the GK differ radically from their Vedāntic successors. Nevertheless, Śaṇkara and his followers do use the term "*advaya*" to refer to their own doctrine of non-dualism, but it is not a technical usage as it is in the GK. Consequently, a general distinction between "*advaya*" and "*advaita*" is not possible, the terms being in most cases largely interchangeable.

Nevertheless, we are in danger of misrepresenting the fourth *prakaraṇa* if we do not see the purpose behind its composition. Although it contains many explicit and implicit metaphysical statements about the nature of reality, I suggest that its primary focus is an analysis of mind and the nature of experience. This is not to say that the author of the fourth *prakaraṇa* is not adhering to a non-dualistic ontology. Considerable time has been spent establishing the idea of non-origination (*ajātivāda*) in the metaphysical sphere with the denial of all creation theories and doctrines of causation in the first three *prakaraṇas*,[70] but it is also important to ground this same insight in the epistemological realm. It is here that we find the development of the Gauḍapādian version of consciousness-only (*citta-mātra*), in the idea of the untouched (*asparśa*) and non-dual (*advaya*) nature of consciousness. The theory outlined and emphasized in the fourth *prakaraṇa*, while having ontological implications (in terms of the doctrine of *advaita*), is established primarily as a phenomenology of consciousness i.e. as an explanation of the phenomenon of conscious experience. It is on the basis of this analysis of the phenomenon of consciousness that the GK expounds its "idealistic" epistemology. However, given the Vedāntic distinction between mundane epistemology (*aparā vidyā*) and non-dualistic gnoseology (*parā vidyā*), this does not entail that the final position of the GK can be adequately labeled a form of idealism without some qualification. The primary reason for the characterization of Gauḍapādian thought as "idealistic" is the equation of the waking and dream states. However, before we can consider the nature of this equation we must first contextualize the GK by discussing the early Yogācāra philosophy which underpins such an equation.

The Yogācāra Phenomenology of Perception

One of the most important features of the Yogācāra "re-formulation" of the Middle Path is a marked movement away from the "negativistic" interpretation of emptiness found in the Madhyamaka school. For Asaṅga there are two types of extreme and erroneous view,

> (1) that one which clings to affirming (*samāropata*) the existence of what are nonexistent individual characteristics, having essential nature only through verbal designation (*prajñapti*) for a given thing. . . and also (2) that one which, with respect to a given thing (*vastu*), denies (*apavadamāno*) the foundation for the sign of verbal designation, which exists in an ultimate sense (*paramārthasadbhūtam*) owing to its inexpressible essence (*nirabhilāpyātmakatayā*) saying "absolutely everything is nonexistent" (*sarvena sarvam nāstīti*).[71]

Thus, for Asanga, a universal denial (*sarva-vaināśika*) of the "bare given thing" (*vastu-mātra*) is a view which strays from the Buddhist path (*Dharma-viṇaya*).[72]

> Neither reality (*tattva*) nor [its] designation (*prajñapti*) would be known when the bare given-thing of form (*rūpa*) and so forth, is denied. Both these views are inappropriate.[73]

An important point to note is that Asaṅga here explicitly criticizes the view that denies that there exists a "bare given-thing" (*vastu-mātra*) as the basis for the *rūpa-skandha*.[74] Indeed, the Yogācāra school seems to have accepted the traditional Sarvāstivāda division of *dharmas* into five categories, i.e. mind (*citta*), mental concomitants (*caitasikā*), form (*rūpa*), compounded-factors independent of the mind (*citta-viprayukta-saṃskāra-dharmas*), and the uncompounded factors (*asaṃskṛta*).[75] This seems to be at variance with the "naive idealism" usually attributed to Yogācāra thought. It should be made clear from the outset then that the Yogācāra school is far more complex in its understanding of the nature of experience than is usually acknowledged.

It must be realized, however, that the abhidharmic taxonomy of the Yogācāra school (usually said to consist of one hundred specific dharmic types) is only provisional. Such conceptual categories are existent only in a purely conventional and nominal sense (*prajñapti-sat*). In his *Abhidharmasamuccaya*, for instance, Asaṅga criticizes the idea that matter (*rūpa*) is a substantial and independent existent.[76] Thus,

> It is said that a mass of matter (*rūpasamudāya*) is composed of atoms (*paramāṇu*). Here the atom should be understood to be without a physical body (*niḥśarīra*). The atom is determined (*vyavasthana*) in the final analysis (*paryantaprabheda*) by the intellect (*buddhyā*), in view of the abandonment (*vibhāvana*) of the notion of an aggregate (*piṇḍasaṃjñā*), and in view of the penetration into the relativity[77] of matter as a substance (*dravyapariniṣpattipraveśa*).

This argument was extended further by Asaṅga's brother Vasubandhu in his *Viṃśatikā*[78] with an attack upon the realist notion of matter (*rūpa*) as a substance existing independently of the experiencing subject. Whether this is a case of idealism depends to a large extent upon one's understanding of the term. Certainly, much of Asaṅga's work presupposes a distinction between material and immaterial, and external and internal. Indeed, in the *Abhidharmasamuccaya*[79] Asaṅga describes the grasping subject of perceptions (*grāhaka*) as the material sense-organ (*rūpīndriya*), the mind (*citta*), and the mental factors (*caitasika*). The inclusion of a gross sense-faculty in the analysis of the subject is hardly what one would expect from an idealistic analysis. Again, in the same work,[80] Asaṅga makes a distinction between internal and external sensations (*ādhyātma/bahirdhā vedanā*). Internal sensation is "that which is produced from one's own body (*kāya*)", while its external counterpart is "that produced by an external body."[81] However, in *Mahāyānasaṃgraha* I.22 the notion of an external seed (*bāhya*) is said to be purely conventional (*saṃvṛta*) while that of an internal seed (*ādhyātmika*) is said to be ultimate (*paramārthika*).[82] Whether Asaṅga is an idealist or not, internal or subjective states (*ādhyātmika*) are given more validity than those based upon external (*bāhya*) stimuli.

Clearly, no category can be left untouched by the Mahāyāna deconstruction of conceptual referents. Thus in the *prakāraprabheda* section of the *Abhidharmasamuccaya* (I.2) Asaṅga considers the *skandhas, dhātus*, and *āyatanas* from sixteen points of view, as substance and designation (*dravya/prajñapti*), conventional and ultimate (*saṃvṛti-sat/paramārtha-sat*), conditioned and unconditioned (*saṃskṛta/asaṃskṛta*), mundane and supramundane (*laukika/lokottara*), time and space, dependent-origination (*pratītyasamutpāda*) etc. with the intention of demonstrating that there is no "self" in any of these factors and that they are thus both empty and without a substantial referent. In such a philosophical environment, neither material form (*rūpa*), nor internal consciousness (*vijñāna*) can ultimately stand the test. All are equally lacking in an abiding or permanent nature (*ātman*).

However, this is not necessarily "idealism" in the strict sense, being more a form of "anti-realist de-constructionism."[83] Nāgārjuna in his *Yuktiṣaṣṭika*[84] also maintains that:

> 34: *mahābhūtadi vijñāne proktaṃ samavarudhyate, tajjñāne vigamaṃ yāti nanu mithyā vikalpitam.*
> Such things spoken of as the great elements, are absorbed in consciousness. They are dissolved by understanding them. Certainly, they are falsely discriminated.

> 37: *jig rten ma rig rkkyen can du // gaṅ phyir saṅs rgyas rnams gsuṅs pa,' di yi phyir na' jig rten' di. rnam rtog yin źes cis mi' thad.*
> Since the Buddhas have stated that the world is conditioned by ignorance, how is it not reasonable that this world therefore is a [result of] discrimination (*vikalpa*).

"*Vikalpa*" is variously rendered as "discursive thought," "conceptual construction" or "discrimination" by western translators. It refers to the cognitive process whereby one "constructs" one's picture of the world. According to the general Buddhist understanding of this process the discrimination of an "object" is fundamentally based upon the function of contrasting and distinguishing it from another "object." Thus, in the discrimination (*vikalpa*) of a table in our perceptions one is involved in a selective procedure whereby the given qualities attributed to that table are established by contrasting them with those of something else (e.g., a chair). This is Buddhist semantic theory (*apohavāda*) applied to the perceptual sphere. The attractiveness of the *apoha* theory for the Buddhist lies in the fact that one can define (either linguistically or experientially) a "given object" without necessarily attributing any substantiality to it. Thus, a "cow" is defined as that which is "not-horse," "not-dog," "not-table," etc. Such a theory allows for the establishment of a world of conceptual boundaries without the necessity of postulating a given substantial basis for those distinctions.

The idea that *vikalpa* (discursive thought) is the cause of the manifestation of *saṃsāra* is nothing new to Mahāyāna Buddhism. Where Asaṅga and his successors are breaking new philosophical ground is in the development of a systematic abhidharma-style analysis of experience based upon the notion that all factors are empty (*sarve dharmāḥ śūnyāḥ*).

In his *Tattvārtha* chapter of the *Bodhisattvabhūmi* Asaṅga describes the eight types of discriminations (*vikalpa*) caused by "incomplete knowledge (*aparijñātatva*) of suchness (*tathatā*)."[85] These *vikalpas* are the source of all samsaric experience. Consequently, their manifestation results in the arising of the three bases (*tri-vastu*) of experience, i.e. the subjective and objective poles of perception, and the primary afflictions (*kleśa*). The following scheme can be outlined from the Tattvārtha[86]:

1. *svabhāvavikalpa*—"discrimination of intrinsic nature."
   This *vikalpa* posits an assumed nature to an object.
2. *viśeṣavikalpa*—"discrimination of particularity."
   This *vikalpa* delineates distinctions and qualities within the given object. It is an awareness of specificity and has the function of particularizing the object of *svabhāvavikalpa*.
3. *piṇḍagrāhavikalpa*—"discrimination grasping a whole."
   This is the reification of a flow of variegated *dharmas* so as to appear as a single entity or compound. Thus, it accounts for our attribution of such terms as "self" (*ātma*), sentient being (*sattva*), living being (*jīva*) to these multiple *dharmas*, as well as our attribution of "house," "army," and "forest" etc.

   These three produce the "given thing" (*vastu*) known as form and so on (*rūpādi*), which serves as the foundation (*adhiṣṭhāna*) and objective-support (*ālambana*) for all conceptual proliferation (*prapañca*). Thus in the *Abhidharma-samuccaya, rūpa* is described as the support of existents (*bhūtāśraya*).[87] One may note at this point that this is little more than a further sophistication and refinement of Nāgārjuna's statement in *Yuktiṣaṣṭika* v.34.

4. *aham iti vikalpa*—"discrimination of 'I'"
5. *mameti vikalpa*—"discrimination of 'mine'"

When a given-thing is grasped (*abhinivișța*), there arise the views of "self" (*ātma*) and "belongs to self" (*ātmīyatā*). This is the reifying view of self (*satkāyadṛṣṭi*), which takes the interdependently-arisen object (*vastu pratītyotpadyate*) to be placed there by one's own view (*svaṃ dṛṣṭi-sthānīyam*). Thus, (4) is the reification of the five *skandhas* in terms of a persisting, independent entity, and (5) is the reification of "objects" as existent in the form in which they are perceived. Together, these two produce the base (*vastu*) which results in the reifying view of self (*satkāyadṛṣṭi*) and the roots of all other views, i.e., pride (*māna*) and egocentricity (*asmi-māna*).

6. *priyavikalpa*—"discrimination of the agreeable."
7. *apriyavikalpa*—"discrimination of the disagreeable."
8. *ubhaya-viparitovikalpa*—"discrimination contrary to these."

These three *vikalpas* and their respective objective-supports (*ālambana*) produce the three primary afflictions (*kleśa*), i.e., desire (*rāga*), hatred (*dveșa*), and delusion (*moha*).

There are many interesting ideas that can be gleaned from an analysis of this scheme. It is clear that the afflictions (*kleśa*) of the unenlightened manifest themselves through our passions, prejudices, and belief-systems. All of these are involved in the process of having an experience, even at the most rudimentary perceptual level. Asaṅga's system allows for a complex understanding of the perceptual process. All experience is conceptual (*savikalpa*) and value-laden (that is "colored" or distorted by the *kleśas*). To adapt a common English expression, we all see the world through "colored spectacles." Nevertheless, one can discern different stages within this process of conceptualization and distortion. In the scheme outlined above, for instance, Asaṅga appears to be differentiating between three "stages" of grasping an object. Firstly, there is the initial imposition of an "intrinsic nature" to the percept. It is the designation of that given-thing as a recognisable and definable (*svalakṣaṇa*) entity (i.e. the awareness of the percept x). Secondly, there is the differentiation of characteristics within the given-thing, (i.e., it is the moment when we are aware for instance that x is blue). Thirdly, we have what Asaṅga calls the "discrimination which grasps a whole" (*piṇḍagrāhavikalpa*). This is the attribution of a persisting and self-identical entity to a flow of percepts (i.e. postulating a substantial object based upon the continuity of percepts, as in the case where we believe that we are looking at a blue disc that is both separate from and a cause of our experience of a series of x's.

These "stages" are followed by (or perhaps simultaneous with) the establishment of the "subjective" and "objective" poles of experience (*aham iti* and *mameti-vikalpas*). The final stage, and the most prevalent, is the emotional reaction to these conceptualizations in terms of the three primary afflictive emotions, i.e. passion (*rāga*), aversion (*dveṣa*), and confusion (*moha*). Of course, like the much older Buddhist scheme of the five *skandhas* that it is intended to supplement, the distinctions between these various stages in the perceptual process are merely heuristic and didactic. Both the eight *vikalpas* and the three bases (*tri-vastu*) which they engender are all mutually related and interdependently-arisen. Thus, desire could not arise unless there was a view of self and vice versa. This is the perpetual wheel of rebirth (*saṃsāra*). Nevertheless, the divisions between the eight *vikalpas* are interesting because they highlight Asaṅga's complex analysis of the perceptual process.[88]

In his *Mahāyānasaṃgraha* (II.20) and again in his *Abhidharmasamuccaya* (III.2),[89] Asaṅga outlines an alternative scheme based upon 10 *vikalpas*. The delight in the composition of comprehensive lists and exhaustive (and often overlapping) categories is a major stylistic feature of Asaṅga's works. His analytical mind was perfectly attuned to the task of compiling a Mahāyāna Abhidharma. One should note, however, that all of these conceptual schemes and analytical lists are purely for didactic purposes; in the Mahāyāna all conceptual systems are ultimately misleading, being based upon distinctions and abstractions that have no basis in reality. This point should not be overlooked when examining Asaṅga's thought. The proliferation of different (yet not contradictory) conceptual schemes is purely provisional, being an example of skill in means (*upāya-kauśalya*). These conceptual schemes are complementary because of their inherently provisional status. As such, they are not seen as attempts to contribute to the incessant proliferation of concepts (*prapañca*) that is the bane of the *bodhisattva's* quest for the universal salvation of all beings. We should not expect Asaṅga to express a clearly defined and consistent set of categories throughout his voluminous literary output since his motive is primarily soteriological and "therapeutic." To miss this fact is to forget that for all Buddhists, the alleviation of suffering is the *raison d'être* of philosophical speculation. It would not be overly strange then, given the Mahāyāna de-construction of all postulated entities and the consequent provisional nature of all conceptual systems, to see the utilization of a number of "methods" of teaching. Janice Dean Willis, for instance, suggests that Asaṅga utilized a number of different methods (*upāya*) in his exposition of the Dharma.

> One was the invention of an "ontological psychological" model for explaining the bifurcation of apparent reality into a subject and an object. . . Another was what might be called a nominalist approach. . . Yet another was the extremely important introduction of a new schema in which the model of the so-called "three natures" (*trisvabhāvas* or *trilakṣaṇa*) is used to extend and supplement the older Mahāyāna formula of the "two truths."[90]

Nevertheless, this is not to say that Asaṅga is a "sloppy" and uncritical thinker. In fact, on the contrary, he was clearly one of the greatest systematizers that Buddhism and India have ever produced. Nor is it to suggest that the classical Yogācāra of Asaṅga and Vasubandhu has nothing to say on the philosophical problems of the day; indeed, as should already be clear, the Yogācāra upholds a complex theory regarding the nature of consciousness and the perceptible world upon which it "feeds." What must be remembered, however, is that for the Mahāyānist ultimately all theories are means (*upāya*) to an end; maps for the following of the path (*mārga*). Like all maps, theories have little use outside their essentially provisional and indicative (*prajñapti*) purpose. This is because from a Mahāyāna point of view conceptual systems are necessarily distorted representations (*vijñapti*) of the actual state of things (*yathābhūta*). This is the nature of language and all purely intellectual attempts to grasp perfect wisdom.

In the *Tattvārtha* chapter of the *Bodhisattvabhūmi*, Asaṅga outlines the complex process whereby the individual perpetuates his or her experience of the wheel of *saṃsāra*.

> this whole process is composed of two elements only: discursive thought (*vikalpa*), and the given thing (*vastu*), which then becomes the mental support (*ālambana*) of discursive thought and the foundation of discursive thought. It should be understood that these two are mutually caused (*anyonya hetuka*) and without beginning in time.[91]

From this, the following scheme can be outlined:

vastu	»»»	ālambana	»»»	vastu	»»»	ālambana
	(vikalpa)		(vikalpa)		(vikalpa)	

Note that *vikalpa* and *vastu* are mutually interdependent (*anyonya-hetuka*). There can be no discursive thought without a given thing as its basis. Nevertheless (and this is the primary insight of the Buddhist notion of experience), the perception of a given thing is distorted by the individual's attachment to the constructions of the discursive mind. This is dependent-origination (*pratītyasamutpāda*) explained in an experiential context.

As we have seen, *vikalpa* is the conceptualizing tendency of the mind which categorizes and reifies the given-thing (*vastu*), which is actually nothing other than a stream of perceptions, so as to appear as a subsisting, permanent, and independent object (*artha*). These perceptions, under the influence of such false conceptual constructions, become an objective-support (*ālambana*) of consciousness and a subsequent source of attachment (*abhiniveśa*). Each experience leaves a subliminal impression (*vāsanā*) in the individual's "subconscious" (the *ālayavijñāna*) that acts as a seed (*bīja*) for the future ripening of further experiences of a like nature (the arising of the *vipākavijñāna* or "fruition-consciousness"). Each new perception (the purely given-thing or "*vastu-mātra*"), is the coming to fruition (*vipāka*) of a stored (*ālaya*) memory (*smṛti* or *vijñāna*) or karmic trace (*vāsanā*) caused by our persistent attachment to the constructed (*parikalpita*) aspects of perception. This leads to an interminable vicious circle, that can only be relinquished upon the realization that our perception is just that and nothing else (*vijñaptimātra*). This is the "establishment" (a misnomer if ever there was one) of the *bodhisattva* in *apratiṣṭhita nirvāṇa* (unfixed *nirvāṇa*) and the realization of *nirvikalpa-jñāna* (non-conceptual knowledge). Thus, the *bodhisattva* being "of no fixed abode," rides the waves of *saṃsāra*, being "in" it and yet "beyond" it.

Thus, with regard to the *bodhisattva*, Asaṅga declares that:

> Moreover, because discursive thought (*vikalpa*) does not arise, there is no future generation of a given-thing (*vastu*) having that as its support (*ālambana*). Thus for him discursive thought, along with the given thing, ceases (*nirodha*). This should be understood as the cessation of all proliferation (*prapañca*).[92]

Classical Yogācāra, in its de-construction of accepted Abhidharmic concepts, continues in the tradition of the Prajñāpāramitā. Asaṅga and Vasubandhu both attack the notion of the independent existence of material form (*rūpa*). However, despite the fact that *rūpa* is not an ultimate category (there being no ultimate categories for the Mahāyāna), there is nevertheless "something there" as the basis of the *rūpa-*

skandha. In the assertion of a basis (*āśraya*) of a given-thing (*vastu*), we have here a radical departure from the Madhyamaka tradition that preceded Asaṅga. Thus, the *Tattvārtha* declares that:

> Hence, whenever a *dharma* is termed (*saṃjñakaṃ*) form etc. (*rūpādi*), that given-thing is void of identity (*ātmanā śūnyaṃ*) with the verbal designation "form" etc. Then, what remains in that place when a given-thing is termed "form" etc? As follows: just the basis (*āśraya*) of the verbal designation "form" etc., When one know both those as they really are—namely, that there is just a given-thing (*vastu-mātra*) and there is just a verbal designation (*prajñapti-mātra*) for just a given-thing—then he neither affirms (*samāropayati*) the existence of what is non-existent nor denies what is existent.[93]

For Asaṅga, although material form does not ultimately exist, the *dharmas* which form the basis of its designation nevertheless remain. This is the inexpressible nature of all *dharmas* (*nirabhilāpya svabhāvatā*). All *dharmas* are momentary (*kṣaṇika*) and so cannot be pinpointed or given a "name"; nevertheless they are present and as such provide the perceptual basis for the attribution of names. This is Asaṅga's understanding of the Middle Path being an avoidance of the extremes of "realism" (*astivāda*) and nihilism (*vaināśika, prajñapti-mātra-vāda*). Soteriologically, it means that liberation (*nirvāṇa*) is not to be found in the relinquishment of *saṃsāra*, but in the "detached" immersion of the *bodhisattva* in the whirlpool of existence. This is the motif adopted in the Heart-Sutra (*Hṛdayasūtra*) and the Diamond-Sutra (*Vajracchedikaprajñāpāramitāsūtra*), where we find the same "spiral-staircase" of dialectical reasoning, where accepted categories are refuted, then fully comprehended, and then re-affirmed from a higher perspective (that of perfected wisdom). Thus,

> *iha Śāriputra rūpaṃ śūnyatā śūnyataiva rūpaṃ*
> Here, O Śāriputra, form is emptiness, and emptiness is form.

This brief phrase sums up the characteristic style of the shorter Prajñāpāramitā texts and indeed of the Prajñāpāramitā as a whole. Wayman suggests that the shorter texts, and the *Vajracchedika* in particular, show the influence of Yogācāra ideas.[94] Certainly the verse just mentioned can be reconciled to Asaṅga's qualified denial of the *rūpa-skandha*, (combined with the affirmation of its perceptual support, devoid of *prapañca*).

Through the dialectical method endorsed in the Prajñāpāramitā one first negates the categories of the world. Then, through a thorough understanding of emptiness, one realizes that it is only because everything is empty that anything can be said to come into existence in the first place. This isn't so much a real negation, as an acceptance that emptiness is the only manner in which something can be said to "exist." This is in fact what Nāgārjuna means when he says that emptiness is dependent origination (*MMK 24.18*), and is one of the primary reasons why *śūnyatā* is not nihilism. Form can only be understood if it is understood to be empty of its own being. For the Yogācārins form (*rūpa*) exists but only as an unreal construction (*abhūta-parikalpa*). *Saṃsāra* then is an evanescent bubble that needs pricking. However, once the bubble's evanescence is realized there is no longer any need to prick it since it no longer holds any sway over us. The consequences of this is that in the last analysis even the *via negativa* endorsed by the Prajñāpāramitā is itself superseded. The affirmation, initially made from an ignorant point of view is re-affirmed but from a new and higher perspective (that of the ultimate truth gained through perfect wisdom). One way of expressing the Prajñāpāramitā position is to say that it does not deny the existence of form (*rūpa*), but in fact re-affirms it from the standpoint of the emptiness of form. It is only because something is empty that it can even be said to exist. This is a thorough-going attack on the presuppositions of "substantialist" thought.

Experientially, perfect wisdom is the consequence of *śamathavipaśyanāyuganaddha* or "tranquility combined with insight." Having seen the evanescence of all *dharmas* and thereby negating them, one then returns to one's original position, but this time with the benefits of the new meditative insight (*prajñā*). *Dharmas* are still "there," but now it is understood that they are not the self-sufficient "entities" that they were once thought to be. This is experiencing with complete insight (*vipaśyanā*) and yet remaining unaffected and unpeturbed (*śamatha*). This is also penetration into the selflessness or emptiness of all *dharmas*, and correlates with the Mahāyāna idea that there is no difference between *saṃsāra* and *nirvāṇa*. Such an insight is the ultimate redemption of the conventional realm. For the Yogācārin in particular, but by no means exclusively, it is the question of the difference between a defiled and ignorant mind and a pure and enlightened mind. The *bodhisattva* as an example of the latter, remains in *saṃsāra*, but is always "above it."

The *bodhisattva*, as an enlightened being, is in a state of complete tranquility conjoined with insight (*śamathavipaśyanāyuganaddha*). Such a being understands that all *dharmas* are evanescent yet nevertheless continues to experience them. Thus, the *bodhisattva* is said to reside in the *nirvāṇa* of "no fixed abode" (*apratiṣṭhita nirvāṇa*). The philosophical problems of how someone devoid of all discursive thought (*vikalpa*) could then continue to experience a world of conceptual constructions was one that provided the focus for some debate in the Yogācāra school.[95]

In this section we have considered the Yogācāra understanding of perception and have come to the conclusion that the description of the school as "idealistic," while an understandable interpretation, is problematic to say the least. The early texts of the Yogācāra school display an interest in the nature of experience which largely "brackets out" discussion of the reality or unreality of an external world. Asaṅga is primarily interested in the dynamics of experience and as such restricts the parameters of legitimate philosophical discourse to "that which is given [in experience] and nothing else" (*vastu-mātra*). We are now in a position to consider the applicability of the term "idealism" again—this time in the case of the GK. In examining the early Advaita position it should be noted that the early Yogācāra thought to which the GK is indebted might be more accurately described as "phenomenological" rather than "idealistic" since ontological assertions (*samāropa*) and negations (*apavāda*) of an independently existing external world are avoided ("bracketed out"?) in the Yogācāra's quest to avoid extremes and remain true to the experiential event. This should be kept in mind when considering the use of Yogācāra ideas in the *Gauḍapādīya-kārikā*.

The Non-Veridicality (Vaitathya) *of Waking and Dream Experiences in the GK*

> Just as a dream and illusion and a castle in the air are seen, so is seen this whole universe by those well-versed in the Vedāntas.[96]

The idea that the world is like a dream is given philosophical backing in the second and fourth *prakaraṇas* where the GK continues its exposition of the truth of non-origination through an analysis of the waking and dream states of consciousness. Between them, these two states constitute our entire experience of diversity. Thus, any attempt to derive the doctrines of non-origination (*ajātivāda*), and non-dualism (*advaita*) from empirical experience must deal with the appearance of such diversity.

The common sense realist argues that waking and dream experience fundamentally differ. Perceptions in the waking state correspond to a real, substantial, and external world, while experiences in the dream state are figments of our imagination, merely existing "in the mind." The author of GK II subverts this distinction with a series of arguments designed to show the similarity of the two states.

Waking experience is claimed to have a practical utility and a continuity that is not found in a dream. Against this it is argued that the utility of waking experience is in fact contradicted by virtue of the fact that it is constantly interrupted by dreams.[97] The commentator (Śaṅkara?) points out that just as eating food in a dream will not satisfy the waking person, one can eat a huge meal while awake and yet still dream that one has not eaten for days. If dreams displayed no coherence for the agent, it would be impossible to make any sense of such experiences while they were occurring.

The weird and wonderful character of dreams is determined by the particular state of the dreaming subject (*sthānidharmā*). What is strange from the perspective of the waking state is in fact a normality for the dreamer.[98] Even the distinction between inner thought and outer perception can be found in the dream state.[99] If this were not so, one would always be a lucid dreamer i.e. one would always know that one was in a dream, and this is quite obviously not the case. The same distinctions can be found in both the waking and the dream states. Thus the two states are taken to be one.[100]

According to this analysis the correct criterion for dismissing dream experiences as non-veridical (*vitathā*) is their lack of continuity, i.e. at some time or other the dream world is contradicted by the experience of the other states of consciousness. This criterion of course also applies to the waking state. The only time that we "step outside" waking experience is when we are in one of the other states of consciousness, i.e. dream, deep sleep, or meditation (*samādhi*). In all three of these other spheres, the world as we experience it in the waking state is contradicted.

GK IV.25 concords with this analysis, suggesting that,

> From a logical point of view it is held that a designation (*prajñapti*) has an objective reference (*nimitta*);
> from the point of view of reality, it is said that [there is] no objective-reference for an objective-referent.[101]

There are in fact no objective grounds from which we can validate our own experience. With regard to the dream and waking states, both are false since both are limited, having a beginning and an end. Reality must always be. The only thing which stands the test is Brahman, which is eternally unborn. All dualistic experience is false because it fails to live up to the standard of immutability. Thus, throughout the second, third, and fourth *prakaraṇas* we find our authors stating that,

> That which does not exist in the beginning and end, also [does not exist] in the present.[102]

This is one of the most frequently repeated phrases of the *Gauḍapādīya-kārikā*; for something to be real, it cannot ever have come into existence, or ever cease to be.[103] It is a succinct statement of *ajātivāda*, the doctrine of non-origination.

"Enclosure" and the World within the Mind

The second *prakaraṇa* states that the cause of the unreality of objects in the dream state is their "enclosure" (*saṃvṛtaḥ*), that is their "location within" (*antaḥsthāna*). Karmarkar says that "Things seen in a dream are admitted to be false, because they are seen within the body in a very limited space."[104] Virtually all commentators follow this line of interpretation, stemming as it does from Śaṅkara's(?) commentary. There it is explained that objects experienced in a dream are unreal for "mountains or elephants cannot possibly exist within the limited space of a body."

However, in GK II.4 the same reason is given for the unreality of objects in the waking state. What sense are we to make of the statement that external objects are unreal because they are "enclosed" within the body? Although the "spatial limitations" argument can be used against the veridicality of dream experiences (there being no problem here since common sense beliefs do not attribute externality to dream objects), the same argument fails to stand up to rational consideration when applied to waking experience.[105] In the fourth *prakaraṇa*, the falsity (*mṛṣā*) of the dream state is argued for on just such grounds, again using the term *saṃvṛta*, "enclosed." Thus, IV:33 says:

> All *dharmas* in a dream are false on account of their perception within the body. How can there be the perception of existing things within this confined space?[106]

"Enclosure within the body" can hardly be the meaning of the term in the context of GK II.4 since it would make no sense to argue that the "external" world of waking experience existed within our own body because the body itself is a material object and part of that world. Besides, IV.33 is discussing *dharmas* not *bhāvas*, which may be a different case altogether.[107] In this context, therefore, it seems more likely that the argument refers to "enclosure within" the mind.[108] This makes statements such as IV.36—"all things perceived by the mind (*citta*) are insubstantial,"[109] appear more appropriate. On this understanding of the verses, it is our error in attributing "otherness" to the world that is called into question. The problem amounts to mistaking the experiences of the mind as something other than the mind. The denial of "otherness" or separation is a basic tenet of the non-dualistic (*advaita*) tradition and here the author of GK IV is establishing *advaita* through a critique of correspondence theories of perception.[110]

The Status of the Waking and Dream Worlds in Classical Advaita Vedānta

In his *Brahmasūtrabhāṣya*, Śaṅkara clearly differentiates dreaming and waking experience in that dreams are false and illusory whereas waking experience is veridical, having an external cause.[111] The authors of the second, third, and fourth *prakaraṇas* of the GK, however, do not accept the distinction between waking and dream experience. The equality of the two states of consciousness is argued for in the fourth *prakaraṇa* in terms of a theory of perception that has clear antecedents in the Yogācāra school of Mahāyāna Buddhism. According to the GK, consciousness never actually comes into contact with an external object. Neither waking nor dream experience "touches" an external world.

This in itself does not necessarily prevent a conventional (*saṃvṛti-satya*) distinction between waking and dreaming experience being drawn, a point emphasized by Śaṅkara. It may still be the case that there is an independent and external world that corresponds in some way to our waking experience of it, while in the case of dream experiences there is no such external correspondence. The point of the arguments in the second and fourth *prakaraṇas* is that such a distinction has no independent means of corroboration. It cannot therefore be an ultimate truth (*paramārtha-satya*). This is the point stressed in GK IV.25 (previously quoted). From a logical (or perhaps "common-sense") point of view (*yukti-darśana*), it would be a mistake to say that a designation (*prajñapti*) has no objective referent. Nevertheless, such referents themselves have no objective means of verification.[112]

The only manner in which one could validate the postulated correspondence between experience and object would be to "step outside" the confines of that experience. The GK's point is that every time this is done we find ourselves confronted with a conflicting set of data, that is, we find ourselves in the states of sleep, dream, or *samādhi*, none of which substantiate waking experience. For the GK then, all experience is "state-bound;" the only way in which the veridicality of an experience can be validated is to be literally "out of one's mind." This is the "*metanoia*" (*amanastā*) of the enlightened being and is to be achieved through the practice of *yoga*. It is only then that Brahman, the ultimate reality, can be directly perceived.

The arguments that are put forward in the GK establish the reasons why we take dream experiences to be false (when we are awake). Those reasons are not based upon the fact that our experiences correspond to a world of real, external objects, but upon the coherence of each experience in relation to our general set of experiences (and the presuppositions and prejudicial views that go along with them). This is a "coherence" rather than a "correspondence" theory of perception. The idea that the mind could ever come into contact with an external and independent reality is a fallacious one.

In this case, one can agree with Stephen Kaplan's "phenomenological interpretation" of these *kārikās*.[113] The basic thrust of the equation of waking and dream experiences is the realization that these two types of experience are equal in the sense that what we perceive is the appearance (*ābhāsa*) of an object and not the object itself. This is not so much a denial of an independent world of objects but rather a denial that such a world could have any bearing upon experience, which is wholly an activity of consciousness.

It may well be the case that the description of the philosophy of the *Gauḍapādīya-kārikā* as "idealistic" is as misleading as it is for the works of the early Yogācārins Asaṅga and Vasubandhu.[114] This is a problem that has found its way to the forefront of Western approaches to Indian philosophy and I suggest that the question can never be adequately resolved until we are more precise about the meaning of the term "idealism." Many of the philosophical systems that developed in India were closely linked to a religious tradition and consequently cannot be understood purely in terms of the western term "*philosophia*"—the love of wisdom for its own sake. In Vedānta and Buddhism wisdom procures liberation. The soteriological intent of much of Indian philosophy is a point that has been stressed in the past to the point of banality. Nevertheless, it is a fact that should not be overlooked. In understanding Indian systems of thought from a Western perspective, it is important to acknowledge the background of many doctrines and theories in actual religious practice. In the case of the Yogācāra school, for instance, Schmithausen has demonstrated the way in which the school's distinctive philosophical position is established as a result of reflection upon the nature of the meditative experience (*samādhi*) and its consequences for so-called "normative" states of mind.[115]

Both the Yogācāra and Vedānta systems place a great deal of importance on the attainment of some form of non-discursive (*nirvikalpa*) "enlightenment" experience, sometimes referred to as *yogi-pratyakṣa*, the direct-perception of reality by the yogin. Such an experience is claimed to be of a radically different order when compared to the experiences of most human beings. Indeed, the distinction between the enlightenment-experience of insight (*prajñā*) and the everyday experiences of unenlightened individuals is vitally important to the social structure of the religious community in India. Sociologically, the difference between levels of attainment and knowledge clearly demarcates the religious specialist i.e. the *bhikṣu* or the *saṃnyāsī*, from the lay community at large. For the religious layperson, such a distinction provides an ideal or an archetype to be lived up to and respected in others, while for the religious specialist it functions as a religious "status symbol," providing a clearly defined and hierarchical path of meditative attainment.

The distinction between "mundane" (*aparā*) and "supramundane" (*parā*) levels of knowledge (*vidyā*) is found throughout Indian religious thought and Buddhism and Vedānta are no exceptions. The distinction is often expressed in terms of the axiological polarity between defiled and pure states of mind, or sometimes between mundane consciousness (*vijñāna : episteme*) and supramundane insight (*jñāna : gnosis*).[116] It is in the context of this distinction that the question of the appropriateness of the Western term "idealism" is to be considered in relation to these philosophical systems.

The GK has an idealistic epistemology, that is it propounds a theory of (mundane) knowledge (*pramāṇa*) in which the objects of experience are said to be "constructed" in some manner by the dispersive mind (*vijñāna*). The world of our experience is nothing more than a series of images (*ābhāsa*) caused by the fluctuations of consciousness (*vijñāna-spandita*). This is where the idea of an independent and external world of objects comes from. Clearly then in our everyday experience of waking, dreaming, and sleeping we are living a lie; we are ignorant in that we fail to realize that the objective world that confronts us is made up of images caused by our own disturbed state of mind.

This all sounds remarkably like straightforward idealism. Nevertheless, the GK maintains that there is a wholly different type of "experience." This is the fourth state of awareness (*turīya*) discussed in GK I. In this supramundane state of knowledge the ignorance (*avidyā*) and constructed ideality (*vikalpita*) of the so called "normative" states of experience are completely absent. In *turīya* or *samādhi* the yogin has a direct perception (*pratyakṣa*) of "things as they are" (*yathābhūta*). This *gnosis* (*jñāna*) is a direct apprehension of Brahman, the supreme reality. The distinction between epistemological idealism (i.e. the theory that "normative" experience is a product of a vibrating consciousness or *vijñāna*) and a "gnoseological" realism (i.e. the theory that a substantive and mind-independent reality is directly perceived in supramundane *gnosis* or *jñāna*) is crucial to a correct appraisal of the sophistication of Gauḍapādian thought.

The unqualified description of the philosophy of the GK as idealistic is inappropriate insofar as the text posits a substantial reality (Brahman) wholly independent of the mind and its constructions. Nevertheless, the text also suggests that the world as we know it in mundane and unenlightened experience is largely an idealistic construction. The world as experienced by the religious specialist (the enlightened one, *buddha*), however, is not one of ideality (*vikalpita*). It is in fact a direct perception of "reality as it is" (*yathābhūta*). So from the GK's point of view all unenlightened individuals are idealists, in practice if not in theory, in that they experience a realm of ideality constructed by their own minds. In contrast to this all enlightened individuals experience reality not ideality.

As we have seen, the *Gauḍapādīya-kārikā* consistently denies that the world is an idealistic creation of the individual.[117] Nevertheless, all that the unenlightened mind comes into contact with in the so-called "normative" states of consciousness (i.e. the waking, dream, and deep sleep states) are the activities (*spandita*) of the mind itself. This is the adoption of the Yogācāra notion of *Vijñaptimātratā* by the *Gauḍapādīya-kārikā*, a point perhaps noted by the commentator, who describes Gauḍapāda's position as "*jñaptimātra*."[118] For the commentator these arguments are adopted from the "*Vijñānavādins*" to combat realism and as such they seem to have been understood to be of a provisional nature.[119] From the text of the GK, however, there is no evidence to suggest that this is not the author's own definitive position (*siddhānta*).

Māyā *in the* Gauḍapādīya-kārikā

This brings us to another important notion in the *Gauḍapādīya-kārikā*—that of *māyā*. The authors of the GK do not develop the notion of *māyā* to any great extent. This is probably because they had little interest in the idea, the primary focus of the GK being the truth of non-origination. Equally, the reason the notion of *māyā* shows little in the way of systematic development may reflect that fact that for the authors of the GK *māyā* is, in the final analysis, incomprehensible (*acintya*).[120] This could be seen as a possible precursor of the classical Advaita Vedānta doctrine of the indeterminability of *māyā* (*māyā-anirvacanīya-vāda*). However, one should beware of reading back views into the *kārikās* for there is no consistently developed doctrine of *māyā* in the *Gauḍapādīya-kārikā*. Debate about the nature of *māyā* was left to the GK's successors.

Nevertheless, one can discern certain key points in the GK's conception of *māyā*. Traces of Vedic influence can be found in certain references to *māyā* as some sort of "divine power" of *ātman* in the second and third *prakaraṇas*.[121] Notable is a quotation referring to the birth of Indra through *māyā* in GK III.[122] In GK I.17, however, the existence of the world is rejected on the grounds that it is "merely *māyā*" (*māyāmātra*). This accords with GK III.27 where *māyā* is placed in direct opposition to *tattva*, reality. It is this opposition, *māyā :: tattva* which is central to the Gauḍapādian understanding of the term.

> The birth of an existent is, in fact, only reasonable through *māyā*, and not in reality. [Him] for whom [the existent] is born in reality, the [already] born would be born.[123]

The verse following this (in the third *prakaraṇa*) is illuminating since it denies that a non-existent thing can come into existence, even through *māyā*. *Māyā* then has more provisional status than the "son of a barren woman," which cannot even be perceived.[124]

The frequent occurrence of the term "*māyā*" in the instrumental case throughout the text points to its position as the means by which the world appears as it does. It is through *māyā* that the mind vibrates into the duality of a perceiver and a perceived.[125] The frequent juxtaposition of *māyā* and "dream" (*svapna*) also alludes to the "dream-like" status of the world.[126] In post-Gauḍapādian Vedānta, *māyā* is increasingly given the status of a specific power (*śakti*), through which Brahman apparently creates (*vivartate*) the manifold world. In GK II and III we find the term utilized in a cosmological context as the *ātman*'s power of self-delusion; while in GK IV and the latter part of GK III, *māyā* is used in a psychological context as the delusory capacity of the individual mind to construct a static world picture from the flux of experience.

> Just as an illusory elephant is said to exist owing to the perception [of it] and common consent, likewise it is said that an object exists on account of its perception and common consent.[127]

In IV.58, *māyā* is aligned with the notion of *saṃvṛti*, the concealing and conventional level of truth. Origination can only occur in the saṃvṛtic world, that is in the realm of *māyā*, but not in reality. However, *māyā* itself does not exist, being mere appearance. Consequently, people who see origination are seeing a "footprint in the sky."[128]

A more comprehensive understanding of the status of *māyā* can be drawn from an analysis of the *Gauḍapādīya-kārikā's* use of analogies. The relationship between the world and Brahman is like that between a rope and its false appearance as a snake. Thus,

> As a rope not clearly seen in the dark, is falsely imagined to be things like a snake or a stream etc., so likewise is *ātman* falsely imagined.
>
> Just as the imagined thing (*vikalpa*) disappears when the rope is clearly seen as a rope, so is *ātman* clearly seen as the non-dual (*advaita*).[129]

The world of diversity has the status of a false imagination (*vikalpa*); it is like the snake, a misconception, which nevertheless has its basis in the rope.[130]

Māyā is also comparable to the image (*ābhāsa*) caused by a moving firebrand—it is a false appearance projected upon the screen of reality. Both the firebrand and the rope-snake analogy imply that behind all appearances there is an unchanging and unaffected substratum, just as behind the snake and the image there is a rope or a firebrand. The world is not real, just as the snake and the image are not real, yet what status they do have (as appearances) is dependent upon the substrative reality underlying them.[131] This is classic Vedānta in that the world can only appear because Brahman supports it. Thus, we can discern in the Gauḍapādīan notion of *māyā*, the stirrings of a philosophical position that predominated in the later Śaṅkarite school and that is the idea that the relationship between *Brahman* and the world is indeterminable (*anirvacanīya*) and inexpressible in terms of the categories of "existence" and "non-existence." In the firebrand section of the fourth *prakaraṇa*, the author argues that:

> When consciousness (*vijñāna*) is vibrating, the images do not derive from anywhere else. When it is not vibrating, [they] do not reside elsewhere, nor do they enter consciousness.
>
> [The images] do not go out from consciousness, owing to their insubstantiality. Because of the absence of a relation between cause and effect, they are ever incomprehensible (*acintya*).[132]

The Firebrand Analogy in GK IV as Explanation of the Experience of Duality

The world is a dualistic construction caused by the oscillation of consciousness (*vijñāna/citta-spandita*). These vibrations of the mind create the images of a perceiver and a perceived. Anything that the mind appears to come into contact with is in reality only an image caused by the mind's own tendency to fluctuate. These images are likened to those caused by a moving firebrand.

> Just as with a moving firebrand there are straight and crooked images etc., likewise with vibrating consciousness (*vijñāna*) there are the images of a perceiver and a perceived.[133]

The analogy of a "wheel of fire" (*alātacakra*) was originally used by Buddhists to explain how a series of discrete "flashes of light" could appear as a single persisting entity. When a firebrand is moved in a circular motion there appears to be a wheel of fire hovering in the air. The illusion of permanence is created by the firebrand's swift movement.

In his *Abhidharmakośabhāṣya*, Vasubandhu (*qua* Sautrāntika) criticizes the Vaibhāṣika's acceptance of shape (*saṃsthāna*) as a substantial entity (*dravya-sat*). In order to illustrate his point, the author refers to the evanescence and insubstantiality of the various shapes caused by the whirling of a firebrand.

> Seeing a firebrand [moving] in one direction, from one spot to the immediately adjacent one, quickly and without interruption, one recognizes (or ascertains) "length," seeing it thusly in all directions, one recognizes "round." Shape is [therefore] not substantial (*na dravyasat saṃsthānam*).[134]

Interestingly, the author of GK IV uses the analogy to make the opposite point. The single firebrand when moved does indeed create various images. These images depend upon the firebrand for their appearance, yet they are not real. As such, they are neither part of the firebrand itself, nor are they different from it. This use of the analogy is ingenious and it is interesting to compare this to the Buddhist version of the analogy because it shows the differing interests of the two camps. The Buddhists are primarily interested in explaining how a stream of discrete perceptions can create the illusion of a permanent self. The author of GK IV, however, wishes to establish the non-dual substratum of the world appearance. To do this the author emphasizes the role of the firebrand as the non-dual reality behind the fluctuating images.

The terms "*cittaspandita*" and "*vijñānaspandita*," denoting the "vibration" or "oscillation" of consciousness, are of some interest given the importance of the term "*spanda*" in the (subsequent?) traditions of Kashmir Śaivism. The term has no obvious antecedents in this context and is perhaps being used by the authors of the *Gauḍapādīya-kārikā* instead of the more obvious Yogācāra term "*vijñānapariṇāma*"—the "transformations of consciousness." Vasubandhu (*qua* Yogācārin) is responsible for the establishment of this phrase as a technical term explaining the manifestation of subject-object dichotomies in experience. According to the opening verse of the *Triṃśikā*, both the idea of a subjective self (*ātman*) and of an object of perception (*dharma*) are caused by *vijñānapariṇāma*.[135] Thus the term performs the same function as the GK's term "*vijñānaspandita*." The advantage of the latter term is that it explains the manifestation of dualism without necessitating an actual transformation (*pariṇāma*) thereby conforming to the doctrine of non-origination (*ajātivāda*) which is central to the philosophical perspective of the GK as a whole.

Nevertheless, the important point to note about the notion of the vibrations of consciousness is that it is a metaphorical expression. One cannot take the "vibration" or "oscillation" motif too seriously since it provides nothing more than an analogical explanation of the way in which consciousness can appear as two (subject and object). Notice for instance that the term "*spandita*" is only introduced *after* the simile of the firebrand. The idea of consciousness-vibration, therefore, is only valid as an explanation of duality if seen as an analogy based upon our experience of the images created by a moving firebrand.[136]

It is clear that the entire philosophy of the *Gauḍapādīya-kārikā* is based upon the conception of an unchanging and non-dual reality. GK II.12, for instance, declares that "*ātman* deludes itself through its own *māyā*". The inevitable questions arise as to how and why the non-dual and omniscient *ātman* could possibly "delude itself." The upshot of *ajātivāda* is that all attempts at explaining creation are doomed to failure from the start because they take creation to be a real and not an apparent transformation. There can be no attributable reason for the creation of the universe. Thus, in the first *prakaraṇa* it is noted that,

> Creation is for the sake of enjoyment (or experience)—so say some. Others say it is for the sake of sport. This again is the lordly own-nature of the divine, for what desire is there for the one who has obtained all wishes?[137]

The world can only appear insofar as it conforms to the very nature of Brahman itself. *Māyā* as such is inexplicable—it is "there" in the sense that we experience it but it is not reality, being mere appearance. As such, it is directly comparable to the status of dreams as seen from the perspective of waking consciousness.[138]

It has been suggested that the term "*māyā*" derives from the root *mā*, "to measure."[139] *Māyā* is the construction of boundaries and distinctions (*vikalpa*) in that which has none (*nirvikalpa*);[140] it is a measuring (*mā*) of the immeasurable (*amātra*).[141] *Māyā* cannot be ultimately real because it is sublatable i.e. it is capable of being overturned by a higher form of knowledge. Dream experience contradicts waking experience and vice versa. More importantly, however, the realization of non-duality contradicts both.

Diversity appears to be caused by the faulty apprehension of the individual. This is what the authors of the *Gauḍapādīya-kārikā* are getting at when they say that the world is enclosed within the mind.[142] We cling to non-existent entities (*abhūtābhiniveśa*),[143] and construct a duality based upon these attachments. Through misconception (*viparyāsa*) we experience "contact" with the "incomprehensible" (*acintya*).[144] Our experience as individuals then is a peculiar construction of our own tendencies and dispositions. Each person's perception of reality is conditioned by the memory of past experiences. Thus, in the second *prakaraṇa* it is said that:

> First [*ātman*] imagines the *jīva*, and then various known entities, [both] external and internal, for as with one's knowledge, so is one's memory.[145]

The Meaning of the Term "Asparśayoga"

There appear to be three possible meanings of the term "*asparśayoga*" in the *Gauḍapādīya-kārikā*. They are:

1. A technical term for the practice of yoga. Thus Mahadevan (1960) notes:

> *Asparśayoga* is the yoga of transcendence, whereby one realizes the supra-rational reality. . .The purpose for which this yoga is to be resorted to is the same as that which is set forth in the *Pātañjalasūtra* as the goal of yoga, i.e., to stem the tide of the surging psychoses of mind and gradually attain thereby a state of mindlessness.[146]

2. A description of the highest form of *samādhi*. Thus Bhattacharya (1943) suggests that:

> The word *asparśayoga* literally means the yoga, in which there is no contact, or the faculty of perception by touch or connection with anything. The author himself says (III.37), it is a *samādhi* "profound or abstract concentration," and very difficult to realize. It points to what is *asaṃprajñāta samādhi* (*Yogasūtra*, I.2, 18, 51 with the scholiast Vyasa), or *nirvikalpa samādhi* (*Pañcadaśī* II.28) of yogins.[147]

3. A reference to the GK's perceptual theory of no-contact. We find Hixon maintaining that:

> *asparśayoga* is a path of insight which does not involve trance-states at all, or at least does not regard the highest realization as a trance-state. We propose that *asparśa* is synonymous with *asaṅga* or *niḥsaṅga* as the terms are used in *Gauḍapādakarikā* IV.72 and IV.79, to refer to the absence of an object. . .this understanding of the mind does not apply only to trance-states but to the nature of mind and its objects in any and all states of consciousness.[148]

These options, however, are not mutually exclusive. Given the emphasis placed upon meditative techniques throughout the GK, it seems likely that "*asparśayoga*" is a technical term which defines the nature of the practice of yoga in terms of its final goal, the realization that the mind never comes into contact with an external world. In this case, it is rather similar to Vyāsa's definition of yoga (in *Yogasūtrabhāṣya* I.1) as *samādhi*; the definition favored by the GK being that yoga is "*asparśa*."[149] It should not seem strange to find yogic practices being described in terms of their final goal. After all in the case of many meditative paths, it is the description of the goal that most clearly differentiates the philosophical position of one yogic school from another.

To accept the first option to the exclusion of the others is to avoid the fact that the *kārikā* states that "this is *asparśayoga*" (III.39) immediately after a description of *nirvikalpa samādhi* (III.37–38). Nevertheless, options (2) and (3) are also too narrow by themselves since it is equally clear that the *Gauḍapādīya-kārikā* encourages the utilization of certain meditative techniques to control and unify the fluctuating mind. This has lead Colin Cole to suggest that:

> there are two meanings of the term *Asparśa Yoga*. On the philosophical level, the term implies the realization of non-duality, i.e., of *Turīya* or Brahman. In this sense it could be called the "No-dual Yoga" or the "Yoga of the Non-dual." On the level of religious practice, the term refers to discipline, path, method or process whereby the *sādhaka* attains this condition of being one with Ultimate Reality.[150]

To deny that *asparśayoga* is an explicit reference to a set of meditative practices or that it refers to a state of realization is to fly in the face of the evidence. The confutation of goal and method in the GK is not surprising given its radical absolutism. The most plausible explanation of the term "*asparśayoga*," therefore, is that it refers both to a form of meditative practice (yoga) and to the goal of that practice (*samādhi*). As such, it also presupposes a specific epistemological theory—the theory that the mind does not touch an external object. This explanation, I suggest, most readily accommodates the multivalented nature of the term "*asparśayoga*" as it occurs in the *Gauḍapādīya-kārikā*.

CHAPTER

6

Gauḍapādian Inclusivism and the Mahāyāna Buddhist Tradition

It is well known that Śaṅkara was criticized by later (rival) Vedāntins as a crypto-Buddhist (*pracchana bauddha*). What is less well known is that before the time of Śaṅkara, the Mādhyamika Buddhist philosopher Bhāvaviveka countered the inverse claim that the Mahāyāna is really a form of crypto-Vedānta. As we shall see, Bhāvaviveka's response to this accusation is of great interest and highlights many of the issues concerning the relationship between these two religious and philosophical traditions. However, accusations of crypto-Buddhism or crypto-Vedāntism fail to take into account the sense in which members of the various Indian religious and philosophical movements lived in a context of continual and largely unspoken interaction with one another, sometimes no doubt on a day-to-day basis. Despite the recent rise of certain Hindu movements with a more exclusivist attitude, the dynamic and fluid nature of Indian religion remains to this day in India where Hindus, Buddhist, Jainas, and Muslims interact on a number of different levels, including the philosophical or the doctrinal. This is frequently overlooked by scholars of Indian philosophy who, in focusing upon a de-contextualized philosophical text, forget that it has been abstracted from its original cultural and temporal milieu where interactions between Buddhist and Vedāntins might well have been commonplace and perhaps not so controversial as is often suggested in the literature on this subject.

Probably the most notable features of the *Gauḍapādīya-kārikā* relevant to the question of the alleged crypto-Buddhism of Advaita Vedānta are the Buddhistic terminology of the text (especially in the fourth *prakaraṇa*), the doctrinal emphasis upon non-origination (*ajātivāda*) and the assertion of the equality of the waking and dream states. As a result of these features of the text, it has been argued that Gauḍapāda is a crypto-Buddhist (deriving *ajātivāda* from the Madhyamaka school and the doctrine of the equality of waking and dream states from the Yogācārins). That the GK has been influenced by Buddhist ideas is, of course, beyond question. However, the issue of the apparent crypto-Buddhism of the text depends partly upon one's definition of what Buddhism is and partly upon an appraisal of the GK's own conception of Buddhism and its relationship to that tradition.

The Gauḍapādian Conception of Buddhism

In GK IV.25 the author rejects the ultimacy of the dependently-existent realm (*paratantrāstitā*). This view is stated in opposition to the classical Yogācāra position that is put forward as the *pūrvapakṣa* in the preceding verse. Thus,

> *prajñapteḥ sanimittatvam anyathā dvayānāśataḥ, saṃkleśasyopalabdheś ca paratantrāstitā matā.*
> [Yogācārin]: "It is admitted that a designation (*prajñapti*) has an objective cause (*sanimittatva*) otherwise the duality (*dvaya*) [of perceiver and perceived] would not be in existence; the experience of afflictions (*saṃkleśa*) also exists dependent (*paratantra*) [upon this objectivity]."

> *prajñapteḥ sanimittatvam iṣyate yuktidarśanāt, nimittasyānimittatvam iṣyate bhūtadarśanāt.*
> From the perspective of common sense it is held that a designation has an objective cause, [however], from the perspective of the actual state of things [there is] no objective cause for the objective cause [itself].

Prima facie the denial that designations (*prajñapti*) have some form of objective cause or reference (*nimitta*) might be misleading since it is clear that words do have some sort of reference. However, the referents themselves (*nimitta*) have no "referential objectivity" (*animittatva*) from an ultimate point of view. Upholding the ultimate non-objectivity (*animittatva*) of referents, however, does not necessitate a denial of their conventional efficacy (*saṃvṛti/vyavahāra*).

The GK's refusal to accept the ultimate objectivity (*nimittatva*) of designations places it in general agreement with the position of the Madhyamaka school (*pace* Yogācāra). Nevertheless, it should be pointed out that the fundamental reasons behind their respective refutations substantially differ. All Buddhist schools accept the validity of the scheme of inter-dependent-origination (*pratītyasamutpāda*) upholding what might be called a "non-substantial" view of reality. The Vedāntic authors of the GK, however, are firm adherents of a "substance" view of reality and avoid all terms that might imply such a conception (note the absence of the notions of *pratītyasamutpāda, niḥsvabhāvatā, śūnyatā*, etc). In fact throughout the GK one finds a consistent (if implicit) rejection of the mutual-dependency model (*pratītyasamutpāda*) accepted by the Buddhists. That the authors never confront these issues head on reflects the intention of establishing a Vedāntic type of absolutism based upon Mahāyāna arguments. In IV.25, however, the author explicitly rejects the Yogācāra view that mutual-dependency actually exists (*paratantrāstitā*). The Mādhyamikas, of course, also refuted the Yogācāra notion that the paratantric realm actually existed but not for the absolutistic reasons of the GK. From the Madhyamaka point of view those Yogācāra texts which asserted the "existence" of the *paratantra-svabhāva* were guilty of reification, thus straying into the extreme of eternalism (*śāsvata-vāda*).[1]

In IV.87–88 the GK distinguishes between different levels of knowledge. The scheme outlined is substantially based upon Mahāyāna divisions of the Buddhist path.

1. "Dualistic mundane" knowledge (***laukika***), that has both an object and a perception of that object.
2. "Pure mundane" knowledge (***śuddhā-laukika***), that is a perception of the world without a corresponding object.
3. "Supra-mundane" knowledge (***lokottara***), that has neither an object nor a perception.

"Pure mundane" knowledge seems to conform to the Yogācāra realization of *vijñapti-mātra* in that it is a realization that one experiences representations (*vijñapti*, "percepts") of objects and not the objects themselves. The supra-mundane knowledge corresponds to the final stage of enlightenment outlined by Asaṅga and Vasubandhu where even the notion of representation is relinquished. For how can you talk of representation (*vijñapti*) in the absence of an object that is being represented?[2]

GK IV.90 then states that much knowledge can be gained from the "Agrayāna":

heyajñeyāpyapākyāni vijñeyāny agrayānataḥ, teṣāṃ anyatra vijñeyād upalambhas triṣu smṛtaḥ.

From the Agrayāna one should know that which is to be abandoned, that which is to be known, that which is to be acquired and that which is to be perfected. Excepting that which should be known (*vijñeya*), perception of these is said to occur in the three [levels of knowledge].

That the term "*agrayāna*" denotes the Mahāyāna schools can be gleaned from such texts as the *Ratnagotravibhāga* and the *Mahāyānasūtrālaṅkāra*. This verse would seem to imply that although much can be learned from Mahāyāna Buddhism, it is not the tradition of the author. On this interpretation the author of GK IV did not conceive of himself as a Mahāyānist; the traditions in fact are to be clearly differentiated. Thomas Wood, however, suggests that the term "*agrayāna*" means "the first vehicle" and is a reference to the "Hīnayāna" and not the Mahāyāna tradition.[4] "*Agra*" denotes "that which comes first" and *prima facie* the translation "the first vehicle" seems appropriately enough to denote the non-Mahāyāna traditions of Buddhism, accepted as a preliminary stage on the path by the Mahāyāna tradition. However, "*agra*" often denotes primacy in an evaluative sense, as in "foremost," "chief," or "best."[5]

It is unlikely, therefore, that the author of GK IV would have referred to the non-Mahāyāna ("Hīnayāna") Buddhist tradition as the "foremost vehicle" since his philosophical interest is clearly in the Mahāyāna schools. Wood fails to provide any evidence of the term being used to denote the "Hīnayāna" tradition. Indeed, the citations mentioned by Bhattacharya point to the fact that the Mahāyāna texts that use the term understand the "*agra*" of "*agrayāna*" to be a synonym for "*mahā*" (great) and thus use it to denote the "Great vehicle" (Mahāyāna) to which they belong. It seems more likely then that the term "*agrayāna*" in GK IV.90 is a reference to the scheme of the three levels of knowledge (dualistic mundane, pure mundane, and supramundane) mentioned in the previous verses which are derived from the author's knowledge of Mahāyāna Buddhist categories. That the author is differentiating his own position from that of the Agrayāna (from whom, nevertheless, he thinks one can learn a lot) is clear from this verse.

The fourth *prakaraṇa* begins with an invocation to "the greatest of bipeds" (*dvipadāṃ varaḥ*). The traditional commentator suggests that the author is here paying homage to Nārāyana, often described as "Puruṣottama." There is no evidence within the text, however, that would provide any support for this traditional interpretation of the verse. The verse could be a reference to the author's *guru* (perhaps even to the author of earlier *prakaraṇas* of the GK?). Bhattacharya though suggests that the invocation is paying homage to the Buddha.[6] The verse in fact says:

> I salute that greatest of bipeds, who, through a knowledge (*jñāna*) like space (*ākāśa*, or the sky) and non-different from its object, is fully-enlightened (*saṃbuddha*) about the *dharmas* resembling the sky.

Our understanding of the meaning of this verse will be greatly improved if we consider the use of "*buddha*" and its cognate terms and the "*jñāna*" mentioned in this verse. *Jñāna* is a technical term in the GK denoting the attainment of gnosis, where it is sometimes contrasted with *vijñāna* (denoting mundane consciousness). In GK IV.1 the gnosis (*jñāna*) of the "greatest of bipeds" is likened to the sky or space (*ākāśa*), presumably insofar as it is is undifferentiated and unmodified by apparent changes (this is the sense in which the term *ākāśa* is used in GK III.3–9). Such a gnosis is said to be non-different from that which is known (*jñeya*). This would appear to establish the *jñāna* under discussion in this verse as the supramundane knowledge (*lokottara jñāna*) of GK IV.88. The attainment of this state is clearly linked up with the practice of *asparśayoga* which is accordingly mentioned in the second verse. Our analysis of the epistemology of the GK has established that it upholds the view that knowledge (*jñāna*) does not "proceed outward," being unrelated (*asaṅga*) to an object (i.e. a denial of "realist" epistemologies, see GK IV.96). The mind, therefore, never comes into contact with mental objects (*dharma*) (IV.26 *et al*). The final gnosis (*jñāna*) envisaged by the GK, therefore, is a non-dual awareness devoid of subject-object distinctions (*advaya*).

Let us consider the instances when GK IV refers to the "enlightened ones" (*buddhas*). The *buddhas* are referred to in IV.19 where they are said to proclaim *ajātivāda* and again in IV.42 where it is said that they teach origination to those who are afraid of *ajātivāda*. In IV.80 the supramundane gnosis of IV.1 and IV.89 is mentioned again where it is described as an unmoving, objectless state, being unborn, self-identical, and non-dual (*advaya*). This gnosis again is said to be the sphere (*viṣaya*) of the *buddhas*. In IV.98 those who lead others to liberation (*nāyakāḥ*) are said to know (*budhyante*) that all *dharmas* are without covering, pure by nature, liberated and enlightened from the very beginning (*ādi-buddha*). To whom does the term "*nāyakāḥ*" refer? The use of the term "*buddhyante*" in this context could be interpreted as a disrespectful jibe at the Buddhist tradition. On this view the author of GK IV is using Buddhistic terms such as "*buddha*," "*budhyante*," and "*nāyakāḥ*" to refer to his own Vedāntic tradition to the detriment of Buddhism. This, however, does not appear to be the author's attitude to the Buddhist tradition. Throughout the text we see a keen interest in Mahāyāna ideas and the author is clearly indebted to the Mahāyāna for many of his fundamental ideas. It is unlikely, therefore, that the author of GK IV is here distinguishing the views of his own teachers from those expounded in the Buddhist tradition. If this were the author's intention the use of the term "*buddha*" would not have been used as this obscures rather than clarifies the distinction between his own tradition and that of the Buddhist. One must conclude then that in IV.98 the term "*nāyakāḥ*" is not being used specifically to distinguish the author's own teachers from the Buddhists. It merely refers to those who know (*budhyante*).

In the following *kārikā*, the penultimate verse of the fourth *prakaraṇa* (*IV.99*), it is said that neither *jñāna* nor *dharmas* (here "mental-objects") pass over to one another. The verse then states that "the Buddha did not say this."

> *kramate na hi buddhasya jñānaṃ dharmeṣu tāyinaḥ, sarvadharmās tathā jñānaṃ naitad buddhena bhāṣitam.*
> The gnosis (*jñāna*) of the enlightened (*buddha*) holy man does not proceed toward *dharmas*. All *dharmas* are like gnosis [in this respect]. This was not stated by the Enlightened One (*buddha*).[7]

The occurrence of the term "*tāyin*" here is interesting. According to Edgerton the term can be used to refer to a "holy" or "religious" person or "one who protects himself and others" such as the Buddha or a Jina, but does not necessarily designate a particular individual such as Gautama the historical Buddha.[8] Consequently, one cannot definitively say, as some have, that this verse is a specific reference to the founder of the Buddhist tradition. Nevertheless, the non-Vedāntic nature of the term and its frequent occurrence as an epithet of the Buddha (as well as Buddhas and Bodhisattvas in general) is highly suggestive of such a reading. Taking the verse at face value would seem to suggest that the term "*buddha*" in this *kārikā* denotes the founder of the Buddhist religion and is probably not being used in a non-specific sense to denote an "enlightened" person. Such a conclusion might lead one to think that this establishes beyond question that the author of GK IV differentiates his own view from that of the Buddha. This indeed is the traditional view accepted by the Vedānta school and supported by scholars like T. M. P. Mahadevan and R. D. Karmarkar.[9] However, Vidhushekhara Bhattacharya has put forward the view that the statement "the Buddha did not say this" (*naitad buddhena bhāṣitam*) is not a denial of the Buddhist view but rather an expression of the transcendental and ineffable nature of the Buddha's teaching. This is the Buddha's teaching but he did not say this because such an insight cannot be verbalized or taught to another! He further suggests that this statement is based upon two fundamental principles:

1. *pratyātmadharmatā*, i.e. that the ultimate truth can only be attained individually and cannot be instructed by one person to another, and
2. *purāṇasthitidharmatā*, i.e. that the true nature of reality remains the same whether it is taught by a Buddha or not.[10]

Examples of this approach to the transcendental and intuitive nature of central Mahāyāna doctrines can be found throughout the Mahāyāna literature. In chapter eight of the *Vimalakīrtinirdeśa* for instance, Vimalakīrti asks an assembled group of venerable bodhisattvas to explain the "entry into the teaching of non-duality" (*advaya-dharma-mukha-praveśa*). Upon the completion of their exposition Mañjuśri, the *bodhisattva* exemplifying wisdom (*prajña*), asks Vimalakīrti for his own views on this subject. Vimalakīrti responds by remaining silent (*tūṣṇībhūto 'bhūt*) and is thereby praised for his great profundity. In MMK 25.24, Nāgārjuna makes a similar point with regard to the Buddha's own teaching:

> *sarvopalambhopaśamaḥ prapañcopaśamaḥ śivaḥ, no kvacit kasyacit kaścid dharmo buddhena deśitaḥ.*
> The quiescence of perception, the benign quiescence of conceptual proliferation,—no *dharma* was taught by the Buddha to anyone anywhere.

In the *Vajracchedikaprajñāpāramitāsūtra* we find the following statement,

> The Lord asked: What do you think, Subhūti, does it occur to the Tathāgata, "by me has *dharma* been demonstrated?" Whosoever, Subhūti, would say "the Tathāgata has demonstrated *dharma*," he would speak falsely, he would misrepresent me by seizing upon what is not there. And why? "Demonstration of *dharma*, demonstration of *dharma*," Subhūti, there is not any *dharma* which could be got at as a demonstration of *dharma*."[11]

In the *Saptasaptati* (*Seventy-Seven Stanzas*), a short commentary on the *Vajracchedika* traditionally ascribed to Asaṅga, the following comments are made on this section of the *Sūtra*

> *nairmāṇikena no buddho dharmo nāpi ca deśitaḥ, deśitas tu dvayāgrāhyo 'vācyo 'vākpathalakṣaṇāt.*
> By the fact of being apparitional, the apparitional body is not really the Buddha, nor any Law [i.e. *dharma*, teaching) has been taught by it; on the contrary it has been taught that no *dharma* can ever be grasped in either way, i.e. either (as *dharma* or as non-*dharma* as stated before) and that it is therefore inexpressible because it transcends the path of words.[12]

Thus, there is an established trend within Mahāyāna Buddhism, no doubt influenced by the early tradition of the Buddha's silence with regard to certain questions (the *avyākṛta* or "unanswered" questions), that expresses the transcendental nature of the *Dharma* by stating that the Buddha in fact did not teach anything. The author of GK IV is aware of the Mahāyāna attempts to avoid all extremes (see GK IV.57–60, 82–84) and displays a keen awareness of Mahāyāna doctrines and scholastic controversies (see especially GK IV.24–25, 73–74). It is likely, therefore, that he was aware of this view within the Mahāyāna tradition.

One of the main reasons for the Mahāyāna view was a concern to avoid all grasping after *dharmas* and the intention to avoid all conceptual proliferation (*prapañca*). This is the attainment of "unsupported thought" (*citta-apratiṣṭhita*) that the *Vajracchedika* describes as that

> "which is unsupported by forms, sounds, smells, tastes, touchables, or mind-objects, unsupported by *dharma*, unsupported by no-*dharma*, unsupported by anything. And why? All supports have actually no support."[13]

Thus, one should not become attached to *dharmas* nor to their non-existence (non-*dharmas*). This, in fact, is also the position expounded in GK IV (see GK IV.79, 82, 96, 97, 99). One should not allow the mind to project itself outward and grasp onto a mental object (*dharma*). It is clear then that the GK follows the Perfection of Wisdom texts in the view that one should not grasp after *dharmas*. This state of non-attachment is said by the author of GK IV to be attained in the final gnosis (*jñāna*) of the Buddhas, being in fact the sphere of activity (*viṣaya*) of the *buddhas* (IV.80). Indeed for the GK *dharmas* can neither be described as substantial nor insubstantial (IV.53cd), an echo perhaps of the refusal of the Perfection of Wisdom texts to assert either the existence or non-existence of *dharmas*. Taking this into account, I am inclined to agree with those who suggest that the author of GK IV is using the term "*buddha*" unambiguously to refer to the founder of the Mahāyāna Buddhist tradition in *kārikā* 99.

Whatever one's view on the figure denoted by *kārikā* IV.99, it is difficult to accept (as some have) that the term *buddha* mentioned in IV.99ab denotes a different personage to the *buddha* of IV.99d. This would make little sense unless the author deliberately intended to deceive the reader. IV.99ab declares that the *buddha*'s transcendental gnosis (*jñāna*, established as a transcendental and *nirvikalpa* knowledge in IV.96, 80; III.32–34, 37–38) does not carry over to *dharmas*. This is the view already expounded throughout the text, as we have seen. Following on from this, the *kārikā* then suggests that the same is the case (*tathā*) with regard to *dharmas*—they also do not proceed toward the transcendental gnosis (*jñāna*) of the *buddha*. This is a statement to the effect that the *buddha*'s gnosis (*jñāna*) is unrelated (*asaṅga*) to a mental object (*dharma*) in conformity with the non-contact theory of perception outlined in the preceding verses (see III.45; IV.26, 79, 96, 97).

It is likely, then, that in GK IV.99 the author of the text is not distinguishing his own view—that *dharmas* and *jñāna* do not "cross over to one another"—from that of the "*buddha*," since the text asserts that this is indeed what "the *buddha*" himself realized (IV.99ab; see also IV.80). This would also seem to suggest that the "fully-enlightened" (*saṃbuddha*) figure revered as the "greatest of bipeds" in IV.1 is indeed this same *buddha*, since this figure is also said to have realized the *jñāna* which is non-different from the known. The *jñāna* in IV.1 and the *jñāna* in IV.99 appear to be the same. Thus, analysis of the occurrences of the terms *jñāna* and *buddha* in GK IV appears to establish a connection between the "*dvipadāṃ varaḥ*" revered in GK IV.1 and the *buddha* in IV.99. Both realize the unrelated (*asaṅga*) and non-dual *jñāna* which is non-different from the known (*jñeya*, IV.1) and, therefore, cannot be said to proceed toward any mental-object (*dharma*, IV.96, 99.) Indeed, for the author of the GK the Mahāyāna Buddhist endorsement of this view is further proof that the *buddhas* also proclaim non-origination (GK IV.19, 42).

We have seen that the view that gnosis (*jñāna*) and *dharmas* do not come into contact with one another has some basis in the Perfection of Wisdom texts themselves and that GK IV seems to associate this insight with the "*buddhas*." It seems possible, therefore, that Bhattacharya is correct when he suggests that "*naitad buddhena bhāṣitam*" in GK IV.99 is a statement referring to the transcendentality of the Buddha's teaching and not an attempt to differentiate the authors own view from that of the Buddha. I do not think that it is easy, however, to make a firm conclusion with regard to either this verse or the invocation at the beginning of the fourth *prakaraṇa*. Nevertheless, it would seem that the author's attitude to Mahāyāna Buddhism is expressed in IV.90, which acknowledges the debt owed to the Mahāyāna (or Agrayāna) and a respectful admission that much can be learned from it.

This is not to suggest, however, that GK IV sees the two traditions as identical. The author's attitude to Mahāyāna Buddhism is expressed in IV.90, which is an acknowledgment of the debt he owes to the Mahāyāna and a respectful admission that much can be learned from it. Evidently, the author does not consider himself a Mahāyāna Buddhist. This is perhaps not overly surprising given that his Vedāntic absolutism is something of a reversal of the orthodox Mahāyāna position. As Thomas Wood has suggested,

> The ALP (i.e. GK IV) was undoubtedly not written by a Buddhist author and it is not a Buddhist text. No alert, orthodox Buddhist could ever have accepted the ALP's interpretation of *prakṛter anyathābhāvo na hi jātūpapadyate* from MMK XV.8, for in this passage the author of the ALP is trying to turn Nāgārjuna on his head.[14]

Whether the author of the GK was aware of the difference between the Vedāntic and Mahāyāna philosophies on this fundamental issue is a moot point. GK IV.90 establishes that the two traditions are to be differentiated in some sense, but the grounds for such a distinction are never elucidated. The author of the text believed that his own view of non-origination was also upheld by the *buddhas* and as such seems to have held an absolutistic interpretation of Buddhism. Indeed, given the inclusivism of Gauḍapādian thought, as expressed in the view that *ajātivāda* is the final resting place (*siddhānta*) of all doctrines, it would be fair to say that the GK upholds an absolutistic interpretation of all doctrines!

Taking all of these factors into account, GK IV appears to have been written to facilitate a *rapprochement* of Vedānta and Buddhist philosophy. It is for this reason that the author of the text is interested in proving that his views do not fall into the Buddhist heresies of eternalism or nihilism and not because of any definitive allegiance to the Buddhist tradition. Perhaps the author of GK IV is attempting to "woo" Mahāyānists toward the Vedānta by establishing the sense in which Gauḍapādian doctrines conform to Mahāyāna ideas. As we have seen, however, the absolutism of Gauḍapādian thought owes more to the Vedāntic tradition than it does to the scholastic works of Mahāyāna

Buddhism. From a Madhyamaka and Yogācāra point of view the GK's acceptance of an unchanging Absolute supporting the world of appearances is a form of eternalism (*śāsvata-vāda*) despite Gauḍapādian protestations to the contrary.

In the third *prakaraṇa ajātivāda* is established on the basis of the *śruti* of the Vedānta school.[15] In the fourth *prakaraṇa* the same doctrine is established on the basis of Buddhist arguments and categories. Of course the previous *prakaraṇa*s are also reliant upon Buddhist philosophy; their focus, however, is firmly on the Vedānta tradition, its methodology, its fundamental texts, and its fundamental presuppositions. In this I am in basic agreement with the work of Vidhushekhara Bhattacharya, who states that:

> In Book IV Gauḍapāda has discussed nothing directly of the Vedānta, as nothing Vedāntic will be found therein. In explaining the Vedānta in accordance with his own light he establishes the *ajātivāda* in Book III. . .Then in Book IV he supports the same view independently of the Vedāntists.[16]

This situation is reflected in the absence of Vedāntic terms such as "*ātman*." The occurrence of the phrase "*brāhmaṇyaṃ padam*" in GK IV.85, while reconcilable with Buddhist meditative terms such as "*brahma-vihāra*:" the divine or blessed abodes, has clear Vedāntic overtones. Bhattacharya, however, is too presumptuous in his statement that there is no evidence of the Vedānta in GK IV; the absolutism expounded throughout the *prakaraṇa* is clearly Vedāntic. He is generally correct, however, in his view that the fourth *prakaraṇa* was written with a view to establishing non-origination on Buddhist grounds and as such avoids Vedāntic terms wherever possible. One should also note the absence of the term "*advaita*" in GK IV, all instances of non-duality being expressed by the term "*advaya*." This omission cannot be seen as an attempt to "hide" the Vedāntic undercurrents of Gauḍapādian thought since it is clear that at this time the term "*advaita*" was used by Buddhists and was not specifically associated with the Vedānta traditions. Indeed, our analysis suggests that the reason for the predominance of the term "*advaya*" is the phenomenological subject matter of GK IV. The text, as well as displaying Buddhist inclinations, is a discussion of the non-dual nature of experience (*advaya*) and not an exposition of non-dualistic ontology (*advaita*) (see chapter 5).

Considered in its entirety the fourth *prakaraṇa* of the *Gauḍapādīya-kārikā* is an attempt to establish a philosophical dialogue between the Vedānta and Mahāyāna traditions. The Vedānta tradition before the composition of the GK does not appear to have been active as a philosophical school (*darśana*). The Buddhist doxographer and philosopher Dignāga (480–540) compiled a comparative study of Indian epistemologies known as the *Pramāṇasamuccaya*. In it he discusses the views of the Nyāya, Vaiśeṣika, Sāṃkhya, and Mīmāṃsā schools. The omission of the Vedānta suggests that it had not developed a systematic epistemology (*pramāṇa*) of its own at this time. One should note that even in the *Gauḍapādīya-kārikā* epistemological discussion is largely derivative in the sense that it is dependent upon the doctrines of the Yogācāra school. Nevertheless, what we find in the four *prakaraṇas* of the GK is a philosophical school in the early stages of its development.

The Theory of Non-Conflict (*Avirodhavāda*) in the GK

The dialectical critique of causality, formulated in the MMK and adopted in the GK, draws attention to logical discrepancies in the causal theories of *satkāryavāda* and *asatkāryavāda*. The authors of the GK have shrewdly picked up on the Madhyamaka critique and accept that the problem of change subverts the Vedāntin's reliance upon *satkārya-vāda*.[17] However, this is not an acceptance of the Buddhist position. A recourse can be made to the Vedāntin's substrative metaphysics by the acceptance of *satkāraṇavāda* (the doctrine of the sole reality of the cause) as the logical consequence of a dialectical analysis of *satkāryavāda*. This step marks the beginning of the *vivarta* tradition in Vedānta (although the term is not used in this sense until after Śaṅkara). Whether it is philosophically sound to maintain a substrative line given that the manifold that is to be supported is denied is a moot point. One's answer to this question will decide which side of the fence one stands on in the Buddhist (*anātman/niḥsvabhāvatā*)—Vedānta (*ātman/svabhāvatā*) debate.

In the third *prakaraṇa* it is declared that *ajātivāda* is the supreme view of reality because it does not conflict with dualistic views. Thus, *kārikās* 17 and 18 state that:

> *svasiddhāntavyavasthāsu dvaitino niścitā dṛḍham, parasparaṃ virudhyante tair ayaṃ na virudhyate., advaitaṃ paramārtho hi dvaitaṃ tadbheda ucyate, teṣāṃ ubhayathā dvaitaṃ tenāyaṃ na virudhyate.*

> The dualists are firmly convinced in the establishment of their own conclusions and contradict one another; but this [view] does not conflict with them. Non-duality is indeed the ultimate reality; duality is said to be a differentiation of it. For them [the dualists] there is duality both ways; therefore this [view] does not conflict [with theirs].

This is reaffirmed in the fourth *prakaraṇa* (v. 4–5):

> *bhūtaṃ na jāyate kiñcid abhūtaṃ naiva jāyate, vivādanto dvayā hy evam ajātiṃ khyāpayanti te. khyāpyamānām ajātiṃ tair anumodāmahe vayam, vivadāmo na taiḥ sārdhaṃ avivādaṃ nibodhata.*
> Neither does an existent nor a non-existent originate in any manner [whatsoever]. Those dualists (*dvaya*), [through their] disputing, in fact reveal Non-origination. We approve of the Non-origination revealed by them;we do not dispute with them. Know how it is free from dispute (*avivāda*)!

At face value it appears that the authors of GK III and IV are suggesting that, insofar as they display the inherent contradictions of each other's positions, the dualists have established the doctrine of non-origination by default. Traditionally these verses are said to point to the fact that the GK upholds the two-truths doctrine. Thus, the GK accepts the conventional truth (*saṃvṛti-satya*) of duality but its definitive position (*siddhānta*) is that ultimate reality (*paramārtha-satya*) is non-dualistic.

However, it would seem that the GK's reasons for saying that *ajātivāda* does not conflict with other views are much more complex than this. Immediately following the declaration of non-conflict between dualism and non-dualism (III.17 and 18) the text again re-affirms the fundamental basis of its philosophy, the impossibility of a change in nature (III.20–22; IV.7–9). "How can the immortal become mortal? how can the intrinsic nature of a thing change? By changing its nature it becomes something else, and we are once again left with the problems already encountered by the dualistic theories of cause and effect. The repetition of this principle is not coincidental, it is again evidence of the primacy with which the principle is held.

Having examined the basic presuppositions of Gauḍapādian doctrine, we are now in a position to see precisely why *ajātivāda* is not in conflict with other views. Like Nāgārjuna, the authors of GK III and IV believe that we can realize the truth through the application of a dialectical method of analysis. The mutual contradictions found in all theories of causality lead one to the inevitable conclusion that the very ideas of "cause" and "effect" are self-contradictory. It is at this point that we can see the relevance of this section to the GK's syncretistic attitude to other doctrines. If we can be lead to the truth by a dialectical analysis of any doctrine then *ajātivāda* can be placed upon a pedestal and said to be the final resting place of all seemingly disparate and conflicting doctrines. *Ajātivāda* becomes the *siddhānta* of all *siddhāntas*, the final position of all doctrines. Understood as such non-origination is beyond the disputations of competing philosophies for it is both their beginning and end points. The credit for most of the hard work in establishing this fact must go to Nāgārjuna for pointing out that all views presuppose *svabhāva* (intrinsic nature) and that *svabhāva* must be by definition unchanging. The credit for applying this Buddhist insight to support Vedāntic absolutism must go to the authors of the *Gauḍapādīya-kārikā*.

Inclusivism in the Gauḍapādīya-kārikā

Following the arguments found in Nāgārjuna's MMK,[18] it becomes clear that some form of absolutism (*ajātivāda*) is a logical consequence of a *svabhāva* view of reality (which amounts to all views of reality since all views presuppose "own-nature" in some form). In GK II the misapprehension of *ātman* as various different entities (*bhāva*) is explained in terms of the analogy of the rope and the snake. Following on from this, the second *prakaraṇa* lists a variety of views concerning the nature of reality. What is interesting about this list is the fact that the author understands these views to be views about the nature of *ātman*. Thus, in verse 19 of the second *prakaraṇa*,

> *prāṇādibhir anantais tu bhāvair etair vikalpitaḥ, māyaiṣā tasya devasya yayāyaṃ mohitaḥ svayam.*
> But [*ātman*] is wrongly understood to be *prāṇa* and other innumerable entities (*bhāvas*). This is the *māyā* of the divine one (*tasya devasya*), by which it itself has been deluded.

GK II spends the next 9 verses listing some of the "innumerable things" that people assume *ātman* to be. Thus,

> The *Prāṇa* knowers call it "*Prāṇa*;" The guna-knowers call it "*Guṇas*;" "*Tattvas*" say the knowers of them; "Sense-objects" (*viṣaya*) say the knowers of "sense-objects," and [likewise] "gods" (*deva*) say the knowers of them.[19]

And so on.

Yet all of these things are really just the non-dual *ātman*. This idea is little more than an extension of *Māṇḍūkya Upaniṣad* 2,

> *sarvaṁ hy etad-brahma-(ayam ātmā brahma).*
> All this is truly Brahman. (This *ātman* is Brahman).

The misapprehension of *ātman* as various different entities is explained rather cryptically in verse 29 of the second *prakaraṇa*.

> Whatever *bhāva* (entity) is shown to one, that entity is what one sees; that [*ātman/bhāva*?], protects him, having become it. Possessed by that [idea], it absorbs him.

It is difficult to grasp the precise meaning of this verse, but taking into account what we already know about the nature of "Gauḍapādian" thought, the verse would seem to imply that the world that we experience is determined by our past experience (that is, "whatever is shown to one"). Experience then is largely a product of karmic attachment; *saṃsāra* continues for as long as one is attached to the notions of cause and effect (GK IV.55, 56). Release from the apparent bonds of *saṃsāra* is the realization of the impossibility of causal relationships. This is the realization of *ajātivāda*—non-origination. The world can never really have come into existence since the relationship between a cause and its effect is an impossibility.

As we have seen, the authors of GK III and IV do not see themselves as disputants or debaters (*vādin*) in the usual sense of the term. "*Ātman*" here does not refer to the *jīvātman*, the individual "self," rather, it appears to be synonymous with reality itself. Whereas one might say that different philosophical schools have different views about the nature of reality, the authors understand these doctrines to be different conceptions of the non-dual *ātman*. One of the reasons for this appears to be the author's keen interest in the debate about intrinsic nature (*svabhāva*) instigated by the Buddhists. *Ātman* no longer refers to the "subjective self" (*ādhyātma*); it is the "self-nature" or "essence" of reality. *Ajātivāda* from this perspective is not a competing theory fighting for recognition alongside other doctrines, but a "meta-theory," implicitly assumed by and explains the nature of "other" theories.

All views then, insofar as they are about reality, are partial attempts at understanding the non-dual *ātman*. The focus of the debate has been moved from "what is the relationship between myself and the absolute, my *ātman* and Brahman?", to a debate about the nature of reality itself. The move is subtle but effective. Of course, such inclusivism is apparent in the author's own Vedāntic background. Thus, the Ṛg Veda states that "Him, who is the One existent, sages name variously" (I.164.46). A similar attitude can be found in the *Bhagavadgītā* where Kṛṣṇa declares that:

> VII.21: *yo yo yāṁ tanuṁ bhaktaḥ śraddhayā 'rcitum icchati, tasya tasy 'ācalāṁ śraddhāṁ tām eva vidadhāmy aham.*
> Whatever form a devotee with faith desires to honor, that very faith do I confirm in him [making it] unswerving and secure.
>
> IX.23: *ye 'py anya devatā bhakta yajante śraddhayā 'nvitāḥ, te 'pi mām eva kaunteya yajanty avidhi pūrvakam.*
> Even those who are devoted to other gods and worship them with faith are really worshipping me, though not in the proper way.
>
> X.20: *aham ātmā, Guḍākeśa, sarva bhūtāśaya sthitaḥ, aham ādis ca madhyam ca bhūtānām anta eva ca.*
> I am the *ātman* established in the heart of all beings: I am also the beginning, middle, and end of all beings.
>
> X.21: *ādityānām ahaṃ viṣṇur jyotisāṃ ravir aṁśumān, marīcir marutām asmi nakṣatrāṇāṃ ahaṃ śaśī.*
> Among the Ādityas I am Viṣṇu, among lights the radiant sun. Among the Maruts I am Marīci, among the stars I am the moon.[20]

What makes the theory of non-conflict (*avirodhavāda*) in the GK of particular interest, however, is the authors' attempt to ground these syncretistic tendencies in philosophical arguments derived from Nāgārjuna's *MūlaMadhyamakakārikā*.

The philosophical basis for Gauḍapādian inclusivism thus is derived mainly from a reading of Nāgārjuna's MMK. This is not to say that the GK is a Buddhist text. Clearly it is not. Nor am I suggesting that important precursors of *advaita-vāda* and *ajātivāda* cannot be found in the Upaniṣadic literature. Clearly in some form they can. Nevertheless, the form taken by the subsequent Advaita Vedānta *darśana* is somewhat dependent upon the fact that it was influenced in its formative years by the philosophical perspectives of Mahāyāna Buddhism. This influence is a contingent and not a necessary one. In an abstract sense it is conceivable that an uncompromising *advaita-vāda* could have developed on the basis of Vedāntic sources alone. Such a view, however, would be historically inaccurate for two reasons. First, Mahāyāna influence upon the GK is beyond reasonable doubt. Second, the view that a religious tradition can develop in a cultural vacuum, unaffected by contemporaneous traditions and movements is methodologically and historically unsound. Despite the GK's obvious reliance upon Buddhist ideas, *ajātivāda* is still founded upon the primacy of the Vedāntic absolute, i.e. Brahman, as the non-dual and unborn support of all appearances.

For both the Mādhyamika and the authors of the GK the method of *reductio ad absurdum* (*prasaṅga*) establishes the impossibility of a change in nature (*prakṛti/svabhāva*). Such a philosophical critique establishes *ajātivāda* as the final position (*siddhānta*) of all doctrines of "own nature" (*svabhāva*). For the authors of the GK this shows that the fundamental presuppositions of all dualistic theories logically result in their own position, an absolutism of the unoriginated. All diverse objects appears only insofar as they have an unborn intrinsic nature (* *ajāta-svabhāva*), that is an unoriginated absolute to support their manifestation. Thus the text states that "there is no doubt that in the waking state the non-dual appears as the dual."[21] It is only by virtue of non-duality (*advaya*) that entities are imagined—"The entities exist as the non-dual as it were."[22] For both the MMK and the GK all views presuppose "own-being" (*svabhāva*) and thus necessitate the acceptance of an "absolute" and unchanging reality. Both texts assert that all views entail absolutism. For Nāgārjuna, the contradiction between the premise and the conclusion is grounds for the rejection of the entire schema of *svabhāva-vāda*, while for the authors of the GK it is the final vindication of absolutism since all roads can now be said to lead to Advaita. Armed with such all encompassing authority it is not surprising that we find the GK frequently adopting non-Vedāntic terms in the exposition of its own philosophical position.

In the Madhyamaka school *śūnyatā* is clearly distinguished from the theories of other schools which are characterized by the acceptance of "own being" (*svabhāva*). This is reflected in the eagerness with which all views are described as *aśūnyavāda* in the MMK. Nāgārjuna's grounds for doing so are elucidated in MMK 24:20f and they amount to the fact that all views when dialectically analyzed are seen to lead to absolutism (*ajātivāda*). The GK's grounds for the acceptance of *ajātivāda* are precisely the same insight, namely that all views entail it. It is at this fundamental level that we appear to encounter the root of the distinction between the *ātman* and *anātman* traditions.

The Bhāvavivekan Response to the Vedāntic Inclusivism of the GK

The first Buddhist scholar to consider the doctrines of the Vedānta as an established philosophical school (*darśana*) was Bhāvaviveka. As we have seen Bhāvaviveka criticizes doctrines which are unique to the GK (e.g. the concept of *ajātisamatā*). In his auto-commentary (*Tarkajvālā*) to MHK 8.54 Bhāvaviveka has the Vedāntin explain the variety of descriptions given of the *ātman* in the following manner:

> Those who do not see Reality see it in many forms: Some say that it is all-pervasive (*sarvatraga*), some say that it is just the extent of the body (*deha*), others again think that it just has the nature of an atom (*paramāṇu*). Like the elephant's intrinsic-nature (*svabhāva*), it is just one (*eka*), but like the major and minor limbs (*aṅga/pratyaṅga*) of the elephant (*hastin*), it is also many.[23]

As we have seen, the idea that difference in opinion reflects the degree to which one has truly apprehended the *ātman* is expounded in GK II.19–30. The inclusivistic nature of the Vedānta school that Bhāvaviveka addresses is criticized later in his chapter on the Vedānta. The Vedānta school is in fact nothing more than a "completely heterogenous" (*atyantātulyajātīya*) amalgam of the doctrines of other schools.[24] This criticism suggests that Bhāvaviveka was aware of the apparent similarity of many Buddhist and Vedāntic doctrines.

In chapter four of his *Madhyamakahṛdayakārikā* (on the *śrāvaka-yāna*) Bhāvaviveka puts forward a *śrāvaka* objection to the Mahāyāna on the grounds that it is a form of crypto-Vedāntism.

> *na buddhoktir mahāyānaṃ sūtrāntādāv asaṃgrahāt, mārgāntaro-padeśād vā yathā vedāntadarśanam.*
> [*Śrāvaka* objection]: The Mahāyāna cannot represent the teaching of the Buddha, either because it is not included amongst the *Sūtrāntas* etc., or because it teaches the heretic paths of salvation, thus being similar to the Vedānta system.[25]

The example given in the commentary upon this verse is that the Vedānta teaches that bathing in rivers, fasting, and incantations can lead to the removal of sin. This is said to be a practice held in common by the Mahāyānists. Bhāvaviveka's reply, however, is that

> *Vedānte ca hi yat sūktaṃ tat sarvam buddhabhāṣitam.*
> Whatever is well said in the Vedānta has all been taught by the Buddha [already].[26]

In chapter III of the same text, Bhāvaviveka discusses the transcendental and ineffable nature of the *dharmakāya*. Positive statements that are used to express the highest level of attainments, he suggests, are, in actuality, beyond the scope of words. Silent realization (*jñāna-mauna*) of this is identical with the quiescent, benevolent, and unoriginated *dharmakāya*. Finally, Bhāvaviveka states that

> *kiṃcit kathañcin nā'py asmāj jāyate vyajyate'pi vā, nā'trā'vatiṣṭhate kaścin nā'pi kaścit pralīyate.*
> Nothing and in no way is anything born from, or manifested by, it. There is none here, who either endures or perishes.

> *idaṃ tat paramam brahma brahmādyair yan na gṛhyate, idaṃ tat paramam satyam satyavādī jagau muniḥ.*
> This is the great Brahman, which cannot be grasped by the (god) Brahmā and others. This is the great truth, declared by the Sage, who always speaks the truth.[27]

The commentary on the final verse states that "Brahman" means both "Lord of living beings" (*prajāpati*), as well as "cessation" (*nirvāṇa*). However, Bhāvaviveka notes that "Brahman" should only be understood to denote the latter, that is *nirvāṇa*. The gods such as Brahmā, Viṣṇu, Maheśvara, etc. are deluded by their own notions of self-existence and so do not understand the true meaning of "Brahman." Returning to the text of the MHK, Bhāvaviveka then suggests that

> *āryāvalokiteśāryamaitreyādyāś ca sūrayaḥ, anupāsanayogena munayo yad upāsate.*
> [It is this] which the learned seers, like Ārya Avalokiteśa, Ārya Maitreya, and others adore by the method of non-adoration.[28]

The primary connotation of the term "Brahman" is that of "expansion" or "creation," (from the root "*bṛh*"). This is in sharp contrast to the "blown-out" connotation of "*nirvāṇa*." Nevertheless, the two terms are sometimes found together in the compound "*brahma-nirvāṇa*" (e.g. *Bhagavadgītā* 2.72; 5.24–26.). Bhāvaviveka's statement, however, is remarkable since he appears to be suggesting that the term "Brahman" can be equated with the Buddhist *nirvāṇa* if understood correctly.[29]

In the conclusion to his critique of Vedānta philosophy, Bhāvaviveka suggests that if by "self" (*ātman*) the Vedāntin means the universal characteristic of "lacking an own-nature" (*niḥsvabhāva*) then the Mahāyāna and the Vedānta are in agreement.[30] Thus he enjoins the Vedāntins to join him in tasting the sweet nectar of truth (*tattvāmṛta*) provided by the teaching of the Buddhas (MHK 8.97). The tone of the discussion suggests that Bhāvaviveka is parodying the inclusivism of the Vedāntins by playing them at their own game. His "tongue-in-cheek" inclusivism, however, is further acknowledgment of the perceived similarity between the two systems at this time.

The author of GK IV seems to believe that both Buddhism and Vedānta, despite their differences (see GK IV.90), proclaim the self-same doctrine of non-origination (*ajātivāda*). Such a syncretistic view is refuted by Bhāvaviveka who puts it forward as an objection to his Buddhist re-interpretation of *ātman* in terms of *niḥsvabhāvatā*. In the MHK, Bhāvaviveka has the Vedāntin suggest that if *ātman* and *anātman* mean the same thing then the final positions (*siddhānta*) of the two systems are equal.[31] Bhāvaviveka, however, firmly rejects any attempt to conflate the two traditions. He argues that when it is said that entities do not arise it is not because of their unchanging intrinsic-nature but because they fundamentally lack any such nature![32] This is the basis of the distinction between the two systems and Bhāvaviveka is here suggesting that the two perspectives (*darśana*) as they stand are incommensurable. For Bhāvaviveka, therefore, the Vedānta notion of a self (*ātman*) is nothing more than the superimposition of a conceptual construction (*kalpanāsamāropa*).[33] As such, the school is criticized for its false clinging (*asadgrāha*) to the notion of a self (*ātmatva*).[34]

The GK as a whole, while accepting much of the argumentation and style of Mahāyāna philosophy, aligns itself firmly with the *ātman* (*svabhāvatā*) tradition of Vedānta. The Gauḍapādian view of *ātman*, however, is inspired by an absorption of the Madhyamaka method of dialectical refutation (*prasaṅga*). Both the GK and the Madhyamaka school establish their positions with regard to the impossibility of a change (*na anyathābhāva*) in nature (*prakṛti/svabhāva*). For the Mādhyamika this entails *niḥsvabhāvatā*; for the authors of the GK it establishes the absoluteness of *svabhāvatā*. Both accept that the belief in an "own nature" (which amounts to all views of reality) entails a non-active, unchanging absolute. The Mādhyamika takes this as grounds for a rejection of *svabhāvatā*, while the GK accepts this as proof of its ultimate reality. Thus, the Mādhyamika denies the possibility of an underlying and unchanging substratum behind all manifestations, opting instead for a view of reality based upon inter-dependent origination. The world appears as it does because of the inter-dependency of its constituent factors. The authors of the GK, however, argue that for there to be an appearance there must be a substantial entity that appears. It is this point, the debate over *ātman-svabhāva:: anātman-niḥsvabhāva* at its most fundamental level, that provides the philosophical dividing line between the philosophies of the Mādhyamika Buddhist and the Advaita Vedāntin.

The GK, however, does not appear to be aware of the underlying conflict between the Vedānta and Madhyamaka traditions on this basic paradigmatic issue. There is no evidence of a reactionary attitude to Buddhist philosophical ideas within the text; indeed they are often wholeheartedly endorsed, if often adapted to give a more Vedāntic conclusion. The GK, therefore, is an example of an early stage in the development of Advaita Vedānta. The conciliatory attitude of the text towards Buddhism reflects the authors' fundamental reliance upon Buddhist ideas and arguments for the formulation of their own distinctive position. For anti-Buddhist polemic one needs to look slightly later in the tradition—at the works of the more famous Śaṅkara, traditionally upheld as the founder of the Advaita Vedānta school but dependent upon the GK for the central doctrines of non-dualism (*advaita*) and non-origination (*ajātivāda*). Despite this, scholars have continued to overlook the *Gauḍapādīya-kārikā* in their attempt to understand the roots of early Advaita Vedānta.

The extent to which the GK is reliant upon the Mahāyāna Buddhist philosophical schools should by now be abundantly clear. In the main the twin focus of the GK—the ontological denial of origination (*ajātivāda*) on the one hand and the epistemological denial of subject-object duality (*advaya-vāda*) on the other are dependent upon the Madhyamaka in the case of the former and the Yogācāra in the case of the latter.[35] In the final chapter, however, we shall consider the possibility that the extent of Mahāyāna influence upon the GK goes beyond a reliance upon the respective philosophies of these two schools of thought.

CHAPTER

7

Absolutism in the GK and the Mahāyāna: the Tathāgatagarbha Texts

When considering the philosophical doctrines of Indian Mahāyāna Buddhism it has often been deemed adequate to consider the two main schools of thought, i.e. the Madhyamaka and Yogācāra perspectives. One must be aware, however, of the great complexity of the Mahāyāna tradition, partly stemming no doubt from its multifarious origins. The Mahāyāna texts that we have considered so far are scholastic in orientation and, insofar as they reject any form of absolutism, are at variance with the Brahmanical tradition to which the authors of the GK align themselves. Previous studies of the *Gauḍapādīya-kārikā* and its relationship to Mahāyāna thought have palpably failed to consider the complexity and multifarious nature of Mahāyāna thought. Restricting the scope of analysis to the Madhyamaka and Yogācāra scholastic works is historically narrow in that it does not acknowledge the existence of other strands of thought within the Indian Mahāyāna tradition that perhaps were not adequately represented in a scholastic form.

Our analysis of the GK in the light of Madhyamaka and Yogācāra ideas has also left certain questions largely unanswered. The author of GK IV is clearly acquainted with the central themes of the Madhyamaka and Yogācāra schools, even to the extent of discussing an inter-scholastic debate of the fifth century CE concerning the status of the *paratantra-svabhāva* of the Yogācāra school (see GK IV.24, 25). The author of GK IV is also clearly a Vedāntin. This can be deduced from his wholesale endorsement of a Vedāntic absolutism and the distinguishing of his position from that of the "Agrayāna" (the Mahāyāna, see GK IV.90). However, given that the author has a great familiarity with Mahāyāna philosophical concepts and arguments, it is odd to find him interpreting those ideas in an absolutistic manner. It is even stranger to find the author of GK IV suggesting that the Buddha himself was an absolutist of the same degree (see GK IV.19, 42). We have already seen how the authors of the *Gauḍapādīya-kārikā* use Mahāyāna arguments to fit their own absolutistic presuppositions. The question remains—why bother? If an absolutistic interpretation of the Mahāyāna was out of the question in India at this time there would seem to be little point in putting such an interpretation forward. One answer to this question is to point to the fact that, from a Gauḍapādian perspective, *all* systems of thought are, in the final analysis, forms of absolutism (see GK III.17, 18, IV. 4, 5). This is perhaps part of the motivation behind the composition of the fourth *prakaraṇa*, namely to provide an absolutistic interpretation of Buddhism based upon the view (already established in GK III and GK II.19–28), that all doctrines presuppose an absolute. It has already been suggested that the authors of the GK derive this view from the arguments of Nāgārjuna in his MMK. Therein, such a doctrine was put forward as a criticism of all views; in the GK, however, its seen as an all-embracing (and inclusivistic) endorsement of them.

It would be a mistake, however, to suggest that the philosophical doctrines of the Madhyamaka and Yogācāra encompass the entirety of Indian Mahāyāna thought in the pre-Gauḍapādian era. In this chapter we shall consider the perspective of certain texts which focus upon the notion of a "*tathāgatagarbha*," that is a "buddha-seed" inherent within (or perhaps even identical with) all sentient beings. It will become clear that these texts are more amenable to an absolutistic interpretation than the scholastic works of the Madhyamaka and Yogācāra in the pre-Gauḍapādian period. Thus, the possibility remains that the author of GK IV derived his own absolutistic interpretation of the Mahāyāna from such a "strand" of thought within the Buddhist tradition itself.

The *Tathāgatagarbha* Texts

It is difficult to over-estimate the extent to which the Prajñāpāramitā doctrine of the emptiness of all *dharmas* revolutionized Buddhist thought in India. It would be misleading, however, to suggest that Indian Mahāyānists were universally concerned with the abstrusities of the concept of emptiness as understood in the Prajñāpāramitā texts.[1] To many Mahāyānists the abstrusities of the Prajñāpāramitā texts must have seemed at best perplexing and at worst downright nonsensical. "If all is empty," Nāgārjuna has an opponent ask, ". . . how can there be either suffering or the cessation of it?"[2] Nevertheless, even among those texts that do discuss the notion of emptiness, there appears to have existed a strand of Mahāyāna thought in India that opened up the possibility of an absolutistic interpretation of Buddhism. This movement is represented primarily by certain texts that focus upon the notion of the *tathāgatagarbha*. Here a different conception of emptiness is at work; one, in fact, that appears more consonant with Gauḍapādian absolutism.

The "*tathāgatagarbha*" texts were part of the second phase of development of Mahāyāna texts, being compiled after the early *Prajñāpāramitā*, *Saddharmapuṇḍarika*, and *Avataṃsakasūtras*, and so probably arose in response to this intial phase of Mahāyāna ideas and themes.[3] William Grosnick has suggested that there are two important meanings to be found in the term "*tathāgatagarbha*" and its various synonyms (e.g., *buddhatā, buddhadhātu,* the latter of which Grosnick suggests is the most frequent Sanskrit original for the Chinese term for "Buddha-nature," *fo-hsing*).[4] The first is an affirmation of the *ekāyana* principle that all beings are someway along the path of the *Buddha-yāna* and secondly he maintains that "such expressions seem to have been intended in what is perhaps a deeper sense: to point to the ultimate nature of things. . ."[5] Grosnick also suggests that the original meaning of the phrase "*tathāgatagarbha*," rather than denoting a "seed" within beings, actually referred to the beings themselves.[6]

The term "*garbha*" (from *grabh*: "to conceive") originally seems to have denoted a "womb," but it soon came to refer to the interior of anything. The term was also used to denote a "foetus" or "embryo."[7] As such the compound "*tathāgatagarbha*" has generally been translated as "embryo," "seed," "womb," or "matrix" of the Tathāgata.[8] Jikido Takasaki[9] favors the translation "matrix of the Tathāgata," but is criticized by Brian Brown[10] who finds the implications of a "container" misleading, preferring those translations which emphasize the *tathāgatagarbha* as an embryonic seed. That Brown has made a salient point can be seen from an analysis of the nine analogies adopted in the *Tathāgatagarbhasūtra* (Sanskrit now lost), one of the earliest texts to utilize the notion. These analogies are set out and explained in the *Ratnagotravibhāga* (RGV)[11] and can be seen from the following table:

Kleśa	Tathāgatagarbha
1. Withered Lotus flowers	Buddha in the petals
2. swarm of honey bees	honey
3. outer husk	inner kernel
4. dirt	gold
5. ground of a poor man's hut	jewels buried below the ground
6. bark-covering of a seed	the seed
7. discarded/tattered garment	jewel-studded image wrapped within it
8. pregnant, abandoned woman	future emperor in embryonic form
9. clay mould	priceless golden statue of *tathāgatadhātu*

Brown maintains that all nine analogies suggest that the *tathāgatagarbha* is to be seen as a content enclosed within rather than as a container.

> Interpreted spatially, each represents an interior condition, a position within something else. And in the eighth example there is an explicit distinction between the embryo (representing the immaculate *Tathāgatadhātu*) and the womb which carries it. This latter, signifying the woman, is a direct referent to impurity. These two factors (the concept of content in general, and the image of the embryo specifically) help to convalidate the overall interpretation of *tathāgatagarbha* as "embryo" rather than "womb" of the Tathāgata.[12]

However, one should note (as indeed Brown himself does) that it is only the sixth and eighth analogies that can properly be said to express the idea of the *tathāgatagarbha* as a dynamic and progressive "seed"; the remaining analogies all suggest that the Buddha-nature is already present in full form, merely obscured from sight by impurities. These seven analogies all have the common feature of denoting something that is substantial and intrinsically of value, namely a treasure of some sort. This "treasure" (denoted by the notions of honey, the inner kernel of a seed, gold, a jewel-studded icon, a golden statue of the Tathāgata, the Buddha himself, and buried jewels), is hidden by the defilements (*kleśa*) which are in actual fact extrinsic (*āgantuka*) to it. This would seem to suggest that the *dharmakāya* (that which is to be attained) is something that is essentially present from the beginning, being obscured by ignorance and the other defilements (*kleśa*). Indeed, the idea of being enlightened from the very beginning (*ādibuddha*) became a major theme of East Asian Mahāyāna Buddhism, and a subject of much controversy in Tibet, China, and Japan. The idea, however, was current in India as early as the fourth century CE,[13] since it is discussed in the *Mahāyānasūtrālaṃkāra*, a central text of the early Yogācāra school.[14] In this text the concept of being "primevally enlightened" (*ādibuddha*) is criticized on the grounds that Buddhahood requires not only the gradual accumulation of knowledge and work, but also the existence of another Buddha to inaugurate one's career as a *bodhisattva*.[15] GK IV, however, appears to endorse the implications of this notion since *kārikā* 92 states that,

> All *dharmas* by their nature (*prakṛti*) are well established as enlightened from the very beginning (*ādibuddha*). One who has such self-sufficiency (*kṣānti*) is fit for the deathless state.

The endorsement of the concept of *ādibuddha* should be seen in the light of the following verse (GK IV.93) which appears to be a reformulation of *Mahāyānasūtrālaṃkāra* XI.51 in the light of a *svabhāva* rather than a *niḥsvabhāva* way of thinking. Thus, whereas as the *Mahāyānasūtrālaṃkāra* states that,

> *niḥsvabhāvatayā siddhā uttarottararaniśrayāt, anutpādānirodhādi-śānti prakṛtinirvṛtiḥ.*
> From their lack of own-nature, one gradually establishes that there is neither arising nor cessation, that [*dharmas*] are originally quiescent and essentially in *nirvāṇa*.[16]

GK IV.93 states that,

> *ādiśāntā hy anutpannāḥ prakṛtyaiva sunirvṛtāḥ, sarve dharmāḥ samābhinnā ajaṃ sāmyaṃ viśāradam.*
> By their very nature all *dharmas* indeed are quiescent from the very beginning, non-arising, liberated, and homogenous. [Reality is] non-separate, devoid of fear and uniformly unoriginated.

Here the author of GK IV appears to be endorsing the concept of *ādibuddha* in the light of his absolutistic view that all things, insofar as they possess a *svabhāva*, are unoriginated and already essentially in *nirvāṇa*. Thus, a view that in the *Mahāyānasūtralaṃkāra* is put forward on the grounds that all *dharmas* lack a *svabhāva* is reformulated in the GK on the grounds that all *dharmas* possess an unoriginated *svabhāva*![17]

Although Trevor Ling suggests that the concept may have originated in Bengal (Gauḍadeśa perhaps?), *ādibuddha* only appears to have gained great prominence in East Asian Mahāyāna. In Indian Mahāyāna it was the concept of the *tathāgatagarbha* that came to the fore in the post-Nāgārjunian period. One of the earliest and most notable texts of this ilk is the *Śrīmālādevisīṃhanādasūtra*, which remains one of the primary Indian sources of *tathāgatagarbha* thought. The text was probably composed in the third century CE, the first Chinese translation of the *sūtra* (now lost) being carried out by Dharmakṣema in the early part of the fourth century CE.[18] The *Śrīmālāsūtra* is quick to distinguish the *tathāgatagarbha* from any notion of a self (*ātman*).

> World-Honored One, the Tathāgata-embryo is not a self, a personal identity, a being, or a life. The Tathāgata-embryo is not in the domain of sentient beings who believe in a real self, whose thinking is confused, or who cling to the view of emptiness.[19]

According to the *Śrīmālā*, the *tathāgatagarbha* is profound and subtle and was explained by the Buddha through the teaching of the four noble truths. Both teachings in fact are "beyond the scope (*viṣaya*) of the *śrāvakas* and *pratyekabuddhas*," since they are "beyond the realm of thought and speculation, and transcend the credence of the world."[20] Unenlightened disciples of the Buddha are to accept the existence of the *tathāgatagarbha* on faith (*śraddhā*) alone, true knowledge being the exclusive preserve of the fully enlightened.[21]

The *Śrīmālā*, in fact, re-formulates the traditional scheme of the four noble truths so as to allow for two levels of understanding their import (the constructed—*kṛta*, and the unconstructed—*akṛta*).[22] The constructed (*kṛta*) noble truths present the exoteric and superficial meaning of the teaching, expounded for the sake of the limited comprehension of the *śrāvakas* and *pratyekabuddhas.* The unconstructed noble truths, however, are without limitations since they do not presuppose the need for a refuge. This, maintains the *Śrīmālā*, is the only way to truly understand and eradicate suffering since one has relinquished all dependence. In effect then the *Śrīmālā* expounds a theory of eight noble truths, four constructed and limited and four unconstructed and definitive. Only the *Tathāgata* can understand the unconstructed noble truths since "*nirvāṇa* is not to be realized by any *dharma*, whether superior or inferior, whether, low, middle or high."[23]

What are the implications of such a view? The *Śrīmālā* suggests that the third noble truth—"the cessation of suffering" does not in actual fact entail the real destruction of anything since it is merely a name for the *dharmakāya* of the Tathāgata. This *dharmakāya* has

> no beginning, no action, no origination, and no end; it is ever abiding, immovable, intrinsically pure and free from the shell (*kośa*) of defilements. . .when this Dharma-body (*dharmakāya*) is not apart from defilements, it is called the *tathāgatagarbha*.[24]

This is the closest the *Śrmālā* comes to identifying the Tathāgata's *dharmakāya* with the *tathāgatagarbha*. However, the precise relationship between the two is never completely specified. The text denies that the *tathāgatagarbha* is a personal self and yet accepts the description of the *dharmakāya* as the "perfection of self" (*ātmapāramitā*). The partial acceptance of the validity of *ātman* terminology, at least with regard to the *dharmakāya*, is something of a departure from what might be called the "mainstream" textual tradition of Indian Buddhism that accords great philosophical and symbolic significance to the concept of no-self (*anātman*). Within the classical Indian context, the Buddhist concept of *anātman* functions as a symbol of intransigence in the face of Brahmanical speculation about the nature of the self. That the *Śrīmālā* refers to the *dharmakāya* (that it equates with the final *nirvāṇa* of the cessation of suffering) as the perfection of self (*ātmapāramitā*) is a distinct movement away from the traditional view that *nirvāṇa* (along with everything else) fundamentally lacks a self. The *Śrīmālā*'s statement that the *tathāgatagarbha* is not a self, however, clearly suggests that it still remains somewhat reticent about the unqualified use of *ātman* terminology.

Nevertheless, other evidence from the *Śrīmālā* suggests the possibility of a movement toward a more absolutistic conception of reality. The *Śrīmālā* maintains that of the four noble truths, only the truth of cessation is true in the ultimate sense.

> Lord, of those four noble truths, three truths are impermanent, and one truth is permanent. Why? The three truths [of suffering, the cause of suffering, and the path leading to the cessation of suffering] belong to the realm of conditioned *dharmas*. What is conditioned is impermanent, and what is impermanent is destructible. What is destructible is not true, not permanent, and not a refuge. Therefore, in the ultimate sense, the three noble truths are not true, not permanent, and not a refuge.
>
> World-Honored One, the noble truth of the cessation of suffering is beyond the realm of conditioned *dharmas*. What is beyond the realm of conditioned *dharmas* is ever abiding by nature. What is ever abiding by nature is indestructible. What is indestructible is true, permanent, and a refuge. For this reason World-Honored One, the noble truth of the cessation of suffering is in the ultimate sense true, permanent, and a refuge.
>
> World-Honored One, this noble truth of the cessation of suffering is inconceivable.[25]

Given that the *Śrīmālā* identifies the "truth of cessation" with the *dharmakāya*, this statement is a declaration of the sole reality of the *dharmakāya* of the Tathāgata. All other factors (*dharmas*), including the first, second, and fourth noble truths (i.e. *duḥkha*, suffering, *samudāya*, its cause and *mārga*, the path leading to liberation) are compounded (*saṃskṛta*) and thus, according to the *Śrīmālā*'s own arguments, ultimately unreal. This sounds remarkably like the radical absolutism of the *Gauḍapādīya-kārikā* in the denial of the reality of conditioned factors coupled with an assertion of the ultimate reality of the unconditioned *dharmakāya*.

Let us briefly consider the *Śrīmālā*'s view in the light of the "mainstream" philosophical tradition of the Mahāyāna. The view that conditioned factors are impermanent and therefore not ultimately real would be acceptable to both the Madhyamaka and the classical Yogācāra, but the postulation of an unconditioned ultimate reality is, as we have seen, exceedingly problematic. Indeed the primary focus of much of Nāgārjuna's critique of others is that their postulation of a *svabhāva* is tatamount to the belief in an unconditioned absolute. The *Śrīmālā* in asserting the ultimate reality of the *dharmakāya* appears to be doing precisely that. This fundamentally differs from the positions outlined in the philosophical texts of both the Abhidharma and the Mahāyāna schools,[26] but does parallel somewhat the absolutism of the *Gauḍapādīya-kārikā*.

Undeterred by the apparent philosophical consequences of this position, the *Śrīmālā* maintains that the *tathāgatagarbha* is the base, (*āśraya, niśraya*), support (*ādhāra*) and foundation (*pratiṣṭhā*) of all constructed natures (*saṃskṛta*),[27] a substrative position that is also reminiscent of the Vedāntic view that Brahman is the unconditioned reality that supports all conditioned things. The *Śrīmālā* in fact maintains that

> the *Tathāgatagarbha* is not born, does not die, does not pass away to become reborn. The *Tathāgatagarbha* excludes the realm with the characteristic of the constructed. The *Tathāgatagarbha* is permanent (*nitya*), steadfast (*dharma*), and eternal (*śāsvata*).[28]

One hardly need mention the similarity between this mode of expression and the exposition of *ajātivāda* in the *Gauḍapādīya-kārikā*. In both cases the non-originated, subjacent ground (*tathāgatagarbha*:: Brahman) supports a constructed realm that in actual fact does not really exist. Whether a substrative metaphysics can be maintained given the ultimate non-reality of that which is supported is a moot point. This question lies at the heart of the conflict between non-absolutistic and absolutistic systems of thought. Clearly, however, the perspective of the *Śrīmālā* is not easily reconciled with the mainstream Madhyamaka position. The denial of the ultimate reality of the constructed and the concomitant assertion of the ultimate reality of the unconstructed (*asaṃskṛta*, i.e. the *dharmakāya*) is a definite movement away from the Madhyamaka understanding of the universality of *dharma-nairātmya*. From a Madhyamaka perspective the *dharmakāya* is as empty of *svabhāva* as everything else. That the *Śrīmālā* does not understand emptiness and no-self in this manner can be gleaned from the following statement,

> Lord, the *tathāgatagarbha* is void of all the defilement stores, which are discrete and knowing as not liberated [or "apart from knowledge that does not lead to liberation"][29] Lord, the *tathāgatagarbha* is not void (*aśūnya*) of the *Buddha dharmas* which are nondiscrete, inconceivable, more numerous than the sands of the Ganges, and knowing as liberated.[30]

The *tathāgatagarbha*, as support or substratum for the manifestation of *saṃskṛta dharmas*, is thus devoid (*śūnya*) of them. Of course this follows from the fact that the *tathāgatagarbha* is real and the *saṃskṛta dharmas* (which it somehow supports), are not. Nevertheless, the *Śrīmālā* qualifies the scope of emptiness by stating that the *tathāgatagarbha* is not empty (*aśūnya*) of the pure *buddha-dharmas* that constitute the *dharmakāya* of the Tathāgata. Despite this, the text makes it clear that one must resist the temptation of ascribing self-hood to the *tathāgatagarbha*, arguing that this would be an extreme view (as indeed are the views of "those who cling to the view of emptiness").[31]

Despite the possibility of an absolutistic reading of the *Śrīmālāsūtra*, there is enough evidence in the text to suggest that the *tathāgatagarbha*, far from being a static absolute, is in fact a dynamic and developmental reality. Nowhere does the *Sūtra* explicitly state that sentient beings are "enlightened from the beginning" (*ādibuddha*). The *tathāgatagarbha* is the "seed of Buddhahood" of all beings. As such it is a developing potential and is not to be confused with a self (*ātman*) of any sort. To account for the dichotomy between enlightenment and ignorance, the *tathāgatagarbha* is described as the base, support, and foundation of both enlightenment and of the constructed *dharmas* of the saṃsāric world. Thus the *tathāgatagarbha* is both intrinsically pure (being the embryo of the *dharmakāya*), and yet at the same time apparently contaminated by adventitious defilements (*āgantuka kleśa*).

The author of the *Śrīmālā*, however, seems unaware of, or perhaps unwilling to draw, philosophical consequences from certain statements made within the text. Notably there is no development of the notion that what is constructed (*saṃskṛta*) does not really exist. This may stem from the unsavory consequences of postulating such a view. A wholesale denial of the reality of the constructed (*saṃskṛta*) would seem to lead to the unfortunate conclusion that suffering is in fact not real.[32] Such being the case, there would be no necessity for a Mahāyāna path since only the *dharmakāya* really existed anyway! Such a view, however, can be discerned implicitly in the text when the *Śrīmālā* argues that the factors of the constructed realm (specifically the first, second, and fourth noble truths) do not ultimately exist because they are impermanent (*anitya*) and lacking a self (*anātman*). The view that there is no religious path, no bondage, and no liberation, since all of these are impermanent and thus not ultimately real, is in fact the view of the *Gauḍapādīya-kārikā*, as expressed, for instance, in GK II.32:

> Neither cessation nor origination, neither one bound nor one practicing spiritual discipline, neither one aspiring for liberation nor one who is liberated. This is the supreme truth.

Of course we have already encountered a similar *via negativa* in the Prajñāpāramitā literature; in these texts, however, there was no question of this path leading to the affirmation of an unconditioned, absolute reality. The *Śrīmālā* leaves certain fundamental questions about the nature of the *tathāgatagarbha* unanswered. It does not make any serious attempts to reconcile the notion of an intrinsically pure mind with that of the existence of defilements. The text also does not deal with the problem of the relationship between the *tathāgatagarbha*'s twin functions as the store of the pure *buddha-dharmas* on the one hand and as the support of the constructed world on the other, nor is its relationship with ignorance ever clarified (both being described as the source of the world's manifestation).[33]

For the Madhyamaka and classical Yogācāra schools the question of the relationship between the mind and the factors that defiled it was something of a pseudo-problem since both consciousness (*vijñāna*) and defilement (*kleśa*) were fundamentally empty and so ultimately without basis. The problem arose for the *tathāgatagarbha* texts, however, because they seem to have accepted neither the Madhyamaka conception of universal emptiness nor the Yogācāra position that the mind (*citta*) and its concomitant factors (*caittas*) were basically one and the same phenomenon (i.e., just-mind, *citta-mātra*). For those texts that focus upon the notion of the *tathāgatagarbha*, the reality of an intrinsically pure mind was a basic presupposition of their perspective, grounded as it was in a firm belief in the possibility of salvation and a religious orientation toward the spiritual catharsis of an apparently defiled consciousness. As such, their major philosophical concern was the attempt to delineate the relationship between an ultimate reality (i.e. the intrinsically pure mind or *dharmakāya*) and a conventional reality (the constructed factors or *saṃskṛta dharmas* and the adventitious defilements or *āgantuka kleśa*).

The emphasis upon the *tathāgatagarbha* as an embryonic and processive factor not to be mistaken for a self, despite its permanent and indestructible nature, and the text's recourse to the doctrine of the momentariness of consciousness suggest that the *Śrīmālā* was unwilling to endorse a fully blown absolutism based upon the sole reality of the *dharmakāya*. Notable, however, is a shift in perspective away from the universality of emptiness as expounded in the Madhyamaka and classical Yogācāra schools.

We have briefly considered the philosophical perspective of the *Śrīmālāsūtra* and suggested that in some respects it can be compared to the absolutism of the *Gauḍapādīya-kārikā*. Nevertheless, there is no evidence to suggest any connection between the *Śrīmālā* and the GK as such other than the former's partial acceptance of *ātman* terminology and its equivocal and somewhat tentative movement toward a form of absolutism. It is unlikely, therefore, that the author of GK IV derived his absolutistic interpretation of the Mahāyāna tradition from the *Śrīmālāsūtra*.

The *Śrīmālāsūtra*'s unwillingness to relinquish wholeheartedly the language of no-self (*anātman*) shows an awareness of the importance of the concept as a symbol of Buddhist identity in contrast to the Brahmanical *ātman* traditions in India. The *Mahāparinirvāṇasūtra*, however, appears to find no difficulty in the utilization of "self" (*ātman*) terminology in relation to the *tathāgatagarbha*. The *Sūtra*, translated into Chinese by Dharmarakṣa c. 412 CE, appears to have been compiled some time in the fourth century. Today only Sanskrit fragments remain of what is a somewhat complex and heterogenous text. The "Northern edition" (*Hokuhon-Nehan*) of the text appears to be the original translation by Dharmarakṣa, but a "Southern edition" (*Nanpon-Nehan*) incorporating translations of later sections of the *Sūtra* also exists. Although the origin of these later sections is historically rather obscure, this latter edition is particularly noteworthy for its explicit references to the universality of the *tathāgatagarbha*, including even the *icchantikas* (i.e. those felt to be beyond the hope of salvation).[34]

The *Mahāparinirvāṇasūtra* is the Mahāyāna equivalent of the pre-Mahāyāna canonical text of the same name (Pali: *Mahāparinibbāna Suttanta*), that claims to be an authentic record of the last days of the Buddha. The Mahāyāna text, however, places little emphasis upon the historical Buddha declaring that "the Tathāgata is eternal and unchanging."[35] In the Chapter on "Grief" the four "upside down" or erroneous positions (*viparyāsa*) are discussed. The Buddha praises his followers for meditating on the sorrowful (*duḥkha*), the impermanent (*anitya*) and the selfless (*anātman*), but then declares that there is a superior form of meditation, i.e. that which focuses upon the permanent, the blissful, the pure, and the "self."[36] This theme is developed further in the larger heterogenous text where the Buddha declares that:

> The thought of self against no-self and the thought of no-self against self are the upside downs. The people of the world say that there is self, and within Buddhism, too, we say that there is self. The people of the world say that there is self, but there is no Buddha Nature (*buddhadhātu*?). This is the raising of thought of self in [what is] no-self. This is an upside-down. The self talked about in Buddhism is the Buddha Nature. The people of the world say that there is no self in Buddhism. This is a thought of no-self in [what is] the self.[37]

The *Mahāparinirvāṇasūtra* clearly differs from the *Śrīmālā* in its description of the *tathāgatagarbha* as a self. In the chapter "On the Nature of the Tathāgata"[38] the *Sūtra* declares that " 'Self' (*ātman*) means '*tathāgatagarbha*.' Every being has the Buddha Nature. This is self."[39] The text also expresses disapproval of those who understand the Tathāgata to be a conditioned being

> What is a right thing to say is "The Tathāgata is definitely an uncreate". . .One may well throw away one's own self, but not say that the Tathāgata is equal to what is created. One must say that the Tathāgata is an uncreate. By saying that the Tathāgata is an uncreate, one attains the unsurpassed *bodhi*.[40]

It would seem that the *Sūtra* wishes to establish the view that the Tathāgata is an essentially unconditioned (*asaṃskṛta*), unchanging, and eternal reality. It is possible then that Paul Williams is correct when he suggest that,

> The *Mahāparinirvāṇa Sūtra* teaches a really existing, permanent element (Tibetan: *yang dag khams*) in sentient beings. It is this element which enables sentient beings to become Buddhas. It is beyond egoistic self-grasping—indeed the very opposite of self-grasping—but it otherwise fulfills several of the requirements of a Self in the Indian tradition. Whether this is called the Real, True Transcendental Self or not is as such immaterial, but what is historically interesting is that this *Sūtra* in particular (although joined by some other *Tathāgatagarbhasūtras*) is prepared to use the word "Self" (*ātman*) for this element. However one looks at it the *Mahāparinirvāṇa Sūtra* is quite self-consciously modifying or criticizing the no-Self traditions of Buddhism.[41]

Like the *Śrīmālāsūtra*, there is no evidence to suggest any specific connection with the doctrines of the *Gauḍapādīya-kārikā*. Nevertheless, the possibility of an absolutistic strand of thought within Indian Mahāyāna does suggest a more general source for the GK's absolutistic use of Mahāyāna philosophical ideas. It is our view that an implicit (and sometimes explicit) absolutism is detectable in a number of Mahāyāna texts which utilize the notion of a *tathāgatagarbha*. This is not to suggest that all such texts are absolutistic, only that some of them can, and thus in all probability were, understood in such a manner in Buddhist circles at the time of the composition of GK IV.

As we have seen, the *Śrīmālāsūtra* does not make explicit the precise relationship between the *tathāgatagarbha* and the *dharmakāya*. This produces a variety of doctrinal and hermeneutical problems. How, for instance, is one to reconcile the statements in the *Śrīmālā* that the *tathāgatagarbha* is not a self to the declaration that the *dharmakāya* is the perfection of self (*ātmapāramitā*)? To further exacerbate the situation, there is also the problem of reconciling this position to the apparently conflicting statements made by the *Mahāparinirvāṇasūtra*, which has little or no reservations about the use of *ātman* terminology to describe the *tathāgatagarbha*.

The Systematization of Indian *Tathāgatagarbha*: The *Ratnagotravibhāgaśāstra*

The *Ratnagotravibhāga* (RGV) is unique as the only Indian *śāstra* devoted specifically to an exposition of the *tathāgatagarbha* doctrine. No doubt one of the reasons behind the composition of the *Ratnagotravibhāgaśāstra* was to overcome the various doctrinal variations and inconsistencies presented by this group of texts. It seems likely that the RGV originally consisted of a number of *kārikās*, attributed to Maitreya by the Tibetan traditions, and later expanded to include a verse and prose commentary (*vyākhya*) written in all probability by the text's redactor Saramati.[42] The final text of the *Ratnagotra* (including the commentary) was translated into Chinese in 511 CE. It seems likely then that the final version of the text was completed sometime in the late fourth to early fifth century CE,[43] thus placing it in a period before the composition of the fourth *prakaraṇa* of the GK. However, judging by the frequency with which the *śāstra* is quoted in other Mahāyāna works, it does not seem to have been an important influence in Indo-Tibetan thought prior to the eleventh century CE. The sub-title of the RGV is the *Mahāyānottaratantraśāstra* or "The text on the final teaching of the Mahāyāna." This name reflects the fact that the text was intended by its author(s) (and/or redactors) to be the definitive interpretation of Buddhist teachings. The copious and diverse quotations, taken from Prajñāpāramitā Sūtras and from other Mahāyāna texts, point to the RGV's expressed intention of explaining the correct interpretation of diverse elements of Buddhist thought. The most common thread in the text, however, is a persistent emphasis upon the *tathāgatagarbha* doctrines and their greater clarification. As such, the primary scriptural authority for the *Ratnagotra* is the *Śrīmālāsūtra*, a text which it quotes more than any other.

The RGV explains the relationship between *dharmakāya* and *tathāgatagarbha* through the delineation of two specific "modes" of suchness (*tathatā*): defiled (*samalā*) and undefiled (*nirmalā*). In the *Śrīmālāsūtra*, the *tathāgatagarbha* was the embryonic seed or potential that existed within every sentient being. The actualization of this potential was the realization of the *dharmakāya* of the Tathāgata. The *Ratnagotra* emphasizes the identity of these two factors through the unifying concept of Suchness (*tathatā*). Thus, Suchness with defilements (*samalā tathatā*) is the *tathāgatagarbha* while Suchness free from defilements (*nirmalā tathatā*) is the *dharmakāya*.

As we noted earlier, only two of the nine metaphors utilized in the *Tathāgatagarbhasūtra* (and cited in the RGV) refer to the *tathāgatagarbha* as a dynamic, embryonic, and developmental "potential" within sentient beings. The remaining seven metaphors all suggest that the *dharmakāya* is already present, obscured from clear vision by what the *Śrīmālāsūtra* calls the "underlying defilement of ignorance." This idea is developed further in the RGV through the notion of the non-origination (*ajāti*) of discursive thought (*vikalpa*)[44] and the idea of an intrinsically pure mind obscured by adventitious defilements. Let us consider these two themes in order to throw more light upon the philosophical position of the RGV.

According to the RGV, irrational thought (*ayoniśomanasikāra*) or discursive thought (*vikalpa*) are the cause of all mental, bodily, and verbal activities. They are, however, ultimately non-existent. Thus, through knowing this fact, neither discursive thought (*vikalpa*), duality (*dvaya*) nor suffering can arise. To substantiate this position the RGV quotes the *Śrīmālā*'s explanation of the "Truth of cessation" as nothing more than a name for the *dharmakāya*, and the following statement from the *Jñānālokālaṅkārasūtra* (Taisho, XIII, No. 357, v. 247a):

> O, Mañjuśri, . . . there is neither origination nor extinction, mental actions as mind, intellect, and consciousness (*citta-mano-vijñāna*) never take place. Wherever no mental action takes place, there is no false imagination by which they would think irrationally. One who applies himself with rational thought never makes Ignorance arise. Non-arising of Ignorance means non-arising of the Twelve Parts of Existence (*dvādaśa-bhavāṅga*), [i.e., the *pratītyasamutpāda* cycle beginning with ignorance]. It is called "non-birth" (*ajāti*).[45]

Thus, we find the RGV referring to non-origination (*ajāti*), a major theme of both the Mahāyāna schools and of the *Gauḍapādīya-kārikā*. Does the RGV's understanding of non-origination conform to that of the Madhyamaka or is it more conducive to an absolutistic interpretation along the lines of the GK? According to the RGV the realization that irrational thought (*ayoniśomanasikāra*) does not actually exist is the means whereby the *tathāgatagarbha* (defiled Suchness) realizes itself as the essentially undefiled (*nirmalā*) *dharmakāya* of the Tathāgata. This insight is explained in terms of the irruption of the causal chain of conditional arising (*pratītyasamutpāda*) and the realization that, with the non-arising of ignorance, none of the other factors of existence can arise either. Thus the non-existence of ignorance (as the "basis" of the dependent-origination chain) necessitates the non-existence of the factors which arise in dependence upon it. This is the RGV's explication of the fundamental Madhyamaka insight that dependent-origination (*pratītya-sam-utpāda*) is in fact no origination (*an-utpāda*) at all.

However, while the RGV clearly endorses the Madhyamaka interpretation of the *pratītyasamutpāda* scheme and while this interpretation of the scheme is the central insight of that school, it is also clear that the text does not take the Madhyamaka doctrine of *śūnyatā* to be its final position. All of the "limbs" (*aṅga*) in the *pratītyasamutpāda* scheme are examples of conditioned phenomena. This is true by definition since *pratītyasamutpāda* means "conditioned-co-arising." The RGV seems to be suggesting that it is only *conditioned* factors that are denoted by the adjective "dependently-co-arisen" (*pratītyasamutpanna*). In sharp contrast to these factors then, it argues that the *dharmakāya* is unconditioned (*asaṃskṛta*), permanent (*nitya*), pure (*śubha*), blissful (*sukha*), and self-existent (*ātma*).[46] On this view the *pratītyasamutpāda* scheme is only valid as an explanation of the origination of conditioned phenomena (*saṃskṛta dharmas*). This is a focal point of the RGV analysis for it means that "selflessness" and "emptiness" can only refer to conditioned phenomena and not to the unconditioned absolute (the *dharmakāya*). As we have seen, this view was prefigured in both the *Śrīmālā* and *Mahāparinirvāṇasūtras*.

Such a view clearly differs from that of the Madhyamaka school for which all conceptual dichotomies (e.g. *bhāva—abhāva; saṃskṛta—asaṃskṛta*) operate within a state of mutual interdependence (i.e. they are *pratītyasamutpanna*). Thus, the notion of "non-existence" (*abhāva*) implies and is conceptually reliant upon the contradictory notion of "existence" (*bhāva*) and *vice versa*. The entire structure of conceptual proliferation (*prapañca*) operates within a "play" of conceptual (*prajñapti*) and conventional (*saṃvṛti*) "entities," mutually supporting each other but having no ultimate support for themselves—a conceptual circularity with no beginning or end points. For the Mādhyamika, this analysis is valid across the entire conceptual spectrum, leaving no stone unturned. Thus, even the notion of "unconditioned" (*asaṃskṛta*) is conceptually dependent upon the notion of a "conditioned" (*samskṛta*). Take away one piece from the house of cards and the whole edifice falls! But this does not entail, so the Mādhyamika argues, that any one card can be said to be more "real," substantial or supportive than any other. The RGV, however, seems to disagree and in its postulation of a self-existent (*ātma*), permanent (*anitya*), and unconditioned (*asaṃskṛta*) reality, it appears to be endorsing an absolutistic understanding of *ajātivāda* more akin to the GK than the Madhyamaka.

In the *tathāgatagarbha* texts the description of traditional Buddhist teachings such as the three "marks" of existence (i.e. *duḥkha, anitya,* and *anātman*) and the four Noble Truths as provisional, or valid only with regard to the conditioned factors of the conventional world (*saṃvṛti-sat*), is a clear devaluation of the act of contemplating the suffering, impermanence, and selflessness of experience. As we have seen, "emptiness" has been re-interpreted in these texts to refer to the emptiness of compounded or conditioned *dharmas*. For the RGV and its related texts, contemplation of these conditioned factors was simply not sufficient in the quest for enlightenment.[47] Progress upon the Mahāyāna path also requires personal experience of the *tathāgata-garbha* as the base, locus, and substratum for these suffering, impermanent, and constructed *dharmas*. The RGV, following the traditional Buddhist position, argues that it is wrong to describe compounded forms as permanent (*nitya*), blissful (*sukha*), self-established (*ātma*) or pure (*śubha*). It describes such misplaced attribution of "positive" characteristics as the fourfold delusion (*viparyāsa*). The truth, therefore, is that all compounded factors are impermanent (*anitya*), subject to suffering (*duḥkha*), lacking an abiding-self (*anātma*), and impure (*aśubha*). These are the traditional three marks of existence (*tri-lakṣaṇa*) with an additional fourth declaring the impurity of all such phenomena. So far nothing has been stated that might contravene the views of the "mainstream" textual tradition of Buddhism. However, the RGV then suggests that the four "erronous positions" (*viparyāsa*), become non-erronous (*aviparyāsa*) when applied to the *dharmakāya*, which can therefore be legitimately described as permanent (*nitya*), blissful (*sukha*), self-established (*ātma*), and pure (*aśubha*). Thus,

> "Being the Antidote to this notion, there is established the fourfold Supreme Virtue of the Absolute Body [i.e. the *dharmakāya*] of the Tathāgata. That is to say, the Supreme Eternity (*nitya-pāramitā*), the Supreme Bliss (*sukha-pāramitā*), the Supreme Unity (*ātma-pāramitā*), and the Supreme Purity (*śubha-pāramitā*).[48]

The four positive "antidotes," of course, are already to be found in the early texts of the *tathāgatagarbha* tradition where they exemplify a radical revolution in the approach to traditional Buddhist concepts and meditative practices. This has created a problem when attempting to reconcile these texts to the mainstream emphasis upon *duḥkha, anitya,* and *anātman*.

The RGV also maintains that the intrinsically pure mind is without modification (*avikāra*). Thus, it is likened to space (*ākāśa*) in that it is not compounded (*saṃskṛta*) and is not subject to origination or destruction, being stable in its own essence (*svarasa-yogena*).[49] Contrary to this, all the defilements, that apparently pollute the mind, are conditioned factors that never actually come into contact (*asaṃbaddha*) with the "innately pure mind" (*citta-prakṛti-viśuddhi*). The RGV describes this innate mind in the following terms,

It has neither origination nor destruction, nor even stability [between two points].
The innate nature of the mind is brilliant and, like space, has no transformation at all;
It bears, however, the impurity by stains of desires etc.,
Which are of accident and produced by wrong conception.[50]

We have already seen the basis of this view in the *Śrīmālāsūtra*. In that particular text the mind was seen as essentially momentary and for that reason untouched by defilements. In the RGV, however, the mind has clearly taken on a pre-eminent status as an unconstructed element and, far from being momentary, is now the permanent and unchanging factor that supports the arising of defilements. In the *Śrīmālā*, the *tathāgatagarbha* notion was brought into play to account for the possibility of retaining the experience of suffering given that the mind was essentially momentary. This was necessary because the *Śrīmālā* accepted the traditional Buddhist denial of a persisting personal self (*pudgala-nairātmya*) and as such had to deal with the problems of identity entailed by that position. In the RGV this problem is seen to have been overturned. It is still the case that there is no individual self, given that all separate and conditioned factors are impermanent and selfless; however, each individual being (*sattva*) has the unconditioned *dharmakāya* as its intrinsic nature (*svabhāva*). This *dharmakāya* is, of course, the intrinsically pure mind—untouched by the adventitious defilements (*āgantuka kleśa*).

A Question of Hermeneutics: Is There a Mahāyāna Absolutism?

The description of the "*tathāgatagarbha* texts" as absolutistic in contrast to the prevailing Mahāyāna rejection of absolutism has been criticized by a number of scholars in an effort to reconcile apparent doctrinal differences between various Mahāyāna texts. Sallie King in a discussion of this issue has suggested three "ways out of this problem."[51] First, there is the suggestion that many *tathāgatagarbha* statements are not ontological proclamations at all but are merely soteriological in intent. The second hermeneutical possibility, she suggests, is that the texts are "non-dualistic" not "monistic." Presumably by this King means that the *tathāgatagarbha* texts do not posit a substantialist monistic ontology, but instead expound the doctrine of non-duality (*advaya*) found in many Buddhist texts. Non-duality on this view is the denial of the reality of the subject-object bifurcation (as in the Yogācāra school) on the one hand, and the denial of the two types of extreme view (the positivistic and the negativistic) on the other. The third option, and this is the one that King seems particularly interesting in developing, is the idea that the *tathāgatagarbha* notion denotes an "active self," but not thereby a substantialist one. The various references to "self" etc. in *tathāgatagarbha* texts are said to be used to express the dynamic and transformative nature of the Buddhist path. Thus, King suggests that:

> Buddha nature is expressly identified with such acts as wisdom, non-attachment and compassion. It is never represented as possessing a substantive thing-like character or attribute. It is specifically said that the "functions" of the Buddha nature are its "essence." It is this identification. . .which makes possible the affirmation of such a thing as the Buddha nature despite the emphasis on *anātman* and *śūnyatā* in the history of Buddhism. The Buddha nature functions as a metaphor for the efficacy and desirability of the Buddhist path without creating a substantial "thing" to which persons could become attached. As an "active self," the Buddha nature is not an entity, but an identity comprised of certain acts.[52]

This is a non-absolutistic interpretation of the notion of "Buddha nature" that conforms nicely to mainstream Mahāyāna ideology. More recently, David Seyfort Ruegg has suggested two ways in which the "positivistic" notions of the *tathāgatagarbha* texts can be reconciled to the traditional Buddhist approach.[53] They are:

1. that *tathāgatagarbha* texts are intentional (*ābhiprāyika*) texts that require further interpretation (*neyārtha*).[54]
2. that *tathāgatagarbha* texts are texts of definitive meaning (*nītārtha*) but are nevertheless "meta-theoretical" in their scope.

Ruegg's analysis is preferable to that of King's since it succinctly enunciates the hermeneutical possibilities that were considered by Buddhist exegetes themselves.

What then is meant in the RGV and other such texts by the term "perfection of self" (*ātma-pāramitā*)? Are we encountering a form of absolutism akin to the Vedāntic view expounded in the *Gauḍapādīya-kārikā* (and thus a potential source of the GK's own view)? Brown argues, for instance, that the "perfection of self" is nothing more than the realization that one has no self. In other words, the term "self" (*ātma*) is being used in a propadeutical and essentially metaphorical sense as a corrective to the dangers of interpreting *śūnyatā* in an overly negative and ontological sense.[55] Again, in relation to the "perfection of permanence," Brown argues that *nitya-pāramitā* does not imply a "concrete attribute, qualifying some quintessential concrete hypostasis." Rather,

> the *śāstra*'s major intent in advancing the four *guṇapāramitā* is more properly pastoral and spiritually pedagogical, than it is ontological.[56]

John P. Keenan also argues that the interests of the "*tathāgatagarbhavādins*" lay in the practical and not the theoretical sphere.

> The aim of the *tathāgatagarbha* literature is then not to offer a rival synthesis to either Madhyamaka or Abhidharma, but to develop a practical doctrine that will encourage people to follow the path . . . this does not mean that *tathāgatagarbha* is directly opposed to Madhyamaka. Again there is a shift in the context of meaning. For the majority of people, reading the tracts of Nāgārjuna will probably always remain meaningless, for they have not experienced the all encompassing vision that leads to mystic consciousness. . .Thus, *tathāgatagarbha* functions in the main in the common sense context of meaning.[57]

This corresponds to Ruegg's second option, the meta-theoretical interpretation of *tathāgatagarbha* texts, and is in fact how the Tibetan dGe lugs pa (Prāsaṅgika Madhyamaka) school generally explained the apparent doctrinal discrepancies between *tathāgatagarbha* and mainstream Madhyamaka texts. On this view, *tathāgatagarbha* doctrines are the utilization of a cataphatic language adopted in order to alleviate the suffering of those beings who cannot understand that "all is empty." All such works, therefore, were classified as texts of definitive meaning (*nītārtha*) since they dealt directly with the notions of no-self (*nairātmya*) and emptiness (*śūnyatā*).[58]

The other and *prima facie* the most obvious explanation of the various *tathāgatagarbha* texts is that they are texts requiring further interpretation (*neyārtha*), that is, that they were written with an intentional purpose (*ābhiprāyika*), so as to draw those people to the Buddhist path who could not understand the complexities of the notions of no-self and emptiness. This view is put forward in the *Laṅkāvatārasūtra* that suggests that the *tathāgatagarbha* notion is taught as a self for the sake of non-Buddhists.[59] That this explanation is not appropriate in the case of the RGV should be clear from a careful reading of the text and from an awareness of the text's expressed position as the "final doctrine" (*uttaratantra*). Thus, if we are to take the RGV's doctrines at face value—there being no internal evidence to the contrary, we must inevitably draw the conclusion that the text represents a wholly different approach to the problems encountered by Buddhist philosophy than that exemplified by the texts of the Madhyamaka, Yogācāra, and Abhidharma schools in India.

Ruegg, however, follows the dGe lugs pa commentators in describing the *tathāgatagarbha* texts as meta-theoretical works. In contrast to these, the śāstric works of Nāgārjuna etc. are said to provide an insight (*prajñā*) into emptiness and no-self within a theoretical context. Thus the (Prāsaṅgika) Mādhyamika utilizes the *prasaṅga* (*reductio ad absurdum*) technique in refuting the theories of others. In this way the philosophical texts of the Madhyamaka point to emptiness through a radical de-constructionism of conceptual entities. The *tathāgatagarbha* texts, however, are said to deal with the same basic insights but from an essentially meta-theoretical context. The emphasis is upon *praxis* and not theory.

Keenan suggests that there has been "a shift in the context of meaning" in the transition from Madhyamaka to *tathāgatagarbha* ideas. This is undoubtedly the case but does not in itself mean that the views outlined in Madhyamaka and *tathāgatagarbha* texts are beyond meaningful comparison, despite the probability that they were intended for different audiences or the fact that they exhibit different approaches or "meaning contexts." Keenan argues that the *tathāgatagarbha* tradition was not a scholastic movement in India and so was not a legitimate "rival" of either the Madhyamaka or Yogācāra positions. Despite this, it is my view that the texts of this "strand" of Mahāyāna Buddhism do possess a distinctive philosophical position; one, in fact, that is structurally different in both form (as Keenan, Grosnick,[60] and Brown accept) and content (which they do not). The existence of the *Ratnagotravibhāga*, itself a philosophical *śāstra*, suggests that *tathāgatagarbha* ideas can be, and indeed were, meaningfully compared to the philosophical positions of the Madhyamaka and Yogācāra schools.

Whether the *Ratnagotravibhāga* was intended for a different audience or written for a different reason is largely beside the point for the text clearly distances itself from the Madhyamaka conception of *śūnyatā*, arguing that the *tathāgatagarbha* is empty of defilements (*kleśa*) but not empty of pure *buddha-dharmas*. Ruegg, following the dGe lugs pa commentators, is misleading in his suggestion that the *tathāgatagarbha* ideas are "explicated in such a manner as to be consonant with the definitive teachings of *nairātmya* and *śūnyatā* according to the criterion established by the *Akṣayamatinirdeśasūtra* and the *Samādhirājasūtra*.''[61] The Tibetan hermeneutical principle to which Ruegg refers is basically the view that a Buddhist text that discusses the notions of *nairātmya* and *śūnyatā* must, by definition, be definitive in its meaning. While it is true that the *tathāgatagarbha* texts do fulfill the formal requirements of the hermeneutical principle laid down in those two texts insofar as they discuss both the doctrines of no-self and emptiness, in terms of philosophical content it is difficult to reconcile the standard Madhyamaka conception of emptiness with the notion as it is understood within the *tathāgatagarbha* tradition. The incommensurability of the two perspectives remains despite an orthodox ''massaging'' of the texts.

The view that *tathāgatagarbha* texts are definitive in meaning but meta-theoretical in approach presents us with another hermeneutical possibility. Sallie King argues (cp. Keenan) that the ''*tathāgatagarbha*'' notion is basically soteriological in intent; it is the idea of an ''active self'' following the Mahāyāna path to transformation (*āśraya-parāvṛtti*). This is an attractive interpretation. However, it seems more appropriate to acknowledge the possibility of divergent ''strands'' within the Buddhist tradition. To argue that all of the *tathāgatagarbha* texts were written with a propadeutical and didactic purpose (and therefore did not intend to postulate some form of hypostatized absolute in the form of the *dharmakāya*), is somewhat problematic. Ruegg himself, despite his own attempts to reconcile *tathāgatagarbha* ideas to mainstream Madhyamaka philosophy, acknowledges that

> the question may even arise as to whether the name ''Buddhism'' denotes one single entity rather than a classification embracing (more or less polythetically) a very large number of strands held together by family resemblances.[62]

One suspects that the situation in Buddhist India was somewhat akin to that of modern Buddhist scholarship—a healthy plurality of perspectives upon the tradition. For some scholars the Buddhist tradition consistently upholds an absolute, while for others there is no absolute to be found, everything being in a state of flux (*anitya*) and insubstantiality (*nairātmya*). It is likely that neither of these perspectives fully encapsulates the diversity of Mahāyāna thought in India. As I have argued in previous chapters, the ''non-absolutistic'' interpretation of Buddhism is an appropriate way of understanding the perspectives of ''mainstream'' textual Buddhism.[63] Nevertheless, each text should be examined on its own merits. As Paul Williams has suggested, scholars should resist the temptation of reducing Mahāyāna philosophy to "a series of footnotes to Nāgārjuna."[64] To argue that all Indian Mahāyānists agreed unanimously in the interpretation and meaning of fundamental Buddhist doctrines is to fail to acknowledge the diversity of human expression and the pluralistic nature of the Mahāyāna movement.[65]

Nevertheless, one can accept the view that *tathāgatagarbha* ideas often occur in a "cathartic" and practical rather than an epistemological and theoretical context without assuming that this thereby restricts the sense in which they can be meaningfully compared with other "philosophical" aspects of the tradition. The professed practical orientation of the *tathāgatagarbha* texts does not preclude them from expressing philosophical positions that differ from that of the "mainstream." While a number of thematic links can be established between the *tathāgatagarbha* texts and the developing Yogācāra school, there is a clear divergence in their respective philosophical positions.[66] Even if not as systematically developed as the philosophical views of the Mahāyāna schools, the Indian *tathāgatagarbha* texts that we have been considering seem, at least at face value, to uphold a form of absolutism based upon the hypostatization of the unconditioned (*asaṃskṛta*) *dharmakāya*.[67] Consequently, one can say that these texts and the movement that they represent provide a potential source for the absolutistic conception of the Mahāyāna found in the GK.

Tathāgatagarbha *and Two Types of Emptiness in Tibetan Mahāyāna*

Later Tibetan exegesis of the Mahāyāna tradition saw the elucidation of two distinctive conceptions of emptiness. The first, *raṅ stong pa* (*svabhāva-śūnyatā*), or "emptiness-of-self," denotes the selflessness of all *dharmas* and corresponds to the position of the Indian Madhyamaka school in particular. This is generally regarded to be the position upheld by Tsong kha pa and his school, the dGe lugs pa (Prāsaṅgika Madhyamaka). The second position, *gzhan stong pa* (*paradharma-śūnyatā*), or "emptiness-of-other," denotes the selflessness of compounded *dharmas*. In Tibet, the school most readily associated with this point of view was the Jo naṅ pas, who are criticized by their opponents for upholding an apparently eternalistic position. Thus, Ruegg notes that

> Their fundamental doctrine was the Void-of-the-other (*gzhan ston*), that is, an absolute which is established in reality and is Void of all heterogenous relative and phenomenal factors, as against the Void-of-

> Own-being (*raṅ stoṅ, svabhāvaśūnya*) of the Mādhyamika which the Jo naṅ pas considered to be a merely preliminary or lower doctrine bearing on the relative (*saṃvṛti*) and not on the absolute Meaning (*paramārtha*). Although, the Jo naṅ pas none the less considered themselves true Mādhyamikas, the Tibetan Mādhyamikas who follow Candrakīrti—in other words the majority of Tibetan scholars—resolutely oppose and refute their theories.[68]

The upholders of *gzhaṅ-stong* argue that the self-emptiness model (*raṅ stong*) is adequate as a *description* of the nature of the saṃsāric world but that it cannot explain its appearance. Provisionally then, all *gzhaṅ-stong* theorists accept *raṅ stong pa*.[69] However, they would contend that one must understand that behind this empty world there exists the pure Buddha-mind. Thus, as Williams notes:

> The *gzhan stong* tradition shows a clear tendency towards creating an ontological absolute through the hypostasization of experience. . . Inasmuch as there is a direct denial of the anti-ontological expressions of the dGe lugs pa, and in speaking of the ultimate as primevally existing, permanent, self aware, and self luminous, not empty but rather enjoying a fundamental ontological status, so the *gzhan stong* has created an ontology of the (transcendental) subject. This is an ontology which postulates as a substratum to a denial of a self-luminous, albeit depersonalized, awareness cleared of adventitious defilements.[70]

Gzhaṅ stong pa, of course is at variance not only with the dGe lugs pa tradition of Tibet but also with the Indian Madhyamaka and Yogācāra schools, both of which place a great emphasis upon the universality of the *pratītyasamutpāda* scheme for explaining the appearance of the world in terms of the inter-dependent arising of *dharmas*. Nevertheless, the perspective that precipitated *gzhaṅ stong pa* is an archaic one and can be traced back to various statements in the texts of early Buddhism.[71] The most likely direct antecedents of the *gzhaṅ stong* position, however, appear to be the various *tathāgatagarbha* works of Indian Mahāyāna, that clearly understands emptiness to refer to compounded *dharmas* alone. This is interesting since, as Ruegg notes, these are precisely the texts appealed to by the Jo naṅ pas.[72]

For the Jo naṅ pas, the unconditioned Buddha-nature is unaffected by the fluctuations of the empty and impermanent *dharmas* of saṃsāric experience. The defilements are seen as adventitious elements that never actually came into contact with the intrinsically pure mind. This view is in marked contrast to the prevailing view of scholastic Buddhism in India, that envisaged consciousness as a phenomenal mixture of pure and impure elements (*dharmas*).

We should note at this point that whereas the *tathāgatagarbha* strand of Buddhist thought seems more amenable to the latter interpretation (*gzhaṅ stong*—"other-empty") and to that extent upholds a form of absolutism based upon the reality of the intrinsically pure mind (*cittaprakṛtiviśuddha*), the Madhyamaka (*raṅ stong*—self-empty) does not.[73] The accommodation of these two trends within the wide spectrum of Buddhist thought is a testament to the "open-endedness" of the Buddhist approach to doctrinal matters and to the overwhelming importance of *upāya*—using the means available—in order to alleviate suffering.

As we have seen, one of the primary reasons for the development of *tathāgatagarbha* ideas was the attempt to "save" the concepts of "suffering" and "liberation" from the nullification of the emptiness doctrine. Universal emptiness (*sarva-dharma-śūnyatā*) was seen by some to circumvent the very possibility of salvation and so, in order to correct this "extreme," the notion of emptiness was qualified so as to refer to the constructed realm of *saṃsāra* alone. However, the final consequence of this view is that, from the *gzhaṅ stong* point of view, ultimately there is no *saṃsāra* or bondage since everything is essentially in *nirvāṇa*. All beings are already enlightened (*ādibuddha*).[74] One should note the similarity between this view and the absolutism of the Advaita Vedānta school. As we have seen, the *Gauḍapādīya-kārikā* also declares that everything is essentially enlightened (IV.92); all is Brahman!

From the perspective of the self-emptiness view (*raṅ stong pa*), however, the postulation of an unconditioned reality is superfluous since the world can be explained in terms of the interdependence (*pratītyasamutpāda*) of its constituents. This eradicates the need for a creative or supportive principle. In fact, according to these thinkers, the appearance of *saṃsāra* cannot be explained adequately in any other way. The upholders of *gzhaṅ stong pa* thus have the problem of explaining the relationship between an unconditioned and essentially pure reality and the defiled world of *saṃsāra*. This is a problem for all substrative philosophies of this kind. In the Vedānta tradition, for instance, a similar objection is raised in *Brahmasūtra* 2.1.26. If the whole of Brahman transforms it becomes another, rendering Brahman non-existent, and yet if only a part of Brahman is transformed, this contradicts the unity and partlessness of Brahman. In the *Śrīmālāsūtra*, the problem of the relationship between the pure mind and the adventitious defilements is also at the forefront of the author's mind. Both the *Brahmasūtra* and the *Śrīmālāsūtra*, however, refuse to respond to the problem suggesting that the disciple should accept the existence of the *tathāgatagarbha*/Brahman on faith alone. Neither *sūtra* was prepared to embrace the radical absolutism of the *Gauḍapādīya-kārikā* which does attempt to overcome the problem. From the GK's point of view, Brahman (the absolute) has never actually transformed itself into a created realm and so the problem of its relationship to that realm cannot even arise.

In the Mahāyāna movement, therefore, there appear to be (at least) two widely differing conceptions of the Buddhist Path. Etienne Lamotte has formulated the distinction between these "strands" as perspectives exemplified by the "cessation of mental activity" (*acitta*) on the one hand and "the innate purity of mind" (*citta-viśuddhi-prakṛti*) on the other.[75] Both approaches claim to be the definitive statement of the Buddha's teachings and both lead to contrasting explanations of the Buddhist message. It is interesting to note that both approaches explain away the texts of the other through misinterpretation or by assigning them the status of a text requiring further interpretation (*neyārtha*). This is not the place to become embroiled in the debate concerning the true intent of the Buddha's original message, suffice it to say that these two interpretations of Buddhism correspond to the two main "schools" of interpretation in Buddhist scholarship today (i.e. the absolutists and the non-absolutists).

Many proponents of the absolutistic approach to Buddhism argue that the Buddha did not in fact deny a self but was merely denying that the self can be found *in* the five *skandhas*. These scholars point to the frequent occurrence of reflexive pronouns such as "this" (*idam*) as evidence that the Buddha's "no-self" statements were referring to a self in this empirical world and were not denials of the possibility of a "trans-empirical" or "supramundane" self. Thus the Buddha was not denying that a self exists, rather his was a denial of a self within the five *skandhas* of saṃsāric experience. Daisetz Suzuki, for instance, argued in his *Outlines of Mahāyāna Buddhism* that the Buddhist and Vedāntic uses of the term "*ātman*" differ; the former being understood as an empirical and personal ego (*pudgala*) and the latter being understood as an "abstract metaphysical substance." Consequently, Suzuki could then argue that the two views were essentially compatible.[76] There are, of course, many possible permutations of this approach, but their one distinguishing feature is the tendency to provide either an "absolutistic" or an "agnostic" interpretation of the Buddha's teaching concerning the status of the self.

The most famous quotation from the scriptures of early Buddhism that is often used to support the "absolutistic" tendencies of the pure-mind "strand" is that found in *Udāna*,

> There is, brethren, an unborn, a not-become, a not-made, a not-compounded. If there were not, brethren, this that is unborn, not-become, not-made, not-compounded, there could not be made any escape from what is born, become, made, and compounded. But since, brethren, there is this unborn. . . therefore is there made known an escape from what is born, become made, and compounded.[77]

This can be interpreted as a succinct expression of the dependence of the conditioned world of saṃsāric appearance upon the unconditioned reality that supports it as its *raison d'être*. It should be noted, however, that an ontological interpretation of the verse is by no means the only possibility. The verse may simply be making the point that the two realms "*saṃsāra*" and "*nirvāṇa*" are mutually dependent and not that *saṃsāra* is in any way dependent upon a subjacent ground known as *nirvāṇa*.

The second interpretation of *anātmavāda* takes the assertion of "no-abiding-self" in a more literal and straight-forward sense. Proponents of this view argue that the Buddha's statements should be taken at face value and that he is declaring his opposition to all theories based upon the conception of a "self." These scholars point to the analysis of the individual into five *skandhas* as the Buddhist explanation of how a succession of momentary "heaps" (*skandhas*) can appear as a composite and unified individual (*pudgala*). The distinction between these two interpretations is not always clear and it would seem that many are unsure or even unaware that there are two distinctive traditions of interpretation at work here. The important point to note at this point, however, is that there is a "strand" of thought[78] within the Buddhist tradition that finds no difficulty in the adoption of "self" (*ātman*) terminology to describe the ultimate truth. This tradition was most notably exemplified in Indian Mahāyāna by the *tathāgatagarbha* texts and in Tibet by the Jo naṅ pas (who no doubt were not the only representatives of this position).

The *Gauḍapādīya-kārikā* and *Tathāgatagarbha* Buddhism

From where does the author of GK IV derive his absolutistic conception of the Buddhist tradition? One potential source could have been those Indian Mahāyāna texts that focus upon the notion of "*tathāgatagarbha*." Certain of these texts approach the major themes of the Buddhist tradition (*anātmatā, śūnyatā, anityatā* etc.) from an apparently absolutistic perspective. Various explanations for this have been put forward by scholars attempting to reconcile divergent trends within the Mahāyāna tradition, but it seems likely that some Indian Mahāyānists upheld a form of absolutism in their belief that uncompounded or unconditioned (*asaṃskṛta*) Buddha *dharmas* are not in themselves empty (*aśūnya*). One should note, however, that the *tathāgatagarbha* notion never precipitated a philosophical movement of its own within Indian Buddhism, although in the Tibetan Jo naṅ pa school we appear to have a later example of just such a development. The degree to which the early *tathāgatagarbha* texts were taken to be straightforwardly orthodox by the Mahāyāna scholasts probably reflects the fact that absolutism was never a viable alternative for the Mahāyāna philosopher since the scholastic tradition largely structures its own position in contrast to what it sees as the absolutism of the Brahmanical (especially the Vedāntic) traditions. In Tibet and the Far East, however, the symbolic (and paradigmatic) opposition between the two traditions was not a predominating factor. Therefore, it became possible for the innovations and philosophical distinctiveness of some of the *tathāgatagarbha* texts to be fully appreciated and intellectually developed in scholastic directions (i.e. as *darśanas*).[79]

In Tibetan Buddhism the disputes between the dGe lugs pas and the Jo naṅ pas reflect an antagonistic clash between constrasting philosophical paradigms (although, in the case of Tibetan Buddhism many scholastic disputes were also fueled by political considerations). Retrospectively then, one can see structural similarities between the absolutism of the GK and the conception of reality endorsed by some *tathāgatagarbha* texts. Both the GK and the *tathāgatagarbha* texts deny the independent-existence (*svatantrika*) of the individual self (*jīvātman, pudgala*).[80] The Mahāyāna schools deny the independent existence of all contingent entities (*bhāva*) on the grounds that everything is dependently-originated (*pratītyasamutpanna*). In the GK and the subsequent Advaita Vedānta school, however, Brahman is affirmed as the (sole) ultimate reality on the grounds that it is an independent and self-established existent. In the postulation of an independently existing and unconditioned realm of pure *asaṃskṛta* (Buddha) *dharmas* the underlying paradigm of the *tathāgatagarbha*-texts is structurally similar in that it too posits the existence of an independent existent or absolute reality—the *dharmakāya*—underlying apparent defilements. In the final analysis, in fact, all is the *dharmakāya*, which seems to play the same part in this perspective as the supreme self (*paramātman*) in the Advaita Vedānta system. As the essential ground or nature (*dharmadhātu/dharmatā*) of things all distinctions between *dharmas* are denied (all *dharmas* being *asaṃskṛta* and *nirvṛti*, i.e. essentially in *nirvāṇa*). Such a view can even be described as non-dualistic. All of these structural similarities suggests Vedāntic influences upon the *tathāgatagarbha* texts themselves. This line of thought should not be readily dismissed. No movement develops in a cultural vacuum; interaction and mutual influence between Buddhist and Hindu schools has no doubt been a feature of the traditions from the beginning. Discussion of specific Vedāntic influence upon the *tathāgatagarbha* texts, however, is beyond the scope of the current study that is specifically concerned with the *Gauḍapādīya-kārikā* and its Buddhist influences. Nevertheless, it is an interesting area, deserving of further research.

The apparent similarities between the Vedāntic perspective of the GK and that of the *tathāgatagarbha* texts, however, should not be over-emphasized. As we have already noted, the predominant interpretation of the notion of "*tathāgatagarbha*" in India understood the notion to be entirely orthodox in the Mahāyāna avoidance of absolutism. It is possible that many of these texts do not endorse absolutism and are in fact merely adopting a more cataphatic approach to the central themes of Mahāyāna Buddhism. Given the complexity and wide-ranging nature of the Mahāyāna tradition, however, it would be misleading to suggest that all Mahāyāna texts are speaking from a common philosophical perspective. The scholar must remain aware of the extent to which the notions of *ekayāna* and *upāya-kauśalya* have been used by Mahāyānists to harmonize philosophical divergences within the tradition. It seems highly probable that many Mahāyāna Buddhists understood (and still do understand) their tradition in broadly absolutistic terms. The extent to which this was or continues to be a predominant orientation is beyond our concern since this is not an exercise in counting heads. Given the complexity of such notions as *śūnyatā* etc., it would be ridiculous to assume that all Mahāyāna Buddhists had a satisfactory grasp of the "mainstream" import and significance of these terms. It is important to acknowledge, however, that in the philosophical and scholastic texts that we have considered (that represent the "mainstream" textual tradition) absolutism is consistently rejected as an extreme view based upon (and leading to) attachment. Upon closer examination then, the absolutism that scholars such as T. R. V. Murti find in the mainstream philosophical texts of Indian Mahāyāna Buddhism simply is not present!

As we saw in the previous chapter, the fourth *prakaraṇa* of the GK, in common with the work of modern scholars such as T. R. V. Murti, appears to endorse an absolutistic view of the Mahāyāna. This interpretation, while incorrectly attributed to "mainstream" Indian

Mahāyāna (i.e. philosophical or ''darśanic'' Buddhism), may have come from the author's reading of such texts as the *Śrīmālāsūtra*, the *Ratnagotravibhāgaśāstra*, and the *Mahāparinirvāṇasūtra*. There is little textual evidence, however, that might suggest that the author has been specifically influenced by the notion of the *tathāgatagarbha* or by texts which utilize that notion as their central concept. The adoption of the rare term ''*Agrayāna*'' to refer to the Mahāyāna in GK IV.90, however, may very well derive from its occurrence in texts such as the *Ratnagotravibhāga* and the *Mahāyānasūtrālaṅkāra*—both pre-Gauḍapādian compositions that freely utilize the notion of the *tathāgatagarbha* to a great degree. Nevertheless, Indian Mahāyānists themselves do not seem to have been terribly aware of any conflict between the views propounded in these texts and those found, for instance, in the Prajñāpāramitā *sūtras* and other texts interpreting the Buddhist tradition from a ''mainstream'' (*dharma-nairātmya*) Mahāyāna perspective. The explicit development of the *tathāgatagarbha* orientation was left to Mahāyāna philosophers in Tibet, China, and Japan. It remains a distinct possibility, nevertheless, that GK IV derives its own absolutistic reading of the Mahāyāna from the author's awareness of Mahāyāna texts such as the *Ratnagotravibhāga* and the *Mahāyānasūtrālaṅkāra*. Acknowledgment of the existence of a form of absolutism (albeit not the ''mainstream'' view) within the Mahāyāna tradition makes this possibility all the more likely.

Conclusions

The Date and Authorship of the *Gauḍapādīya-kārikā*

In chapter 1 we examined the text of the GK and considered questions of date and authorship. The traditional view of the text as the unitary composition of a figure known as Gauḍapāda is represented by the work of Mahadevan (1952) and Karmarkar (1953). The analysis therein, however, suggests that the text is composite in nature, a view shared by Vidhushekhara Bhattacharya (1943), (though he does not develop the point), Alexander Hixon (1976), Tilmann Vetter (1978), and Thomas Wood (1990). GK I can be reconciled with the other *prakaraṇas* but not easily and so is likely to be a separate (and more straightforwardly Vedāntic) text, integrated at some later date with the other chapters. GK II, III, and IV clearly uphold the same general philosophical position (*ajātivāda*, the equality of waking and dream states etc.) and thus are likely to be the work of members of the same philosophical school (probably established in Bengal—hence the name "Gauḍa"). I have also suggested (*pace* Hixon and Vetter) that GK IV is the latest and most sophisticated of the *prakaraṇas*. This view is based upon a detailed philological examination of the GK and a consideration of its relationship to the work of the sixth century Buddhist doxographer Bhāvaviveka. The relationship between the GK and Bhāvaviveka's *Madhyamakahṛdaya-kārikā* (MHK) is a complex one. GK III appears to be one of many sources for the chapter on the Vedānta in the MHK (and so must be pre-Bhāvavivekan), while GK IV is aware of the sixth century Madhyamaka-Yogācāra controversy over the status of the *paratantra-svabhāva* (GK IV.24,25). Christian Lindtner has noted the latter in a recent article but his short and equivocal comments concerning its relevance are hampered by a failure to consider the composite nature of the GK.[1] It was also suggested in chapter 1 that the entire text of the GK, despite its composite nature, is pre-Śaṅkarite since it shows no evidence of any influences in the post-sixth century era. This indeed is the most commonly held view among scholars in this field, though recently Thomas Wood (1990) has voiced his dissent.[2]

All four *prakaraṇas* display evidence of Buddhist influence. Most notably in GK I are the references to *prapañca* and *vikalpa* and the doctrine of non-origination (see especially GK I.16, 17, and 18). The second *prakaraṇa* displays evidence of an implicit Yogācāran influence in its interpretation of the *Bṛhadāraṇyaka* analysis of the dream and waking states. Again Mahāyāna influence is clearly present in verses such as II.31 and 32, and the chapter's general acceptance of *ajātivāda* further substantiates this view. I have also attempted to demonstrate that the syncretism of GK II is related to the view (expressed later in GK III and IV) that *ajātivāda* does not conflict with any other doctrine. This is itself dependent upon the analysis of views (*dṛṣṭi*) found in Nāgārjuna's *MūlaMadhyamakakārikā*. In GK III we find the utilization of Buddhist terminology and doctrines in a text that is largely concerned with Vedāntic topics and themes. In particular, one should note the acceptance of the equation of waking and dream states and the doctrine of non-origination. Clearly, however, the most obvious examples of Buddhist influence are to be found in the fourth *prakaraṇa*. Here we find explicit citations and allusions to Buddhist texts alongside discussions of the equality of the dream and waking states, the doctrine of the non-duality (*advaya*) of consciousness—i.e. the denial of the validity of subject-object divisions in experience, (both Yogācāra-inspired themes), a Madhyamaka-style critique of causality, and the endorsement of the Mahāyāna doctrine of the non-origination of *dharmas*. The second, third, and fourth *prakaraṇas*, nevertheless, overlap with each other insofar as they all share certain "family resemblances." The overlapping of themes between these three chapters suggest common lineage but not common authorship. It is because of the doctrinal and thematic commonalities between these three *prakaraṇas* in particular that one can meaningfully refer to "Gauḍapādian thought" without thereby implying unity of authorship. The term does, however, imply that there is a strand of thought that can be discerned from the *prakaraṇas* when taken *in toto*. One can say then that "Gauḍapādian thought" refers to the fundamental perspective of the school of thought represented by the *prakaraṇas* (particularly the last three) of the *Gauḍapādīya-kārikā*.

The Nature of Gauḍapādian Thought

Our analysis of the contents of the *Gauḍapādīya-kārikā* has highlighted the centrality of two doctrinal themes within the text. These are the doctrine of non-origination (*ajātivāda*) on the one hand and the concept of *asparśayoga* on the other.

Ajātivāda in the GK

My analysis of the Gauḍapādian doctrine of non-origination concords with that of Tilmann Vetter (1978) in suggesting that it is dependent upon the Madhyamaka understanding of the non-arising (*anutpāda*) of *dharmas*. This, of course, is hardly a controversial statement! Previous studies of the GK, however, have failed to discuss the nature of this dependence and its implications for the relationship between the philosophies of the GK and the Mahāyāna. Both the Gauḍapādian doctrine of non-origination and the text's belief that it is not in conflict with any other view are drawn from an absolutistic (mis-)reading of Nāgārjuna's arguments in the MMK. The GK takes Nāgārjuna's rejection of all views (*dṛṣṭi*) as incipient forms of absolutism and adopts it for its own purposes. All views, the authors of the GK argue, entail an unoriginated absolute. This is seen as the final vindication of *ajātivāda*.

Analysis of the GK and some pertinent comments by the Mādhyamika philosopher Bhāvaviveka have highlighted the direction in which the Madhyamaka-Vedānta debate can most fruitfully progress. It would seem that the two schools reach a philosophical impass precisely over the question of "*svabhāva :: niḥsvabhāva*" and that this points to the incommensurability of the two approaches. The GK upholds a philosophical position that is structured in direct opposition to the *dharma-nairātmya* paradigm of the Madhyamaka and early Yogācāra schools (whether the author of the fourth *prakaraṇa* in particular is aware of this fact is indeed a moot point). This reflects the fact that historically the Advaita Vedānta perspective (*darśana*), as espoused in the *Gauḍapādīya-kārikā*, initially arose within a context of Mahāyāna philosophical hegemony.

It is largely in response to the prevailing Buddhist paradigms that the early Advaita Vedānta of the GK structures its own position. This, for instance, has been shown through an analysis of MMK chapter XXIV and GK III. 17 and 18. Nāgārjuna rejects all views insofar as they presuppose a *svabhāva* and therefore entail absolutistic consequences. In contrast, the author(s) of the GK accept all views for the self-same reason. In a sense one might say that the authors of the MMK and the GK are looking at the same picture from opposite sides of the mirror. Their presuppositions (and therefore their conclusions) are thus diametrically opposed. Paradoxical as this may seem, it is because of the "directly facing" nature of the two systems that the Mahāyāna and Advaita traditions are so often confused; in many respects their discussions and conclusions are mirrored in the views of the other. Mirror images are, of course, reversals of the things which they reflect. One must not take this analogy too seriously however. I am not suggesting that Advaita Vedānta distorts or merely reflects Mahāyāna themes and approaches. One must not forget the rich tradition of Vedāntic speculation that preceded the GK (see chapter 2). Rather, my position is merely that the *prima facie* similarity of Advaita and Mahāyāna ideas, in actuality, reflects their direct incommensurability. This relationship reflects the historical roots of the early Advaita Vedānta paradigm, that is the GK's philosophical reliance upon Mahāyāna themes and perspectives. I do not propound the thesis that the GK is dependent upon Buddhist sources either as a means of denigrating Advaita Vedānta as a living philosophical and religious tradition, or in order to prove some claim of Buddhist philosophical superiority. My thesis, then, is intended to be primarily historical rather than ideological in intent (though I am aware that such a distinction is somewhat naive). Theoretically, Advaita Vedānta could have developed independently from a particular reading of Brahmanical sources such as the Upaniṣads. My work merely suggests that, historically, such a view ignores the cross-fertilization of ideas that undoubtedly occurred between the different religious schools in the Gauḍapādian era, and the strong evidence that suggests that early Advaita (as exemplified by the GK) constructed its own basic paradigm in dialectical relationship with prevailing Buddhist philosophical ideas.

At an early stage in its development the characteristic features of the Vedānta movement (as exhibited for instance in the *Brahmasūtra*) were structured in contra-distinction to, and reflect an ongoing debate with, the Sāṃkhya school. Likewise, the philosophical paradigm outlined in the early Advaita Vedānta of the GK, while wholeheartedly Vedāntic in its absolutistic premises, reflects the contemporaneous Buddhist context of the debate. One should note, however, that the antithetical atttitude toward Buddhism found in the works of Śaṅkara and most of his disciples reflects the reactionary nature of the Advaita Vedānta paradigm upon its further establishment. In this later stage of development the school more clearly distinguishes itself from the Mahāyāna influences of the earlier stages. This antithetical attitude is not to be found in the earlier stage as exhibited by the GK, one reason being the absolutistic interpretation of the Buddhist tradition upheld by the author of the fourth *prakaraṇa*. By contrast, the Śaṅkara of the *Brahmasūtrabhāṣya* (and other clearly authenticated works) tends to treat the Buddhists as arch nihilists. However, neither this, nor the Gauḍapādian interpretation of mainstream Mahāyāna as absolutistic, are appropriate.

Nevertheless, the philosophical perspective of the GK reflects a very early stage in the historical development of the Advaita Vedānta *darśana*. Further systematization and differentation from Buddhist sources, however, was left to Śaṅkara and his successors. The importance placed upon the great systematizers of the post-Gauḍapādian Vedānta tradition should not prevent us from acknowledging the importance of the *Gauḍapādīya-kārikā* as an innovative and seminal text of the Advaita Vedānta school.

Asparśayoga in the GK

This study of the classical Yogācāra of Asaṅga and Vasubandhu has pointed to the dangers of an unqualified designation of this school as a form of idealism. A distinction must be made between the idealistic epistemology of the early Yogācāra and its final position, which seems more phenomenological than idealistic in its attitude to the external world.[3] Likewise, I have also suggested that Gauḍapādian thought, as found in the fourth *prakaraṇa* at least, might be more accurately designated "phenomenological" than "idealistic" given the author's reliance upon Yogācāra theory and *praxis* and the denial of the ultimate reality of mind (*amanastā*). My analysis suggests that the discussion in GK IV is phenomenological, insofar as it is an examination of the nature of experience in the light of the non-origination of *dharmas* and not specifically ontological in import. Vetter has noted the philological distinction between the terms "*dharma*" in GK IV and "*bhāva*" in GK II and III, but fails to consider the philosophical implications of this for the "question of idealism" in the text.[4] In fact the whole question of "idealism" is methodologically problematic in Indian context. The distinction in Vedānta between *para vidyā* and *apara vidyā* is based upon the belief in the primacy of "yogic" states of consciousness (a similar distinction is found in Buddhism). One needs to take this yogic context into account when classifying Indian philosophy in terms of western categories. For GK IV everyday experience (*aparā vidyā/vijñāna*) is "idealistic," but the yogic / enlightenment experience (*parā vidyā/jñāna*) of Brahman is not!

The central connecting term in the fourth *prakaraṇa*'s phenomenology of experience is "*asparśa-yoga*," that I have suggested is a multi-valented concept designating a thorough-going *praxis* (i.e. a dynamic interaction of philosophical reflection and meditative practice). This view is an integration of the narrower conceptions of the notion as discussed by 1). Bhattacharya and followed by Hixon (i.e. that *asparśayoga* is a description of a non-dual state of consciousness), 2). Mahadevan *et al*. (that *asparśayoga* is a type of yoga), and 3). That *asparśayoga* is related to a specific theory of perception (a point acknowledged by Cole (1982), for whom *asparśayoga* is a combination of 1 and 3). My view is that *asparśayoga* is intrinsically linked to all three.

The Nature of the Fourth Prakaraṇa of the GK

GK IV is a separate text written by a member of the same Vedāntic school of thought as the author(s) of GK II and III.[5] Vetter is correct to point out that the entire GK is dependent upon the Mahāyāna doctrine of the non-origination of *dharmas*, but this does not necessitate that GK IV (which discusses this issue) is thereby the earliest of the *prakaraṇas*. GK IV pays homage to the Buddha at the beginning of the text[6] and sees a great similarity between Vedānta and Buddhism. As Thomas Wood has recently argued, the author of GK IV has an absolutistic view of the Mahāyāna.[7] The significance of this has not been noted before since previous scholars studying the relationship of the GK to Buddhism have been insufficiently aware of the absolutist :: non-absolutist distinction. The author of GK IV does, however, acknowledges his reliance upon the Mahāyāna at IV.90.

GK IV and *Tathāgatagarbha* Buddhism

Previous work on the GK has worked on the philosophically narrow and historically misleading assumption that the Madhyamaka and Yogācāra schools are the only Mahāyāna influences upon the philosophy of the GK. This reflects an inadequate grasp of the absolutistic :: non-absolutistic divide between Advaita Vedanta and scholastic Mahayana on the one hand, and a failure to appreciate the diversity of the Mahayana (encompassing absolutistic approaches also) on the other. In chapter 7 we considered certain pre-Gauḍapādian texts of the Mahāyāna tradition that appear at times to uphold a form of ontological absolutism akin to the doctrines of the GK. It was suggested that the imposition of a non-absolutistic orthodoxy upon all Mahāyāna texts is misleading both philosophically and historically, despite the many attempts by traditional Mahāyāna scholasts and modern academics to reconcile the texts with the mainstream position. A brief consideration of the later Tibetan debates over "self-emptiness" (*raṅ stong*) and "other-emptiness" (*gzhaṅ stong*) suggests that the *tathāgatagarbha* texts conform to the latter (absolutistic) doctrine of emptiness and thus do not conform to the "mainstream" Madhyamaka/Yogācāra rejection of absolutism, (that is more characteristically *raṅ stong*).[8] The possibility remains, therefore, that the absolutistic conception of the Mahāyāna in GK IV may derive from the author's acquaintance with the *tathāgatagarbha* strand of Indian Mahāyāna. There is, however, little philological evidence to substantiate this hypothesis.

Nevertheless, the imposition of an absolutistic ontology onto the mainstream (non-absolutistic) philosophical texts of the Madhyamaka and Yogācāra schools by the author of GK IV is itself an unwarranted step. Further research needs to be carried out concerning the nature of the relationship between the absolutistic and non-absolutistic strands of the Mahāyāna.[9] Nevertheless, a few preliminary suggestions have been made concerning the differentation of these traditions and their direct confrontation in later Tibetan debates concerning the nature of emptiness.

Appendix

A Running Translation of the *Gauḍapādīya-kārikā*

The Āgama-prakaraṇa

The Three States (pāda) of Experience (1–5)

Viśva, [is] the all pervading knower of the external [world]; *Taijasa* (the radiant), [is] knower of the internal [world]; and likewise *Prājña*, [is] a mass of cognition. [Through these states] one [entity] is known as three. [1] As three is it situated in the body. The opening (*mukha*) for *Viśva* is the right eye; for *Taijasa* it is in the mind; for *Prājña* it is in the space in the heart. [2] *Viśva* always experiences the gross [object], *Taijasa* the subtle and likewise *Prājña* experiences bliss. [Thus, one should] know that experience is three-fold. [3] The gross [object] satisfies *Viśva*, the subtle [object] *Taijasa*, and likewise bliss satisfies *Prājña*. [Thus, one should] know that satisfaction is threefold. [4] He who knows both the [object of] experience and the experiencer as they have been described to be in the three states, though experiencing, is not contaminated. [5]

Analysis of Creation Theories (6–9)

It is the firm conclusion [of wise men] that [there must be] an origin of all existing entities. *Prāṇa* creates the universe [and] *Puruṣa* creates separately the rays of consciousness (i.e. the individual *jīvas*). [6] Some creation-theorists, however, consider creation [to be] an outflowing (emanation). Creation is imagined by others as having the same form as dream and illusion (*māyā*). [7] Creation is merely the will of the Lord (*prabhur*) so [think others who have] a firm conviction about creation and the time-theorists (*kālācintakā*) consider the creation of beings [to be] from time. [8] Creation is for the sake of enjoyment (or experience), so say some. Others say for the sake of sport. This again is the lordly own-nature of the divine, for what desire is there for the one who has attained all wishes? [9]

Turīya *and the Three States of Experience (10–15)*

The All-pervading One is traditionally known as *turīya* (the Fourth), the Powerful, capable of bringing about the cessation of all suffering, the immutable and non-dual God (*deva*) of all beings. [10] These two, *Viśva* and *Taijasa*, are taken to be conditioned by cause and effect but *Prājña* is conditioned by cause [alone]. However, in [the case of] *turīya* neither of those two (i.e cause and effect) is established ("*sidhyataḥ*"). [11] Neither self nor others, neither truth nor untruth—*Prājña* does not apprehend anything. That *turīya* [however] is always all-seeing. [12] Non-grasping of duality [is] common to both *Prājña* and *turīya*. *Prājña* [is] associated with the causal state of sleep, while it does not exist in *turīya*. [13] The first two [states] are associated with dream and sleep, *Prājña*, on the other hand is associated with dreamless sleep. The firmly convinced ones see in *turīya* neither sleep nor again dream. [14] Dream [is] for one who apprehends reality other [than it is]; sleep for one who does not know reality. When the errors in these two become extinct one attains to the Fourth stage. [15]

*The Nature of Reality for the Awakened Individual (*jīva*) (16–18)*

When the individual self (*jīva*), asleep due to beginningless *māyā*, is awakened then he realizes the unborn, sleepless, dreamless, non-duality. [16] There is no doubt that if the multiplicity (*prapañca*) were existing it would cease to be [upon such realization]. This duality is only *māyā*; ultimately [there is only] non-duality. [17] If discursive-thought (*vikalpa*) were [really] imagined (*kalpita*) by someone it would undoubtedly disappear. This doctrine is for the sake of instruction. When known, duality does not exist. [18]

*The Equation of the States (*pāda*) with the Syllable Om (19–23)*

When there is the desire to state that *Viśva* has A-ness, the common quality [of] being the first [would be] prominent; and for the equating of [*Viśva*] with the [syllabic] portion [A in Aum], the common quality of pervading, itself [would be prominent]. [19] As regards the knowledge of *Taijasa* being possessed of U-ness [the common quality] superiority [or posteriority] is distinctly seen; for the equating of [*Taijasa* with] the [syllabic] portion [U in Aum] [the common quality] the nature of being both, could be of the same type [that is, is distinctly seen.] [20] As regards *Prājña* possessing the state of M, the common quality, the measure [by which the remaining two are measured is] prominent; for the equating of [*Prājña* with] the [syllabic] portion [M in Aum] on the other hand, the common quality, merging, itself [is prominent]. [21] The man of conviction knows the equal common quality in the three abodes, he, the great sage, is worthy of worship and adoration by all beings. [22] The syllable A leads on to *Viśva* and the syllable U as well, from *Taijasa*, and the syllable M again to *Prājña*. There is no path towards that which has no [syllabic] portions. [23]

The Fruits of Meditation on Om (24–29)

One should know the syllable Om, quarter by quarter. Without doubt the quarters [are] the [syllabic] portions. Having known the *Oṃkāra* quarter by quarter, one should reflect upon nothing [else] whatsoever. [24] One should fix the mind upon *Prāṇava* [the syllable Om]; *Prāṇava* [is] Brahman void of fear; for him ever fixed upon *Prāṇava*, there is no fear anywhere. [25] *Prāṇava* indeed [is] the lower Brahman, *Prāṇava* also (*ca*) [is] the higher [Brahman]. Beginningless, without inside, without outside, unique, [and] immutable [is] *Prāṇava*. [26] *Prāṇava* indeed [is] the beginning, middle, and likewise the end itself of everything. Having indeed known *Prāṇava* thus, one attains to it immediately. [27] One should indeed know *Prāṇava* as the Lord (*īśvara*) established in the heart of all. Having thought of the all-pervading *Oṃkāra*, the wise one does not grieve. [28] He who knows the *Oṃkāra*, portionless and possessed of infinite portions, the [cause of] cessation of duality, [and] auspicious, [is] the sage, and none other. [29]

The Vaitathya-Prakarana

The Falsity of External Objects in Waking and Dreaming States (1–10)

The wise speak of the unreality of all entities in dream, on account of their location within, owing to their being enclosed. [1] And owing to the shortness of time, one does not see the places one has gone to [in a dream], and moreover, when awakened, everyone is not in that region. [2] The non-existence of chariots and other [things] is attested in the *śruti* from the standpoint of logic. They say that the unreality, proven by that [statement] is evident in dream. [3] [The falsity] of diverse things in the waking state is traditionally known from their location within (*antaḥsthāna*). As it is there [in the waking state], so is it in dream, the difference is in the state of enclosure. [4] The wise say that the dream and waking states are one. On account of the similarity of diverse things [in the two states] on the strength of reason. [5] That which does not exist in the beginning and end is so also in the present. Being like the unreal, things are taken as not unreal. [6] The utility [of things in the waking state] is contradicted in dream; thus, on account of [their] having a beginning and end they are regarded as false and nothing else. [7] The strange thing is a normality for the agent (*sthānidharma*) [in dream] as for the dweller in heaven. This [person dreaming] sees those [things] having gone [there] as a well-trained person does here. [8] Even in the dream state, what is imagined inwardly by the consciousness (*antaścetas*) is [regarded as] non-existing; what is grasped outwardly by the consciousness is [regarded as] existing [but] the unreality of these two is seen (*dṛṣṭa*). [9] In the waking state also, what is imagined by the mind as interior is [regarded as] unreal and what is grasped by the mind as exterior is [regarded as] real [but] the unreality of these two is logical. [10]

Nature of Perception of Objects in Both States (11–18)

If there [is] the unreality of diverse things in both states, who cognizes these things? Who indeed is their imaginer? [11] The effulgent (*deva*) *Ātman* imagines itself through itself by its own *māyā*. It alone cognizes things. This is the conclusion of the Vedānta. [12] [The *Ātman*], outward-minded, diversifies other objects existing within the mind and fixed ones; in this way does the powerful one (*prabhu*) imagine. [13] Those that exist within for as long as the thought lasts (lit. thought-timers) and those which are external and exist in two points of time (lit. "duality-timers"—to be understood in terms of the duality of *grāhya-grāhaka* or grasped and grasping) are all merely imagined. [Their] differentiation is not due to any other factor. [14] Those again that are unmanifest within and those that are manifest outwards—all those are all imagined, [their] differentiation is [by means of] the different sense organs [with which they are cognized]. [15] [The *ātman*] first imagines the *jīva* (individual soul), and then different things, external and internal (objective and subjective); as one knows so does one recollect. [16] As a rope not definitely ascertained in the dark, is imagined to be things like a snake or a line of water, so likewise is the *ātman* imagined. [17] When the rope is definitely ascertained the imagined thing disappears and there is non-duality in the form of the

Rope alone; likewise is the ascertainment of *ātman*. [18] [*Ātman*] is imagined to be *Prāṇa* and other innumerable things. This is the *māyā* of that shining one ("*tasya devasya*") by which it itself has been deluded. [19]

List of Various Views of Nature of Reality (20–30)

As *Prāṇa*, the *Prāṇa*-knowers imagine [*Ātman*]; and as elements those who know the elements (*bhūta*); as *guṇas*, those who know the *guṇas*; and as *tattvas* the knowers of them. [20] As the quarters (*pāda*) the knowers of the quarters; as sense-objects (*viṣaya*) the knowers of objects; as worlds (*loka*) the knowers of the worlds; and as gods (*deva*) the knowers of them. [21] As Vedas, the Veda-knowers; and as sacrifices, the knowers of them; as the Enjoyer, the knowers of the Enjoyer; and as the object of Enjoyment by the knowers of it. [22] As subtle, the subtle knowers [imagine *ātman*], as gross the knowers of the gross. As form say those who know form, and as formless say those who know the formless. [23] As time, the knowers of time; and as the four directions, the knowers of them; as theories, the theory-knowers; as (the fourteen) worlds the knowers of them. [24] Those who know the mind [imagine *ātman*] as the mind; as Intellect, by the knowers of the Intellect; as consciousness, the knowers of consciousness; as merit and demerit the knowers of them. [25]

Some speak [of *ātman*] as constituted of twenty-five, and others as constituted of twenty-six; some as constituted of thirty-one; and as endless by others. [26] Those knowledgeable about people, [imagine *Ātman*] as people; as stages of life, the knowers of them. The grammarians [imagine it] as male, female, and neuter; and others as the higher and lower [Brahman]. [27] As creation, the knowers of creation; and as dissolution, the knowers of dissolution; as subsistence the knowers of subsistence, and all these [imaginations] are always here. [28] Whatever entity may be shown to one, one again sees that entity; and that [*ātman*], protects him, having become him. Possessed by that [idea], it absorbs him. [29] This [*ātman*] is pointed out as though indeed separate, due to these entities that [are really] non-separate. One who knows thus truly imagines without hesitation. [30]

The True Nature of Reality (31–38)

As are seen dream and illusion and a castle in the air, so also is this whole universe seen by those well-versed in the Vedāntas. [31] Neither cessation nor origination, neither one bound nor one practicing spiritual discipline, neither one aspiring for liberation nor one who is liberated. This is the supreme truth. [32] And this is imagined to be non-existing entities themselves by means of the non-dual (*advaya*). The [dual] entities exist only by means of the non-dual. Therefore there is auspicious non-duality. [33] This universe is not manifold either due to the nature of *ātman* or even its own nature. Nothing whatsoever is separate or non-separate—this the knowers of reality know. [34] By the sages, free from desire, fear and anger, having reached the further shore of the Vedas, is seen the non-dual and non-conceptual cessation of the multiplicity (*prapañca*). [35] Therefore, having known this, one should fix one's memory on non-duality. Having attained non-duality, one should behave in the world like an inert object. [36] Disassociated from praise, salutation, and the utterance of the *svadhā* [at the *śrāddha* funeral ceremony], having no fixed abode, one should become an ascetic acting according to circumstance. [37] Having seen the reality inwardly and reality outwardly, having become the reality, delighting in it, one should not deviate from reality. [38]

The Advaita-Prakarana

Opening Remarks (1–2)

The duty (*dharma*) of practicing worshipful contemplation (*upāsanāśrita*) arises when Brahman is [taken to be] born. Before birth all is unborn, for this reason such a practice is regarded as pitiable (*kṛpaṇa*). [1] Therefore I shall speak of that which is not pitiable, established as the self-identity of the unoriginated (*ajātisamatā*), which [though appearing] born everywhere is [in fact] not born in any manner. [2]

The "Space in Pots" Analogy (3–9)

Ātman, like space, rises up in the form of *jīvas* in the same way as spaces enclosed by clay jars, and as composite things like jars, etc. This is the illustration of birth. [3] When the jars, etc. are destroyed the space within the jars merge into space, so do the *jīvas* [merge] here in *Ātman*. [4] Just as when one of the spaces enclosed in a jar is connected with dust, smoke, etc., not all are connected with them, so are the *jīvas* with regard to happiness, etc. [5] Indeed forms, functions, and names differ here and there but there is no differentiation of space, likewise is the conclusion with regard to the *jīvas*. [6] As the space within a jar is neither a modification (*vikāra*) nor a part of space, so a *jīva* is neither a modification nor a part of *Ātman*. [7] As the sky becomes darkened by impurities [in the opinion of] children, similarly *Ātman*, [in the opinion of] the unenlightened, becomes tainted with impurities. [8] In death and in birth, in going and coming as well as in standing [still], in all bodies it is not unlike space. [9]

*Māyā and the Tradition of Vedic Revelation (*śruti*) (10–16)*

All composite things are like dreams, projected by the *māyā* of *Ātman*. [As regards their] superiority or the equality of all there is no valid ground [to prove that the composite things exist]. [10] The sheaths, consisting of the essence [of food], etc. that are fully dealt with in the *Taittirīyaka* [*Upaniṣad*], the *Ātman* is clearly shown as the supreme *jīva*, like space. [11] In the *Madhu-jñāna* (i.e. the *Madhu-vidya* section of *Bṛhadāraṇyaka Upaniṣad* II.5) in each of the pairs the supreme Brahman is shown, just as space is shown in the earth and in the stomach [to be the same]. [12] That the identity of *jīva* and *Ātman* without any difference is praised and diversity is censured—that is rational only thus [on this view]. [13] The separateness of *jīva* and *Ātman* before creation that has been declared, is figurative referring to the state to come, its primary sense does not fit [the facts]. [14] The creation that has been expounded in various ways with [the illustrations of] earth, metal, sparks, etc. that is a means of introduction [into the true position]. No difference whatsoever exists. [15] There are three stages, having low, middle, and supreme vision. This worship is prescribed for them out of compassion. [16]

Advaita is Avirodhavada (17–22)

The dualists are firmly convinced in the establishment of their own conclusions and contradict one another; but this [view] does not conflict with them. [17] Non-duality is indeed the ultimate reality; duality is said to be a differentiation of it. For them [the dualists] there is duality both ways; therefore this [view] does not conflict [with theirs]. [18] The unborn indeed becomes different through *māyā*, not through any other circumstances. If indeed it was differentiated in reality the immortal would undergo death. [19] The disputants wish [to establish] the birth of an unborn thing. How can a birthless and [thus] deathless thing pass on to death? [20] The deathless does not become subject to death, just as an entity subject to death does not become deathless. The mutation of a thing's nature in no way takes place. [21] He, for whom an entity immortal in its own nature, goes to its death—how will his immortal [being], becoming a product, remain changeless (lit. unmoving)? [22]

Creation in the Śruti (23–28)

The *śruti* is equal with regard to whether creation occurs from the existent or from the non-existent. Only that which is associated with logical reasoning and firmly ascertained is appropriate. [23] From the sacred text "There is no plurality here, etc." and "Indra on account of *māyā*, etc." [it is to be known that] "He being unborn is however born in various ways through *māyā*." [24] From the refutation of birth, origination is negated and by "Who indeed would produce this" the cause [of origination] is denied. [25] The explanation "This is not this, not that. . ." denies explanation, by reason of its incomprehensibility, the unborn [nature] of all shines forth. [26] The birth of the existent is indeed reasonable through *māyā*, but not in reality. For whom [i.e. in whose opinion] is born [the existent] in reality, for him the [already] born is born. [27] The birth of the non-existent is not reasonable through *māyā* nor in reality. The son of a barren woman is not born either in reality or even through *māyā*. [28]

Manas *in Waking, Dream, and Deep Sleep—the Realization of No-Mind (29–38)*

As in a dream, the mind vibrates with the image of two (perceiver and perceived) through *māyā*, so in the waking states does the mind vibrate with the image of two through *māyā*. [29] There is no doubt that in dream the non-dual (*advaya-manas*) mind appears as a duality. Similarly, there is no doubt that in the waking state the non-dual appears as a duality. [30] This duality in whatever manner, comprising of the moving and the motionless, is perceived by the mind, for when the mind has become non-mind (*amanībhāva*) duality is no longer experienced. [31] When by knowledge of the truth of *ātman* [the mind] ceases to imagine it goes to the state of non-mind (*amanastā*); it is without cognition in the absence of a cognizable entity. [32] They say that the unborn *gnosis* (*jñāna*), free from imagination, is not different from the known. Brahman is the known, the unborn, and the permanent. So the unborn is known by the unborn. [33] But the state of the mind— completely controlled, free from conceptualization and endowed with discernment, is particularly to be known; in deep sleep it is different and is not like that [of the controlled mind]. [34] For in deep sleep it fades away, but it does not fade away when completely controlled. That itself is Brahman devoid of fear, with the illumination of *gnosis* (*jñāna*) all around. [35] [It is] unborn, without sleep, without dream, nameless, formless, ever illumined, omniscient. There is no practice in any way whatsoever. [36] [It is] enstatic-concentration (*samādhi*), devoid of all expression, risen above all thought, completely quiescent, ever effulgent, unmoving, and fearless. [37] Where there is no thought, there is no grasping] and no letting go. At that time the gnosis established in itself (*ātmasaṃstha*) attains the self-identity of the unoriginated (*ajāti-samatā*). [38]

Asparśa-yoga—*i. Controlling the* Manas *(39–43)*

This is "*asparśa-yoga*" by name, difficult to be realized by all yogins. Yogins are afraid of it, seeing fear where there is no fear. [39] For all yogins, depending upon the complete control of the mind (*manas*), are fearlessness, the removal of suffering, complete enlightenment, and eternal quiescence itself. [40] Like the draining of the sea by a drop [at a time] by the tip of [a blade of] *kuśa* grass, so is the control of the mind (*manas*) without all out diligence. [41] By the [proper] means one should control [the mind] distracted in desire and enjoyment and also at great ease in deep sleep, for the sleeping state is as [bad as] desire. [42] Constantly remembering that all is suffering one should turn back from desires and enjoyments; having constantly remembered all as unborn one does not see anything born. [43]

ii. The Realization of the Motionless Citta (44–48)

One should fully awaken consciousness (*citta*) in sleep, when distracted one should pacify it again. One should know it [to be] with passion and not cause it to fluctuate when established in equilibrium (*samaprāpta*). [44] There one should not enjoy happiness; by wisdom (*prajñā*) one should be free from attachment. One should unify, with effort, the steadied mind (*citta*) that is intent on going out. [45] When the mind is not asleep and is also not distracted, it is motionless and without image. Then it becomes Brahman. [46] They say it is quiescent within itself, calm, in *nirvāṇa*, indescribable, ultimate bliss (*sukha-uttama*), the unborn known by the unborn, the omniscient. [47] No *jīva* whatsoever is ever born; there is no origin of it. This is that ultimate truth where nothing whatsoever is born. [48]

The Alātaśānti-Prakaraṇa

Opening Salutations (1–2)

I salute that greatest of bipeds, who, through a knowledge (*jñāna*) comparable to space (or the sky) and non-different from its object, is fully enlightened about the *dharmas* comparable to the sky. [1] I bow to the Yoga of Non-Contact (*asparśa-yoga*), indeed so named, taught for the happiness of all beings, beneficial, free from dispute and opposition. [2]

The Dualists and the Basis of Non-Origination (3–10)

Some disputants indeed wish for the birth of an existent thing; other wise ones for a non-existent thing. [Thus] they dispute with one another. [3] An existent does not originate nor does a non-existent originate in any manner. Those dualists (*dvaya*), indeed disputing reveal Non-origination. [4] We approve of the Non-origination revealed by them; we do not dispute with them, know how it is free from dispute. [5] The disputants wish [to establish] the birth of an unborn thing (*dharma*). How can a birthless and [thus] deathless thing pass on to death? [6] The deathless does not become subject to death, just as an entity subject to death does not become deathless. The mutation of a thing's nature in no way takes place. [7] He, for whom a *dharma*, immortal in its own nature, goes to mortality—how will his immortal [*dharma*], becoming a product, remain changeless? [8] That should be known as nature which is permanently established, intrinsic, innate, not produced, [and] that which does not abandon its own nature (*svabhāva*). [9] All *dharmas* are by their very nature (*svabhāva*) free from old age and death. Wishing for old age and death they deviate owing to that very thought. [10]

Critique of Various Theories of Causation (11–23)

For whom the cause indeed is the effect (i.e. the *satkāryavādin*), for him the cause is originated. How is it originated when unoriginated and how is that modified when permanent? [11] If there is non-difference from the cause and the effect is unoriginated, how is your cause eternal (*dhruva*) when the effect is originated? [12] For whom [the effect] is originated from the unoriginated there is no illustration [to support his view]; and [the case] of [the effect] being originated from the originated [also] leads to no solution. [13] For whom the effect is the origin of the cause and the cause the origin of the effect how can the beginninglessness of the cause and the effect be described by them. [14] For whom the effect is the origin of the cause and the cause the origin of the effect, there would be birth in the same way as the birth of the father from the son. [15] As regards the origination of cause and effect, the order has to be found out by you, for with simultaneous origination [there is] no relation like horns [of a cow]. [16] Your cause, coming into being from [its] effect, does not come into existence; how will the cause that has not come into existence produce [its] effect? [17] If the subsistence of the cause is from the effect and the subsistence of the effect is from the cause, which is produced first, whose subsistence is dependent [upon the other]? [18] Incapacity [to answer this problem], incomplete knowledge or again violation of sequence, in view of this indeed non-origination has been elucidated by the enlightened ones (*buddha*). [19] The illustration known as "the seed and the sprout" indeed is always equal to [a thing] yet to be proven. Surely a reason yet to be proven is not to be used for the establishment of a thing in question. [20] Incomplete knowledge about the priority and posteriority [of cause and effect] is the illuminator of non-origination; how [is it that] the [thing] prior to a *dharma* that is being originated is not grasped? [21]

Nothing (*vastu*) whatsoever is originated either from itself or from something else; nothing whatsoever existent, non-existent, or both existent and non-existent is originated. [22] By [their] own nature (*svabhāvataḥ*) the cause and the effect, being beginningless, do not come into being. For which there exists no beginning, there exists no source. [23]

*Cognition and the Problem of Objective Reference (*nimitta*) (24–28)*

[Some say:] "It is admitted that cognition (*prajñapti*) has an objective referent (*sanimittatva*) otherwise there would be a disappearance of the two (i.e. perceiver and perceived); the experience of impurities (*saṃkleśa*) exists dependently (*paratantrāstitā*)." [24] From a logical perspective it is held that cognition has an objective referent, from the perspective of the actual state of things the objective referent [itself has] no objective referent. [25] The mind (*citta*) does not make contact with an object nor even the appearance of an object. The object is non-existent (*abhūta*) and so its appearance is not different from it (or perhaps from the mind). [26] Never in the three divisions [of time] does the mind make contact with an objective referent (*nimitta*) how would there be a misconception without an objective referent. [27] Therefore the mind (*citta*) is not originated, nor are the things perceived by the mind originated. Those who see its origination are seeing a foot [-print] in the sky. [28]

Further Analysis of Waking and Dream Experience (29–37)

Inasmuch as it is the unoriginated that is originated, non-origination is [its] very nature. There is not any change in nature whatsoever. [29]

It would not be established that beginningless *saṃsāra* has an end, nor would there be the endlessness of a liberation (*mokṣa*) with a beginning. [30] That which does not exist in the beginning and end is so also in the present. Being like the unreal, things are taken as not unreal. [31] The utility [of things in the waking state] is contradicted in dream. Thus, on account of [their] having a beginning and end they are regarded as false and nothing else. [32] All *dharmas* in dream are false on account of their perception within the body. How [can there be] the perception of existing things within this confined space? [33] The perception [of things] by going [to them] is not reasonable owing to [there being] no fixed rule of time for the act of going. Moreover, when awakened everyone is not in that place. [34] Having conferred with friends and others, when awakened one does not find [them]; and furthermore, whatever had been held, one [when] awakened does not see it. [35] The body in a dream is insubstantial (*avastuka*) owing to another body being perceived [as] different [from it]; as [with] the body, so is everything perceived by the mind (*citta*) insubstantial. [36] Due to the similar apprehension [of things in dream] to the waking state, dream is held to have that [waking state] as [its] cause. Owing to it having that as its cause, the waking state is held to be real for him (i.e. the agent) alone. [37]

Denial of Theories of Causality (38–41)

As production is not established, all is declared as unoriginated; and there is no birth in any way of the non-existent from the existent. [38] Having perceived the non-existent in the waking state, being deeply absorbed [by it], one sees it in dream; and having perceived the non-existent in dream also, when awakened one does not see [it]. [39] There is not a non-existent with a non-existent cause, likewise there is not an existent with a non-existent cause. Where is the non-existent with an existent cause? [40] As in the waking state, through misconception one may come into contact with unthinkable [things] as real, similarly in dream, through misconception, one sees objects (*dharma*) there. [41]

The Basis of Belief in Origination (42–44)

Origination has been taught by the enlightened for those who, from perception (*upalambha*) and common consent (*samācāra*), assert that substantiality (or objectivity) exists (*astivastutvavādin*) and are afraid of non-origination. [42] For those who, being afraid of non-origination, go astray due to the perception [of things], the evil due to [belief in] origination will not attain fruition. The evil again will be small. [43]

As the illusory elephant is said to exist owing to the perception [of it] and common consent, likewise it is said that a given-thing (*vastu*) exists, on account of [its] perception and common consent. [44]

Analysis of Everyday Consciousness (vijñāna)*—How Duality Appears (45–54)*

The images of origination, movement and substance, are the unoriginated and motionless, insubstantial, quiescent and non-dual (*advaya*) consciousness (*vijñāna*). [45] Thus consciousness (*citta*) does not originate; thus *dharmas* are traditionally known as unoriginated; those knowing [this] thus indeed do not fall into error. [46] Just as with the moving firebrand there are straight and crooked images, etc. likewise with the vibrating consciousness (*vijñāna*) there are images of perceiver and perceived. [47] As the unmoving firebrand is imageless and unoriginated, the consciousness that is not moving [and] imageless, likewise [is] unoriginated. [48] When the firebrand moves the images are not from anywhere else. When it is not in motion they are not anywhere else, nor do they enter the firebrand. [49] [The images] do not go out from the firebrand, owing to their insubstantiality (lit. "their connection with the absence of substantiality"). Similarly with consciousness also for the image is not different [in nature from the image of the firebrand]. [50] When consciousness is vibrating the images are not from anywhere else. When it is not vibrating [the images are] not anywhere else, nor do they enter consciousness. [51] [The images] do not go out from consciousness, owing to their insubstantiality; because of the absence of a relation of cause and effect they are ever incomprehensible. [52] A substance may be the cause of another substance, and the other (i.e. non-substance) the cause of another (non-substance) indeed, [but] it cannot be shown that *dharmas* have the nature of substantiality or other [than that]. [53] Thus, *dharmas* are not originated by consciousness (*citta*), nor is consciousness originated from *dharmas*. Thus, the wise affirm (lit. "enter into") the non-origination of cause and effect. [54]

Causation is the Result of Attachment (aveśa) *to a Causal View (55–60)*

As long as there is attachment to cause and effect (*hetuphalāveśa*), so long is the arising of cause and effect; when the attachment to cause and effect ceases there is no arising of cause and effect. [55] As long as there is attachment to cause and effect, so long is *saṃsāra* spread out; when attachment to cause and effect ceases one does not attain to *saṃsāra*. [56] All is born according to the conventional; therefore, in fact there is no eternal. In terms of reality, all is unborn; thus, there is no annihilated. [57] Those *dharmas* said to be born by convention are not born in reality. Their birth is like *māyā*, and that *māyā* itself does not exist. [58] Like a *māyā*-made seed, a sprout of the same nature is born. It is neither permanent nor destructible; so likewise is it for *dharmas*. [59] The terms "eternal" (*śāsvata*) and "non-eternal" do not apply to all the unoriginated *dharmas*. Where words do not function (lit. exist) discrimination (*viveka*) is not spoken of. [60]

Further Analysis of Citta*—Perception in the Waking and Dream States (61–72)*

Just as consciousness (*citta*) moves in dream with the appearance of two (i.e. perceiver and perceived) through *māyā*, likewise in the waking state consciousness moves with the appearance of the two through *māyā*. [61] There is no doubt that in dream the non-dual consciousness (*advaya citta*) has the appearance of two. Similarly in the waking state the non-dual consciousness has the appearance of two. [62] While moving in a dream the dreamer constantly sees egg-born, moisture-born, and other *jīvas* located in the ten directions. [63] Perceived by the consciousness (*citta*) of the dreamer, they do not exist apart from it. Similarly the perceived object is held [to be] this consciousness of the dreamer alone. [64] While moving in the waking state the waking one constantly sees egg-born, moisture-born, and other *jīvas* located in the ten directions. [65] Perceived by the consciousness (*citta*) of the waking one, they do not exist apart from it. Similarly that which is perceived by it (i.e. the mind) alone is said to be the waking consciousness. [66]

Both [consciousness and its object] are understood (lit. "seen") in terms of each other. What is it then that [really] exists? This is not uttered (*na ucyate*). Both, devoid of characteristics (*lakṣaṇaśūnya*) are only [to be] grasped through the other. [67] As a dream-made *jīva* is born and also dies, likewise all these *jīvas* exist and then do not exist. [68] As a *māyā*-made *jīva* is born and also dies, likewise all these *jīvas* exist and then do not exist. [69] As a *jīva* made by supernatural means is born and also dies, likewise all these *jīvas* exist and then do not exist. [70] No *jīva* whatsoever is born; no origination of it is found. This is the final truth that nothing whatsoever is originated. [71] This duality of perceiver and perceived is merely vibration of consciousness (*cittaspandita*). This consciousness is declared to be unrelated to an object (*nirviṣaya*), permanent and non-relational. [72]

The Mundane, Pure Mundane, Supra-mundane, and the Omniscient State (87–90)

That which has an object and [its] perception is regarded as "dualistic mundane" (*dvaya laukika*). That which is without an object [but] with the perception is regarded as "pure mundane" (*śuddha laukika*). [87] That which is without an object and [its] perception is traditionally known as "supramundane" (*lokottara*). Knowledge, the object of knowledge and the knowable (*vijñeya*) are always proclaimed by the Enlightened Ones. [88] When the threefold [nature of] knowledge and the objects of [that] knowledge are known in succession, omniscience, of its own accord, emerges everywhere to the wise one. [89] From the Agrayāna ("*agrayāṇa*": the Mahāyāna tradition?) one should know that which is to be abandoned, that which is to be known, that which is to be acquired and that which is to be perfected. Excepting that which should be known (*vijñeya*), perception of these is said to occur in the three [levels of knowledge]. [90]

The Non-originated, Non-relational, Ever-enlightened Dharmas *(91–100)*

All *dharmas* are known to be naturally beginningless like space (or the sky). For them, there is found no multiplicity whatsoever anywhere. [91] All *dharmas* by their nature are well determined as enlightened from the very beginning (*ādibuddha*). One who has such self-sufficiency is fit for the deathless state. [92] All *dharmas* indeed are quiescent from the very beginning, unoriginated, and happy by nature itself, homogenous, and non-separate, [reality is] fearless and unoriginated sameness. [93] But truly there is no fearlessness for the one who always moves in [the world] of difference. Those who hold the doctrine of separateness are inclined to make distinctions; therefore they are of limited understanding. [94] But those who are firmly established in the unoriginated sameness are possessed of great knowledge in the world. The world, however, does not delve into it. [95] It is said that the unoriginated *gnosis* (*jñāna*) does not proceed to unoriginated *dharmas*. Since [such] *gnosis* does not proceed it is declared [to be] non-relational. [96] If for the unwise one there is the slightest [belief in] origination for any *dharma* there is never the non-relational state. How then can there be the removal of the veil (*āvaraṇa*) [for such a one]? [97] All *dharmas* are without covering, naturally without impurity; enlightened as well as liberated from the beginning, so enlightened are the Masters. [98] The gnosis (*jñāna*) of the enlightened holy man (*buddha*) does not proceed toward *dharmas*.

All *dharmas* are like gnosis [in this respect]. This was not stated by the Enlightened One (*buddha*) [99] Having realized the state, difficult to be seen, profound, unoriginated, homogenous, fearless, without multiplicity, we praise it to the best of our ability. (100)

Notes

Introduction

1. Surendranath Dasgupta (1922), *The History of Indian Philosophy* (Indian Edition, 1975, Motilal Banarsidass, Delhi) Vol I, pp. 420–429.

2. Karl Potter (ed.), (1981), *Encyclopaedia of Indian Philosophies Vol III: "Advaita Vedānta up to Śaṃkara and his pupils"* (Motilal Banarsidass), pp. 103–114.

3. Bhattacharya (1943), Mahadevan (1952), Karmarkar (1953), Conio (1971), and Hixon's unpublished Ph.D. thesis (1976). As yet, the second volume of H. Nakamura's *Early Vedānta Philosophy,* which spends some time considering the GK, is yet to become available in English translation and so I have been unable to consult it. This study is the work of a Japanese scholar and so does not contradict the sorry state of affairs in terms of western scholarship in this area.

4. Mahadevan (1952), pp. 222–223.

5. Mahadevan (1952), ibid., p. 240.

6. See Conio (1971), p. 196.

7. See Hixon (1976), p. 303.

8. For instance, Hixon suggests that GK II.13 has a different author from GK II.1–12 since we find in the verse the introduction of "*bhāva*" for "*bheda*" and "*citta*" for "*cetas,*" see Hixon (1976), p. 175.

9. Colin Cole (1982), p. 61.

10. For example, consider Cole's unquestioned acceptance of the view that Gauḍapāda upholds the (Sāṁkhya-based) conception of the empirical self (*jīva*) outlined in Śaṅkara's commentary on MU 3. There is no evidence in the text to substantiate this view. See Cole (1982), ibid., p. 57.

11. e.g. Willis (1979), Kochumottum, (1981).

12. See Karl Potter (1979), "Was Gauḍapāda an Idealist?" in Nagatomi, Matilal, Masson, and Dimock (eds.), (1979), *Sanskrit and Indian Studies*, (D. Reidel Publishing Company), pp. 183–199.

13. For a fuller appraisal of Fort's work see my review of *The Self and Its States* in *Scottish Journal of Religious Studies* Vol XII. No. 1 (Spring 1991), pp. 65–67.

Chapter 1 The Date and Authorship of the *Gauḍapādīya-kārikā*

1. Some scholars have suggested that the *Paramārthasāra* is pre-Gauḍapādian. The text discusses the four states of consciousness using the GK's "*viśva*" in place of the Upaniṣadic "*vaiśvānara*," so a relationship between the GK and the *Paramārthasāra* is likely. A verse from the latter is quoted in the *Yuktidīpikā*, an early commentary on the *Sāṃkhyakārikā*. The date of composition of the *Yuktidīpikā* has been assigned to the sixth century CE. Erich Frauwallner for instance suggests that (*History of Indian Philosophy* Vol I, translation by V. M. Bedekar (1970, Motilal Banarsidass), p. 226: "Many commentaries of the *Sāṁkhyakārikā* are handed down. By far the most important among them is the *Yuktidīpikā* ('Light of Argumentation'), of an unknown author; this commentary must have originated about 550 A.D. All the remaining commentaries are clarifications of the original *kārikā* but they are poor in content and have little to offer beyond the text." A. Wezler, however, has convincingly shown that the *Yuktidīpikā* is not original insofar as it contains within it an earlier text known as the *Rāja Vārttika* ('Some Observations on the *Yuktidīpikā* in *Zeitschrift der Deutschen Morgenlandischen Gesellschaft*, Supplement II, pp. 434–455). Thus, one cannot safely use the *Yuktidīpika* as evidence of the early date of the *Paramārthasāra* since it is composite in nature.

2. The twenty-nine verses of the first *prakaraṇa* of the GK are traditionally interspersed with the 12 prose passages of the *Māṇḍūkyopaniṣad* (MU) in the following manner: *Māṇḍūkyopaniṣad* 1–6 followed by *Gauḍapādiya-kārikā* I.1–9, *Māṇḍūkyopaniṣad* 7 followed by *Gauḍapādiya-kārikā* I.10–18, *Māṇḍūkyopaniṣad* 8–11 followed by *Gauḍapādiya-kārikā* I.19–23, and finally, *Māṇḍūkyopaniṣad* 12 followed by *Gauḍapādiya-kārikā* I.24–29.

3. *Prima facie* the reason for this would seem to be the fact that the first *prakaraṇa* of the GK forms something of a commentarial expansion on the main themes of the *Upaniṣads*. The various *kārikās* of the first *prakaraṇa* are introduced after the *Mandukya's* passages with the phrase "*atraite ślokā bhavanti*" ("here are these verses"). Vidhushekhara Bhattacharya, however, maintains that GK I is in fact older than the MU, and so therefore cannot be commenting upon it. As evidence for this he suggests that the GK fails to explain or even mention certain problematic terms in the MU, such as "*saptāṅga*:" "with seven limbs" and "*ekonaviṃśatimukha*:" "with nineteen mouths" (in MU 3–5). "Why should the *kārikās*, that are supposed to have been written

in order to explain the text i.e., the prose passages, omit these two important words." See Bhattacharya (1943), *The Āgamaśāstra of Gauḍapāda*, (University of Calcutta), p. xl, and Mahadevan, (1952), pp. 32–54.

4. Surendranath Dasgupta, *History of Indian Philosophy* Vol I, pp. 420–429.

5. Thomas E. Wood (1990), *The Māṇḍūkya Upaniṣad and the Āgama-Śāstra: An Investigation into the Meaning of the Vedānta* (University of Hawaii Press, Monographs of the Society for Asian and Comparative Philosophy, no. 8) pp. 130–131.

6. Wood (1990), ibid., pp. 131–132.

7. For an informative and balanced discussion of these legends see Mahadevan (1952), *Gauḍapāda A Study in Early Advaita*, pp. 1–13.

8. Walleser (1910), *Der Altere Vedānta. Geschichte, Kritik und Lehre* (Heidelberg).

9. The author(s) of the *Gauḍapādiya-kārikā* are referred to three times by Sureśvara: as "Gauḍas" in *Naiṣkarmyasiddhi* IV.44; as "Gauḍācārya" in *Bṛhadāraṇyaka Upaniṣadbhaṣyavārttika* II.1.386, and as "Gauḍapāda" in *Bṛhadāraṇyaka Upaniṣadbhāṣyavārttika* IV.4.886.

10. Hixon (1976), maintains that the GK is a text compiled by a Bengali school of early Vedānta. In fact the relative prominence of Buddhism in the Bengali region of India in the pre-Śaṅkarite period would account for the GK's interaction with Buddhist ideas. Bengal appears to have been a major Buddhist center, receiving royal patronage under the Pāla dynasty. Rājabhaṭta, a member of the Khaḍga dynasty, ruled Southern and Eastern Bengal in the latter part of the seventh century CE and was a committed Mayāyānist reciting the *Mahāprajñāpāramitāsūtra* and refering the figure of Avalokiteśvara, see L. Joshi (1977), *Studies in the Buddhistic Culture of India* (Second Edition, Motilal Banarsidass), pp. 34–36. Joshi notes that "Although Buddhism is supposed to have lasted longer in eastern India, up to as late as the thirteenth century AD, yet contemporary records point out that the condition of Buddhism in the seventh century AD was hardly enviable in this part of the country." (ibid., p. 300). This suggests that if the *Gauḍapādiya-kārikās* derive from the Bengali region of eastern India, their interest and adoption of Buddhistic terminology would only have been likely to have occurred in the period preceding the seventh century CE. This hypothesis fits the internal evidence of the text itself, which not only places the fourth (and most overtly Buddhistic) *prakaraṇa* as the last to be composed, but also establishes the composition of the entire text in the pre-Śaṅkarite period.

11. Sangamlal Pandey (1974) suggests the following correspondences between the GK and the *Brahmasūtra* GK I.18:: BS I.1.14; GK IV.30:: BS II.1.35; GK III.26:: BS III.2.22 and GK I.6:: BS I.1.23. (Pandey, ibid., p. 79). None of

these verses, however, are suggestive of any link between the two texts, merely that a common point or subject is being discussed. It seems unlikely that the author(s) of the GK were influenced by the BS, although possibly aware of its existence.

12. The predominant viewpoint of pre-Śaṅkarite Vedānta seems to have been based upon the conception of creation as a real transformation (*pariṇāma*) of Brahman into the world. The relationship between this effect and its underlying cause was said to have been one of "difference-non-difference" (*bhedābheda*). Many different permutations of this view are possible. For instance, it may be that the individual self (*jīvātman*) is different from Brahman while in bondage, but non-different once liberated (this appears to be the view of the pre-*Brahmasūtra* Vedāntin Auḍulomin, see BS IV.4.6). Again, Brahman may only appear as this or that from the point of view of its manifestation, in itself it is non-different from the self (the view of Āśmarathya, see BS I.4.20; I.2.29; Śaṅkara's commentary on BS I.4.22). It is easy to see how *bhedābhedavāda* could lend itself to a more radically advaitic interpretation once one accepts a distinction between levels of truth. Difference is thereby relegated to the level of worldly or empirical truth and non-difference exhalted as the ultimate truth. This development within Vedāntic circles became inevitable once the conception of the two truths was introduced.

13. Śāntarakṣita, roughly contemporary with Śaṅkara, criticized the Vedānta philosophy, but declared that compared to the Buddhists, the school had only a little error (*alpāpāradha*).

14. "*etaddvayematamadvaitākhyevicārayiṣye*." See Conio (1971), *The Philosophy of the Māṇḍūkya-Kārikā*, (Arun Press, Varanasil), p. 55.

15. Karmarkar, ibid., p. 60.

16. This is made even more likely if we consider the possibility that at this early stage of speculation a clear distinction between *pariṇāma* (real-transformation) and *vivarta* (apparent-transformation) had not yet been made. This is true also of the authenticated works of Śaṅkara, where there appears to be a very real discrepancy in his perspective unless one accepts that the *pariṇāma-vivarta* distinction had not yet been established. See also the discussion of this in relation to the *Brahmasūtra* in the next chapter.

17. Note also that the title of Bhāvaviveka's chapter on Vedānta philosophy in his MHK (which quotes GK III.5) is called "*Vedāntatattvaviniścaya*."

18. Note that in GK I.7cd some editions have *māyāsarūpa* (See Karmarkar, Gambhīrānanda, Wood), while Bhattacharya's edition (1943) has *māyāsvarūpa* (without a reference to any variant). Of the two, *māyāsvarūpa* would seem to be preferable.

19. Karmarkar, ibid., p. 61.

20. Bhattacharya, ibid, p. 3.

21. Hixon, ibid., p. 158.

22. Wood, ibid., p. 10.

23. Wood, ibid., p. 119.

24. Wood, ibid., p. 123.

25. Wood, ibid., pp. 158–159.

26. Wood, ibid., p. 156.

27. See my "Brahman and the World: Immanence and Transcendence in Advaita Vedānta—a Comparative Perspective." *Scottish Journal of Religious Studies* Vol 12 No.2 (Autumn 1991), pp. 107–126. Here I suggest that the Advaita Vedānta school adopts three basic conceptual models for explaining the relationship between Brahman and the world. These are (i) the Delusion model (duality is caused by the ignorance of the *jīvātman*); (ii) the Illusion Model (duality is caused by something objective which causes the *jīvātman* to see reality incorrectly); and (iii) the Non-difference Model (the non-dualistic world is non-different from Brahman). Each model has its advantages and disadvantages and Advaitins use analogies conforming to each of these conceptual models when they wish to make a particular point. No model is used exclusively in classical Advaita Vedānta and the adoption of a variety of models reflects the Advaitin's wish to use the languages of immanence and transcendence while upholding a radically non-dualistic ontology.

28. Karmarkar (ibid., p. 62) points out that these thinkers are not merely astronomers.

29. Here the more technical philosophical usage of "*bhogārtha*" meaning "for the sake of experience" is preferred given that it is distinguished from the second view which itself expresses the idea of "enjoyment." The second line of this verse is quoted and accorded the status of *śruti* in Madhva's *bhāṣya* on BS II.1.33.

30. Note that I have emended *devasyaiṣa* to *devasyaiśa*. I am indebted to Dr. Friedhelm Hardy (Kings College, University of London) for suggesting this reading. Compare this with the statement in GK IV.85: "Having attained complete omniscience. . .(*prāpya sarvajñatāṃ kṛtsnām*). . .what does one strive for after this? (*kim ataḥ param īhate*)"

31. e.g. *Taittirīya Upaniṣad* 2.6.

32. Wood, ibid., p. 10.

33. Questions do arise, however, even if one denies that creation is an ultimately real event. If the world is laboring under some form of cosmic illusion (*māyā*) how did this occur? How can the *ātman* delude itself? See GK II.12,

16, 19, for an outline of this problem. Basically, the GK's answer is that there is no explanation of creation. This leads one onto the doctrine of non-origination (*ajātivāda*).

34. The term *paramārthatā* is a substantive and not an adjective and so means "ultimateness"' with this in mind we can see what the author of first *prakaraṇa* is getting at—the duality we experience in the three "worldly" states of consciousness is merely an appearance of the non-dual Absolute (another term that may be used as a translation of *paramārthatā* in this instance), thus the ultimate essence of multiplicity (*prapañca*) is non-dual. The entire dualistic world, when examined in terms of its "ultimate nature" (again, *paramārthatā*) is seen to be fundamentally non-dualistic, therefore there can be no conflict between *dvaita* and *advaita* since the former dissolves into the latter upon rigid examination. The explicit formulation of the GK's general acceptance of the non-conflictory (*avirodha*) nature of *advaita* is to be found in verses GK II: 20–30 and in GK III: 17–22. However, it is to be noted at this point that the very foundations of duality are believed to be grounded in non-duality, and that this viewpoint is at the basis of the Gauḍapādian exposition of *advaita*.

35. Wood. ibid., p. 14.

36. That Wood has not considered the idealistic epistemology of the GK is clear from his discussion of the *bhāṣya-kāra*'s exposition of an argument occurring at GK II.4. The verse says

> II.4: *antaḥsthānāt tu bhedānāṃ tasmāj jagarite smṛtam, yathā tatra tathā svapne saṃvṛtatvena bhidyate.*
> [The falsity] of diverse things in the waking state is traditionally known from their location within. As it is there, so is it in dream, the difference is in the nature of the enclosure.

The commentator outlines an argument in syllogistic form, which he (wrongly) takes to be the import of GK II.4. Thus,

1. *Pratijñā* (proposition to be established): "objects perceived in the waking states are illusory."
2. *Hetu* (reason): "Because they are perceived."
3. *Dṛṣṭānta* (Illustration): "they are like the objects in a dream."
4. *Upanaya* (Relation between the two): "they are both perceived."
5. *Nigamana* (conclusion): "Therefore, objects perceived in the waking state are illusory."

While this argument is, as Karmarkar suggests (Karmarkar p. 73), "cumbrous and confusing," it is premature to suggest, as Wood does, that "it is a transparently fraudulent argument." (Wood, p. 110). The argument elucidated in GK II.4 and (poorly) expounded in the commentary on this verse is compact and presumes an idealistic epistemology. Perception (i.e. seeing) is the activity whereby consciousness is made aware of an object. But for the GK consciousness never touches an external object (GK IV.26, 27, 41, 66). Therefore perception and experience have nothing to do with an independently existing external world, but are established within (*antaḥsthāna*) consciousness itself. Anything that is perceived therefore is an object of consciousness and not an external reality.

37. Wood, ibid., p. 193.

38. The author of GK I, firmly grounding his philosophy in non-difference (*abheda*) and non-origination (*ajāti*) maintains that our attempts to place non-duality in opposition to duality are based upon a gross, logical fallacy. One does not necessarily negate the other since duality is of a thoroughly different order. *Advaita* is ultimate (*paramārtha*), whereas *dvaita* exists only in the subordinate realm of *māyā*.

39. For more on this see Karl Potter, "Was Gaudapada an Idealist" in Nagatomi, Matilal, Masson, and Dimock (ed.), (1979), *Sanskrit and Indian Studies*, (D. Reidel Publishing Company), pp. 183–199.

40. Vetter, (1978), "Die Gauḍapādīya-Kārikās: Zur Entstehung und zur Bedeutung von (A)dvaita" in WZKS XXII, pp. 95–133. See pp. 104–108.

41. Hixon, 1976, pp. 230–231.

42. Vetter (1978), ibid., p. 96.

43. It is possible that GK III.39–48 or even III.29–48 are interpolations composed by the author of GK IV. But note that Sureśvara quotes GK III.46 as a *śloka* of Gauḍapāda in BV IV.4.888. By Sureśvara's time then one can assure that GK I, II, and III have been grouped together and assigned to a specific source. Whether that source is a single figure or a school of "Gauḍa" *ācaryā*s is a moot point since the use of the Sanskrit plural form often reflects deference toward a single teacher rather than reference to a number of teachers.

44. A prime example of Buddhist influence upon the third *prakaraṇa* is verse 10 which states that all composite entities (*saṅghāta*) are like dreams projected by the *māyā* of *ātman*. This is clearly a Vedāntic verse but the use of "*saṅghāta*" is strongly suggestive of Buddhist influence in that the notion of the composite (and, on Mahāyāna grounds, ultimately illusory) nature of objects presupposes the Buddhist analysis of the world into compounded and uncompounded *dharmas*.

45. See MHK 8.13. References are to the Sanskrit edition and translation of the eighth chapter of the *Madhyamakahṛdayakārikā* by Olle Qvarnström (1989), entitled *Hindu Philosophy in Buddhist Perspective: the Vedānta tattvaviniścaya Chapter of Bhavya's Madhyamakahṛdayakārikā*, (Lund

Studies In African and Asian Religions Vol 4, Lund Plus Ultra). See also Nakamura (1983), *Early Vedānta Philosophy* Vol I, pp. 182–219.

46. Walleser, *Der Altere Vedānta. Geschichte, Kritik und Lehre* (Heidelberg 1910), p. 18.

47. Vidhushekhara Bhattacharya (1943), ibid., p. 52.

48. See Yuichi Kajiyama, "Bhāvaviveka, Sthiramati, and Dharmapāla" in *Wiener Zeitschrift für die Kunde Südund Ostasiens* 13 (1969), pp. 193–203.

49. For example, *Chāndogya Upanisad* IV.10.4; VI.4.2.

50. As Qvarnström suggests it is likely that Bhāvaviveka was already aware of this analogy from his own tradition. This is implied by *Tarkajvālā* 8.64 which suggests that the pot-space analogy is accepted by both the Buddhist and Vedānta tradition. Qvarnström points out that the analogy can be found in the Buddhist text known as the *Āryasatyadvayāvatārasūtra*, see Qvarnström pp. 109, 113.

51. See Krishnamurti Sharma, "New Light on the Gauḍapāda-Kārikās" in *Review of Philosophy and Religion* 1931, pp. 35–56.

52. See Potter, *Encyclopaedia of Indian Philosophies* Vol I: *Bibliography*, pp. 265–266.

53. Sharma ibid., pp. 46–47.

54. Larson and Bhattacharya, *Encyclopaedia of Indian Philosophies* Vol IV: Sāṁkhya, p. 654, note 8.

55. MHK 8.15, Qvarnström p. 30 and p. 68.

56. 558c 25–26: see Lindtner "Bhavya's Controversy with Yogācāra in the Appendix to *Prajñāpradīpa*, Chapter XXV" in Ligeti (1984), *Tibetan and Buddhist Studies: Commemorating the 200th Anniversary of the Birth of Alexander Csoma De Koros* Vol XXIX/2, pp. 77–97; see in particular p. 81 and p. 82 note 26. Also see Lindtner, "Remarks on the *Gauḍapādīya-kārikās*," in *Indo-Iranian Journal* 28 (1985), pp. 275–279.

57. Lindtner (1985), "Remarks on the *Gauḍapādīya-kārikās*" in *Indo-Iranian Journal* 28, p. 278.

58. For a comprehensive discussion of Candrakīrti's disputations with the Yogācāra school in his *Madhyamakāvatāra*, see C. W. Huntington, Jr. (1989), *The Emptiness of Emptiness: An Introduction to Early Indian Mādhyamika* (University of Hawaii Press), especially pp. 60–68, 162–167; see also Lindtner, "Bhavya's Controversy with Yogācāra in the Appendix to *Prajñāpradīpa*, Chapter XXV," ibid.

59. Recent research on the Yogācāra school has established that there are two "traditions" within the school. One tradition is that of the early school of Asaṅga and Vasubandhu and is represented in the Chinese translations of

Yogācāra texts by Paramārtha (although even in Paramārtha's works we find a tendency to conflate Yogācāra with *Tathāgatagarbha* notions). The other tradition, maintaining that the external world is a "transformation of consciousness" (*Vijñānapariṇāma*), is represented by Dharmapāla. This latter tradition is the one that most readily deserves the epithet "*Vijñānavāda*," since it is clear that this strand of Yogācāra thought differs from the works of the early Yogacarins, in upholding the ultimate reality of consciousness. See Ueda's article "Two Main Streams of Thought in Yogācāra Philosophy" in *Philosophy East and West* Vol 17, (1967), pp. 155–165. What Bhāvaviveka appears to be criticizing in his works is the fully fledged idealism of Dharmapālan Yogācāra (*Vijñānavāda*). Work by Thomas Kochumottum (*A Buddhist Philosophy of Experience*, 1982) and Janice Dean Willis (*On Knowing Reality*, 1979) among others has also drawn attention to the possibility that it may be inappropriate to describe the early formulations of Yogācāra (as found in Asanga and Vasubandhu) as "idealistic."

60. GK IV.25.

61. Qvarnström translation, p. 91.

62. Lindtner (1985), ibid., p. 276.

63. The critique of *ajātisamatā* is absent in Tibetan manuscripts. Consequently, we also do not have Bhāvaviveka's auto-commentary (the *Tarkajvālā*) on these verses. See Qvarnström, p. 24.

64. See Qvarnström, ibid., p. 24 and footnote 16.

65. Qvarnström, pp. 109–110.

66. This appears to be a reference to *Puruṣasūkta* (Ṛg Veda X.90), verse two.

67. The analogy of the spider and its thread is found in *Bṛhadāraṇyaka Upaniṣad* 2.1.20, *Muṇḍaka Upaniṣad* 1.1.6, and *Svetaśvatāra Upaniṣad* VI.10.

68. For example Bhāvaviveka refers to various interpretations of the nature of the self within the Vedānta school in his commentary on MHK 8.54; see also Qvarnström, p. 111.

69. Grosnick (1979), unpublished Ph.D. thesis, p. 82n.

70. Williams (1989), ibid., p. 78.

71. See Williams (1989), ibid., p. 81–82. Lamotte notes that Sthiramati was professor at the University of Valabhī in Kāthiāvār. (Etienne Lamotte, *La Somme Du Grand Véhicle DAsaṅga* Vol II, p. viii.). Dharmapāla and his pupil Śīlabhadra held the chair at Nālandā in the time of Bihar.

72. Richard Robinson, *The Buddhist Religion*, 3rd edition, 1982, p. 91.

73. Edward Conze (1980), *A Short History of Buddhism*, p. 78.

74. See Ruegg (1981), *The Literature of the Madhyamaka School of Philosophy in India*, p. 87.

75. See Wood, ibid., pp. 140f.

76. Even Sadānanda in his fifteenth century text the *Vedāntasāra* quotes verses 45 and 46 from the third *prakaraṇa*, again omitting any mention of GK IV.

77. Whether the *Gauḍapādīyakārikābhāṣya* is by Śaṅkara is an important issue, but one to which we do not have time to do justice. The text, even if not by Śaṅkara himself shows a näivety with regard to Buddhism and a lack of awareness of post-Śaṅkarite ideas, which suggest that it is also an early (i.e. pre-Śaṅkarite) text of the school. If it is by Śaṅkara (and many respected and able scholars suggest that it is, see for instance Mayeda (1967–68), Hacker (1972) and Vetter (1978)), then it is likely to be an early commentary—not showing the intellectual maturity of the BSBh. For a discussion of the authenticity of the commentary see Paul Hacker "Notes on the *Māṇḍūkyopaniṣad* and Śaṅkara's *Āgamaśāstravivaraṇa*," and Sengaku Mayeda, "On the Author of the *Māṇḍūkyopaniṣad* and the *Gauḍapādīyabhāṣya*," in *Adyar Library Bulletin* 31–32, (1967–68), pp. 73–94.

Chapter 2 The Vedānta Heritage of the *Gauḍapādīya-kārikā*

1. The concept of non-human revelation was a doctrine of the Karma-Mīmāṃsa school, adopted by its "sister school" the Vedānta.

2. Early names for the Vedānta school were "Upaniṣadic ones" (*aupaniṣada*) "the doctrine of the end of the Vedas" (*Vedānta-vāda*), "the doctrine of Brahman" (*brahma-vāda*), "the doctrine that Brahman is the cause [of everything]" (*brahma-kāraṇa-vāda*). Śaṅkara has various names for his own school: "the doctrine of non-dualism" (*advaita-vāda*), "the school of non-difference" (*abheda-darśana*), "the doctrine of the denial of dualism (*dvaitavādapratiṣedha*), and "Non-dualism of the Isolated" (*kevalādvaita*). The term *advaita* first occurs in a recognizably Vedāntic context in the prose of *Māṇḍūkya Upaniṣad* 7, although it is to a certain extent prefigured in the *Chāndogya Upaniṣad*'s statement that Brahman is "one without a second" (*ekam advitiyam*).

3. There is also the *Mahānārāyaṇa Upaniṣad*, a composite text constituting part of the *Taittirīya Āraṇyaka*.

4. For a more sophisticated chronology see Nakamura (1983), *A History of Early Vedānta Philosophy*, Vol 1, p. 42.

5. See Deussen (1906), *The Philosophy of the Upanishads*, pp. 9–10. For an alternative historical analysis see Nakamura, ibid., p. 44.

6. The distinction between Pūrva-Mīmāṃsa and Uttara-Mīmāṃsa corresponds in Brahmanical circles to the sections of the Vedas dealing with ritual action and injunction (*karma-kāṇḍa* or *vidhi-kāṇḍa*) and knowledge (*jñāna-kāṇḍa*).

7. P. T. Raju (1985), *Structural Depths of Indian Thought*, (South Asian Publishers, New Delhi), p. 25.

8. See *Kaṭha Upaniṣad* I.iii.3–9, and following discussion.

9. This is an idea taken up by Śaṅkara in his notion of *adhyāsa*. The discrimination (*viveka*) of the self from what is not-self is also an important feature of the Sāṃkhya philosophy.

10. See for instance *Kauṣītakī Upaniṣad* I.2–3.

11. *Bṛhadāraṇyaka Upaniṣad* III.9.

12. Translation in Hume (1931), p. 241.

13. *Taittiriya Upaniṣad* II.6; see also II.7; Hume trans., p. 287.

14. *Bṛhadāraṇyaka Upaniṣad* III. vi; trans. Madhavananda, p. 342–343.

15. *Chāndogya Upaniṣad* III.14.1,4.

16. *Chāndogya Upaniṣad* VI.12ff; cf also *Taittirīya Upaniṣad* I.8: "Om is Brahman. Om is all this," *Aitareya* III.1.3; *Īśa Upaniṣad* 5; *Muṇḍaka Upaniṣad* II.2.11.36. *Bṛhadāraṇyaka Upaniṣad* IV.4.5, 6.

17. *Bṛhadāraṇyaka Upaniṣad* III.2.13.

18. It has been argued by some scholars (e.g. Richard Gombrich (1988)), *Theravāda Buddhism* (Routledge, p. 66) that it is the Buddha who is primarily responsible for "ethicizing" of the concepts of *karman* (action) and *saṃsāra* (rebirth), to denote the intention or volition (*cetanā*) being actions and not the actions themselves. While this is a clear feature of the Buddha's teachings, the verse quoted from the *Bṛhadāraṇayaka Upaniṣad* suggests that the move pre-dates Śakyamuni. It would also be unwise to assume that the mental state of the agent performing a sacrifice was of no relevance in pre-*Bṛhadāraṇyaka* Vedic passages.

19. *Kāṭha Upaniṣad* I.i.1–II.iii. 19.

20. *Kāṭha Upaniṣad* I.iii. 3–4.

21. See also *Kāṭha Upaniṣad* IV.1–2.

22. *Bṛhadāraṇyaka Upaniṣad* VI.1.

23. See *Kauṣītakī* I.6, III.3, IV.20; *Kāṭha* II. ii.3; Isa 4; *Muṇḍaka* III.1.8, III.2.7; *Praśna* V.11.

24. *Kauṣītakī* IV.19, 20.

25. *Bṛhadāraṇyaka Upaniṣad* IV.iv.

26. The doctrine that the world is a creation of individual experience is also not a position endorsed by the *Gauḍapādīya-kārikā*, see for instance GK I.18, or by any of the major exponents of Advaita philosophy until perhaps Prakāśānanda in the sixteenth century.

27. So in fact, while it may be true that in an ultimate sense *karman* is, in Eliot Deutsch's words, "a convenient fiction" for the Advaita Vedāntin, the doctrine provides an explanation of an individual's (*jīva*) faulty apprehension of reality. As such, Deutsch suggest that *karman* is "a theory that is undemonstrable but useful in interpreting experience." See Eliot Deutsch (1969), *Advaita Vedānta: a Philosophical Reconstruction*, East-West Center Press, Honolulu, (1969), p. 69.

28. *Bṛhadāraṇyaka Upaniṣad* IV.iii.6.

29. *Bṛhadāraṇyaka Upaniṣad* IV.iii.14.

30. *Bṛhadāraṇyaka Upaniṣad* IV.iii.18.

31. *Bṛhadāraṇyaka Upaniṣad* IV.iii.21–32.

32. *Bṛhadāraṇyaka Upaniṣad* IV.v.13. Translation by Madhvānanda, p. 542.

33. *Chāndogya Upaniṣad* VIII.11.1.

34. *Chāndogya Upaniṣad* VIII.12.1.

35. *Chānodgya Upaniṣad* VIII.12.1; translation by Hume, p. 272.

36. GK I.15. See also GK III.34–36.

37. GK II.3 specifically refers to *Bṛhadāraṇyaka Upaniṣad* IV.iii. Linda Kay Barabas Mackey (1983), *Reflections on Advaita Vedānta: The Approach of the GauḍapādaKārikā on the Māṇḍūkyopaniṣad with Śaṅkara's Commentary* (unpublished Ph.D. thesis, University of Texas at Austin), p. 28f., argues that GK II.3cd (*vaitathyaṃ tena vai prāptaṃ svapna āhuḥ prakāśitam*) is deliberately ambiguous in that it can be understood to mean "the established illusoriness has been shown in dream" or "the illusion being thus established, they declare the light in dream." She suggests that the second is the primary meaning (p. 29). Thus, "An examination of the dream state can clarify our understanding of the nature of the light of experience because in this state the light is not confused with the activities of the senses and the external lights. . .The third verse of the *kārikā* refers to this part of the *Bṛhadāraṇyaka Upaniṣad* because here it is shown that the internal light of the dreamer must necessarily be self-luminous since there is no other light by which the dream is seen." (pp. 59–60).

38. See GK II.9.

39. This term is used by Andrew Fort (1989), *The Self and Its States*. See p. 16 *et passim*.

40. See *Bṛhadāraṇyaka Upaniṣad* IV.iv.5.

41. *Kāma* is used in this cosmogonic sense in *Ṛg Veda* X.129; X.190.

42. *Bṛhadāraṇyaka Upaniṣad* III.vi.

43. *Bṛhadāraṇyaka Upaniṣad* III.vii.

44. The text of the *Māṇḍūkya Upaniṣad* is as follows:

1. *aum ity etad akṣaram idaṃ sarvam tasyopavyākhyānam bhūtam bhavad bhaviṣyad iti sarvam auṁkāra eva yac cānyat trikālātītaṁ tad apy auṁkāra eva.*
2. *sarvaṁ hy etad brahma ayam ātmā brahma so'yam ātmā catuṣpāt.*
3. *jāgarita sthāno bahiṣprajñaḥ saptāṅga ekonaviṁśati mukhaḥ sthūla bhug vaiśvānaraḥ prathamaḥ pādaḥ.*
4. *svapna sthāno 'ntaḥ prajñaḥ saptāṅga ekonaviṁśati mukhaḥ pravivikta bhuk taijaso dvitīyaḥ pādaḥ.*
5. *yatra supto na kaṁcana kāmaṁ kāmayate na kaṁcana svapnam paśyati tat suṣuptam suṣupta sthāna ekībhūtaḥ prajñānaghana evānanda mayo hy ānanda bhuk ceto mukhaḥ prājñas tṛtīyaḥ pādaḥ.*
6. *eṣa sarveśvaraḥ eṣa sarvajñaḥ eṣo 'ntaryāmi eṣa yoniḥ sarvasya prabhavāpyayau hi bhūtānām.*
7. *nāntaḥ prajñam na bahiṣ prajñam nobhayataḥ prajñam na prajñāna ghanam na prajñam naprajñam adṛṣṭam avyavahāryam agrāhyaṃ alakṣaṇam acintyam avyapadeśyam ekātma pratyaya sāram prapañcopaśamam śāntam śivam advaitam caturtham manyante sātmā sa vijñeyaḥ.*
8. *so 'yam ātmādhyakṣaram auṁkāro 'dhimātram pādā mātrā mātrāś ca pādā akāra makāra iti.*
9. *jāgarita sthāno vaiśvānaro 'kāraḥ prathāmā mātrā'pter ādimattvād vā'pnoti ha vai sarvān kāmān ādiś ca bhavati ya evaṁ veda.*
10. *svapna sthānas taijasa ukāro dvitīyā mātrotkarṣat ubhayatvādvotkarṣati ha vai jñāna saṁtatiṁ samānaś ca bhavati nāsyābrahmavit kule bhavati ya evaṁ veda.*
11. *suṣupta sthānah prājño makāras tṛtīyā mātrā miter apīter vā minoti ha vā idaṁ sarvam apītiś ca bhavati ya evaṁ veda.*
12. *amātraś caturtho 'vyavahāryaḥ prapañcopaśamaḥ śivo'dvaita evam auṃkāra ātmaiva saṃviśaty ātmanā'tmanaṁ ya evaṁ veda.*

45. This phrase is borrowed from *Bṛhadāraṇyaka Upaniṣad* IV.iii.19.

46. MU 3; see also GK I.3,4.

47. See *Bṛhadāraṇyaka Upaniṣad* IV.iii.9.

48. Wood, ibid., p. 59.

49. Wood, ibid., pp. 11–12.

50. See Wood, ibid., pp. 54–56.

51. The interest of the author of GK I in meditation upon Om may reflect his practical orientation and interest in the practice of yoga. This interest cannot be found in the mature works of Śaṅkara, who perhaps not surprisingly does not place as much emphasis upon the practice of yoga. See Andrew Fort (1989), *The Self and its States*, p. 344: "it seems that Śaṅkara sees om analysis as secondary, necessary only for the weaker devotees, those who need a support to know brahman." See also chapter 5 of this work.

52. Raghunath Damadar Karmarkar (1953), *The Gauḍapāda-kārikā* (Govt. Oriental Series – Class B, No. 9, Poona, Bhandarkar Oriental Research Institute).

53. See Sangamlal Pandey (1974) *Pre-Śaṅkara Advaita Philosophy*.

54. e.g. *Chāndogya Upaniṣad* III.14; *Kaṭha Upaniṣad* II.iii.17; *Svetāsvatāra Upaniṣad* 3.20, 4.17.

55. *Kaṭha Upaniṣad* I.2.22; II.1.4, and II.3.6.

56. See especially BG VIII.6, but also BG IV.11; VII.21–23; IX.16–25; X.2 and X.20–39.

57. Cf. BG VII.24, which says that the higher state is changeless (*avyaya*). See also XIII.31. *Bhagavadgītā* discusses the unchanging and static nature of Brahman in XIII.12–17.

58. e.g. see BG VIII.22; IX.27.

59. BG VII.5; VIII.20; XV.16–17.

60. Translation by R. C. Zaehner (1969), *The Bhagavad Gītā* (Oxford University Press). Compare this reference to Brahman as the womb with *Brahmasūtra* 1.1.2.

61. *Brahmasūtrabhāṣya* I.3.30 and II.1.37.

62. *Upadeśasāhasrī* I.16; 67.

63. Sangamlal Pandey (1974), *Pre-Saṃkara Advaita Philosophy*, p. 127.

64. BS I.2.28; I.2.31; I.3.31; I.4.18; III.2.40; III.4.2; III.4.18; III.4.40; IV.3.12; IV.4.5; and IV.4.11. See Nakamura (1983), *Early Vedānta Philosophy*, Vol I, p. 401.

65. Nakamura, ibid., p. 407.

66. Ibid., p. 423.

67. Ibid., p. 433.

68. Ibid., p. 432 and p. 436.

69. Both Rāmānuja and Nimbārka consider the "*atha*" (now) to refer to the fact that knowledge of Brahman comes "after the knowledge of *karman* and its fruits." Śaṅkara considers the term to be referring back to the four prerequisites for knowledge of Brahman, i.e. discrimination between the eternal and the non-eternal, aversion to the enjoyment of sense-objects, the attainment of self-restraint and tranquility, and the desire for liberation. Madhva is not specific as to the reason for the occurrence of the term, while Vallabha takes "*atha*" in the sense of "*adhikāra*," that is as the beginning of a new topic requiring no pre-requisities. See V. S. Ghate, *The Vedānta: A study of the Brahmasūtras with the bhāṣyas of Samkara, Rāmānuja, Nimbārka, Madhva and Vallabha*, (3rd edition, 1981, Bhandarkar Oriental Research Institute, poona), p. 55.

70. See Nakamura, ibid., p. 415.

71. Ibid., p. 520.

72. Ibid., p. 484.

73. The term "*brahman*" originally denoted the *mantra*, the sacred Vedic utterance. As a result it was soon conflated with the revelatory word of the Vedas themselves (*śabda*). This early connotation is also present in two subsequent developments—first in the equation of Brahman with the syllable Om, found throughout the Upaniṣadic literature, (but see in particular the *Māṇḍūkya Upaniṣad* and *Gauḍapādīya-kārikā* I), and second in Bhartṛhari's notion of *śabda-brahman*—the Absolute as Sound.

74. Cf. GK I.9.

75. Maṇḍana-Miśra deals thoroughly with the issue of Brahman as "bliss" (*ānanda*) in his *Brahma Siddhi*.

76. Nakamura, ibid., p. 472.

77. Ibid., p. 473.

78. For example, the usage of the term "*puruṣa*" to denote the self, the adoption of the theory of *triguṇa*, etc. See Nakamura, ibid., p. 146 and p. 154.

79. This in itself seems to derive from *Kauṣītakī Upaniṣad* 4.19.

80. Nakamura, ibid., *passim*.

81. For example, the debate between the Parmenidean and Heraclitean points of view in pre-Socratic Greece, and later the debate between Cratylus

and Plato in *Cratylus*. The classic alternatives in this debate in an Indian context can be seen in the respective positions of Nāgārjuna and Gauḍapāda, see my "*Śūnyatā* and *Ajāti*: Absolutism and the Philosophies of Nāgārjuna and Gauḍapāda" in *Journal of Indian Philosophy* 17. No. 4 (1989): pp. 396ff., and chapter 4 of this monograph. In a more contemporary, Western setting this problem was tackled from the point of view of the absolutist by the English philosopher Francis Herbert Bradley (see Bradley's *Appearance and Reality*, Oxford Clarendon Press, 1893, p. 40f).

82. Nakamura, ibid., pp. 495–496.

83. *Brahmasūtrabhāṣya* III.ii.3, translation by Gambhirānanda, p. 590.

84. For example see *Brahmasūtrabhāṣya* I.iv.23–27.

85. GK II.4.

86. For a concise discussion of *bhedābheda-vāda* see Madan Mohan Agrawal, "The Origin and Development of the Doctrine of Difference and Non-difference," in *Aspects of Indian Philosophy* (1986, Shree Publishing House, New Delhi, India), chapter 1, pp. 1–23.

87. Śaṅkara uses the term *vivartate* in BSBh 1.3.39, 2.2.1 (disputed reading), and *Taittiriya Upaniṣad-bhāṣya* 1.6.2. The term *vivarta* is never found in any clearly authenticated works of Śaṅkara.

88. See *Brahma Siddhi* 7.23–8.10; 18 1–3; 19.1–4; *Vibhramaviveka* 36. See also Thrasher's "*Vivarta* According to Maṇḍana-Miśra" in *Wiener Zeitschrift für die Kunde Süd-und Ostasien*. Maṇḍana seems to get the term "*vivarta*" from Bhartṛhari.

89. *Vākyapadīya* 3.7, 105, p. 246.

90. Cf. *Yoga Sūtra* I.3: liberation is the *Puruṣa* abiding in its own-form (*svarūpa*).

91. This idea is prefigured in the *Upaniṣads* by such statements as "to know Brahman is to be Brahman" (*Muṇḍaka Upaniṣad*).

Chapter 3 The Abhidharma Context of Non-Origination (*Ajātivāda*)

1. A common name for Śaṅkara's doctrine is *kevalādvaita*—the non-dualism of the alone; this conforms very nicely with the Latin derivation of the English term "absolute."

2. As is the case with the translation of all technical terms from the original Sanskrit, one has to be aware of the loss of some of the meaning by the utilization of one fixed English equivalent. In this case the use of own, self

or intrinsic "nature" palpably fails to display the connection of the term *svabhāva* with the question of being itself (*bhāva*). Thus, I have adopted the policy of freely rendering *svabhāva* as "intrinsic nature," own nature," "own being," "self-establishment," and "self-sufficiency" etc., according to the context, in order that the wide connotations of this term will be taken on board by the reader. That this is fair can be ascertained from the fact that in virtually all cases these terms are exchangeable without a change in meaning.

3. *Svabhāva* and the related notion of *prakṛti* (nature) occur in the following verses of the *Gauḍapādīya-kārikā-* I.23, II.34, III.32, IV.7–10, 23, 29, 57, 81, 86, 91–93, 98.

4. Both the Sthaviras and the Sarvāstivādins agree that the *bhikkhu* Śāriputra was, during the Buddha's lifetime (he died six months before the Buddha), instructed to carry out elaborations along Abhidharmic lines. Yet the summaries (e.g. Vaiśali) may well be apocryphal. The *Suttanipāta*, one of the earliest Pali collections, contains hardly any of the well-known doctrinal formulations found in the other *sūtras*. They are also absent from the Aśokan edicts (which were probably intended for the laity in any case). It could be argued, therefore, that the *mātṛkās* are fairly late compositions. Watanabe, however, cite the occurrence of the term "*mātikā*" in the *Vinaya* and *Sutta piṭakas*, and maintains that in the earliest period *mātṛkās* were "rehearsed in *abhidhamma* study." Despite attempts at a reconstruction of these "proto-Abhidharmic" lists, however, little can be deduced about their doctrinal intent.

5. Warder, argues that it is probable that the earliest form of the *Abhidharmapiṭaka* consisted of a set of *Mātṛkā* readings, perhaps even propounded by the Buddha himself, and that it was only later that these heading developed into the systematic Abhidharma taxonomies. See Warder, *Indian Buddhism* (Second Edition), p. 10.

6. See Takakusu (1956), *The Essentials of Buddhist Philosophy*, (EBP), (Honolulu), pp. 58–59. See also Watanabe (1983), *Philosophy and its Development in the Nikāyas and Abhidhamma*, pp. 42–43 and p. 45, section 4.4.

7. See Bareau, *Les Premiers Conciles Bouddhiques* (Paris, 1955), pp. 115–118 and Bareau *Les Sectes Bouddhiques du Petit Véhicule*, (Paris, 1956) p. 33.

8. Warder, ibid., p. 274.

9. Takakusu (1956), *The Essentials of Buddhist Philosophy*, p. 58.

10. Takakusu "On the Abhidharma Literature of the Sarvāstivādins" in *Journal of the Pali Text Society*, (1904–1905), p. 71.

11. Warder, *Indian Buddhism*, p. 342; Takakusu (1956), *The Essentials of Buddhist Philosophy*, p. 59.

12. Dutt, *Buddhist Sects in India*, pp. 152–158.

13. See Thomas Dowling (1976), *Vasubandhu on the Avijñapti-Rūpa: A Study in Fifth-Century Abhidharma Buddhism*, (unpublished Ph.D. thesis, Columbia University) p. 18.

14. See Conze, *A Short History of Buddhism*, p. 56.

15. Murti, ibid., p. 69n.

16. See also *Saṃyuktāgama* III, 14. For a brief discussion of the scriptural foundations for the Sarvāstivāda position see Venkata Ramanan (1975), *Nāgārjuna's Philosophy as presented in the Mahāprajñāpāramitāśāstra*, (Motilal Banarsidass, Delhi) pp. 346–347, note 163.

17. Murti, T. R. V. (1955), *The Central Philosophy of Buddhism: A Study of the Mādhyamika System* (Allen and Unwin, Great Britain), p. 67.

18. Murti, ibid., p. 4.

19. Translation by Dowling, ibid., p. 46.

20. See Dowling, ibid.

21. Warder, ibid., p. 318.

22. Translation by Herbert Guenther (1976), *Philosophy and Psychology in the Abhidharma* (Routledge and Kegan, USA), p. 5.

23. See Asaṅga's *Abhidharmasamuccaya, passim*.

24. Piatigorsky (1984), *The Buddhist Philosophy of Thought* (Curzon Press), pp. 188–189, 6.11.1, and 6.11.3.

25. For example, see Venkata Ramanan (1975), *Nāgārjuna's Philosophy as presented in the Mahā-Prajñāpāramita-Sāstra*, (Motilal Banarsidass, Delhi), p. 43.

26. See also Guenther (1976), ibid, pp. 192–193.

27. MMK 22.11.

28. Piatigorsky (1984), ibid., p. 187, section 6.9.

29. Piatigorsky (1984), ibid., p. 188, section 6.11.

30. Lamotte, *History of Indian Buddhism*, (English trans. 1988, p. 600), French edition, p. 664–665.

31. Guenther, (1976), ibid., p. 193.

32. *Visuddhimagga* 16.67 sq.

33. See for instance the use of "*apātubhāva*" in *Aṭṭhāsalinī* III 468 among others.

34. Takasaki, (1987), ibid., p. 119.

35. Piatigorsky (1984), *The Buddhist Philosophy of Thought*, p. 177, section 6.0.6.9.

36. Dowling, ibid., pp. 153–154. Alfonso Verdu points out that: "The present existence of *dharmas* is momentary inasmuch as they are manifested in association with one another; their evanescence is thus merely restricted to their actualized manifestation in bundles or aggregations (*saṃghāta*) in the indivisible moment of the present. Thus, the Sarvastivādins seem to adjudicate the *dharmas* an ultimate, timeless, and transcendent though potential availability." (Verdu (1985), *Early Buddhist Philosophy in the Light of the Four Noble Truths*, (Motilal Banarsidass, Delhi), p. 15; *Abhidharmakośa* II.46 ab.

37. Anacker (1984), ibid., p. 123 note 5a.

38. *sati viṣaye vijñānaṃ pravartate, nāsati/yadi cātītānānāgataṃ na syād asadālambanaṃ vijñānaṃ syāt/tato vijñānaṃ eva na syād; ālambanābhāvāt/. . .yadi cātītam na syāt subhāśubhāṣya karmaṇaḥ phalam ayatyāṃ katham syāt; na hi phalotpattīkāle varttamāno vipākahetur astīti/tasmād asty evātītānāgatam iti vaibhāṣikāḥ*. See Williams (1981), p. 251, n. 10.

39. Williams (1981), p. 230.

40. See Warder, ibid., p. 345.

41. Warder, *Indian Buddhism*, p. 346; see Takakusu "On the Abhidharma Literature of the Sarvāstivādins" in *Journal of the Pali Text Society*, (1904–1905), p. 121, and Dowling, ibid., p. 20.

42. Translation, Dowling, p. 46.

43. See Dowling, p. 47.

44. See *Abhidharmakośabhāṣya* II.36, and Dowling, p. 56–57.

45. Dowling, p. 66.

46. See Verdu, *Early Buddhist Philosophy*, pp. 130ff., esp. p. 136f.

47. The Sautrāntika interpretation of no-abiding-personal-self (*pudgala nairātmya*) can be classified as an acceptance of the following two positions:

1. all *asaṃskṛta dharmas* are empty of self (*asaṃskṛtadharmābhāva/nairātmya*).
2. all *saṃskṛta dharmas* have no personal self (*pudgala nairātmya*).

Interestingly the Sautrāntika view of *pudgala nairātmya* is structurally opposite to the *pudgala nairātmya* of many of the *Tathāgatagarbha* texts, in which the *skandhas* (*saṃskṛtas*) are ultimately non-existent (*abhāva*), and the *asaṃskṛta dharma* i.e. *nirvāṇa*, (the third noble truth), alone is real, see chapter 7.

48. See Jaini's "The Sautrāntika Theory of Bīja" in *Bulletin of the School of Oriental and African Studies*, vol. XXII, pp. 236–249; and the Mahāyāna tradition that Vasubandhu converted from Sautrāntika to Yogācāra. The author of the *Abhidharmakośabhāṣya*, in fact, sometimes appears to attack the Vaibhāṣika position from a broadly Mahāyāna perspective in his elucidation of the Sautrāntika position. Thus, Yuichi Kajiyama notes that in *Abhidharmakośa-bhāṣya* I, v. 20ab, Vasubandhu criticizes the Sarvāstivāda doctrine that the *skandhas* are real. He argues that if "*skandha*" means "heap," it cannot be a reality, but rather a nominal existent (*prajñāptisat*) because it is only the assemblage of many real entities (*anekadravyasamūha*) and has no reality itself. Thus, as Kajiyama notes on p. 24, "for Vasubandhu the criterion for reality or existence is causal efficiency (*karaṇabhāva, śakti*)." (See "The Atomic Theory of Vasuhandhu, the Author of the Abhidharmakośa" in *Journal of Indian Buddhist Studies* 19 (1970–71), pp. 20–24.)

49. See Warder "Was Nāgārjuna a Mahayanist?" in Sprung (ed.), *The Problem of Two Truths In Buddhism and Vedānta*. It may be that in the MMK Nāgārjuna is "wooing" the Sautrāntikas (if he is not a Sautrāntika himself), but the problem of how the *Sūtra* based Sautrāntika could influence the development of a plethora of new "revelatory" texts (the *vaipulya sūtras*) remains a difficult obstacle to any attempts at deriving Mahāyāna ideas from Sautrāntika roots.

50. It is clear that the doctrine of *dharma nairātmya*, often said to be a characteristically Mahāyāna doctrine is also found in non-Mahāyāna schools of thought. See Williams (1989), *Mahāyāna Buddhism*, p. 16. Harivarman for instance appears to uphold such a view in his *Satyasiddhiśāstra*.

51. On the unique particularity of *dharma* see Piatigorsky, ibid., p. 202, n. (26); pp. 190–191, section 6.13).

52. Paul Williams (1980), "Language and Construction in the Madhyamaka" in the *Journal of Indian Philosophy* 8, p. 17.

53. See the commentary on *Hastabālaprakaraṇa* (which the Tibetans attribute to Āryadeva). This text attacks the notion of an "atom," as does Āryadeva's *Catuḥśataka* 9.12–15; 13.4–6. See also Śāntideva, verses 94–96. Criticism of the notion of "atoms" (*paramāṇu*) is also to be found in the Yogācāra school, e.g. Vasubandhu's *Viṃśatikā* 11–15.

54. See the discussion of "change" in the Abhidharma schools. For a discussion of the Abhidharma view concerning the nature and status of *saṃskṛta dharma* see also Conze (1962), *Buddhist Thought in India*, p. 223–224.

55. Piatigorsky (1984), ibid., p. 184, section 6.2.3. and p. 203 n. 40.

56. See Conze (1975), *The Large Sutra on Perfect Wisdom*, p. 102, P135. "The nonappropriation and the nonabandonment of all *dharmas* that is Perfect Wisdom."

57. Translation in Conze, *The Short Prajñāpāramitā Texts* (1973), p. 124; *Buddhist Wisdom Books*, (1988), second edition (revised), p. 34.

58. Conze, *The Prajñāpāramitā Literature*, p. 7–8.

59. Paul Williams (1989), ibid., p. 46.

60. For example see Conze (1975), *The Large Sūtra*, pp. 120–123, P164–169.

61. Translation in Conze (1975), *The Large Sūtra*, p. 103, P138.

62. For example see Conze (1973), *The Perfection of Wisdom in Eight Thousand Lines*, p. 99.

63. See *Vajracchedikaprajñāpāramitāsūtra*.

64. See for instance Conze (1975), ibid., P247.

65. These two languages (roughly categorizable as "emptiness : no distinctions language" and "emptiness : no restrictions" language) are irreducible to each other. This would seem to be the case given that they lead to parallel and complementary types of language (apophatic and cataphatic). Both function on the same level as axiomatic developments of the notion of emptiness. Nevertheless, I do not think that this precludes the possibility of explaining one in terms of the other, as long as this is not taken in a causal sense (that is that one relies exclusively upon the other), for, since both are axiomatic, both can be complemented and explained in terms of the other. Thus,

PREMISE: ALL DHARMAS ARE EMPTY

Apophaticism: [Neither—nor]	Cataphaticism: [Both—and]
No distinctions	No restrictions
Therefore,	Therefore,
All *dharmas* have no restrictions	All *dharmas* have no distinguishing marks

66. Nagao (1989), p. 18–19.

67. For example, see Robinson, (1967), *Early Mādhyamika in India and China* (Motilal Banarsidass, Delhi), p. 44.

68. *Ta-chih-tu lun* T. 1509: 25.229c.

69. Paul Williams (1980), ibid., p. 14. See also p. 39, notes 62 and 63—Candrakīrti's *Madhyamakāvatārabhāṣya* on 6:113; 137–139, and on 6:150 ff.

Chapter 4 Non-Origination in the *Gauḍapādīya-kārikā*: Early Vendāntic Ontology and Madhyamaka Buddhism

1. The distinction between conventional and ultimate truth may be prefigured in the early Buddhist references to an "individual truth" (*paccekasacca*); see Jayatilleke (1963), *The Early Buddhist Theory of Knowledge*, sections 599 ff. Jayatilleke suggests, however, that "there is no clear-cut distinction between these two kinds of truth in the Pali canon" (section 610). Nevertheless, the very fact that the Buddha used personal pronouns and referred to the self in everyday parlance, while stating in his more theoretical moments that there is no-abiding-self (Pāli: *anattā*); suggests an implicit distinction between the everyday and the theoretical contexts of discourse.

2. The conception of the Buddha as a healing physician (and the four noble truths as his diagnosis and cure for the basic condition of life) exemplifies the teacher who teaches according to the spiritual condition of his audience (See *Itivuttaka* 100, quoted in F. L. Woodward's, *Some Sayings of the Buddha* (1973), p. 84.) According to one famous sermon, the *Dharma* is but a raft to be relinquished once one has reached the further shore (*Majjhimanikāya* i.134). From the voluminous evidence of the Buddha's teaching (accepting of course, that much of it is late and perhaps apocryphal), different statements appear to have been made at different times to different audiences. The apparent conflict between these teachings when examined together is overcome by the later Buddhist scholasts via the hermeneutical distinction between definitive and interpretable levels of meaning.

3. There is much evidence of the Buddha adapting his answer to the level of understanding and intent of the enquirer. The most famous incidents are those involving Vacchagotta and Māluñkyāputta. On both occasions, the Buddha refused to be drawn on certain metaphysical questions. These became known as the *avyākṛta* (Pāli: *avyākata*) or "unanswered questions." See *Majjhimanikāya* suttas 63, 72, translation in Henry Clarke Warren's, *Buddhism In Translations*, (1896, Atheneum Press, New York 1962), pp. 117–128.

4. See Collins (1983), ibid., p. 154.

5. *Abhidharmakośa* VI.4, translation by John Buescher (1982), *The Buddhist Doctrine of Two Truths in the Vaibhāṣika and Theravāda schools*, (unpublished Ph.D. thesis, University of Virginia), p. 153.

6. See Williams (1980), "Some aspects of Language and Construction in the Madhyamaka" in *Journal of Indian Philosophy* 8, pp. 1–45.

7. MMK XXIV.8–10

dve satye samupāśritya buddhānāṃ dharmadeśanā, loka saṃvṛtisatyaṃ ca satyaṃ ca paramārthataḥ ye' nayor na vijānanti vibhāgaṃ satyayordvayoḥ, te tattvaṃ na vijānanti gambhiraṃ buddhaśāsane vyavahāram anāśritya paramārtho na deśyate, paramārtham anāgamya nirvāṇaṃ nādhigamyate

8. M. Sprung (1979), *Lucid Exposition of the Middle Way: The Essential Chapters from the Prasannapadā of Candrakirti* (Routledge Kegan and Paul, London), p. 15.

9. See Monier-Williams *Sanskrit-English Dictionary* (1988), p. 1007.

10. See Monier-Williams *Sanskrit-English Dictionary*, p. 1009.

11. See Nagao (1989), p. 39f. and (1991), p. 13–22, for a useful discussion of the meaning of *saṃvṛti* and *saṃvṛtti* in the Mahāyāna schools. My own discussion here is dependent upon the excellent insights of Nagao in this regard.

12. The term *samantād*, ("on all sides") can also be rendered as "everywhere" or as "all-pervasive." See Franklin Edgerton (1953), *A Buddhist Hybrid Sanskrit Grammar and Dictionary Vol. II*, p. 541, on "*Saṃvṛti*."

13. *Madhyamakāvatāra* VI.23.

14. Ibid., *Madhyamakāvatāra* VI.28.

15. MMK 24.10.

16. See Nagao (1991), ibid, pp. 16–22.

17. Cf GK 1V.79—*abhūtābhiniveśa*.

18. GK IV.73cd; see also GK IV.24, 25.

19. The denial of eternalism with respect to *dharmas* suggests a keen awareness of the inter-scholastic controversies of Indian Buddhism. Karmarkar (1973, p. 128) even goes as far to suggest that GK 1V.58 etc. may be an actual reference to (and critique of) the dharmic taxonomy of the Sarvāstivāda school. Compare GK 1V.59 with MMK 18.10 and Candrakīrti's *Madhyamakāvatāra* VI.33 and *bhāṣya* (116).

20. Vidhushekara Bhattacharya (1943), *The Āgamaśāstra of Gauḍapāda*, p. 107.

21. T. M. P. Mahadevan (1954), *Gauḍapāda: A Study in Early Advaita* (Madras University), p. 188.

22. S. S. Roy (1965), *The Heritage of Śaṅkara* (Allahabad, Udayana Publications), p. 15.

23. S. L. Pandey (1974), *Pre-Samkara Advaita Philosophy*, p. 323.

24. GK 111.21. See also GK 1V.7, 29.

25. Richard Robinson (1967), *Early Mādhyamika in India and China* (Mot. Banars, Delhi), p. 44.

26. B. K. Matilal (1977), *The Logical Illumination of Indian Mysticism*, pp. 7–8.

27. Note the background of this view in the Parmenidean—Heraclitean debates of ancient Greece and the similarity between Zeno's paradoxes and the paradoxes generated by Nāgārjuna and his followers. For a brief discussion of this see Elwin W. Jones "Buddhist Theories of Existents: The System of Two Truths" in M. Kiyota (ed) (1978), *Mahāyāna Buddhist Meditation: Theory and Practice*, (University of Hawaii Press, Honolulu).

28. F. H. Bradley (1893), *Appearance and Reality* (Oxford, Clarendon Press), p. 40.

29. Ibid., p. 51–52.

30. MMK XV.3.

31. See Robinson, ibid., p. 48.

32. See Matilal (1977), ibid., for a discussion of the paradox of change and the question of whether it is an antimony or a paradox. See especially footnote 10, p. 35.

33. MMK XXIV.15.

34. MMK XXIV:

20. yady aśūnyam idaṃ sarvam udayo nāsti na vyayaḥ.
22. svabhāvato vidyamānam kiṃ punaḥ samudeṣyate, tasmāt samudayo nāsti śūnyatāṃ pratibādhataḥ.
24. svabhāvye sati mārgasya bhāvanā nopapadyate, athāsau bhāvyate mārgaḥ svābhāvyaṃ te na vidyate.
25. yadā duḥkham samudayo nirodhaś ca na vidyate, mārgo duḥkhanirodhatvāt katamaḥ prāpayiṣyati.
26. svabhāvenāparijñānam yadi tasya punaḥ kathaṃ, parijñānaṃ nanu kila svabhāvaḥ samavasthitaḥ.
27. prahānasākṣātkaraṇe bhāvanā caivam eva te, parijñānan na yujyante catvāry api phalāni ca.
28. svabhāvenādhigataṃ yat phalaṃ tat punaḥ kathaṃ, śakyaṃ samadhigantuṃ syāt svabhāvaṃ parigṛhṇataḥ.
33. na ca dharmam adharmaṃ vā kaścij jātu kariṣyati, kim aśūnyasya kartavyaṃ svabhāvaḥ kriyate na hi.
36. sarvasaṃvyavahārāṃś ca laukikān pratibādhase, yat pratītya-samutpāda śūnyatāṃ pratibādhase.
38. ajātam aniruddhaṃ ca kūtasthaṃ ca bhaviṣyati, vicitrābhir avasthābhiḥ svabhāve rahitaṃ jagat.

For translations and discussion of these verses see Kenneth Inada (1970), *The Mūlamadhyamakakārikā* (Hokuseido Press, Tokyo), pp. 148–152, and David

J. Kalupahana (1986), *Nāgārjuna: The Philosophy of the Middle Way*, (SUNY Press, New York), pp. 342–354. Note that my translation is indebted to the translations of these two authors.

35. MMK XXIV.40.

36. Elwin W. Jones "Buddhist Theories of Existents: The System of Two Truths" in M. Kiyota (ed.) (1978), *Mahāyāna Buddhist Meditation: Theory and Practice*, (University of Hawaii Press, Honolulu), p. 12.

37. F. Streng (1967), *Emptiness: A Study In Religious Meaning* (Abingdon Press), p. 52. In this respect it is also interesting to note the following observation of Streng's "The grammatical character of Nāgārjuna's use of "emptiness" is revealing in that it is always used adjectivally. "Emptiness" is always the emptiness of something; or "emptiness" is always the predicate of something e.g., co-dependent origination of existence or the highest knowledge of no-self-existence." (p. 159).

It is clear then that what we have here is not a reification of "emptiness" which indeed would be an alternative form of absolutism, but the adoption of a practical technique invoking the skillful use of concepts (*prajñaptir upadāya*, MMK XXIV.18). In the same way as the story or question outlined in a Zen *koan* can be said to facilitate a direct realization of enlightenment (*bodhi*) and an insight into the nature of reality without implying the "factuality" of its content, concepts such as emptiness can be used as pointers to the ultimate truth without implying that there is either a substance which is empty or that there is something which can be called "emptiness."

38. Kalupahana renders MMK XVIII.4–5 as follows: "When views pertaining to 'mine' and 'I', whether they are associated with the internal or the external, have waned, then grasping comes to cease. With the waning of that [grasping], there is waning of birth.

On the waning of defilements of action, there is release. Defilements of action belong to one who discriminates, and these in turn result from obsession. Obsession, in turn, ceases within the context of emptiness." (Kalupahana (1986), *Nāgārjuna: The Philosophy of the Middle Way*, pp. 265–266).

39. See MMK 24.18, 22.11.

40. See MMK 22.11.

41. Ruegg, David Seyfort (1986), "Does the Mādhyamika have a thesis and philosophical position?" in Matilal and Evans (ed.) *Buddhist Logic and Epistemology* (Dordrecht, Reidel, 1986), pp. 229–237.

42. For Nāgārjuna's use of *ajāti*, see also *Vaidalyaprakaraṇa padārtha* 6 (*sūtra* 31), where Nāgārjuna denies that he accepts either a *siddhi-ādi* or a *siddha-anta, padārtha* 15 (*sūtra* 68) *jāti* is impossible without *jāta, ajāta*, and *jāyamana*. See also Harsha Narain's "The Nature of Madhyamaka Thought" in *Mādhyamika Dialectic and the Philosophy of Nāgārjuna*, p. 240–242—for

a discussion of the non-absolutism of Nāgārjuna, the provisional nature of definition of *svabhāva* as non-relative and non-artificial, and the denial of origination (*an-utpāda*) as opposed to *anutpāda*—the assertion of an unoriginated).

43. Most "negative" appellations can be understood in this manner. Consider for example the concept of the "beginninglessness" (*anādi*) of *saṃsāra*. In Buddhism this doctrine seems to have been put forward to counter the speculation about the cosmological origins of the universe. (This Buddhist idea is undoubtedly influenced by the general conception of time as a cyclical in nature, a feature of the Indian culture which radically differs from the Judaeo-Christian heritage of the West.) In a non-theistic tradition such as Buddhism (which is not atheistic since it does accept the existence of gods—it merely denies their status as all-powerful and permanent beings), "*anādi*" counters the tendency to postulate a creator who "sets the wheels in motion." However, one can also see beginninglessness in a more positivistic light as the belief that the source or beginning of *saṃsāra* is outside the temporal sphere This interpretation of the concept allows for the possibility of an omnipotent and transcendent cause to the universe's manifestation. Thus there are two possible interpretations of most negative terms corresponding to the two traditional types of negation (implicatory and non-implicatory).

44. See Matilal 1971, pp. 162–165; Ruegg 1981, pp. 78f.

45. See Qvarnstrom, p. 105.

46. See Huntington Jr, p. 206 note. 39 for brief mention of the earliest occurrence of the distinction between Svātantrika and Prāsaṅgika.

47. MHK 8.81, trans. Qvarnstrom, p. 89. This verse in fact appears to be a refutation of the GK's conception of "*ajāti-samatā*." See GK III.38.

48. The term "theism" is here being used in a broad and wide-ranging sense denoting any belief in a divine being or beings. As such it encompasses the wide variety of "theisms," namely polytheism, henotheism, monotheism, panentheism, etc. Such a broad understanding of the term is necessary when dealing with Hindu belief systems because of the flexibility and variety of approaches to the divine.

Chapter 5 *Asparśa-yoga* in the *Gauḍapādīya-kārikā*

1. GK III. 39 and IV.2.

2. GK III. 40.

3. In meditative terms *asparśa-yoga* may also have some connection with the *Yogasūtra* notion of detachment (*vairāgya*). It also connotes the notion of purity in the sense of being untouched by defilements. In the Buddhist *Śrīmālāsūtra* we find the term "*asparśa-dharmin*" used in precisely this sense

to describe the intrinsic purity of the mind: "O Lord, a good mind is momentary (*kṣaṇika*); it cannot be afflicted by defilements. The bad mind is [also] momentary; even this [bad] mind cannot be afflicted by defilements. O Lord, defilements cannot touch that mind. O, Lord, how is it possible that the mind, of untouchable character (*asparśa-dharmin*), can be afflicted by darkness? O Lord, still there is defilement and there is defiled mind. Moreover, O Lord, the meaning that the mind purified by nature is defiled is difficult to be understood." (222 b), translation in Garma Chang (ed.), (1983), *A Treasury of Mahāyāna Sūtras: Selections from the Mahāratnakūṭasūtra* (Pennsylvania State University Press), p. 174–175).

4. See GK III. 31.

5. See my "*Śūnyatā* and *Ajāti*: Absolutism and the Philosophies of Nāgārjuna and Gauḍapādā" in *Journal of Indian Philosophy* 17 (December 1989), pp. 385–405. For a more detailed discussion of this and related issues see chapter 4.

6. *Saṃjñā*, the third of the five *skandhas*, is often translated as "perception," but it denotes slightly more than this, being what we might describe as "notional perception," that is, a cognitive labeling of the given "sensation." It is to a certain extent a subtle evaluation of the experience, and is to be understood as prejudice in the smallest sense of the word.

7. *Abhidharmakośa* II. 24–44d.

8. *Aṭṭhāsalinī* III.77 quoted by Guenther (1976), *Philosophy and Psychology in the Abhidharma* (Routledge and Kegan, USA), p. 32.

9. See Verdu (1985), *Early Buddhist Philosophy in Light of the Four Noble Truths* (Motilal Banarsidass, Delhi), p. 99.

10. The problem of the origins of the term "*asparśayoga*" is that the closest we have to a *locus classicus* for its use in the *Upaniṣads* are such verses as the following from the *Kaṭha Upaniṣad*: "One becomes freed from the jaws of death by knowing that which is soundless (*aśabdam*), touchless (*asparśam*), colorless (*arūpam*), undiminishing (*avyayam*), and also tasteless (*tathā' rasam*), eternal (*nityam*), odorless, without beginning, and without end, distinct from *Mahat* and ever constant." (*Kaṭha Upanisad* I.3.15, translation by Gambhīrānanda (1957) ibid., p. 167.) However, attempts to find the origins of the term in this and other similar verses rest on very shaky ground.

11. In *Yogasūtra* II.54 *pratyāhāra* is said to be the disuniting (*asaṃprayoge*) of sense-faculties from their respective sense-objects.

12. See Karel Werner "Yoga and the Old Upaniṣads" in Connolly (ed.). *Perspectives on Indian Religion: Papers in Honour of Karel Werner*, (Sri Satguru Publications, Delhi, 1986), p. 3.

13. Translation by Gambhīrānanda (1957), ***Eight Upanisads***, Vol I, pp. 208–209. This verse is also quoted in *Maitrāyanīya Upaniṣad* VI. 30.

14. The *Maitrāyaṇīya Upaniṣad* VI.18. Translation by Hume (1931), ***The Thirteen Principal Upanishads*** (second revised edition), p. 435. The *Maitrāyaṇīya Upaniṣads* is of some interest here for a number of reasons. First, it is a composite text which quotes from many older *Upaniṣads* and is clearly aware of the idea of a fourth state of consciousness (*turīya*, see for instance, VI.19). Buddhist influences on this text are unquestionable. Note for instance the text's discussion of the goal of selflessness (*nirātman*, VI. 20). VI. 21 describes a yogic technique of liberation whereby *prāṇa* is conveyed along the *suṣumnā* channel, via concentration on the breath, the syllable Om, and the mind. The conjunction of the senses (*saṁ-yojya*), thus enables the aspirant to attain a state of "selflessness." "Due to the [realization of] selflessness, one becomes a non-experiencer of pleasure and pain; such a one obtains absolute isolation" (Hume's translation, (1931), ibid., p. 437)

15. *Bhagavad Gītā* II.58; V.21, 22, 27. See also II. 68. Translation by Zaehner (1969), The *Bhagavad Gita*, (Oxford University Press). The *Adhyātma-paṭala* of the *Āpastamba* law book (c. 300 BCE according to Leggett, see his *The Chapter of the Self*) uses the term *asparśa* in the following context:

> Verse 7: "He who is constant (*nitya*) in all beings, wise (*vipaścid*), immortal (*amṛta*), firm (*dhruva*), without limbs (*anaṅga*), without sound (*aśabda*), without body (*aśarīra*), without contact (*asparśa*), great, pure—He is all, the highest goal, he is in the center, he divides, he is the city." (Leggett's translation).

16. Although Karmarkar thinks that *Oṁkāraprakaraṇa* is more suitable. See Karmarkar (1973), *The Gauḍapāda Kārikā* (Bhandarkar Oriental Research Institute, Poona), p. xxviii.

17. Although Bhattacharya has argued that the *Upaniṣad* is later than the *prakaraṇa*. See Bhattacharya (1943), *The Āgamaśāstra of Gauḍapāda*, p. xli.

18. *Māṇḍūkya Upaniṣad* 5.

19. See GK IV. 55–56. These verses are important for they link together the two strands of the GK, the ontological critique of causality and non-dualism (*advaita/ajātivāda*) and the phenomenological analysis of the psyche (*advaya-citta/asparśayoga*). Suffering is the result of a deeply rooted psychological attachment to the notions of cause and effect. Simplistically speaking then, *ajātivāda* is the intellectual remedy for all false views, and *asparśayoga* is the practical method for uprooting the afflictions (*kleśa*) which cause these fallacious opinions to arise. The distinction between theory (*ajātivāda*) and practice (*asparśayoga*), however, cannot be strictly enforced, as we shall see.

Asparśayoga involves a theoretical element (a theory of perception), and is not just the practice of *yoga*.

20. GK I.5.

21. GK I.10, 16: *nivṛtteḥ sarvaduḥkhānām īśānaḥ prabhur avyayaḥ, advaitaḥ sarvabhāvānāṃ devas turyo vibhuḥ smṛtaḥ. anādimāyayā supto yadā jīvaḥ prabudhyate, ajam anidram asvapnam advaitaṃ budhyate tadā.*

22. GK I.25, 27: *yuñjīta praṇave cetaḥ praṇavo brahma nirbhayam, praṇave nityayuktasya na bhayaṃ vidyate kvacit. sarvasya praṇavo hy ādir madhyam antas tathaiva ca, evaṃ hi praṇavam jñātvā vyaśnute tad anantaram.*

23. For example, GK II.6.

24. The idea that perception is grounded in the non-dual apprehension of *Brahman* was developed later by Maṇḍana-miśra in his *Brahmasiddhi* (e.g., 71.1–2). Maṇḍana denies that diversity (*bheda*) is given in the immediacy of direct perception. All that is perceived is the bare thing (*vastu-mātra*). Difference is given subsequent to the actual apprehension of an object in perception, being nothing more than a conceptual construction (*vikalpa*).

25. Hixon, (1976), unpublished Ph.D. thesis, "*Mahāyāna Buddhist influence on the Gauḍa school of Advaya Vedānta*," University of Wisconsin, 1976), pp. 217; 234–235.

26. See GK IV.72.

27. For instance, GK III.40–47.

28. The importance of outlining a path for teaching the unenlightened is acknowledged in GK I.18.

29. *Yogasūtra bhāṣya* I.1.

30. e.g., GK III.38.

31. GK II.25.

32. GK III.31, 32: *manodṛśyam idaṃ dvaitaṃ yat kiñcit sacarācaram, manaso hy amanībhāve dvaitaṃ naivopalabhyate; ātmasatyānubodhena na saṅkalpyate yadā, amanastāṃ tadā yatigrāhyabhāve tadagrahāt*. GK III.32d seems to be dependent upon Vasubandhu's *Triṃśikā* 28d (*grāhyabhāvetadagrahāt*).

33. *Bṛhadāraṇyaka Upaniṣad* IV.5.13.

34. *Bṛhadāraṇyaka Upaniṣad* IV.3.21.

35. *Bṛhadāraṇyaka Upaniṣad* IV.3.29; IV.5.15. Translation by Mādhavānanda (1965), *The Brhadaranyaka Upanisad*, (Fourth Edition), pp. 471; 543–544.

36. For a brief discussion of this see Wayman "Nescience and Insight according to Asaṅga" in Elder (ed). *Buddhist Insight*, p. 211. There are a number of interesting terminological features to be gleaned from an analysis of the philosophy of mind expounded in the third and fourth *prakaraṇas* of the GK. Notice for instance the following verses:

> III.29 *yathā svapne dvayābhāsaṃ spandate māyayā manaḥ, tathā jāgrad dvayābhāsaṃ spandate māyayā manaḥ.*
> As in a dream the mind (*manas*) vibrates into the image of two (perceiver and perceived) through *māyā*, so does the mind in the waking state vibrate into the image of two through *māyā*.
>
> III.30 *advayaṃ ca dvayābhāsaṃ manaḥ svapne na saṃśayaḥ, advayam ca dvayābhāsaṃ tathā jāgran na saṃśayaḥ.*
> There is no doubt that in dream a single (*advaya*) mind (*manas*) appears as two. Likewise, there is no doubt that in the waking state the single appears as two.

These verses are repeated verbatim in IV.61–62 with two terminological changes. First, there is the occurrence of "*cal*"—movement in IV.61 in place of the term "*spanda*." This is curious given that "*spanda*" is such a frequent term in GK IV. Secondly, in IV.62 the phrase "*advayacitta*" is used instead of the "*advayamanas*" of III.30. It seems odd for the author of the third *prakaraṇa* to refer to *manas* as non-dual, since from GK III.31 onward the expressed goal is that of the cessation of mental activity (*amanastā*). Is this a terminological oversight, or are *manas, vijñāna,* and *citta* virtual synonyms (as in the *Yogasūtra*)? The phrase "*advayamanas*" also seems out of place since *manas* usually denotes the sixth (mental) sense-faculty. This is clearly an aspect of the dualistic realm and not something one would expect to be described as "non-dual" (*advaya*). One answer is that *manas* has an ambivalent status in the *Gauḍapādīya-kārikā*, being both the cause of apparent bondage and the means to apparent liberation. A more plausible answer, however, is that the third *prakaraṇa* is here moving onto a phenomenological analysis of the nature of the individual psyche (a theme subsequently developed in the fourth *prakaraṇa*). As such, the term "*manas*" is not out of place since the discussion is dealing with the single mind (*advayamanas*) of a single individual (*eka-jīva*), and not discussing questions of ontology.

37. Here it is said that understanding (*vijñāna*) is superior to meditation (*dhyāna*). *Prima facie* this seems to be a reversal of the position of the GK. However, we should be careful in comparing early Upaniṣadic terms with their usage in later philosophical texts. Clearly the terms "*vijñāna*" has none of the "mundane" and "discursive" connotations in the *Chāndogya*. The important point to note is that from an early stage the Vedānta has acknowledged that the gnosis of the sage differs radically from the mundane knowledge of the common man. Note also the distinction between higher (*parā*) and lower

(*aparā*) knowledge (*vidyā*) in the *Upanisads*. A distinction between "ordinary" and "altered" states of consciousness is a distinction made by all who adopt *yoga* as a form of religious practice. This is not surprising since to fail to differentiate between the two is to deny any noetic value to the practice of *yoga*.

38. GK III.35.

39. The Yogācāra equivalent is *āśraya-parāvṛtti*, the "trans-formation" or "con-version" of the consciousness complex (*ālaya-vijñāna*).

40. GK III.35.

41. GK III.37–39: *sarvābhilāpavigataḥ sarvacintāsamutthitaḥ, supraśāntaḥ sakṛjjyotiḥ samādhir acalo 'bhayah.*
graho na tatra notsargaś cintā yatra na vidyate, ātmasaṃsthaṃ tadā jñānam ajāti samatāṃ gataṁ.
asparśayogo vai nāma durdarśaḥ sarvayogibhiḥ, yogino bibhyati hy asmād abhaye bhayadarśinaḥ.

42. Bhattacharya (1943), ibid., pp. 94–100.

43. Griffiths (1986), *On Being Mindless: Buddhist Meditation and the Mind-Body Problem*, (Open Court, Illinois), p. xiv.

44. GK IV.2: *asparśayogo vai nāma sarvasattvasukho hitaḥ, avivādo'-viruddhaś ca deśitas tam namāmy aham.*

45. *Gauḍapādīyakārikābhāṣya* IV.2:
sparś*anaṃ sparśaḥ saṃbandho na vidyate yasya yogasya kenacid kadācid api so'asparśayogo'brahmasvabhāva eva 'vai nāma'iti brahmavidām asparśayoga ity evaṃ prasiddha ityarthaḥ.*

46. GK III.39 and GK IV.2.

47. *Nyayasūtra* I.1.4: *indriyārtha sannikarṣotpannaṃ jñānaṁ avyapadeśyam avyabhichārī vyavasāyātmakaṃ pratyakṣaṃ.*

48. GK IV.26: *cittaṃ na saṃspṛśaty arthaṃ nārthābhāsaṃ tathaiva ca, abhūto hi yataś cārtho nārthābhāsaś tataḥ pṛthak.* The last line of this verse is ambiguous. Are the images non-different from consciousness or are they non-different from the object (insofar as they are both non-existent)? The ambiguity is perhaps intentional (occurring also in IV.26 and IV.50), for it avoids the problem of discussing the precise ontological status of the external world. As we have seen, the world is not merely the product of an individual's imagination. Nevertheless, it is also not ultimately real. As such it is incomprehensible (*acintya*).

49. This argument is also found in various Buddhist texts e.g., Śāntarakṣita's *Madhyamakālaṃkāra* vv. 16–17; *Tattvasaṃgrāha* vv. 2000–2001; Śāntideva's *Bodhicāryāvatāra* 9.93; 9.96–99. The argument that matter and mind are two wholly contrasting types of substance, and therefore cannot "meet" in

perception probably originated with the Sautrantika school. This Buddhist school upheld a correspondence theory of perception, but were indirect representationalists. The Sautrantika position was that consciousness perceived the image (*ākāra*) cast by an object and not the object itself. Nevertheless, the existence of external objects could be known by inference as the cause of the perception.

50. GK IV.66: *jāgraccitteksạṇīyās te na vidyante tataḥ pṛthak, tathā taddṛśyam evedaṃ jāgrataś cittam iṣyate.*

51. GK III.31.

52. GK III.32.

53. III.46: *yadā na līyate cittaṃ na ca vikṣipyate punaḥ, aniṅganam anābhāsaṃ niṣpannaṃ brahma tat tadā.*

54. GK IV.72.

55. GK II.32.

56. This epithet, however, may well be applicable to the later idealism of the Dharmapālan lineage of the Yogācāra, for whom the external objective world was merely a transformation of the ultimately real subjective consciousness. The wide scope of the term "Yogācāra" is clear from the fact that it was originally used in India as a general term for the "practice of yoga" (*yoga-acāra*). Thus, the colophon to the Four Hundred Verses (*Catuḥśataka*) of the Mādhyamika Āryadeva describes the text as "*bodhisattva-yogācāra*." The term seems to have derived its later doctrinal and scholastic specificity from the title of Asaṅga's major work, the voluminous *Stages in the Path of Yoga* (*Yogācārabhūmi*). This work, however, far from being a sectarian exposition of Yogācāra ideas, is a large-scale compendium of the stages of the Buddhist path, of which only a small part is devoted to the specific interests of the Yogācāra school. This is a feature of much of Asaṅga's literary output, the other great example being his *Compendium of the Mahāyāna* (*Mahāyānasaṃgraha*). Although the works of Asaṅga and Vasubandhu do show a marked development of ideas in the delineation and analysis of the yogic path when compared to their Mādhyamika predecessors, this should not necessarily be seen to be characteristic of an antithetical attitude towards the earlier exposition of Mahāyāna ideas. The specific attribution of the term "Yogācāra" or "*Vijñānavāda*" to the thought of Asaṅga and Vasubandhu should always be used with extreme caution, lest one reads back the scholarly controversies of later times into the early development of "Yogācāra" thought. See Richard King (1994), "Early Yogācāra and its Relationship with the Madhyamaka School" in *Philosophy East and West* 44, No. 4, pp. 659–684.

57. *Madhyāntavibhāga* I.7: *upalabdhim samāśritya nopalabdhiḥ prajāyate, nopalabdhim samāśritya nopalabdhiḥ prajayate.*

58. *Madhyāntavibhāgabhāṣya* I.7: *Vijñaptimātra upalabdhim niśritya arthānupalabdhir jāyate. Arthānupalabdhim niśritya vijñapti-mātrasya api anupalabdhir jāyate. Evam asal lakṣaṇam grāhya grāhakayoḥ praviśati.*

59. *Trisvabhāvanirdeśa* v. 36: *cittamātra upalambhena jñeyārthārtha anupalambhatā, jñeyārtha anupalambhena syāc citta anupalambhatā.*

60. *Viṃśatikā 16: pratyakṣa buddhiḥ svapnādau yathā sa ca yadā tadā, na so'rtho dṛśyate tasya pratyakṣatvaṃ kathaṃ matam.*

61. *Mahāyānasaṃgrāha* II (*Jñeyalakṣaṇa*), for instance, mentions dreams as an example to substantiate the Yogācāra thesis of representation-only (*vijñaptimātratā-vāda*), see Lamotte, *La Somme Du Grand Véhicule D'Asanga*, Tome II, p. 92. Hattori notes that in his commentary on *Mahāyānasūtrālaṃkāra* 18 (*Bodhipakṣādhikāra*, v. 43–44), Vasubandhu states that the sensation (*vedanā*) caused by contact between a sense-organ and its object is like a dream, because it is an example of non-veridical experience (*mithyanubhava*) (see Lévi, *Mahāyānasūtralaṃkāra: expose de la doctrine du grand véhicule selon le systeme Yogācāra*, (1907, Paris), p. 141.6) Hattori states that, "Thus, the simile of the dream is, in Vijñānavāda treatises, meant for elucidating that there is in reality no external object and that our daily experience, whether it is pleasurable or painful, is untrue inasmuch as it is based on contact with an unreal object." ("The Dream Simile in Vijñānavāda Treatises" in Hercus et al. (1982), *Indological and Buddhist Studies in honour of J.W. Jong on his sixtieth birthday*, (Australia, p. 237).

Given the importance of the notion of contact [between consciousness and external object] to a "realist" or "correspondence" theory of perception, it seems strange that "*asparśa*" did not become important as a technical term in the Yogācāra critique of such theories. Since it did not, the authors of the *Gauḍapādīya-kārikā* must be credited with its usage in this context.

62. GK III.29.

63. The occurrences of "*dvaita:: advaita*" and "*dvaya:: advaya*" in the GK are as follows:

Chapter	Dvaya/Advaya	Dvaita/Advaita
GK I	NONE	10, 16, 17, 18
GK II	14, 33, 35	17, 36
GK III	29, 30	17, 18, 31
GK IV	4, 45, 61, 62, 72, 75, 80, 85, 87	NONE
Total	14 occurrences	9 occurrences

64. See the denial of the *catuṣkoṭi* in GK IV.83–84.

65. Cf. the Yogācāra notion of *abhūtaparikalpa*, the mental faculty of imagination.

66. GK III.31, 32: *manodṛśyam idaṃ dvaitaṃ yat kiñcit sacarācaram, manaso hy amanībhāve dvaitaṃ naivopalabhyate; ātmasatyānubodhena na saṅkalpyate yadā, amanastāṃ tadā yatigrāhyābhāve tadagrahāt.* Compare GK III.32d (discussing no-mind—*amanastā*) with *Triṃśika* 26d (discussing consciousness-only—*vijñāna-matra*). Both say that this occurs as a result of the absence of a graspable object (*grāhyabhāvetadagrahāt*) and are highly suggestive of selective borrowing on the part of the GK.

67. GK II.32.

68. On the question of the authorship of the fourth *prakaraṇa*, the following points should be noted. The chapter begins with an invocation to the "greatest of all bipeds," who "through a *gnosis* (*jñāna*) comparable to space. . . is fully enlightened (*saṃbuddha*) about the *dharmas* comparable to the sky." The commentator maintains that the author is paying homage to Nārāyaṇa, but the wording and the style of the invocation are close to what is found at the beginning of the *MūlaMadhyamakakārikās*, where Nāgārjuna reveres the "best of all teachers, the fully enlightened one." Weighing this up with the fact that the author of the fourth *prakaraṇa* is clearly aware of Nāgārjuna's ideas, it seems quite possible that the invocation at the beginning of the *prakaraṇa* is directly alluding to Nāgārjuna's own invocation. Both revere the "fully enlightened one" (*saṃbuddha*), but whereas Nāgārjuna speaks of the greatest of all teachers, the author of the GK refers to the greatest of all bipeds. Perhaps this is an attempt to "outdo" Nāgārjuna as it were with a bigger compliment. This may be either because the GK's author distinguishes his own *guru* from the Buddha, or it may be that he felt that "greatest of all teachers" was not reverent enough as an epithet of the Buddha.

Nevertheless, it is unlikely that the fourth *prakaraṇa* is a Buddhist text, for the simple reason that it omits so many of the cardinal concepts of Buddhism. There is no mention of the *bodhisattva*, dependent-origination (*pratītyasamutpāda*), emptiness (*śūnyatā*) etc. (anything, in fact, which could point to a definite Buddhist origin). The absence of certain key Mahāyāna terms (e.g., *abhūtaparikalpa, niḥsvabhāvatā*, etc.,) and the occurrence of others (e.g. *paratantra* (IV.24), *prajñapti* (IV.24.25), *saṃvṛti-paramārtha-satya* (IV.57,58, 73, 74), *catuṣkoṭi* (IV.84), *dharma* (*passim*), etc.) points to the precise selectivity of the author of the fourth *prakaraṇa* (and indeed of the text as a whole). See chapter 1 for a detailed discussion of these issues.

69. Although combined with other evidence (see, for instance, footnotes 63 and 68 of this chapter and chapter 1) there seems to be a good case for arguing for the separate authorship of the fourth *prakaraṇa*. See also note 107.

70. See for instance GK IV.3–23; 40–43.

71. Translation in Janice Dean Willis (1979), *On Knowing Reality: The Tattvārtha Chapter of Asaṅga's Bodhisattvabhūmi*, (Motilal Banarsidass, Delhi), p. 106.

72. See Willis (1979), ibid., p. 106 and Wogihara's edition of the *Bodhisattvabhūmi*, (1930–36) p. 45.

73. Willis (1979), ibid., p. 109 and Wogihara ibid., pp. 45–46.

74. Willis (1979), ibid., p. 21.

75. Compare this with the statement made by Yasomitra in his *Abhidharmakośabhāṣyavyākhya* 1.16: *upalabdhivastumātragrahaṇam vedanāda yas tu caita sā viśeṣagrahaṇarūpaḥ*.

"[The six consciousnesses (*vijñāna*)] apprehend, grasping only the given-thing. However, it is the mental concomitants of sensation that, grasping, specify the form (*rūpa*)."

Williams (*Journal of Indian Philosophy* 8, 1980, p. 15) says that "the distinction between *vijñāna-* and *saṃjñāskandhas* largely marks the difference between apprehending a composite thing and becoming consciously aware of the state of affairs marked by that thing." Compare this also to F. H. Bradley's idealism, where reality is experience or pure apprehension (before the intervention of concepts).

76. Rahula (1971), *Le Compendium de la Super-Doctrine (Philosophie) (Abhidharmasamuccaya) D'Asaṅga*, p. 66.

77. "*A-pariniṣpatti*," literally: "not-absolute" or "not-fulfilled." Rahula translates it as "non-réalité."

78. Thus *Viṃśatikā* vv. 11–14 criticizes "atomic realism" on the grounds that the idea that the sense objects which one apprehends are made up of atoms is not demonstrable on purely experiential (i.e. phenomenological) grounds. Simply speaking it contradicts the given-ness of perception. The concept of a unique and indivisible atom (*paramāṇu*) is also rejected as such an entity would have no facets with which to connect to other atoms. Thus v. 12 states that: "One atom simultaneously conjoined with six other atoms must have six facets. Yet, if they are said to occupy the same space, [being the smallest occupier of space possible], then their aggregate would be no more than a single atom." (*ṣaṭkena yugapadyogāt paramāṇoḥ ṣaḍaṃśatā, saṇṇām samānadeśatvāt piṇḍaḥ syād aṇumātrakaḥ*). See also Williams (1980), ibid., p. 6.

79. Rahula (1971), ibid., p. 32.

80. Rahula (1971), ibid., p. 118.

81. Interestingly, Asaṅga also makes room for a third catgory of sensation, that which is both internal and external. This latter sensation is produced by the interaction of the external sense-spheres (*bāhyāyatana*), that are the support of the sense-organs (*indriyādhiṣṭhāna*), and the "spheres of internal form" (*ādhyātmikāni rūpīṇyāyatanāni*), that constitute the "internal body" (*ādhyātmakāya*).

82. Lamotte, *La Somme du Grand Vehicle D'Asaṅga* (*Mahāyāna-saṃgrāha*), tome II, pp. 39–40.

83. Willis (1979), ibid., p. 25.

84. Translation by Lindtner in *Nāgārjuniana*, (1982), pp. 110–114.

85. Willis (1979), ibid., p. 125.

86. See Willis (1979), ibid., pp. 126–132, and Wogihara ibid., pp. 50–53.

87. See Rahula (1971), ibid., p. 25.

88. Through meditation, one could envisage a stage where there was no attribution of a "self" or an "intrinsic nature" to perception, but merely an awareness of its characteristics. Thus, one could perceive that something is blue but not conceive of it as a blue object (see Vasubandhu's *Abhidharmakośa*, pp. 64. 22–23 etc., see Hattori *Dignaga On Perception*, p. 26 and notes to p. 26), also Candrakirti's *Prasannapadā* to MMK 1.3: *caksuvijñānasāmaṅgī nīlaṃ jānāti no tu nīlam iti* "or again one could perceive the color blue but not attribute an ontic value to this quality, it is merely "the color blue" and nothing else, although this may amount to the same thing."

89. Lamotte, *Mahāyānasaṃgrāha*, tome II, ibid., pp. 112–115; Rahula (1971) ibid., pp. 175–176.

90. An alternative list of ten *vikalpa* is given at *Mahāyānasamgraha* II.20 (Lamotte, ibid., p. 115). In turn, there are 10 distractions (*vikṣepa*) for the *bodhisattva* to overcome (MSG II.21). They are the notions of non-existence (*abhāva*), existence (*bhāva*), affirmation (*adhyāropa*), negation (*apavāda*), unity (*ekatva*), diversity (*nānātva*), own-nature (*svabhāva*), particularity (*viśeṣa*), clinging to the object-as-name (*yathānāmārthābhiniveśa*), and clinging to the name-as-object (*yathārthānāmābhiniveśa*).

91. Willis (1979), ibid., p. 131.

92. Willis (1979), ibid., p. 140 and Wogihara, ibid., p. 55.

93. Willis (1979), ibid., p. 117, and Wogihara, ibid., pp. 47–48.

94. Wayman, "Secret of The Heart Sutra" in Lancaster (ed.), (1977), *Prajñāpāramitā and Related Systems*, p. 137). This is interesting since the *Vajracchedika* appears to have been commentated on by both Asaṅga and Vasubandhu. See Tucci (1956), *Minor Buddhist Texts* Pt 1.

95. For the classic discussion of this problem see *Mahāyānasaṃgrāha*, Lamotte, tome II, pp. 232ff.

96. GK II.31: *svapnamāye yathā dṛṣṭe gandharvanagaraṃ yathā, tathā viśvam idaṃ dṛṣṭaṃ vedānteṣu vicaksaṇaiḥ*. This verse is similar to *MūlaMadhyamakakārikās* VII.34. See also *Catuḥśataka* XIII.25.

97. GK II.7: IV.32.

98. GK II.8.

99. GK II.9.

100. GK II.5.

101. GK IV.25: *Prajñapteḥ sanimittatvam iṣyate yuktidarśanāt, nimittasyānimittatvam iṣyate bhūtadarśanāt.*

102. GK II.6 / IV.31: *ādāv ante ca yan nāsti vartamāne' pi tat tathā.*

103. Cf. *Bhagavadgītā* 2.16–17; 2.20; 7.24; 13.31.

104. Karmarkar (1973), ibid., p. 71.

105. I refer the reader to the parallel discussion in Kaplan (1983), "A Critique of an Ontological Approach to Gauḍapāda's Māṇḍūkya Kārikās" in *Journal of Indian Philosophy* 11, pp. 339–355; Kaplan (1987), *Hermeneutics, Holography and Indian Idealism.*

106. GK IV.33: *sarve dharmā mṛṣā svapne kāyasyāntar nidarśanāt, saṃvṛte' smin pradeśe vai bhūtānāṃ darśanaṃ kutaḥ.*

107. The (originally Buddhist) distinction between elemental factors (*dharmas*) and entities (*bhāvas*) is one that should not be casually overlooked. Note for instance that GK IV.6 repeats III.20 except that "*dharma*" replaces "*bhāva*." This may be seen as an editorial error but for the fact that IV.8 repeats III.22 but with the same change in terminology. I suggest that the reason behind this change in terminology is not so much evidence of separate authorship of the third and fourth *prakaraṇas* (although this remains possible), but that the same point is being made in a different context. In GK IV, in this instance at least, the author is discussing the factors perceived by consciousness. The verses form part of a phenomenological analysis of the workings of the mind. Consequently, the author uses the term "*dharma*" denoting an object of consciousness and not the term "*bhāva*," which denotes a really existing entity. The discussion in IV.6–8 is phenomenological and not ontological.

108. The idea that the world of our experience is "enclosed" (*saṃvṛtyā*) within the parameters of consciousness is closely connected to "*saṃvṛti-satya*," the notion of a conventional and concealing level of truth. It is the veil (*āvaraṇa*) that needs to be lifted, the concealing and enclosing boundaries of our own limited consciousness. It is possible to view the world in (at least) two respects, as an illusion, and secondly as a reality. Neither of these is appropriate for later Advaita Vedānta; Brahman is the sole reality. The world is not an illusion, since we can make a distinction between real and illusory in our everyday lives. The world is not a totally false and unreal "trick," rather it is an ignorant mis-representation of Brahman. The world then is to be transfigured by Brahman in the mystical experience (*anubhava*). For a

discussion of the relationship between Brahman and the created world in classical Advaita Vedānta see my "Brahman and the World: Immanence and Transcendence in Advaita Vedānta—A Comparative Perspective" in *Scottish Journal of Religious Studies* Vol XII. No. 2 (Autumn 1991), pp. 107–126.

109. GK IV.36d: *sarvaṃ cittadṛśyam avastukam.*

110. In the context of this discussion, a "correspondence theory of perception" is any theory which posits an intrinsic and necessary connection or correspondence between veridical perceptions and an independently existing world of external objects. The classic Indian example of this position for instance is that of the Nyāya school (see the definition of perception in *Nyāyasūtra* I.1.4.). Nevertheless, any philosopher upholding the independence of the external world from our perception of it would also thereby be a correspondence theorist. In contrast to this the authors of GK II and IV (in particular) put forward a "coherence" theory of perception insofar as they suggest that the veridicality of experiences is not based upon so-called "objective" criteria but rather on the degree to which that experience remains coherent with one's other experiences. This, however, is not a straightforward form of idealism, simplistically equating the dream and waking states. For the GK the distinction between waking and dream states is one of degree and not of type. The mature Śaṅkara, of course, adopted a thoroughly realist epistemolgy postulating a direct correspondence or contact (*sparśa*) between subject and object in perception. Consequently, the subsequent Advaita Vedānta school rejected both the concept of "*asparśayoga*" and the "idealistic" terminology associated with it. One should note, however, that the Gauḍapādian theory of perception is a rejection of all correspondence theories of perception and the "objective" criteria for distinguishing between waking and dream experiences. For this reason, *asparśayoga* is not mentioned in Advaita circles after the time of Śaṅkara.

111. In *Brahmasūtrabhāṣya* II.2.28 Śaṅkara distinguishes between the waking and dream states on the grounds that [veridical] waking experience corresponds to an independent and external world of objects. This is in stark contrast to the opinion of the commentator on the *Gauḍapādīya-kārikā*, who is traditionally identified as Śaṅkara; see, for instance, the comments on GK II.9–10. Śaṅkara (*qua* commentator on the *Brahmasūtra*) is an epistemological realist, while the author of the GK is an epistemological idealist. This is not to say that the GK upholds a doctrine of unqualified idealism, for, as I have argued, the author of the GK does have a substantive non-dualistic ontology. "Normal" states of perception are idealistic, but enlightenment experiences are realistic.

112. The denial that concepts or designations (*prajñapti*) have some form of objective reference (*nimitta*) is misleading since it is clear that words do have some sort of reference. However, the referents themselves (*nimitta*) have no referential objectivity (*animittatva*) from an ultimate point of view.

Upholding the ultimate non-objectivity (*animittatva*) of referents, however, does not necessitate a denial of their conventional efficacy (*saṃvṛti/vyavahāra*). Such an awareness, perhaps, amounts to what Nāgārjuna would have called a skillful use of concepts (*prajñaptirupadāya*, MMK 24.18), that is, one which knows the nature of the distinction between conventional and ultimate truth (MMK 24.9–10).

113. Kaplan (1983), ibid., pp. 339–344, and Kaplan (1987), ibid., pp. 71–73.

114. See above and also Thomas Kochumottom (1982), *A Buddhist Doctrine of Experience*, (Delhi, Motilal Banarsidass); Janice Dean Wiilis (1979), *On Knowing Reality* (New York, Columbia University Press); Ian Harris (1991), *The Continuity of Madhyamaka and Yogācāra in Indian Mahāyāna Buddhism* (E. J. Brill).

115. Schmithausen, "On the Problem of the Relation of Spiritual Practice and Philosophical Theory in Buddhism" in *German Scholars on India*, Vol II, pp. 235–250.

116. Mundane (*laukika*) and supramundane (*lokottara*). According to the GK, the uprooting of the "object" in perception is called "supramundane" (*lokottara*) perception (see GK IV.87–88). The distinction between mundane and supramundane is also a prominent feature of many Yogācāra texts (e.g. see *Lankāvatārasūtra* III.156, 157).

117. See GK I.17. For a discussion of this problem see Potter, "Was Gauḍapāda an Idealist?" in Nagatomi, Masson and Dimmock (eds). (1979), *Sanskrit and Indian Studies* (Dordrecht, D. Reidel Publishing Company), pp. 183–199.

118. *Gauḍapādīyakārikābhāṣya* III.33.

119. Ibid., IV.28.

120. See GK IV.52: *na nirgatās te vijñānād dravyatvābhāvayogataḥ, kāryakāraṇatābhāvād yato'cintyāḥ sadaivate.*

121. e.g. see GK II.12; II.19; III.10; III.24.

122. GK III.24. This is a quotation from *Ṛg Veda* VI.47; although it is more likely that the author of the *prakaraṇa* is here referring to *Bṛhadāraṇyaka Upaniṣad* II.5.19, that also refers to this verse.

123. GK III.27: *sato hi māyayā janma yujyate na tu tattvataḥ, tattvato jāyate yasya jātaṃ tasya hi jāyate.*

124. See GK III.28.

125. GK III.29–30; IV.61–62.

126. GK II.31; III.10; IV.68–69.

127. GK IV.44: *upalambhāt samācārān māyāhastī yathocyate, upalambhāt samācārād asti vastu tathocyate.* Note that my translation is particularly indebted here to Bhattacharya's that runs as follows: "As an elephant called up by illusion is said to exist owing to perception and common practice, so on the grounds it is said of a thing that it exists." (Bhattacharya (1943), p. 152).

128. GK IV.28.

129. GK II.17, 18: *aniścitā yathā rajjur andhakāre vikalpitā, sarpadhārādibhir bhāvais tadvad ātmā vikalpitaḥ.*
niścitāyāṃ yathā rajjvāṃ vikalpo vinivartate, rajjur eveti cādvaitaṃ tadvad ātma viniścayah.

130. Compare this with Vasubandhu's *Trisvabhāvanirdeśa* (TSN), which appears to be in the background of the GK's conception of the two truths, and his use of the term "*kalpita-saṃvṛti*" in IV.73–74. TSN 30 uses an analogy similar to the rope and the snake to explain the appearance of a world separate from consciousness. A piece of wood is thus made to appear as an elephant by means of a magical incantation, "The root-consciousness (*mūlavijñāna*) is like the incantation, suchness is like the piece of wood, *vikalpa* is like the form of the elephant, and the duality is like the elephant." Thus, the following correspondences are made:

the elephant = *parikalpita* = *dvayagrāhyagrāhaka* (the duality of perceiver and perceived);
the elephant image = *paratantra* = *vikalpa* (the dependency realm of concepts);
the non-existence of the elephant = *parinispanna* (the fulfilled state);
the incantation (the means) = *the mūla-vijñāna* (source-consciousness);
the piece of wood (that is, the substratum wrongly interpreted) = *tathatā* (suchness).

131. For this reason we have to be careful in our translation of the term *māyā*. The English word "appearance" perhaps suits the meaning best in this context as it implies a direct contrast with reality (*tattva*, see GK III.27) without necessarily implying that the world is a complete illusion in a simplistic sense. "Illusion," however, can be used to translate "*māyā*" if it is made clear from the outset that this does not thereby imply that the world is a delusion or a hallucination or that it is merely imagined by the individual (see GK I.18 for a refutation of this doctrine). The idea that *māyā* implies that the world is a subjective delusion, while expounded by some later Advaitins such as Prakāśānanda in the form of the doctrines of *dṛṣṭisṛṣṭivāda*("perceiving is creating," i.e. subjective idealism) and *ekajīvavāda* (solipsism), is not the classical position of Advaita Vedānta.

132. GK IV.51,52: *vijñāne spandamāne vai nābhāsā anyatobhuvaḥ, na tato' nyatra vijñānān na vijñānaṃ viśanti te.* This translation is indebted to that of Swāmi Gambhīrānanda which reads:

> "When consciousness is in vibration, the appearances do not come to It from anywhere else. Neither do they go anywhere else from Consciousness when It is at rest, nor do they (then) enter into It. They do not issue out of Consciousness by reason of their insubstantiality; for they are ever beyond comprehension, being without any relation of cause and effect (with Consciousness)." (Gambhīrānanda (1982), *Eight Upaniṣads* Vol II, pp. 366–367).

133. GK IV.47: *ṛjuvakrādikābhāsam alātaspanditāṃ yathā, grahaṇagrāhakābhāsaṃ vijñāna spanditāṃ tathā.*

134. Translation by Thomas Dowling (1976), *Vasubandhu on the Avijñapti-Rūpa: A Study in Fifth-Century Abhidharma Buddhism* (unpublished Ph.D. thesis, Columbia University), p.139. The firebrand analogy is also alluded to by Āryadeva in *Catuḥśataka* XIII.25, where it is used alongside dream, mirage, and reflection, etc. to explain the status of existence (*bhāva*): "[The cycle of] existence is the same as a firebrand's circle, a magical creation, a dream, an illusion, the moon [reflected] in water, vapor, an echo, a mirage, and a cloud." (translation by Karen Lang (1986), *Āryadeva's Catuḥśataka: On the Bodhisattva's Cultivation of Merit and Knowledge*, (Indiste Studier 7, Copenhagen), pp. 124–125). See also Nāgārjuna's *Śūnyatāsaptati* v. 66.

135. *Triṃśikā* 1: *ātmadharmopacāro hi vividho yaḥ pravartate, vijñānapariṇāme' sau pariṇāmaḥ sa ca tridhā.*

136. Ultimately in the non-dualistic scheme of things there is no recourse to conceptual thinking. The notion of *spandita* or vibration is inconceivable as a precise and literal description of the manifestation of the world given the denial of any dualism or relations. With no point of reference at all there can be no coherent concept of movement or change. Only the non-dual reality exists. The status of the world is inconceivable (*acintya*). Similarly, the concept of *asparśa* falls into oblivion for there can be no concept of "no-contact" without its opposite (that of contact). All attempts to conceptualize reality are doomed to failure from the start. Thus, the author of GK IV says that from the ultimate point of view (*paramārtha*), even the epithet "unborn" (*aja*) is inapplicable to reality since it implies its opposite. (GK IV.74; see also IV.60).

137. GK I.9: *bhogārthaṃ sṛṣṭir ity anye krīḍārtham iti cāpare, devasyaiṣa svabhāvo' yam āptakāmasya kā spṛhā.*

138. GK II.31.

139. See Prabhu Dutt Shastri (1911), *The Doctrine of Māyā* (London, Luzac and Co.), p. 29.

140. All conceptions of reality are approximations in that they attempt to define the infinite in terms of finite categories. For the advaitin then, all views are partial apprehensions of Brahman. The only true "state" of experience (not strictly speaking a state at all) is *turīya*, an unchanging and permanent state of being. This reality is described in GK I.29 as "portionless, yet with unlimited portions" (*amātro' nantamātras*). *Brahman* is the infinite and unborn reality at the beginning, middle, and end of all things. In reality, of course, there are no actual beginning and end boundaries. Our perception of a world of finite and separate objects is our misappropriation of the infinite (*ananta*) and non-different (*advaita/abheda*). Dualistic experience is an inevitable result of any attempts to conceptualize (*vikalpa*) reality. For as we have seen, it is a cardinal principle of non-origination (*ajātivāda*) that anything that has a beginning and an end (both spatially and temporally), is limited and therefore not real.

141. See GK I.29.

142. GK II.1; 4.

143. GK IV.75; 79.

144. GK IV.41.

145. GK II.16: *jīvaṃ kalpayate pūrvaṃ tato bhāvān pṛthagvidhān, bāhyān ādhyātmikāṃś caiva yathāvidyas tathāsmṛtiḥ*. This may constitute the theoretical background to Śaṅkara's notion of superimposition (*adhyāsa*), which is defined by him in his introduction to the commentary on the *Brahmasūtra* as "the apparent presentation of something previously observed in some other thing."

146. Mahadevan (1960), ibid., pp. 181–181. Kaplan agrees that *asparśayoga* denotes a type of meditative path. Kaplan does, however, acknowledge the link with a specific theory of perception. See Kaplan (1987), ibid., pp. 99–100.

147. Bhattacharya (1943), ibid., p. 95.

148. Hixon (1976), ibid., p. 235.

149. This is not dissimilar to the definition offered by the eleventh century Saivite king Bhoja in his commentary on the *Yogasūtra*—"*yogaḥ viyogaḥ*" union (*yoga*) is disjunction (*viyoga*) (see *RājaMārtaṇda* I.1, also called *Bhojavṛtti*). By this Bhoja meant that *yoga* is the pathway to the disjunction of the *Puruṣa* from *prakṛti*. This perhaps shows the important role that philosophical and religious presuppositions play in formulating one's view of the path. Working with broadly Sāṃkhyan principles, yoga is largely a matter of achieving a disjunction (*asaṃyoga* or *viyoga*). From the perspective of the Gauḍapādian philosophy of mind discussed in this chapter, yoga is *asparśa*, the realization that the mind never actually comes into contact with an external object.

150. Colin A. Cole (1982), *Asparśa Yoga: A Study of Gauḍapāda's Māṇḍūkya Kārikā* (Delhi, Motilal Banarsidass), pp. 105–106.

Chapter 6 Gauḍapādian Inclusivism and the Mahāyāna Buddhist Tradition

1. It remains a moot point as to what the Yogācāra school actually meant by the compound "*paratantrāstitā*." Does the term imply the independent existence (*svatantrika*) of a realm of mutual dependency (*paratantra*) or is it a descriptive (but non-ontological) term referring to the inter-dependent nature of existence? On the former interpretation, the Yogācārin does indeed seem to be guilty of reifying the dependency realm itself. On the other hand, the term may simply be an alternative to the Madhyamaka conception of *pratītyasamutpāda*. One suspects that the ambiguity of the phrase is a reflection of the ambivalence of the Yogācāra school itself. Different answers may be given by different members of the school.

2. See *Trisvabhāvanirdeśa* v.36; *Madhyāntavibhāga* I.6 and the *bhāṣya* upon it.

3. See Takasaki (1966), p. 353 and Bhattacharya (1943), p. 199. GK IV.90 echoes verse 558 of the early Buddhist *Suttanipāta*, which reads "What is to be known is known by me; what is to be cultivated is cultivated by me; what is to be destroyed has been destroyed by me. Therefore, O brahmin, I am the Buddha." (translation by H. Saddhatissa (1985), *The Sutta-Nipāta*, p. 66).

4. Wood (1990), ibid., p. 35.

5. See Monier-Williams (1988), Sanskrit-English Dictionary, p. 6.

6. Bhattacharya (1949), ibid., pp. 81–93.

7. Note that my rendering of this difficult verse is indebted to the translations of Bhattacharya and Karmarkar. Bhattacharya renders the verse as follows: "According to the Buddha who instructs the way known to him (*tāyin*), *jñāna* does not approach the *dharmas* (i.e., it does not relate itself to the objects). But all *dharmas* well as *jñāna*—this has not been said by the Buddha." (Bhattacharya (1943), p. 212).

Compare this with Karmakar's translation: "The knowledge of the eternal enlightened one, does not cross over into the entities; all entities likewise [do not cross over into] the knowledge—this has not been declared by the Buddha." (Karmarkar (1973), p. 56).

8. See F. Edgerton (1953), *Buddhist Hybrid Sanskrit Grammar and Dictionary Vol II*, pp. 251–252.

9. See Mahadevan, ibid., p. 214 and Karmarkar, ibid., p. xxiv.

10. Bhattacharya (1943), ibid., p. 214.

11. *Vajracchedika Prajñāpāramitāsūtra* 7e. 21.a; translation in Conze (1973) *The Short Prajñāpāramitā Texts* (Luzac and Company Ltd, London), pp. 134–135.

12. *Saptasaptati* v.15, edition and translation in Giuseppe Tucci (1956), *Minor Buddhist Texts* Part I (Serie Orientale Roma IX, Rome, pp. 61, 100. See also v.19 where it is stated that in the Buddha's realization "there was nothing which was grasped or expressed in words" (*agrāhyānabhilāpyata*), pp. 63, 102.

13. *Vajracheddika* ch. 4, 10c; ch.5, 14e., translated in Conze (1973), p. 129. See also ch. 4, 10c., p. 127. The notion of *apratiṣṭhita-citta* became linked in Mahāyānist thought with the conception of *apratiṣṭhita nirvāṇa*, the *nirvāṇa* of no-fixed-abode, that is the state of liberation attained by the *bodhisattva*, that facilitates a return to *saṃsāra*—being in it and yet beyond it.

14. Wood, ibid., p. 75.

15. See GK III.24–28.

16. V. Bhattacharya (1943), ibid., p. clxiv.

17. See GK IV.11, 12.

18. See especially MMK chapter 24; see chapter 4 for further discussion of this. The logical steps in Nāgājuna's argument as outlined in the MMK are as follows:

i. A. "Own nature" cannot change (15.8).
   B. Emptiness is the relinquishing of all views (13.8) Therefore,
   C. Non-emptiness is the characteristic of all views.

ii. D. Emptiness is a denial of "own nature"—*śūnyatā* = *niḥsvabhāvatā* (13.3) Therefore,
   E. Non-emptiness is the acceptance of an 'own nature" (24.20f), *aśūnyavāda* = *svabhāvavāda* Thus,

iii. From C and E we can deduce that:
   F. All views presuppose an "own nature" (*sarva dṛṣṭi* = *svabhāvavāda*)

iv. From A and E (or F) one can conclude that:
   G. All views presuppose a fixed "own nature," (24.32–38), *sarva dṛṣṭi* = *svabhāva* = *ajātivāda*.

19. GK II.20–21. This list continues up to and including GK II.28.

20. Note that the translations of *Bhagavadgītā* VII.21, and X.21 are from R. C. Zaehner (1969), *The Bhagavad Gita* (Oxford University Press).

21. GK II.33: *bhāvair asadbhir evāyam advayena ca kalpitaḥ, bhāvā apy advayenaiva tasmād advayatā śiva*. And this is imagined to be the non-existing entities themselves by means of the non-dual. The entities exist as the non-dual as it were. Therefore, there is auspicious non-duality.

22. GK III:30—*advayaṃ ca dvayābhāsaṃ tathā jāgran na saṃśayaḥ*.

23. *Tarkajvālā* on MHK 8.54; translation by Qvarnstrom, p. 81.

24. MHK 8.86, 87.

25. MHK 4.7; trans. V. V. Gokhale (1958), "The Vedānta Philosophy Described by Bhavya in His Madhyamakahṛdayakārikā" in *Indo-Iranian Journal*, 2 No. 3, p. 179.

26. MHK 4.56; cited by Gokhale (1958), p. 179.

27. Cited and translated by V. V. Gokhale (1962), ibid.

28. MHK 3.284; cited and translated by Gokhale (1962), ibid., pp. 273, 274.

29. V. V. Gokhale concludes "Thus we have in the above passage a Mādhyamika criticism of the Vedāntic term 'Brahman' which, if properly understood, could be equated with *Nirvāṇa* or *dharmakāya*, according to Bhavya. This proper understanding does, in fact, make all the difference between the Buddhist and the Vedāntic view of the Absolute Reality." (Gokhale (1962) ibid., p. 275).

30. See MHK 8.89–91, 95. Since the GK uses the term *svabhāva* throughout the four *prakaraṇas* (and is in all likelihood dependent upon Nāgārjuna's MMK for this notion), it is also likely that this is a reference to the Buddhistic pretensions of the GK.

31. *Tarkajvālā* ad. MHK 8.99; see Qvarnstrom p. 94.

32. MHK 8.99.

33. MHK 8.103.

34. MHK 8.98; see also *Tarkajvālā* to MHK 8.88.

35. As we have seen *asparśayoga,* as a soteriological discipline provides the conceptual link between the two themes of the non-duality of consciousness (*advaya-vāda*) and non-origination (*ajātivāda*). The cause of suffering (*duḥkha*) is our psychological attachment to a false (dualistic) ontology. When this is overcome, however, through philosophical reflection and the practice of yoga, one can facilitating release from *saṃsāra* (see GK IV.55, 56).

Chapter 7 Absolutism in the GK and the Mahāyāna: the Tathāgatagarbha Texts

1. Despite the fact that emptiness (*śūnyatā*) is often said to be the central concept of Mahāyāna Buddhism, many early Mahāyāna texts shows no particular interest in the concept. In the *Triṣṭubh* verses of the *Saddharma puṇḍarika Sūtra*, that Andrew Rawlinson pinpoints as the earliest stratum of the text, *śūnyatā* is mentioned only once (ch.4 v.45), "and then in an ambiguous passage which seems to equate it with the Ārhat's *Nirvāṇa*" (See A. Rawlinson "The Position of the *Aṣṭasāhasrikā Prajñāpāramitā* in the Development of the Early Mahāyāna" in *Prajñāpāramitā and Related Systems*, 1977, p. 17). In two other instances the term appears in the traditional context of the formula of the three "doors to deliverance" (*vimokṣa-mukhāni*), i.e. wishlessness (*apraṇihita*), signlessness (*animitta*), and emptiness (*śūnyatā*). A specifically Mahāyāna usage of the term does appear in chapter thirteen, but the chapter itself concerns conduct and the term does not seem to suit the context in which it is placed (see Rawlinson's unpublished Ph.D. thesis, Lancaster Univ. 1972, "*Studies in the Lotus Sutra*," para. 1104.) Thus, it is in all likelihood a later interpolation. Texts such as the Pure Land Sūtras show no real interest in the realization of *anātman* and *śūnyatā*. In the *Sukhāvatīvyūhasūtra* the notion of *śūnyatā* is even more scarce, again appearing invariably in a meditative context as one of the *vimokṣa-mukhāni*. The *Sukhāvatīvyūhasūtra*, (the larger version, translated into Chinese c.147–186 CE), describes the splendor of the Buddha fields (*buddha-kṣetra*), and constitutes, in the main, a description and exaltation of the "career" (*cārya*) of a *bodhisattva*. These texts clearly differ in perspective from the Prajñāpāramitā literature.

2. See MMK 24.1–6. It would seem that attempts to safeguard the four noble truths in the light of the emptiness doctrine were at the forefront of the developing *tathāgatagarbha* texts. This reflects, above all else, a failure on the part of the Mādhyamikas in getting their point across. From the Madhyamaka perspective it was argued that *saṃsāra* (bondage) and *nirvāṇa* (liberation) were only attainable if they were both essentially empty (*śūnya-svabhāva*) allowing the possibility of a dynamic movement from one to another. That this explanation remained unsatisfactory to the authors of the *tathāgatagarbha* texts suggest that the philosophical presuppositions of the Madhyamaka school were not shared by this strand of the Mahāyāna movement.

3. It is likely that the *tathāgatagarbha* texts arose in response to the theoretical and practical considerations brought forth by these earlier Mahāyāna texts. Perhaps the most fundamental problem encountered was the question of liberation itself, for the Mahāyāna had opened up the possibility of universal Buddha-hood in a manner that had not previously been emphasized. That this was an important characteristic of the developing Mahāyāna movement can be seen by the increasing emphasis upon the *bodhisattva* as a universal archetype or role-model for all beings and in the growth in importance of the

members of the lay community as full participants in the quest for enlightenment and universal salvation. Thus in the *Saddharmapuṇḍarika*, for example, we find the idea of the one vehicle (*ekāyana*) that encompasses all paths to liberation. The Buddha exercises his skill in means (*upāya-kauśalya*) by teaching a variety of vehicles in order to lead beings of differing inclinations to the *eka-buddha-yāna*.

4. Grosnick (1979), *The Zen Master Dogen's Understanding of the Buddha-Nature in Light of the Historical Development of the Buddha-Nature Concept in India, China, and Japan*, unpublished Ph.D. thesis, University of Wisconsin, pp. 16–17.

5. Grosnick, ibid., p. 38.

6. The earliest occurrence of the term *tathāgatagarbha* appears to have been in the phrase "*sarvasattvās tathāgatagarbhāḥ*." This occurs in a variety of Mahāyāna texts but its first appearance is pinpointed as the *Tathāgatagarbhasūtra* by Takasaki (ibid., p. 196). The prose commentary to *śloka* I.28 of the *Ratnagotravibhāga-śāstra* (RGV) provides a threefold analysis of the formula "*sarvasattvāstathāgatagarbhāḥ*." It suggests that the phrase implies:

1. That the *dharmakāya* of the Tathāgata is all-pervading (*tathāgata-dharmakāya-parispharaṇārtha*),
2. that Suchness and the Tathāgata are undifferentiated (*tathāgata-tathatāvyatibhedārtha*), and
3. that the lineage or "germ" (*gotra*) of the Tathāgata exists in all living beings (*tathāgatagotrasambhavārtha*). (See Takasaki, ibid., p. 197–198).

Of the three, Grosnick suggests that it is the first rendering "all beings are the *garbhas* of the Tathāgata," where *tathāgatagarbha* is a *tatpuruṣa* compound that is the original meaning of the term. See Grosnick, ibid., p. 52, footnote 41, for a grammatical analysis of these renderings.

7. See Monier-Williams (1988), *Sanskrit-English Dictionary*, p. 349.

8. For the various connotations of the term "*tathāgatagarbha*" see Ruegg, (1969), *La Theorie du Tathāgatagarbha et du Gotra*, (Paris), pp. 499–513.

9. See Takasaki, (1966) *Study of the Ratnagotravibhāga*.

10. Brown (1981), *The Buddha Nature: A Study of the "Tathāgatagarbha" and "Ālayavijñāna,"* Ph.D. thesis, New York University, pp. 93–94. Note also that in the Śrī*mālāsūtra* the *tathāgatagarbha* is said to be not empty (*aśūnya*) in so far as "it contains inconceivable *Dharmas* more numerous than the sands of the Ganges." (translation in Chang, *Treasury of Mahāyāna Sūtras* p. 378; cf. Wayman, *The Lion's Roar of Queen* Śrī*mālā*, p. 99). This suggests that the

tathāgatagarbha could be used to denote a container of pure Buddha-*dharmas*. Yet earlier in the same text we find the statement that the *dharmakāya* of the Tathāgata is "free from the shell of defilements" (*avinirmuktakleśakośa*). This is a clear indication that the defilements were seen as impure containers (*kośa*) essentially separate from the innumerable *buddha-dharmas*, that either constituted the *tathāgatagarbha* itself or were themselves "contained" within it.

Clearly there is some confusion as to the precise meaning of the statement that the *tathāgatagarbha* is not empty of the *buddha-dharmas*. On the one hand this may mean that the *tathāgatagarbha* is in fact identical to these *buddha-dharmas*, or alternatively it may mean that the *tathāgatagarbha* is "not empty" in the sense that is contains those same *buddha-dharmas* within itself. The problem perhaps reflects the desire of the authors of these texts to utilize aspects of both the "container" and the "contained" notions of *tathāgatagarbha* (and their appropriate analogies), coupled with an awareness that the *tathāgatagarbha* is essentially beyond the limits of logic and rational discourse. Some later texts, however, exemplify an explicit syncretism of Yogācāra and *tathāgatagarbha* elements, e.g., the *Laṅkāvatārasūtra*. Here the *tathāgatagarbha* is aligned with the *ālayavijñāna*, "store" or "container" consciousness and is described as a womb filled with seeds (*bīja*).

11. See Takasaki, ibid., pp. 268–277.

12. Brown, ibid., p. 204.

13. The earliest references to a "Primordial Buddha" (Ādibuddha) in the Mahāyāna describe this "figure" in a quasi-theistic manner as the primordial source of everything. The term first appears in the *Kāraṇḍavyūha*, a text praising the supremely salvific powers of Avalokiteśvara. This *Sūtra*, that has both a metrical and a prose version, was translated into Chinese c. 270 CE. (See A. B. Keith (1974), *Buddhist Philosophy in India and Ceylon* (Gordon Press, New York), p. 226). The text is notable for its eulogizing of Avalokiteśvara, (himself nothing more than an emanation of the Ādi-Buddha), as the creator of the universe and of the many Hindu gods. Indeed not only is Śiva one of his principal devotees, but Avalokiteśvara himself is called Maheśvara (an epithet of Śiva), taking on many of Śiva's characteristic attributes. (For more on this see Williams (1989), pp. 232–233). The concept of Ādibuddha is an attempt to distinguish between a primeval Buddha-nature (the *dharmakāya*) and the various Buddha figures of the Mahāyāna. As such, it was popular in Nepal where it is associated with the idea of the Buddha as a self-established or absolute being ("self-existent" or "*svayambhu*"). The quasi-theistic connotations of this concept, particularly seen in the light of the *Kāraṇḍavyūha*, suggest that the term arose in a context of Hindu-Buddhistic syncretism.

14. "What is interesting about the *Mahāyānasūtrālaṃkāra* is that it integrates early Yogācāra doctrines with the notion of the *tathāgatagarbha*. Despite its acceptance of a naturally-luminescent mind (*citta prakṛtiprabhāsvaratā*),

and the adventitiousness of defilements (*āgantuka kleśa*), both major themes of the *tathāgatagarbha* texts, the text does not fully integrate *tathāgatagarbha* thought with its own phenomenalistic conception of the *ālayavijñāna*. In fact in the text's suggestion that certain groups (*gotra*) cannot attain enlightenment, we find a rejection of one of the central themes of the *tathāgatagarbha* notion—the doctrine of the "One Vehicle" (*ekayāna*) and the universality of the potential for enlightenment.

15. *Mahāyānasūtrālaṃkāra* IX.77 The text's rejection of *ādibuddha* on the grounds that the attainment of buddhahood is gradual and not already present suggests that the concept can be linked to later controversies within the Mahāyāna tradition concerning the nature of enlightenment and the path leading to it (notably, the "Great Debate" between the subitists and the gradualists in Tibet in the eighth century CE).

16. Lévi, *Mahāyānasūtrālaṃkāra*, vol II, p. 122.

17. Trevor Ling suggests that the occurrence of the concept of Ādibuddha in Java, Nepal, and Tibet points to its origin in the Mahāyāna Buddhism of Bengal. (Trevor Ling (1972), *A Dictionary of Buddhism*, (Charles Scriber Sons, USA), p. 8. We have already noted that the *Gauḍapādīya-kārikā* may derive its name from its origins in the Bengali region (Gauḍa). One can point to the use of the term *ādibuddha* in IV.92 (and *ādaubuddhau* in IV.98), therefore, as supporting evidence for such a geographical link.

18. The *Śrīmālā* presupposes the doctrine of the two bodies of the Buddha (*rūpa-kāya* and *dharma-kāya*) as found in the *Aṣṭasāhasrikā* and other early Prajñāpāramitā *sūtras*, and so probably cannot be placed earlier than the second century CE. The text shows no awareness of the *Avataṃsakasūtra*'s (c. 200–400) doctrine of the three bodies of the Buddha, and must pre-date (at least sections of) the *Laṅkāvatārasūtra* that quotes the *Śrīmālā*. Wayman draws attention to the text's continual reference to the "good sons and daughters" of the congregation, implying the patronage by men and women of high social rank. This leads him to "tentatively place the composition of the *Śrīmālā* within the Īkshvāku rule of the third century A.D." He also suggests that the text derives from the Mahāsaṅghikas of Southern India. (Wayman and Wayman, *The Lion's Roar of Queen Śrīmālā*, pp. 2–3).

19. C. Chang, *A Treasury of Mahāyāna Sūtras*, p. 380, cf. Wayman, pp. 104–106.

20. Chang, p. 377; Wayman, p. 96. Despite their limitations, *ārhats* and *pratyekabuddhas* do experience a form of liberation—the *nirvāṇa* with a remainder (i.e. the cessation of *kleśa*, while the five *skandhas* remain) (see Wayman, p. 91). That this stage of quiescent rest is attained by them is due to the inclusion of the *śrāvaka* and *pratyekabuddha* "vehicles" in the "One-Great-Vehicle, the *eka-mahā-yāna*. However, the *śrāvaka* and the *pratyeka-buddha* can only attain a partial *nirvāṇa* since they are "directed toward the

nirvāṇa realm'' (trans. Wayman, p. 86), i.e. they still meditate upon suffering, its source, its cessation, and the means to that cessation, (i.e. the four Noble Truths), rather than realizing *nirvāṇa* itself.

21. The exhortation to accept *tathāgatagarbha* doctrines on faith alone amounts to a rejection of the very possibility of ''proving'' the *tathāgatagarbha* through logical arguments, (the *tathāgatagarbha* being ''beyond logic''). This attitude alone may have been responsible for the fact that the *tathāgatagarbha* tradition never developed into a distinctive philosophical school of its own, nor drew much attention from scholastic texts that clearly post-date it. The *Śrīmālā* in fact states that: "If a sentient being, out of faith in the Tathāgata, regards the Tathāgata as permanent, joyous, pure, and possessing a self, he does not see [the Tathāgata] wrongly; he sees him correctly.'' (trans. Chang, p. 379; cf. Wayman, p. 102). For further discussion of this issue see David Seyfort Ruegg (1989), pp. 46–49.

22. Aligned with this the *Śrīmālā* also states that there are also two levels of saṃsāric and nirvāṇic attainment: the constructed (*saṃskṛta*) *saṃsāra*, and *nirvāṇa* and the unconstructed (*asaṃskṛta*) *saṃsāra* and *nirvāṇa*. The *śrāvakas* and *pratyekabuddhas* aim for a refuge *nirvāṇa*, while the truly enlightened being needs no refuge since ''the refuge [itself] does not seek a refuge.'' (see Wayman, p. 80). Later Mahāyānists developed the idea that the *bodhisattva* does not reside in a quiescent *nirvāṇa*, but in fact remains active within *saṃsāra*. Perhaps the development of a theory of two types of bondage and liberation was inspired by attempts to differentiate between the enlightened and the unenlightened experiences of *saṃsāra* and *nirvāṇa*. A fully enlightened being, rather than renouncing the world of suffering and entering a *nirvāṇa* of refuge, would remain active and unsupported in the *nirvāṇa* of no fixed abode (*apratiṣṭhita Nirvāṇa*). *Mahāyānasaṃgraha* IX.3 describes such attainment in the following manner: ''When one has produced the knowledge of the identity (*samatājñāna*) of *saṃsāra* and *nirvāṇa*, then, for this reason *saṃsāra* becomes *nirvāṇa*. Consequently, one neither abandons (*tyajati*) nor maintains *saṃsāra*, one neither obtains *Prāpnoti*) nor fails [to obtain] *nirvāṇa*.''

23. Trans. Chang, p. 378; cf. Wayman, p. 97.

24. Chang, p. 378; cf. Wayman, p. 98.

25. Trans. Chang, ibid., pp. 378–379; cf. Wayman, p. 100.

26. The *tathāgatagarbha* strand of themes appears to have been more amenable to the Yogācāra than the Madhyamaka. This may reflect the fact that Yogācāra ideas appear to have arisen at around the same time as those of the *tathāgatagarbha*. Consequently, texts such as the *Mahāyānasūtrālaṃkāra* and Yogācāra thinkers such as Paramārtha both seem to have been greatly influenced by the *tathāgatagarbha* strand of the Mahāyāna. Nevertheless,

tathāgatagarbha ideas do not seem to have been a major force in Indian Yogācāra, though this cannot be said of later East Asian developments. The Madhyamaka school, to an even greater degree, does not seem to have been influenced significantly by *tathāgatagarbha* ideas which are usually viewed as texts "requiring further interpretation" (*neyārtha*). David Seyfort Ruegg, however, speculates as to the possibility of an early Madhyamaka interest in *tathāgatagarbha* ideas in the texts of Rāhulabhadra and Nāga (possibly Nāgārjuna's pupils), see Ruegg (1981), pp. 55–56. This, however, was never a mainstream focus of the Madhyamaka tradition. In fact it is only in the late Madhyamaka of Kumarīla that aspects of the *tathāgatagarbha* strand of thought were integrated into Indian Buddhist scholasticism (see Ruegg (1981), pp. 95; 102–103). This probably reflects scholastic uneasiness with the *tathāgatagarbha* stress on faith (*śraddhā*), and the problems of reconciling the apparent absolutism of these texts with the mainstream Mahāyāna position.

27. See Chang, p. 380, and Wayman, ibid., pp. 104–105.

28. Translation in Wayman, ibid., pp. 104–105. See also Chang, ibid., p. 380.

29. Chang, p. 378.

30. Wayman, p. 99.

31. Chang, p. 380.

32. In fact on this issue of the non-existence of the path compare the view expounded in GK 11.32 with that of the *Ratnagotravibhāga* that describes the fourth noble truth (of the path leading to the extinction of suffering) as a *dharma* of a false and deceptive nature (*mṛṣāmoṣadharmin*) that is untrue (*asatya*). See Takasaki (1966), ibid., p. 182.

33. The *Śrīmālā*'s transitional position leaves certain philosophical problems unresolved. For a more detailed discussion of this see Richard King (1995), "Is 'Buddha-Nature' Buddhist? Doctrinal Tensions in The Śrīmālā Sūtra—An Early Tathāgatagarbha Text" in *Numen* forthcoming.

34. The restriction of salvation to certain individuals, based upon the fact that certain groups were not part of the Buddha's "lineage" (*gotra*), was a feature particularly associated with the Yogācāra tradition, that based itself upon certain references to this idea in the the *Mahāyānasūtrālaṃkāra*. The doctrine of the universality of salvation and the subsequent "redemption" of all beings of whatever doctrinal or ethical persuasion was a feature of the *tathāgatagarbha* texts and caused a stir in Chinese phiiosophical circles when these latter sections were first translated. (We have at the same time in Christian circles a similar controversy based upon Origen's doctrine of universal redemption). See Ruegg (1969).

35. See Kosho Yamamoto, *The Mahāyāna Parinirvāṇa-Sūtra, a Complete Translation from the Classical Chinese Language in Three Volumes*, vol I, (1973), (Karinbunko), Chapter 10, p. 173.

36. Yamamoto, I : p. 53.

37. Yamamoto, I : p. 178.

38. Yamamoto, Vol I, Book VII, p. 12.

39. Yamamoto ibid., I : p. 181.

40. Trans. Yamamoto, I : chapter 2, p. 39.

41. Williams (1989), p. 99.

42. The Indo-Tibetan tradition is unaware of a Saramati and attributes the commentary to Asaṅga. However, despite certain doctrinal elements of the text that presuppose Yogācāra ideas, the *Ratnagotra* is clearly different in approach and interpretation from the works of the Asaṅga-Vasubandhu school. Takasaki in fact believes that the prose section is earlier than Asaṅga but later than Nāgārjuna and Āryadeva, placing it sometime around the middle of the third century CE. Nevertheles, the final version of the *Ratnagotra* seems to presuppose certain ideas of the Yogācāra school and so must be later than the works of Asaṅga and Vasubandhu. See Takasaki (1966), ibid., p. 62.

43. With regard to dating the RGV one shold note that the *Ratnagotra* never refers to the *Laṅkāvatāra Sūtra*, which may have been contemporaneous with it. Brown suggests (ibid., p. 39n.) that the *Ratnagotra* deliberately omits references to the text because it disagrees with its association of the *ālayavijñāna* with the *tathāgatagarbha*. Grosnick (1979, ibid., p. 27 note 43.) suggests that in omitting the *Śrīmālā*'s reference to the *tathāgatagarbha* as the support (*ādhāra*) of saṃsāric *dharmas* (while quoting the verses around it), the RGV may be expressing its disagreement with the *Laṅkāvatāra*. If this were the case, the RGV could not be later than 433 CE since this is the date of the first translation of the *Laṅkāvatārasūtra* into Chinese. Nevertheless, Grosnick's point notwithstanding, there is no internal evidence to support the claim that the RGV presupposes the doctrines of the *Laṅkāvatāra*.

44. Cf. *vikalpa* in the Yogācāra school, see chapter five.

45. Trans. Takasaki, p. 167.

46. See Takasaki, pp. 156–157.

47. e.g. see RGV, Takasaki, p. 297.

48. See Takasaki (1966), *A Study of the Ratnagotravibhāga*, pp. 208–209.

49. Takasaki, ibid., p. 240f.

50. Trans. Takasaki, p. 237.

51. Sallie King, ibid., p. 226.

52. Sallie King, ibid., abstract of thesis.

53. Ruegg (1989), p. 26f.

54. Ruegg here refers us to RGV; pp. 156–157; *LaṅkāvatāraSūtra* ii. p. 78; and Candrakīrti in *Madhyamakāvatāra* VI.95.

55. Brown (1981), ibid., p. 249.

56. Brown (1981), ibid., pp. 154–155. See also his revised publication of this study, (1991, Motilal Banarsidass), pp. 90–91.

57. Keenan (1980), unpublished Ph.D. thesis, pp. 99–100.

58. See Ruegg (1989), p. 37.

59. D. T. Suzuki, *The Laṅkāvatāra Sūtra* ii, pp. 77–78.

60. William Grosnick criticizes interpretations of the *tathāgatagarbha* as some form of "monistic Absolute." He suggests, for instance, that references to the "essential purity of mind" should be regarded as nothing more than a declaration of the absence (or non-arising) of conceptualization (*vikalpa/prapañca*) (see Grosnick, ibid., pp. 60–61). Again this is an example of the cataphatic interpretation of *tathāgatagarbha* texts, that is the view that these texts are expediently making *prima facie* absolutistic statements in an attempt to provide a more positive or cataphatic expression of the Mahāyāna message. This is merely a variation on Tibetan attempts to account for the discrepancy between the Madhyamaka view of emptiness and the views outlined in the various *tathāgatagarbha* texts on the grounds that the latter either "require further interpretation" (*neyārtha*), or were "definitive" (*nītārtha*) but meta-theoretical. The former classification of *tathāgatagarbha* texts is hermeneutically very useful but is rather dubious given the RGV's subtitle as "the final teaching of the Mahāyāna" (*mahāyānottaratantra*). The question of "requiring further interpretation" to understand the *tathāgatagarbha* notion is also firmly denied by the *Śrīmālā* that states that its exposition of "the lion's roar of the Tathāgata's teaching" is based upon the ultimate truth (*nītārtha* see Chang, p. 374; cf. Wayman, p. 88). Indeed for these texts it is the traditional Buddhist emphasis upon impermanence, suffering, and no-self that requires further interpretation and not the *tathāgatagarbha* that is explained via the teaching of the four noble truths (and not *vice versa*).

61. Ruegg, 1989, p. 53; see also pp. 37–38.

62. Ruegg, 1989, ibid., p. 3.

63. The term "mainstream textual Buddhism" is used here to denote the doctrines expounded in the cardinal texts of the three important movements within Indian Buddhist philosophy, i.e. the Abhidharma, the Madhyamaka, and the Yogācāra schools.

64. Paul Williams (1989), *Mahāyāna Buddhism*, p. 132.

65. Acknowledging the possibility of diversity within the Mahāyāna tradition, Gadjin Nagao goes so far as to suggest that the *tathāgatagarbha* emphasis is actually upon non-emptiness (*aśūnyatā*) and not emptiness at all. (Gadjin Nagao, "What Remains in *Śūnyatā* in Mahāyāna Buddhist Meditation (1978), pp. 66–82. See especially pp. 76–77). Appealing to this idea Grosnick notes that, "Consequently, it would seem that the use of the term *śūnya* in the *tathāgatagarbha* literature differs some from the use of the term in the Mādhyamikan treatises and the *Prajñāpāramitāsūtras*, for it does not apply to all *dharmas*, but only to *kleśas*. Moreover, the non-emptiness of the *buddhadharmas* is obviously related to the "existence" (*astitva*) of the *buddhadhātu* [that is, the *tathāgatagarbha*], and this positive assertion of existence would seem to depart from the traditional middle-path doctrine of neither existence nor non-existence, of which the concept of *śūnyatā* was the traditional expression." (Grosnick, ibid., pp. 74–75). Nevertheless, for Grosnick the two conceptions of emptiness are not contradictory since the Madhyamaka usage is philosophical while the *tathāgatagarbha* usage is practical and propadeutical (see also Ruegg (1989), ibid., pp. 8 and 11). However, as we have noted, despite the practical orientation of the *tathāgatagarbha* texts and the emphasis upon the dichotomy between purity and defilement rather than the more philosophical dichotomies, the *tathāgatagarbha* restriction of *śūnyatā* as applicable only to conditioned factors (*saṃskṛta dharmas*) is a clear qualification of the Madhyamaka doctrine of the universality of *śūnyatā*.

66. The RGV defines emptiness in identical terms to *Madhyānta-vibhāga-bhāṣya* I..1 (traditionally attributed to either Asaṅga or Vasubandhu) stating that *yad yatra nāsti tat tena śūnyam iti samanupaśyati, yat punar atrāvaśiṣṭaṃ bhavati tat sad ihāstīti yathābhūtaṃ prajānāti*. "Thus, wherever something is lacking, this is observed as "void" (*śūnya*) in that place (*tena*), whatever remains there, one knows that this being must exist there" (Trans. Takasaki, ibid., p. 301) Asaṅga also defines emptiness in almost identical terms in his *Bodhisattva-bhūmi*. (The only difference being that he substitutes "*na bhavati*" for "*nāsti*" in the first line, see Wogihara's edition of the *Bodhisattva-Bhūmi*, p. 47). Both the Yogācāra and the *tathāgatagarbha* definitions seem to be allusions to the conception of emptiness laid out in the *Cūlasuññatasutta* of the Pali canon (*Majjhima Nikāya* 123, tome III). It is important to note, however, that the context within which the *tathāgatagarbha* texts and Asaṅga utilize the concept of "*śūnyatā*" radically differ. In the *Bodhisattva-bhūmi* Asaṅga uses emptiness in a philosophical and broadly speaking epistemological context to explain the relationship between a designation (*prajñapti*) and its referent (*vastu*). As with the usage of the term in the *Madhyānta-vibhāga-bhāṣya*, Asaṅga's interest is in the status of the "given object" (*vastu*) and its relationship to our perception and

labeling of it. The *paratantrasvabhāva* is empty of *parikalpita* (constructions), but is not totally non-existent. In the *tathāgatagarbha* texts a similar point is made but in this context the unconditioned *dharmakāya* is empty of all constructed factors (*saṃskṛta*). This view would have been unaccepuble to the early Yogācārins, insofar as it postulated an unconditioned ultimate reality.

67. The view put forward in the *tathāgatagarbha* texts represent a radical change in perspective among some Mahāyāna Buddhists with regard to the central insights of the Buddhist tradition, notably the threefold formula of impermanence, suffering, and no-self. Clearly there is a different understanding of *anātman* at work here where no-self is applied to all *saṃskāras* but not to all *dharmas*. Thus the unconditioned or uncompounded *dharmas* remain and emptiness now means "empty of *saṃskṛta dharmas*" and not "empty of *svabhāva*" (which is *asaṃskṛta*).

68. Ruegg (1963), "The Jo naṅ pas : A School of Buddhist Ontologists According to the Grub mthasel gyi me lon" in *Journal of American Oriental Society* 83 p. 74. See also Lobsang Dargyay, "What is Non-existent and What is Remanent in *śūnyatā*" in *Journal of Indian Philosophy* 18 (1990), pp. 81–91.

69. This reflects the incommensurability of the two positions in Tibetan Mahāyāna. Each perspective is contradictory from the point of view of the other. This is also a common feature of philosophy in India where shifting paradigms and philosophical assumptions make previous points of view seem incomprehensible. Although the two perspectives are incommensurable *on the same level* as explanations of the world each tradition can (and indeed does) accept the other on a provisional basis, that is as a step in the right direction.

70. P. Williams (1982), "Silence and Truth—Some Aspects of the Madhyamaka Philosophy in Tibet" in *The Tibet Journal*, Spring/Summer 1982, Vol. VII, pp. 73–74.

71. See for instance Aṅguttara Nikāya I.10 and Majjhima Nikāya I.433 Samyutta nikāya V.92 etc.

72. Ruegg (1963), ibid., pp. 74–75. See also Guenther (1976), Philosophy and Psychology in the Abhidharma, p. 233.

73. See Ruegg (1981), pp. 34 and 35n. for an interesting discussion of Nāgārjuna and *gzhaṅ stong pa*. Nāgārjuna clearly is not an exponent of this latter interpretation of the Buddhist Path, at least in the logical corpus of his texts. Thus in MMK 7:33 he says: "With the non-establishment of origination, duration and destruction, the compounded does not exist; and if the compounded is not established, how can there be an uncompounded?" This statement is a reversal of the position found in the "unconditioned mind"

doctrine where the conditioned (*saṃskṛta*) is said to depend for its existence upon the unconditioned (*asaṃskṛta*).

74. This idea is implicitly pre-figured in the *Śrīmālā Sūtra*, where the noble truths of suffering, the cause of suffering and the path leading to its cessation are all said to be ultimately illusory. This is an astonishing admission for a Buddhist text to make, for it appears to circumvent the very basis of Buddhist soteriology. See Chang, ibid., pp. 378–379.

75. For evidence of these "two traditions" see the introduction to Lamotte, Etienne (1962) *L'Enseignment de Vimalakīrti*, (Louvaine, Bibliotheque de Muséon, Sacred Books of the Buddhists Vol XXXII, Pali Text Society 1976 edition), pp. lxxii–lxxxi.

76. D.T. Suzuki (1907), *Outlines of Mahāyāna Buddhism*, (1963 Schocken Books Inc., pp. 144–145).

77. *Udāna*, p. 80, cap. viii, translation by Woodward, (1973), *Some Sayings of the Buddha*, p. 220.

78. The term "strand" is being used here not to represent self-conscious and philosophically autonomous traditions but rather intertwined streams of thought, that may co-exist across traditional doctrinal and scholastic boundaries.

79. Takasaki suggests that the *Tathāgatagarbha* tradition was prevented from developing into a distinctive school because of the subsequent absorption of many of its basic ideas by the developing Yogācāra. (Takasaki (1966), ibid., p. 58). Post-classical Yogācāra (that is, after Asaṅga and Vasubandhu) appears to diverge into separate strands, each with their own distinctive interpretation of the Yogācāra path. Paramārtha, for instance, shows a great propensity for *tathāgatagarbha* ideas and is likely to have been influenced by them in his postulation of a ninth level of awareness, the *amalavijñāna* or "undefiled consciousness." The idea of the innate purity of mind (*viśuddhi-citta-prakṛti*) is a distinctive feature of the *tathāgatagarbha* tradition and was in many respects already assimilated into the Yogācāra system via such pre-Asaṅgan texts as the *Mahāyānasūtrālaṃkāra* and the *Madhyāntavibhāga* that openly declare the adventitiousness (*āgantuka*) of the defilements (e.g. MV I.23). These texts are at variance with the emphasis upon the purely phenomenal nature of consciousness in the works of Asaṅga and Vasubandhu. However, their brevity and cryptic mode of expression allows for a variety of different interpretations. Thus, in later Yogācāra we have the development of what appears to be a fully blown idealistic system, upholding consciousness as the sole ontological reality (*vijñānavāda*). This is not the position of Asaṅga and Vasubandhu, however, for whom *vijñāna* is merely one of the five *skandhas* and as such is neither an ultimate nor an all-encompassing reality.

80. Despite its apparent absolutism (or perhaps because of it), the *tathāgatagarbha* position appears to conform to the Buddhist *pudgala-*

nairātmya since it denies the reality of a personal and conditioned self (*pudgala*). A systematic rendering of the *tathāgatagarbha* conception of no-self could be analyzed into the following formulae:

i.) "all formations are without self" (*sarva-saṃskārā anātmatāḥ*), and

ii.) "all uncompounded *dharmas* are without a personal self" (*sarva asaṃskṛtā-dharmāpudgalā-nairātmyā*). This remains a form of *pudgala-nairātmya*, but restricts the selflessness of *dharmas* to those which are conditioned (*saṃskṛta*). That which is unconditioned remains an ultimate reality.

Conclusions

1. Christian Lindtner (1985), "Remarks on the *Gauḍapādīya-kārikās*," in *Indo-Iranian Journal* 28 (1985), pp. 277–279.

2. Thomas E. Wood (1990), *The Māṇḍūkya Upaniṣad and the Āgama-śāstra: An Investigation into the Meaning of the Vedānta* (University of Hawaii Press, Monographs of the Society for Asian and Comparative Philosophy, no. 8). Wood's view is that GK IV in particular is a post-Śaṅkarite work. See chapter 1 of this book for more on this issue.

3. See chapter 5. See also the work of Thomas Kochumottum (1982), *A Buddhist Philosophy of Experience: A New Translation and Interpretation of the Works of Vasubandhu the Yogācārin* (Motilal Banarsidass), and Janice Dean Willis (1979), *On _nowing Reality: The Tattvārtha Chapter of Asaṅga's Bodhisattva-bhūmi*, (Motilal Banarsidass, Delhi), and more recently Ian Harris (1991), *The Continuity of Madhyamaka and Yogācāra in Indian Mahāyāna Buddhism* (E J Brill, Leiden, and New York).

4. Tilmann Vetter (1978), "Die *Gauḍapādīya-Kārikā* Zur Entstehung und zur Bedeutung von (A)dvaita" in *Wiener Zeitschrift Kunde Süd-Asien* XXII, pp. 95–133. See especially sections 4.1 and 4.2.

5. Alexander Hixon Jr. (1976), *Mahāyana Buddhist influence on the Gauḍa school of Advaya Vedānta: An Analysis of the Gauḍapāda-Kārikā*, (unpublished Ph.D. thesis, University of Wisconsin), agrees with this statement, suggesting likewise that the GK is a composite work of a Bengali school of Pre-Śaṅkarite "Advaya Vedānta." Hixon, though, has a much more radical conception of the composite nature of the text.

6. Both Bhattacharya (1943) and Hixon (1976) argue that the invocation in GK IV.1 is to the Buddha. This view is, of course, disputed by the traditionalist positions of Mahadevan (1952) and Karmarkar (1953). An analysis of the occurrences of the term *buddha* in GK IV and the references to the non-dual

jñāna of the *buddha* in GK IV.1 establishes the link between the *buddha* of GK IV.1 and the Buddha of GK IV.99 (that even the traditional commentator takes to be a reference to the founder of the Buddhist religion).

7. Thomas E. Wood (1990), *The Māṇḍūkya Upaniṣad and the Āgama śāstra: An Investigation into the Meaning of the Vedānta* (University of Hawaii Press, Monographs of the Society for Asian and Comparative Philosophy, no. 8), pp. 71–81.

8. This is in accordance with the view recently expressed by Paul Williams (1989), (see pp. 105–108), but against David Seyfort Ruegg (1969, 1989), William Grosnick (1979), Brian Brown (1990), and Sallie King (1991). Only Williams and Ruegg fully consider the *tathāgatagarbha* texts in the light of the later Tibetan debates.

9. The view that the *tathāgatagarbha* texts do not conform to the *raṅ stong pa* (self-emptiness view) is put forward by Paul Williams (1989). See also Ruegg (1981), pp. 34–35 for a discussion of this issue.

Bibliography

Agrawal, Madan Mohan (1986), "The Origin and Development of the Doctrine of Difference and Non-difference," in *Aspects of Indian Philosophy* (Shree Publishing House, New Delhi, India): 1–23.

Anacker, Stefan (1984), *Seven Works of Vasubandhu: The Buddhist Psychological Doctor* (Religions of Asia Series No. 4, Motilal Banarsidass).

Bareau, Andre (1955), *Les Premiers Conciles Bouddhiques* (Paris).

Bareau, Andre (1956), *Les Sectes Bouddhiques du Petit Vehicule* (Paris).

Bhattacharya, Vidhushekhara (1943), The *Āgamaśāstra of Gauḍapāda*, (University of Calcutta Press).

Biderman, Shlomo (1978), "Śaṅkara and the Buddhists" in *Journal of Indian Philosophy* 6: 405–413.

Bradley, Francis Herbert (1893), *Appearance and Reality* (Oxford, Clarendon Press).

Brown, Brian (1981), *The Buddha Nature: A Study of the "Tathāgatagarbha" and "Ālayavijñāna"* (Ph.D. thesis, New York University, revised and published by Motilal Banarsidass, 1991).

Buescher, John (1982), *The Buddhist Doctrine of Two Truths in the Vaibhāṣika and Theravāda schools* (unpublished Ph.D. thesis, University of Virginia).

Chang, Garma (1971), *The Buddhist Teaching of Totality: The Philosophy of Hwa Yen Buddhism* (Pennsylvania State University Press).

Chang, Garma (1983) (ed.), *A Treasury of Mahāyāna Sūtras: Selections from the Mahāratnakūṭa-Sūtra* (Pennsylvania State University Press).

Cole, Colin (1982), *Asparśa Yoga: A Study of Gauḍapāda's Māṇḍūkya Kārikā* (Motilal Banarsidass, Delhi).

Collins, Steven (1983), *Selfless Persons: Imagery and Thought in Theravāda Buddhism* (Cambridge University Press).

Conio, C. (1971), *The Philosophy of the Māṇḍūkya-Kāikā* (Arun Press, Varanasi).

Conze, Edward (1953), "The Ontology of the Prajñāpāramitā" in *Philosophy East and West* 3: 117–129.

Conze, Edward (1962), *Buddhist Thought in India* (George Allen and Unwin, London).

Conze, Edward (1967), "The Development of Prajñāpāramitā Thought" in *Thirty Years of Buddhist Studies*: 123–147.

Conze, Edward (1973a), *The Short Prajñāpāramitā Texts* (Luzac and Company Ltd, London).

Conze, Edward (1973b), *The Perfection of Wisdom in Eight Thousand Lines and its Verse Summary* (Four Seasons Foundation, Bolinas).

Conze, Edward (1975), *The Large Sūtra on Perfect Wisdom* (University of California Press, Berkeley and Los Angeles).

Conze, Edward (1978), *The Prajñāpāramitā Literature* (Second Edition, Tokyo, The Reiyukai).

Conze, Edward (1980), *A Short History of Buddhism* (Allen and Unwin, Hemel Hempstead, Great Britain).

Conze, Edward (1988), *Buddhist Wisdom Books* (Second Edition, Unwin Hyman Ltd., New Zealand).

Dargyay, Lobsang (1990), "What is Non-existent and What is Remanent in *śūnyatā*" in *Journal of Indian Philosophy* 18: 81–91.

Dasgupta, Surendranath (1922), *The History of Indian Philosophy* (Indian Edition, 1975, Motilal Banarsidass, Delhi) Vol I–IV.

Deussen, Paul (1906), *The Philosophy of the Upanishads* (1966, Dover Publications, New York).

Deutsch, Eliot (1969), *Advaita Vedānta: a Philosophical Reconstruction* (East-West Center Press, Honolulu).

Dowling, Thomas (1976), *Vasubandhu on the Avijñapti-Rūpa: A Study in Fifth-Century Abhidharma Buddhism* (unpublished Ph.D. thesis, Columbia University).

Dutt, Nalinaska (1978), *Mahayana Buddhism* (Revised edition, Motilal Banarsidass, Delhi).

Elder, George (ed. 1976), *Buddhist Insight: Essays by Alex Wayman* (Religions of Asia Series No. 5, Motilal Banarsidass).

Eliade, Mircea (1963), *Myth and Reality* (translated by Willard R. Trask, New York, Harper & Row).

Fort, Andrew (1990), *The Self and Its States: A States of Consciousness Doctrine in Advaita Vedānta* (Motilal Banarsidass, Delhi).

Frauwallner, Erich (1970), *History of Indian Philosophy* Vol I, translation by V. M. Bedekar (Motilal Banarsidass).

Gambhīrānanda, Swāmi (1957), *Eight Upaniṣads* Vol I (Advaita Ashrama, Calcutta).

Gambhīrānanda, Swāmi (1958), *Eight Upaniṣads* Vol II (Advaita Ashrama, Calcutta).

Gambhīrānanda, Swāmi (1965), *The Brahmasūtrabhāṣya of Śaṅkarācārya* (Advaita Ashrama, Calcutta).

Ghate, V. S. (1981), *The Vedānta: A study of the Brahma-Sūtras with the bhāṣyas of Samkara, Rāmānuja, Nimbārka, Madhva, and Vallabha* (Third edition, Bhandarkar Oriental Research Institute, Poona).

Gokhale, V. V. (1958), "The Vedānta Philosophy Described by Bhavya in His Madhyamakahṛdayakārikā" in *Indo-Iranian Journal* 2 No. 3: 163–180.

Gokhale, V. V. (1962), "Masters of Buddhism Adore the Brahman Through Non-Adoration" (Bhavya, Madhyamakahṛdaya, III) in *Indo-Iranian Journal* 5 No. 4: 271–275.

Gombrich, Richard (1988), *Theravāda Buddhism: A Social History from Ancient Benares to Modern Colombo* (Routledge, London).

Griffiths, Paul (1986), *On Being Mindless: Buddhist Meditation and the Mind-Body Problem* (Open Court, Illinois).

Griffith, Ralph T. (1973), *The Hymns of the Rig Veda* (New Revised Edition, Edited by J. L. Shastri, Delhi).

Grosnick, Willam (1979), *The Zen Master Dogen's Understanding of the Buddha-Nature in Light of the Historical Development of the Buddha-Nature Concept in India, China, and Japan* (unpublished Ph.D. thesis, University of Wisconsin).

Gudmunsen (1977), *Wittgenstein and Buddhism* (New York).

Guenther, Herbert (1976), *Philosophy and Psychology in the Abhidharma* (Routledge and Kegan, USA).

Hacker, Paul (1972), "Notes on the *Māṇḍūkyopaniṣad* and Śaṇkara's *Agamasastravivarana*" in Gaeffke, P. and Ensink, J. (ed.), *India Maior* (Leiden, E. J. Brill, 1972): 115–133.

Harris, Ian (1991), *The Continuity of Madhyamaka and Yogācāra in Indian Mahāyāna Buddhism* (E. J. Brill).

Harrison, Paul (1978), "*Buddhanusmṛtī* in the *Pratyutpanna-Buddha-Sammukavasthita-Samādhi-Sūtra*" in *Journal of Indian Philosophy* 6: 35–57.

Hattori (1968), *Dignāga On Perception: being the Pratyakṣa-pariccheda of Dignāga: Pramānasamuccaya* (Cambridge, Harvard University Press).

Hattori (1982), "The Dream Simile in Vijñānavāda Treatises" in Hercus *et al.* (1982), *Indological and Buddhist Studies in honour of J. W. Jong on his sixtieth birthday* (Australia).

Hirabayashi, Jay and Iida, Shotaro (1977), "Another Look at the Mādhyamika vs Yogācāra Controversy Concerning Existence and Non-existence" in Lancaster, Lewis (ed.) *Prajñāpāramitā and Related Systems: Studies in Honour of Edward Conze.*

Hixon, A. (1976), *Mahāyana Buddhist influence on the Gauḍa school of Advaya Vedānta: An Analysis of the Gauḍapādakārikā*, (unpublished Ph.D. thesis, University of Wisconsin).

Hume (1931), *The Thirteen Principal Upanishads* (Second Revised Edition, Oxford University Press).

Huntington, C. W. Jr. (1989), *The Emptiness of Emptiness: An Introduction to Early Indian Mādhyamika* (University of Hawaii Press).

Inada, Kenneth (1970), *The Mūlamadhyamakakārikā* (Hokuseido Press, Tokyo).

Inazu, Kizow (1967), "The concept of Vijñapti and Vijñāna in the Text of Vasubandhu's Vijñaptimātratāsiddhi" in *Journal of Indian Buddhist Studies* 16:. 474–468.

Ingalls, D. D. (1954), "Śaṇkara's Arguments Against the Buddhists" in *Philosophy East and West* 3, No.4: 291–306.

Jaini, "The Sautrāntika Theory of Bija" in *Bulletin of the School of Oriental and African Studies* vol XXII: 236–249.

Jaini, "*Prajña* and *dṛṣṭi* in the Vaibhāṣika Abhidharma" in Lancaster, Lewis (ed.) *Prajñāpāramitā and Related Systems: Studies in Honour of Edward Conze:* 403–410.

Jayatilleke, K. N. (1963), *The Early Buddhist Theory of Knowledge* (Allen and Unwin Ltd).

Jones, Elwin W. (1978), "Buddhist Theories of Existents: The System of Two Truths" in Kiyota (ed.), *Mahāyāna Buddhist Meditation* (University of Hawaii Press, Honolulu): 3–45.

Joshi, L. (1977), *Studies in the Buddhistic Culture of India* (Second Edition, Motilal Banarsidass).

Kajiyama, Yuichi (1966), "Controversy Between the sākāra- and nirākāra-vādins of the Yogācāra school—some materials" in *Journal of Indian Buddhist Studies* 14: 429–418.

Kajiyama, Yuichi (1969), "Bhāvāviveka, Sthiramati, and Dharmapāla" in *Wiener Zeitschrift Für die Kunde Süd-Und Ostasiens* 13: 193–203.

Kajiyama, Yuichi (1971), "The Atomic Theory of Vasubandhu, the Author of the Abhidharmakośa" in *Journal of Indian Buddhist Studies* 19: 20–24.

Kalupahana, David J. (1986), *Nāgārjuna: The Philosophy of the Middle Way,* (State University of New York Press, New York).

Kaplan, S. (1983), "A Critique of an Ontological Approach to Gauḍapāda's Māṇḍūkya Kārikās" in *Journal of Indian Philosophy* 11: 339–355.

Kaplan, S. (1987), *Hermeneutics, Holography, and Indian Idealism* (Motilal Banarsidass, Delhi).

Karmarkar, R. D. (1953), *The Gauḍapāda-kārikā* (Govt. Oriental Series–Class B, No. 9, Poona, Bhandarkar Oriental Research Institute).

Katsura, Shoryu (1978), "Harivarman on Sarvāstivāda" in *Journal of Indian Buddhist Studies* 26, No. 2: 22–26.

Keenan, John P. (1980), *A Study of the Buddhabhūmupadeśa: The Doctrinal development of the Notion of Wisdom in Yogācāra thought* (unpublished Ph.D. thesis, University of Wisconsin, USA).

Keenan, John P. (1982), "Original Purity and the Focus of Early Yogācāra" in *Journal of the International Association of Buddhist Studies* 5. No. 1: 7–18.

Keenan, John P. (1989), *The Meaning of Christ: A Mahayana Theology* (Orbis Books).

King, Richard (1989), "*Śūnyatā* and *Ajāti*: Absolutism and the Philosophies of Nāgārjuna and Gauḍapāda" in *Journal of Indian Philosophy* 17: 385–405.

King, Richard (1991a), "Brahman and the World: Immanence and Transcendence in Advaita Vedānta—a Comparative Perspective." in *Scottish Journal of Religious Studies* Vol 12 No. 2: 107–126.

King, Richard (1991b), Review of Andrew Fort's, *The Self and Its States* in *Scottish Journal of Religious Studies* Vol XII No. 1: 65–67.

King, Richard (1994), "Early Yogācāra and Its Relationship with the Madhyamaka School" in *Philosophy East and West* 44, No. 4, pp. 659–684.

King, Richard (1994), "Is 'Buddha-Nature' Buddhist? Doctrinal Tensions in The *Śrīmālā Sūtra*—An Early *Tathāgatagarbha* Text" in *Numen*, forthcoming.

King, Sallie (1981), *The Active Self: A Philosophical Study of the "Buddha-Nature Treatise"* (Ph.D. thesis, Temple University, USA).

Kiyoṭa, M. (ed.) (1978), *Mahāyāna Buddhist Meditation: Theory and Practice* (University of Hawaii Press, Honolulu).

Kochumottum, Thomas (1982), *A Buddhist Philosophy of Experience: A New Translation and Interpretation of the Works of Vasubandhu the Yogācārin* (Motilal Banarsidass).

Lamotte, Etienne (1935), *The Saṃdhinirmocana-Sūtra* (Université de Louvaine).

Lamotte, Etienne (1938), *La Somme du Grand Vehicle D'Asaṅga* (Louvaine, Bureaux de Muséon).

Lamotte, Etienne (1958), Histoire de Bouddhisme Indien (1988, English translation, *A History of Indian Buddhism*, by Sara Boin).

Lamotte, Etienne (1962), *L'Enseignment de Vimalakīrti*, (Louvaine, Bibliotheque de Muséon, Sacred Books of the Buddhists Vol XXXII, Pali Text Society 1976 edition).

Lancaster, Lewis (1968), *An Analysis of the Aṣṭasāhasrikā-Prajñāpāramitā* (unpublished Ph.D. thesis, University of Wisconsin).

Lang, Karen (1986), *Āryadeva's Catuḥśataka: On the Bodhisattva's Cultivation of Merit and Knowledge* (Indiste Studier 7, Akademisk Forlag, Copenhagen).

Larson, G. J. and Bhattacharya, R. S. (1987), *Encyclopaedia of Indian Philosophies Vol IV: Sāṁkhya—A Dualist tradition in Indian Philosophy,* (Princeton University Press).

Lesimple, Em. (1944), *Māṇḍūkya Upaniṣad et Kārikā de Gauḍapāda* (Librairie D'Amérique et D'Orient, General Editor: Louis Renou).

Levi, S. (1925), *Mahāyānasūtrālaṃkāra: expose de la doctrine du grand véhicule selon le systeme Yogācāra,* (Paris, H. Champion).

Lindtner, Chr. (1982), *Nāgārjuniana* (Motilal Banarsidass, Delhi).

Lindtner, Chr. (1984), "Bhavya's Controversy with Yogācāra in the Appendix to *Prajñāpradīpa,* Chapter XXV" in Ligeti (1984), *Tibetan and Buddhist Studies: Commemorating the 200th Anniversary of the Birth of Alexander Csoma De Koros* Vol XXIX/2, 77–97.

Lindtner, Chr. (1985), "Remarks on the *Gauḍapādīya-kārikās,*" in *Indo-Iranian Journal* 28 (1985), 275–279.

Mackey, Linda Kay Barabas (1983), *Reflections on Advaita Vedānta: The Approach of the Gauḍapāda-Kārikā on the Māṇḍūkya Upaniṣad with Śaṇkara's Commentary,* (unpublished Ph.D. thesis, University of Texas at Austin).

Mādhavānanda (1965), *The Bṛhadāraṇyaka Upaniṣad,* (Fourth Edition, Advaita Ashrama, Calcutta).

Mahadevan, T. M. P. (1952), *Gauḍapāda: A Study in Early Advaita* (Madras).

Matilal, B. K. (1977), *The Logical Illumination of Indian Mysticism.*

Mayeda, Sengaku (1968), "On the Author of the *Māṇḍūkyopaniṣad* and the *Gauḍapādīyabhāṣya*," in *Adyar Library Bulletin* 31–32: 73–94.

Monier-Williams (1988 edition), *Sanskrit-English Dictionary*.

Murti, T. R. V. (1955), *The Central Philosophy of Buddhism: A Study of the Mādhyamika System* (Allen and Unwin, Great Britain).

Nagao, Gadjin (1978), "What Remains in *Śūnyatā*" in Kiyota (ed.), (1978), *Mahāyāna Buddhist Meditation*: 66–82.

Nagao, Gadjin (1989), *The Foundational Standpoint of Madhyamika Philosophy* (State University of New York Press, New York).

Nagao, Gadjin (1991), *Madhyamika and Yogācāra: A Study of Mahāyāna Philosophies—Collected Papers of G. M. Nagao* (translated by Leslie S. Kawamura, State University of New York Press, New York).

Nakamura, Hajime (1980), *Indian Buddhism: A Survey with Bibliographical Notes* (Motilal Banarsidass).

Nakamura, Hajime (1983), *A History of Early Vedānta Philosophy* Vol 1 (Motilal Banarsidass).

Narain, Harsha (1985), "The Nature of Mādhyamika Thought" in Chhogdup (ed.), *Mādhyamika Dialectic and The Philosophy of Nāgārjuna* (Central Institute of Higher Tibetan Studies, Sarnath, Varanasi): 227–256.

Obermiller, *History of Buddhism by Bu-ston,* Vol I, (Heidelberg, Harrassowitz, 1931).

O'Flaherty, W. D. "Karma and Rebirth in the Vedas and the Purāṇas" in O'Flaherty (1980) (ed.), *Karma and Rebirth in Classical Indian Traditions* (University of California Press, 1980): 3–37.

Osaki, A. (1977–78), "What is meant by destroying the *ālayavijñāna*?" in *Journal of Indian Buddhist Studies* Vol 26 (1977–78): 1064–1069.

Pandey, Sangamlal (1974), *Pre-Śaṇkara Advaita Philosophy* (Allahabad).

Piatigorsky, A. (1984), *The Buddhist Philosophy of Thought* (Curzon Press).

Potter, Karl (1979), "Was Gaudapada an Idealist" in Nagatomi, Matilal, Masson, and Dimock (eds.), (1979), *Sanskrit and Indian Studies* (D. Reidel Publishing Company): 183–199.

Potter, Karl (1970), *Encyclopaedia of Indian Philosophies Vol I: Bibliography* (Motilal Banarsidass, Delhi).

Potter, Karl (1981) (ed.), *Encyclopaedia of Indian Philosophies Vol III: "Advaita Vedānta up to Śaṃkara and his pupils"* (Motilal Banarsidass): 103–114.

Priestley, C. D. C. (1970), "Emptiness in the '*Satyasiddhi*'" in *Journal of Indian Philosophy* 1: 33–39.

Qvarnström, Olle (1989), *Hindu Philosophy in Buddhist Perspective: the Vedāntatattvaviniścaya Chapter of Bhavya's Madhyamakahṛdayakārikā* (Lund Studies In African and Asian Religions Vol 4, Lund Plus Ultra).

Rahula, Walpola (1971), *Le Compendium de la Super-Doctrine (Philosophie) (Abhidharmasamuccaya) D'Asaṅga* (Publications De L'École Française D'Extrême-Orient, Vol LXXVIII).

Rahula, Walpola (1972), "*Vijñaptimātratā* Philosophy in the Yogācāra System—some wrong notions" in *Maha Bodhi* (1972): 324–30.

Rahula, Walpola (1978), *Zen and Taming of the Bull* (Gordon Fraser, London).

Raju, P. T. (1985), *Structural Depths of Indian Thought* (South Asian Publishers, New Delhi).

Rawlinson, Andrew (1972), "*Studies in the Lotus Sutra,*" (unpublished Ph.D. thesis, Lancaster University, Great Britain).

Rawlinson, Andrew (1977), "The Position of the *Aṣṭasāhasrikā Prajñāpāramitā* in the Development of Early Mahāyāna" in Lancaster, Lewis (ed.) (1977), *Prajñāpāramitā and Related Systems: Studies in Honour of Edward Conze:* 3–34.

Robinson, Richard (1967), *Early Mādhyamika in India and China* (Motilal Banarsidass, Delhi).

Robinson, Richard (1982), *The Buddhist Religion: A Historical Introduction,* (3rd edition, Wadsworth Inc., USA).

Roy, S. S. (1965), *The Heritage of Śaṇkara* (Allahabad, Udayana Publications).

Ruegg, David Seyfort (1963), "The Jo naṅ pas: A School of Buddhist Ontologists According to the Grub mthasel gyi me lon" in *Journal of American Oriental Society* 83.

Ruegg, David Seyfort (1969), *La Theorie du Tathāgatagarbha et du Gotra,* (Paris, École Française d'Extrême Orient).

Ruegg, David Seyfort (1981), *The Literature Of The Madhyamaka School Of Philosophy In India* (History of Indian Literature, Vol VII, Fasc. 1, Otto Harrassowitz, Wiesbaden).

Ruegg, David Seyfort (1986), "Does the Mādhyamika have a thesis and philosophical position?" in Matilal and Evans (ed.) *Buddhist Logic and Epistemology* (Dordrecht, Reidel, 1986): 229–237.

Saddhatissa, H. (1985), *The Sutta-Nipāta,* (Curzon Press Ltd.).

Sangharashita (1985), *The Eternal Legacy* (Tharpa Publications, London).

Schmithausen, L. (1973), "On the Problem of the Relation of Spiritual Practice and Philosophical Theory in Buddhism" in *German Scholars on India* Vol II: 235–250.

Sharma, Krishnamurti (1931), "New Light on the Gauḍapāda-Kārikās" in *Review of Philosophy and Religion* 1931: 35–56.

Shastri, Prabhu Dutt (1911), *The Doctrine of Māyā* (London, Luzac and Co.).

Sponberg, Alan (1979), "Dynamic Liberation in Yogācāra Buddhism" in *Journal of International Buddhist Studies* Vol 2. No. 1: 44–64.

Sprung, Mervyn (1979), *Lucid Exposition of the Middle Way: The Essential Chapters from the Prasannapadā of Candrakīrti* (Routledge Kegan and Paul, London).

Streng, Frederick (1967), *Emptiness: A Study in Religious Meaning* (Abingdon Press, Nashville).

Suzuki, D. T. (1907), *Outlines of Mahāyāna Buddhism* (1963, Schocken Books Inc.).

Suzuki, D. T. (1930), *Studies in the Laṅkāvatāra-Sūtra* (London).

Takakusu (1904–1905), "On the Abhidharma Literature of the Sarvāstivādins" in *Journal of the Pali Text Society* 67–146.

Takasaki, J. (1966), *A Study of the Ratnagotravibhāga (Uttaratantra): Being a Treatise on the Tathāgatagarbha Theory of Mahāyāna Buddhism,* (Serie Orientale Roma Vol XXXIII, Istituto Italiano Per Il Medio Ed Estremo Oriente, Rome).

Takasaki, J. (1987), *An Introduction to Buddhism*, translated by Rolf Giebel (Toho Gakkai, Tokyo).

Thurman, Robert (1984), *The Speech of Gold: Reason and Enlightenment in Tibetan Buddhism* (Princeton University Press).

Tucci, Giuseppe (1956), *Minor Buddhist Texts Part I* (Serie Orientale Roma Vol IX, Rome).

Ueda, Yoshifumi (1967), "Two Main Streams of Thought in Yogācāra Philosophy" in *Philosophy East and West* Vol 17: 155–165.

Venkata, Ramanan (1975), *Nāgārjuna's Philosophy as presented in the Mahā-Prajñāpāramitā-Śāstra,* (Motilal Banarsidass, Delhi).

Verdu, Alfonsu (1985), *Early Buddhist Philosophy in light of the Four Noble Truths* (Motilal Banarsidass, Delhi).

Vetter, T. (1978), Die *Gauḍapādīya-Kārikās*: Zur Entstehung und zur Bedeutung von (A)dvaita in *Wiener Zeitschrift für die Kunde Süd-Asiens* Vol XXII: 95–131.

Vetter, T. (1979), *Studien zur Lehre und Entwicklung Śaṅkaras* (Publications of the De Nobili Research Library. Oberhammer, G. (ed.), Indological Institute, University of Vienna, Vol VI. Wien).

Walleser (1910), *Der Altere Vedānta.* Geschichte, Kritik und Lehre (Heidelberg).

Warder, A. K. (1973), "Was Nāgārjuna a Mahayanist?" in Sprung (ed.), *The Problem of Two Truths In Buddhism and Vedānta.* (Dordrecht, Reidel).

Warder, A. K. (1980), *Indian Buddhism* (Second Edition, Motilal Banarsidass, Delhi).

Warren, Henry Clarke (1896), *Buddhism In Translations* (1962, Atheneum Press edition, New York).

Watanabe, (1983), *Philosophy and its Development in the Nikāyas and Abhidhamma* (Motilal Banarsidass, Delhi).

Wayman, Alex (1965), "Review Article of The Yogācāra Idealism" in *Philosophy East and West* 15 no. 1: 65–73.

Wayman, Alex, "Nescience and Insight according to Asaṅga" in Elder (ed. 1976), *Buddhist Insight*: 193–213.

Wayman, Alex, "The Mirror as a Pan-Buddhist Metaphor-Simile" in *History of Religions,* 13.4 (May 1974): 251–269, reprinted in G. Elder (ed., 1976) *Buddhist Insight.*

Wayman, Alex, "The Sixteen Aspects of the Four Noble Truths and Their Opposites" in Elder (ed., 1976), *Buddhist Insight.*

Wayman, Alex (1977), "Secret of the Heart Sūtra" in Lancaster, Lewis (ed.), *Prajñāpāramitā and Related Systems*: 135–152.

Wayman and Wayman, Alex and Hikedo (1974), *The Lion's Roar of Queen Śrīmālā* (New York).

Wayman, Alex, "Yogācāra and the Buddhist Logicians" in *Journal of International Buddhist Studies* Vol 2. No. 1: 65–78.

Werner, Karel, "Yoga and the Old Upaniṣads" in Connolly (ed.) *Perspectives on Indian Religion: Papers in Honour of Karel Werner* (Sri Satguru Publications, Delhi, 1986): 3–9.

Wezler, A. "Some Observations on the *Yuktidīpīka* in *Zeitschrift der Deutschen Morgenlandischen Gesellschaft,* Supplement II: 434–455.

Whaling, Frank (1979), "Śaṇkara and Buddhism" in *Journal of Indian Philosophy* 7: 1–42.

Williams, Paul (1980), "Some Aspects of Language and Construction in the Madhyamaka" in *Journal of Indian Philosophy* 8: 1–45.

Williams, Paul (1981), "On the Abhidharma Ontology" in *Journal of Indian Philosophy* 9: 227–257.

Williams, Paul (1982), "Silence and Truth—Some Aspects of the Madhyamaka Philosophy in Tibet" in *The Tibet Journal,* Spring/Summer 1982, Vol. VII.

Williams, Paul (1989), *Mahāyāna Buddhism: The Doctrinal Foundations* (Routledge and Kegan Paul, London).

Willis, Janice Dean (1979), *On Knowing Reality: The Tattvārtha Chapter of Asaṅga's Bodhisattvabhūmi* (Motilal Banarsidass, Delhi).

Wogihara, Unrai (ed.), (1930–1936), *Bodhisattvabhūmi,* (Tokyo).

Wood, Thomas E. (1990), *The Māṇḍūkya Upaniṣad and the Āgama śāstra: An Investigation into the Meaning of the Vedānta* (University of Hawaii Press, Monographs of the Society for Asian and Comparative Philosophy, no. 8).

Woodward, F. L. (1973), *Some Sayings of the Buddha according to the Pali canon* (Oxford University Press).

Yamada, Isshi (1977), "Vijñaptimātratā of Vasubandhu" in the *Journal of the Royal Asiatic Society* 1977: 158–176.

Yamamoto, Kosho (1973), *The Mahāyāna Parinirvāṇasūtra, a Complete Translation from the Classical Chinese Language in Three Volumes,* Vol I–III (Karinbunko).

Zaehner, R. C. (1969), *The Bhagavad Gītā,* (Oxford University Press).

Index

Abhidharma, 91–118, 120, 128–29, 161, 163, 212, 224, 311n; piṭaka, 91, 94. *See also* Sarvāstivāda; Sautrāntika

Abhidharmakośa, 93, 101, 102, 103, 106, 120, 143; *bhāṣya*, 99, 101, 103, 105, 177, 277n

Abhidharmasamuccaya, 159, 160, 161, 163

Abhūta-parikalpa, 167, 291n, 292n

Absolute, 4, 12, 87, 121, 140, 142, 193, 197, 199, 202, 214, 230, 237, 264n, 274n, 311n

Absolutism, 86, 87–88, 118, 121–22, 129–32, 133; in the *Gauḍapādīya-kārikā*, 68, 69, 86, 98, 114, 128–32, 138, 181, 185, 192–93, 196, 199, 205–7, 209, 212–13, 215, 219, 223, 229, 232, 240; and Mahāyāna Buddhism, 4, 12–14, 87, 98, 111, 114, 121–22, 128, 131–32, 135, 136–37, 139–40, 185, 192–93, 199, 205–7, 209, 211–12, 214, 215, 217, 219, 220, 222–34, 237–39, 240–41, 283–84n, 309n, 311n, 314–15n

Adhyāra, 294n. *See* Samāra

Adhyāsa, 269n, 300n

Ādhyātma, 75, 83, 159, 197

Ādibuddha, 187, 208–10, 213, 229, 257, 306n

Advaita, 10, 20, 28, 41, 42, 48, 64, 65, 67, 78, 82, 85, 88, 90, 141, 142, 153, 158, 168, 169, 171, 176, 193, 194–95, 198, 199, 203, 238, 264n, 286n, 291n, 300n; and Mahāyāna Buddhism, 4, 6, 7, 10, 11–14, 25, 32, 40–41, 87–90, 108, 114, 119, 124–40, 154, 186, 187, 188, 192–94, 198–203, 209, 229–41, 303n; origins of the term, 268n

Advaita Vedānta, 61, 63, 64, 67, 81, 85, 86, 87, 135, 136, 198, 229, 232, 263n, 295–96n; alleged crypto-Buddhism of, 20, 48, 88, 89, 183–184; contemporary, 9; post-Śaṅkarite, 16, 46–47, 48, 51, 67, 69, 77, 84, 86, 131, 157, 175, 176–177, 239, 270n, 296n, 298n, 315n; pre-Śaṅkarite, 2–3, 6, 11, 12, 15, 17, 29, 39, 46, 47, 90, 203, 238

Advaya, 6, 64, 127, 153, 154, 156, 157, 187, 189, 193, 195, 199, 203, 222, 236, 248, 250, 286n, 288n, 291n, 303n

Agnihotra, 74. *See also* Prāṇāgnihotra

Agrayāna, 185–86, 192, 205, 234, 257

Aitareya Upaniṣad, 52, 57, 269n

Agrawal, Madan Mohan, 274n

Ajātisamatā, 34, 41, 42, 45, 151, 200, 209 (ajaṃ samyaṃ), 248, 267n, 284n

Ajātivāda, 7, 12, 13, 22, 26, 29, 34, 41, 45, 48, 49, 65, 88, 90, 126–40, 141, 142, 144, 157, 168, 170, 178, 179, 183, 187, 192, 193, 194–99, 202–3, 212, 213, 218, 219, 235, 236, 237, 264n, 283n, 286n, 299n, 300n, 302n, 303n. *See also* Non-orination; Ātman; Dharmas

Ājivīkas, 53, 92

Ākāśa, 35, 36, 99, 107, 114–15, 187, 221

Index of Verses

Third Prakaraṇa

Fourth Prakaraṇa

10079768R00196

Printed in Great Britain
by Amazon.co.uk, Ltd.,
Marston Gate.